Nietzsche on Art and Life

Nietzsche on Art and Life

EDITED BY
Daniel Came

OXFORD
UNIVERSITY PRESS

OXFORD
UNIVERSITY PRESS

Great Clarendon Street, Oxford, OX2 6DP,
United Kingdom

Oxford University Press is a department of the University of Oxford.
It furthers the University's objective of excellence in research, scholarship,
and education by publishing worldwide. Oxford is a registered trade mark of
Oxford University Press in the UK and in certain other countries

First edition published 2014

Published in the United States of America by Oxford University Press
198 Madison Avenue, New York, NY 10016, United States of America

British Library Cataloguing in Publication Data
Data available

Library of Congress Control Number: 2013943735

ISBN 978-0-19-954596-4

For Martha and Tilly

Contents

Contributors

Daniel Came is Lecturer in Philosophy at the University of Hull.

Adrian Del Caro is Distinguished Professor of Humanities at the University of Tennessee, Knoxville.

A. E. Denham is Associate Professor of Philosophy at Tulane University and Senior Research Fellow in Philosophy at St Anne's College, Oxford.

Ken Gemes is Professor of Philosophy at Birkbeck College, University of London, and Professor of Philosophy at the New College of the Humanities.

Christopher Janaway is Professor of Philosophy at the University of Southampton.

Sabina Lovibond is Emeritus Fellow in Philosophy at Worcester College, Oxford.

Stephen Mulhall is Professor of Philosophy and Tutorial Fellow in Philosophy at New College, Oxford.

Christopher C. Raymond is Assistant Professor of Philosophy at Vassar College.

Bernard Reginster is Professor of Philosophy at Brown University.

Aaron Ridley is Professor of Philosophy at the University of Southampton.

Roger Scruton is Visiting Scholar at the American Enterprise Institute, Visiting Professor of Philosophy and Fellow of Blackfriars Hall, Oxford, and Visiting Research Professor in the Department of Philosophy at the University of St Andrews.

Chris Sykes is currently completing his Ph.D. in Philosophy at Birkbeck College, University of London.

A Note on References

References to Nietzsche's works are incorporated into the text and follow the standard English-language acronym, for example *BGE*, 38. Roman numerals refer to major parts or chapters in Nietzsche's works; Arabic numerals refer to pages not sections (for example, *GM*, III, 28) in all cases except in references to the third of the *Untimely Meditations* where the Arabic numeral refers to the page number of the edition used, for example, *UM*, III, 127. The third chapter of *Ecce Homo* contains parts with separately numbered sections on most of Nietzsche's prior books; these are cited using the abbreviations for those books followed by section number, for example *EH*, III, *BT*, 1.

References to Schopenhauer's works are also incorporated into the text and are cited by abbreviation. In references to Schopenhauer's major work, *The World as Will and Representation*, roman numerals refer to volume number and Arabic numerals refer to page numbers of the standard English-language edition, for example *WWR*, I, 315.

All references to secondary sources follow the Harvard system—with full publication details given at the end of each essay.

Works by Nietzsche

KSA = Reference edition of Nietzsche's works *Friedrich Nietzsche: Sämtliche Werke, Kritische Studienausgabe*. Herausgegeben von Giorgio Colli und Mazzino Montinari. Berlin: de Gruyter, 1967–1977.

BGE = *Beyond Good and Evil*

BT = *The Birth of Tragedy*

CW = *The Case of Wagner*

D = *Daybreak*

EH = *Ecce Homo*

GM = *On the Genealogy of Morality*

GS = *The Gay Science*

HH = *Human, All Too Human*

NCW = *Nietzsche Contra Wagner*

TI = *Twilight of the Idols*

UM = *Untimely Meditations*

WEN = *Writings from the Early Notebooks*

WLN = *Writings from the Late Notebooks*

WP = *The Will to Power*

Z = *Thus Spoke Zarathustra*

Works by Schopenhauer

WWR = *The World as Will and Representation* (Volumes I & II)

Works by Wagner

AP = *Art and Politics*

RA = *Religion and Art*

Introduction

Daniel Came

Nietzsche was not interested in art as such. Nor was he interested in constructing an aesthetic theory of a recognizable traditional sort à la Hume and Kant—that is to say, he was not interested in the internal constitution of aesthetic judgments, or the degree of objectivity attributable to them. Rather, Nietzsche was concerned with 'art from the perspective of life' (*BT*, P, 4), for he regarded the significance of art to lie not in *l'art pour l'art* but in the answers it provides to the problem of how to value human experience.

This is not to deny that Nietzsche's thoughts about art owe a great deal to the experience of art or that he engages in explicit criticism of traditional philosophical conceptions of the aesthetic. There are, for instance, passages in Nietzsche's writings that could be read as addressing questions pertaining to the nature of beauty and whether or not reality includes mind-independent aesthetic properties (e.g., *TI*, IX, 19). But when read in this way, what emerges is a rather unsophisticated and inchoate form of aesthetic anti-realism.

If this way of reading Nietzsche—seeking to extract elements in his thought which intersect with the concerns of traditional philosophical aesthetics—were correct, it would show that his writings on art do not really warrant serious critical reflection. But Nietzsche had very little systematic interest in art and so this mode of engagement with his writings on art runs the risk of short-changing their philosophical value. For—as with all of Nietzsche's concerns—his motivations were practical-existential. That is to say, Nietzsche was interested, not in the nature of art as such, but in the relationship between 'art' and 'life', and in the role that art can play in discharging the principal tasks he set himself as a philosopher—to identify the conditions of the affirmation of life, cultural renewal, and exemplary human living. This volume presents a collection of new essays that engage with Nietzsche's writings on art and the aesthetic from precisely this practical-existential perspective.

The idea that Nietzsche's thought is principally concerned with practical-existential problems might seem obvious. After all, the most famous Nietzschean themes—the death of God, nihilism, suffering, eternal recurrence, self-creation, the affirmation of life—are paradigmatically existential, in the sense that they relate first and foremost to the nature and value of subjective individual existence. But readings that emphasize the practical-existential orientation of Nietzsche's philosophical reflection are rare. There may be sociological reasons for this. Existential concerns are remote from the detached, theoretical interests of mainstream Anglophone philosophy—and the prevailing tendency in recent Nietzsche scholarship has been to attempt to show that Nietzsche's philosophy intersects with these theoretical concerns. For instance, Maudemarie Clark in her seminal *Nietzsche on Truth and Philosophy* claims that Nietzsche's 'perspectivism regarding knowledge... constitutes his most obvious contribution to the current intellectual scene' (Clark, 1991, 127). More recently, Brian Leiter, in his landmark *Nietzsche on Morality*, has argued that Nietzsche deserves recognition as a leading philosophical naturalist and, in more recent work, to be 'a live participant in contemporary debates' in ethics (Leiter and Sinhabubu, 2007, 2).

But attempts to make Nietzsche speak to the concerns of contemporary metaphysicians, epistemologists, and ethicists can lead to neglect or distortion of Nietzsche's deeper interests. Furthermore, Nietzsche was arguably not at his best when addressing the core questions of philosophy, so when read in this way we sometimes get a philosopher less interesting and original than Nietzsche in fact was.[1] Even those questions which could be construed as ethical are generally of derivative importance, and are pursued by Nietzsche in the service of a broader practical-existential imperative.

While Nietzsche does have views on normative and metaethical questions, on free will and the nature of the self, he does not have a systematic interest in these matters. For example, his fundamental objection to the Judaeo-Christian tradition is not that it is false ('it is not error *qua* error that horrifies me at this sight' (*EH*, IV, 7)), but rather that as an expression of the 'ascetic ideal' it is involved in life-denial and nihilism. For Nietzsche, the problem with the Judaeo-Christian tradition is not the putative falsehood of its normative claims and their metaphysical presuppositions, but rather that it manifests an attitude and orientation of hatred towards life—that it 'taught men to despise the very first instincts of life' (ibid.). Interpretations that seek

[1] As Ken Gemes remarks, one problem with seeking to make Nietzsche speak to the concerns of contemporary metaphysicians and epistemologists is that 'it gives us a Nietzsche who is merely rehashing familiar Kantian themes minus the rigor of Kant's exposition' (Gemes, 1992, 48).

to extract a contribution to contemporary discussions on, say, the metaphysics and epistemology (and even semantics) of value involve a certain insensitivity to this wider existential context of Nietzsche's writings.[2]

There is also a tendency in much of the recent English language scholarship on Nietzsche to try to interpret his writings in isolation from his views on art. On the one hand, there might again be sociological reasons for this. Aesthetics in recent Anglo-American philosophy has been generally regarded as the poorer, less sophisticated cousin of ethics. But on the other hand, this particular aspect of the contemporary hierarchical structuring of philosophy might be reflective of the fact that ethics just is more fundamental than aesthetics. Indeed, some have had grave doubts as to whether philosophical aesthetics is a *bona fide* subject at all.[3]

Of course, some kind of link between ethics and aesthetics is implied by the common 'value-judgment' classification. But this classification, those who doubt the legitimacy of aesthetics would argue, merely begs the question of the former's status. While the traditional classification views ethical and aesthetic judgments as two tokens of a quite specific type, ethical judgments usually—perhaps exclusively—concern human conduct, character, and psychological states, whereas aesthetic judgments typically evaluate artefacts and features of the natural world.

As such, the appreciation of art and aesthetic value, as George Santayana once wrote, 'belong to our holiday life' (Santayana, 1955, §3). That is to say, art and the aesthetic belong to those occasions when the burden of necessity and fear is lifted—and in this sense art is merely 'gratuitous'. Ethics, by contrast, is a device by which we try to escape certain ills to which our nature exposes us—death, hunger, disease, weariness, isolation. There are of course negative aesthetic values, of which ugliness is the paradigm example; but occurrences of these are either aesthetically negligible, in the sense that the ugly is not the source of any real pain, or else their significance is primarily practical and ethical, as when we are ethically outraged at the construction of a hideous new building which will cause its inhabitants and their neighbours genuine distress.

If this is right, then it would appear that there is some truth in the received wisdom regarding the relative standing of ethics and aesthetics. But what this piece of philosophical orthodoxy assumes—and this is something that Nietzsche

[2] In contrast May (2002) and Reginster (2009) both identify practical-existential issues—the problem of nihilism and its overcoming through life-affirmation—as Nietzsche's principal concerns. See also Gemes (2008).

[3] See, for example, Hampshire (1954).

would seek to reject—is that the nature of ethical and aesthetic judgment is fixed and immutable. Someone might accept all the points made above, and yet point out that boundaries in this area are not forever fixed by what most people accept, that within certain limits of intelligibility there is room for individuals and communities to negotiate the ethics/aesthetics divide on their own terms; and thus for (more or less reasoned) arguments in favour of a revision in our ordinary practice. Perhaps most of us do tend to keep our ethical and aesthetic faculties in separate boxes, and perhaps we do usually take the deliverances of the former more seriously; but revisionists like Nietzsche will suggest that we shouldn't—either, on realist grounds, because this practice misrepresents the true nature of the respective values, or because it would be more rewarding, or in some other pragmatic sense more valuable, to do things differently.

For Nietzsche, art has a privileged and internal role in his philosophy—and this outlook is expressed not only, as is sometimes supposed, in his early writings. In his first published work, *The Birth of Tragedy*, Nietzsche informs us that 'art is the highest task and real metaphysical activity of this life' (*BT*, 17, 18); a remark somewhat amplified in the brilliant 'Attempt at a Self Criticism', with which he prefaced the 1886 edition of the work: 'art—and not morality—is . . . the real metaphysical activity of man' (*BT*, 8). The book closes with a reiteration of the claim, originally canvassed early on, that 'existence and the world appear justified only as an aesthetic phenomenon' (*BT*, 28).

Regarding the first remark, it is clear from the original context that Nietzsche chiefly intends it as a rebuttal of those who have little respect for aesthetic activity and experience, who 'see in art nothing more than an amusing sideshow, a readily dispensable tinkling of bells to accompany the seriousness of existence' (*BT*, 17). For such people, art could hardly have the function that he wishes to ascribe to it, that of transforming and sustaining an entire culture's sense of itself in relation to the world, of calibrating its members' various impulses so as to enable them to achieve both individual fulfilment and authentic political community. This role is 'metaphysical' in the sense that it facilitates man's most general understanding of the world and his place in it, but also because, as Nietzsche claims repeatedly, the affirmation of life is essentially an aesthetic or artistic stance.[4] This suggestion is made explicitly in *The Birth of Tragedy* (5, 24), and it is found again in *The Gay Science*, in which '*amor fati*' or being 'a Yes-sayer' is said to rest on the ability 'to see as beautiful what is necessary in things' (*GS*, 276; cf. 107). And in *Twilight of*

[4] See, for example, *BT*, 5, 24; *GS*, 276, 10; *GM*, III, 25; *TI*, IX, 22, 24; cf. *WP*, 802, 821–2, 852–3.

the Idols, along with a substantial number of unpublished notes, it is claimed that 'art is the great stimulus to life' (*TI*, IX, 24; cf. *WP*, 802, 821–2, 852–3), and that 'beauty incites' to a continued engagement with it (*TI*, IX, 22).

Furthermore, Nietzsche clearly conceived his own 'positive' ethical ideal as in some sense bound up with art and the aesthetic. The process of self-creation, of giving style to one's character, is an aesthetic enterprise, in the sense that 'to "give style" to one's character' requires a person to 'survey' his various characteristics and 'fit them into an artistic plan' (*GS*, 290; cf. 107; *BGE*, 188; *WP*, 353). Relatedly, in Nietzsche's attempts to elucidate the series of ideal types that permeates his writing, beginning with the noble Hellene of *The Birth of Tragedy*, and developing into the *Übermensch* of *Thus Spoke Zarathustra* and the 'higher man' of the mature philosophy, it is artists—Goethe and Beethoven in particular—who feature most prominently. And as Philippa Foot (1973) points out, the reasons we are given for preferring these higher types to the 'herd' are chiefly aesthetic ones, albeit of a quite sophisticated kind.

Given the priority Nietzsche ascribes to art, understanding his engagement with art is essential for understanding his philosophy *überhaupt*. The aim of this collection is to facilitate such understanding by addressing Nietzsche's account of art and the aesthetic on the practical-existential terms in which he himself engages with art.

The discussion begins with two essays which go to the core of Nietzsche's interest in art—the relation between art and life-affirmation. As we have already noted, Nietzsche claims repeatedly that the affirmation of life is essentially an aesthetic or artistic stance: to affirm life is to come to see it as *beautiful*. Bernard Reginster's paper explores the development and transformations of this claim from its introduction in *The Birth of Tragedy* to Nietzsche's pronouncements on the significance of art in his latest works. Reginster's central contention is that Nietzsche's conception of what seeing life as beautiful amounts to undergoes a subtle, but dramatic shift. In his earliest works, beauty is the character of a 'veil' that *conceals*: it makes the affirmation of life possible by masking its 'terrifying and questionable character'. Nietzsche soon recognizes that such concealment is incompatible with genuine affirmation, however. For this reason, Reginster suggests, in the later works beauty is reconceived as the character of a 'veil' that 'incites' it invites further engagement and exploration of what it covers. According to this new conception, 'having a mysterious allure, which stimulates the spirit of adventure, is an essential feature of the beautiful.' Reginster argues that this conception of beauty allows, *inter alia*, to resolve a perplexing paradox that afflicts Nietzsche's conception of the affirmation of life: on the one hand, he claims that to affirm life is in some way to find it valuable; on the other hand, he also claims that 'the value of life cannot be estimated' (*TI*, II, 2). The paradox dissipates, Reginster concludes, once we recognize that to affirm life is to come to see it as beautiful, and that beauty is 'the quality of that the value of which is uncertain'.

Christopher Janaway's essay addresses the question of the relations between art, truth, and life-affirmation in Nietzsche's early and later writings. There are many passages in Nietzsche's corpus which suggest that, for Nietzsche, the evaluative attitudes to life that may be derived from art are simply a matter of illusion, falsification, and deception. Janaway argues that Nietzsche's construal of the relation of art to truth is always more subtle, and often more unsettled, than that simple impression suggests. In *The Birth of Tragedy* three different relations of art to truth are juxtaposed: the Apollonian, the tragic, and the Socratic. While the Apollonian seeks to conceal the harsh truth of reality behind an illusion, and the Socratic seeks truth at all costs by pure rational enquiry, Nietzsche's vision of tragic art is that it reveals threatening truths in an aesthetic manner that allows the Greeks to rejoice in life. In later works, especially *The Gay Science*, there is much to suggest that art is necessary as the provider of illusions that make life bearable. Yet at the same time, Janaway contends, Nietzsche promotes the 'intellectual conscience' which entails a commitment to affirmation of life 'as it is', without recourse to illusion. Janaway considers ways in which this tension might be resolved, but argues that the relation between art and truth continues to be unstable for Nietzsche, in part because in his later works, with his calling into question of the will to truth and his perspectivist rejection of passive, selfless, detached 'knowing', the very distinction between truth and illusion becomes less stable.

Christopher C. Raymond's essay interprets Nietzsche's account of the value of tragedy as a response to Socrates' challenge in Book 10 of the *Republic*: 'to prove that there's more to it than mere pleasure—that it is also an agent of cultural health and metaphysical consolation'. What unites traditional responses to Socrates' challenge, in Raymond's view, is that they all claim that watching tragedy gives us some knowledge or understanding that contributes to the rational life. This is the case even with Schopenhauer, despite his highly individual conception of what a rational life involves. According to Raymond, Nietzsche is the first major figure in the tradition to respond to Socrates by rejecting the terms on which his challenge is set. Tragedy has value, according to Nietzsche, precisely because it does not benefit us in the way Socrates' challenge demands. Raymond argues that this is because Nietzsche rejects the Socratic project *tout court*. Nietzsche does not think the value of tragedy lies in any knowledge or understanding it gives us about the world and how to live in it. It is in this sense that he rejects Socrates' challenge. Nietzsche thinks it is possible for tragedy to have this effect, but the true value of tragedy depends on its power to give us metaphysical consolation. This, in turn, requires that tragedy show us a world in which there are no rational solutions to the existential problems of life.

It is sometimes claimed that Nietzsche's primary focus was the problem of *suffering*. Against this, Ken Gemes and Chris Sykes argue that Nietzsche's primary focus was the existential lack of *meaning* which he took to be particularly apposite to modern times. Thus, in contrast to Schopenhauer, for Nietzsche suffering as such was never the fundamental objection to life. Gemes and Sykes locate this position in the third essay of *On the Genealogy of Morality* where Nietzsche remarks that 'the meaninglessness of suffering, not suffering itself, was the curse thus far stretched over humanity' (*GM*, III, 28), and they argue that this is also the position of Nietzsche's first published work, *The Birth of Tragedy*. The continuity between Nietzsche's early and later views is thus constituted in the import he gives to the question of meaning. An interpretive offshoot of this analysis is that Wagner is a fundamental inspiration and foil for Nietzsche's thought. While, arguably, the problem of suffering was Schopenhauer's central concern, for Wagner, as Gemes and Sykes argue, the problem of meaning was primary. What is particular to the early Nietzsche, on Gemes and Sykes' reading, is the overt emphasis on the need for mythologizing in the construction of meaning. No longer capable of naïve belief in myth, modern humans need self-consciously to construct myths in order to provide the unity necessary for a new cultural flourishing. The later Nietzsche was much more nuanced on the importance of mythology, tending to emphasize the more general need for illusions. More importantly, the later Nietzsche, in Gemes and Sykes' view, is decidedly more pessimistic about the very possibility of the rebirth of a higher general culture. Where Schopenhauer extolled breaking through the veil of Maya (illusion) in order to realize that life must be denied, Nietzsche, following Wagner, insists that we need to create illusion in order to affirm life.

In 'Orchestral Metaphysics', Stephen Mulhall considers the relationship between Nietzsche's understanding of tragedy in *The Birth of Tragedy* and the particular form of philosophical writing he develops in that work. Mulhall interprets *The Birth of Tragedy* as the site of a 'three-cornered conversation' Nietzsche stages between Aeschylus, Wagner, and Schopenhauer, and hence as an experiment in defining a mode of discourse that makes equal reference to tragic drama, opera, and philosophy. Key ideas in that experiment include the employment of a particular technique Mulhall calls 'metalepsis' (that is, 'Nietzsche's tendency to depict the character and vicissitudes of a phenomenon in terms provided by aspects or elements of the phenomenon itself'), the disclosure of a mythological mode of philosophical thinking, and the elaboration of a critique of Socratic philosophy—as represented by Kant—as privileging Apollo over Dionysus. Mulhall argues that Nietzsche aims not so much to privilege Dionysus instead, but rather to write in a way which amounts to a non-idolatrous acknowledgement of Apollo. Mulhall's concluding claim is that the productive antagonism of Apollo and Dionysus might be thought of as Nietzsche's first attempt to represent the dynamics of the achievement of genuine selfhood as a process of endless self-overcoming. From this broadly perfectionist perspective, Mulhall suggests, Apollo stands for the self's need for individuation, for a fixed structure of values, and Dionysus stands for the self's impulse endlessly to overcome any such structure.

My own essay addresses the question of the relation of aesthetic to ethical value in Nietzsche's early and later writings. My central contention is that Nietzsche wanted to effect a *rapprochement* between aesthetics and ethics, to extend the structure of aesthetic judgment into the ethical domain, and, indeed, to effect the substitution of aesthetic for ethical concepts when dealing with such typically ethical domains as action, motivation, and character, and their adoption as the predominant terms in practical reasoning. The chapter explores the development and transformations of this theme from its introduction in *The Birth of Tragedy*, to Nietzsche's imperative in *The Gay Science* to give 'style' to one's character and thereby 'turn oneself into a work of art' (*GS*, 290). In particular, I am interested in what is distinctive about Nietzsche's aestheticist approach to ethical questions, and in what respects, and to what degree, he extends the norms of aesthetic judgment and practice into the realm of ethical appraisal and practical reason. I argue that Nietzsche saw the individual *qua* agent as an artist, and *qua* bearer of a character and a life as a work of art; but he also saw that this view must lead one to embrace a quite different mode of ethical evaluation. If agents are something like artists and works of art, then being 'good' or 'noble' will be a creative practice, one whose rules and aims are not fixed in advance, but are subject to alteration, expansion, and wholesale reinvention. It also follows, I suggest, that genuine nobility will be different in kind, something available only to a few, not by obedience to any preordained system of rules, but by the selective contravention of existing canons and the invention of new ones. Indeed, the very idea of a 'common morality' must be rejected as expressing a cult of the mediocre, and replaced with a discourse of authenticity and originality exalting just what is uncommon, unexpected, revelatory.

While Nietzsche thought of certain forms of art as uniquely conducive to life-affirmation, he was also prone to denigrate other forms of art as decadent and as in some sense involved in nihilism or the negation of life, or as perpetuating unhealthy, life-denying modes of thought and feeling. Romanticism falls into this latter category. Adrian Del Caro's essay examines Nietzsche's anti-romanticism against the foil of the 'Dionysian classicism', which he favoured and presented as an antidote to the romantic disposition. Del Caro argues that the classical/romantic dichotomy is a major fault line of the modern psyche, helped to prominence by Nietzsche's elevation of the Apollonian/Dionysian dichotomy, and also by his insistence that he had invented a new 'Dionysian classicism' in keeping with his 'anti-romantic self-treatment.' Del Caro treats *Thus Spoke Zarathustra* as a conversation with Goethe's *Faust*, using the lens of anti-romanticism to distinguish between them. According to Del Caro's interpretation, both works compete 'beyond good and evil' for the honour of 'most life-affirming', each modelling a romantic vision of the fulfilled, consummated life, yet each rejecting romanticism as a weak, pathological element suggestive of life-denial and nihilism. Nietzsche was fond of quoting *Faust* throughout his works, but increasingly he took issue with Faust as an exemplar of humanity. Del Caro's critical examination of these works, approached from the standpoint of anti-romanticism, reveals competing versions of the *Übermensch*, the first literally proposed by Goethe in the context of the Earth Spirit, the latter posited as an alternative by Nietzsche, who elevated the *Übermensch* to 'the meaning of the earth.'

One of Nietzsche's central contentions regarding the practical-existential import of art relates to his idea of aesthetic *transfiguration*, the capacity of art to alchemize the meaningless sufferings of mere natural existence into the aesthetically magnificent struggle that is human life. In A. E. Denham's essay, she argues that Nietzsche's phenomenology of aesthetic experience—and in particular his idea that aesthetic transfiguration can invest human experience with positive value—is essentially continuous with Schopenhauer's. Like Nietzsche, Schopenhauer assessed 'art from the perspective of life'. As Schopenhauer is standardly read, however, his conception of aesthetic experience has little in common with that offered by Nietzsche. *Contra* the standard reading, Denham argues that Nietzsche parted ways with Schopenhauer with respect to the normative implications he drew from their common phenomenology: he found a different moral in the story of aesthetic experience. Nonetheless, the story itself was one which he inherited directly from Schopenhauer, and which pervades his account of art's transfigurative powers—from its origins in *The Birth of Tragedy* to its culmination in *Twilight of the Idols*. The idea that aesthetic transfiguration can invest human experience with positive value—that despite its suffering, strife, and pointlessness life can be 'aesthetically justified'—is in fact a natural extension of Schopenhauer's account of artistic activity. Hence, on the account Denham develops, *both* Schopenhauer and Nietzsche emerge as offering powerful strategies for resisting a 'moral interpretation' of life.

Sabina Lovibond explores the theme of 'distance' (see e.g., *GS*, 15, 60; *BGE*, 257) in Nietzsche's writings—that is to say, the idea that many things can be seen, or in general experienced, to the best advantage by standing back. Several remarks in the early books of *The Gay Science* show distance to be important for Nietzsche, in the first place, as a necessary condition for attaining an adequate view of a given phenomenon, but also as a template for our view of ourselves and of human character in general. An individual's character, Nietzsche contends, tends to look better when viewed from a position of distance. Lovibond examines the wide-ranging influence Nietzsche's esteem for distance exerts on his aesthetic reflections. Her suggestion is that distance is the value which links Nietzsche's aesthetics with his ethical and political attitudes, and also with his attitudes to communication and truth. According to Lovibond, what Nietzsche admires at the level of 'thick' aesthetic value is associated with *noblesse* as opposed to 'plebeianism', and thus he articulates an aesthetics based on reaction against modern (democratic) ideas. In a similar vein, Lovibond suggests that Nietzsche's critique of truth is accompanied by a notion of truths which are available only to the few, and which are not intended to feature in an egalitarian mode of discourse that is common or accessible to all.

The last two chapters address issues pertaining to Nietzsche's views on music. Within the context of his wider existential concern with questions relating to our evaluative stance towards human life and experience, Nietzsche clearly assigns music a privileged and internal role. 'Without music', he famously writes, 'life would be a mistake' (*TI*, I, 33). In Aaron Ridley's essay, he attempts to explicate the character of music's significance for Nietzsche, and to suggest ways in which an understanding of Nietzsche's engagement with music is essential for an understanding of his broader project. Ridley suggests that what makes Nietzsche's thought about music distinctive is his connection of music with questions concerning the *valuation* of life. Nietzsche's main objection to modern culture derives from the idea that it is in thrall to a set of moral values that lead us to denigrate and deny life and the world in favour some non-existent metaphysical realm. In Nietzsche's view, therefore, those values stand in need of 'revaluation'—'*the value of these values themselves must*... *be called into question*' (*GM*, P, 6)—as part of an attempt to institute a new system of values through which, without appeal to the metaphysical, life might be celebrated and affirmed. Ridley argues that to that task Nietzsche regards music as having an especially important contribution to make. 'What does all art do?', he asks: 'does it not praise? does it not glorify? does it not select? does it not highlight? By doing all this it *strengthens* or *weakens* certain valuations' (*TI*, IX, 24). The non-musical arts achieve this strengthening or weakening of valuations through their employment of ordinary referential meanings that may be derived from the form that has been imposed. In music, by contrast, the strengthening or weakening is achieved much more powerfully and directly in virtue of its uniquely intimate connection to the inner life. Music, on Ridley's view, 'echoes, and so causes to resonate in the listener, particular evaluative dispositions of the soul'. It thus constitutes a potent medium for the reconfiguration of our evaluative commitments. Indeed, as Ridley concludes, it might be possible that an individual could, through acquaintance with the appropriate works, become so imbued with life-affirmation that this became second nature. Accordingly, music might even be the agent by which we may finally overcome the life-denying values of traditional morality.

One of Nietzsche's most distinctive claims about traditional aesthetic theory is that it has unjustifiably privileged analysis of the spectator over that of the artist. Of particular importance is the claim that works of art are to be judged in terms of the life contained in them, which in turn is taken to be an expression of the underlying health or decadence of the artist. The artist that figures most prominently in Nietzsche's writings is Richard Wagner. Indeed, Wagner was probably the greatest single influence on Nietzsche, and was the inspiration behind *The Birth of Tragedy*. The anthropological approach to ancient religion that Nietzsche adopted in that work was also due to Wagner. As is well known, however, Nietzsche turned against Wagner, criticizing not just the Wagnerian conception of the hero, but also the flawed music, as he saw it, in which that conception was embodied. His response to *Parsifal* was one of dismissive mockery, and he found little or nothing to admire in the conception of life that is presented in the *Ring* tetralogy.

In Roger Scruton's essay, he presents Nietzsche's criticisms of Wagner, assesses them, and asks what exactly a work of music would have to be like if it were to meet Nietzsche's fundamental requirements of the modern work of art. Scruton suggests that within the context of Nietzsche's attack on Wagner, he gives the *central* place in aesthetic judgment to the distinction between healthy and sickly forms of human life. Wagner's music, he suggests, is, in Nietzsche's view, the cause and effect of a sickness. This is largely because the Wagnerian idea of redemption closely corresponds to the Christian one. For Nietzsche, the whole idea of redemption, conceived in that way, is a denial of life and an invocation to decadence. Consequently, the Wagnerian hero is not a hero at all but an *entartete Mensch*. Scruton argues that such far-reaching claims place an enormous critical onus on Nietzsche, and further argues that Nietzsche does not discharge that onus. That is, Nietzsche fails to demonstrate that the Wagnerian philosophy of redemption is either decadent in itself or aesthetically destructive. Scruton concedes that the guiding idea of Nietzsche's approach to aesthetic judgment in terms of health and decadence is sound, noting that the belief that music has a moral and character-forming potential is at least as old as Plato; and the belief that works of art are to be judged in terms of the life contained in them has survived into our times is a critical commonplace. However, Scruton says that this idea stands in need of a philosophical underpinning—something which, he concludes, Nietzsche fails to provide.

References

Came, D. 2009. 'Disinterestedness and Objectivity', in *The European Journal of Philosophy*, 17/1: 91–100.

Clark, M. 1991. *Nietzsche on Truth and Philosophy* (Cambridge: Cambridge University Press).

Foot, P. 1973. 'Nietzsche: The Revaluation of Values', in Solomon, R. C. (ed.), *Nietzsche: A Collection of Critical Essays* (Garden City, NY: Anchor Books): 156–68. Reprinted in Richardson, J. and Leiter, B. (eds.), *Oxford Readings in Philosophy: Nietzsche* (New York and Oxford: Oxford University Press): 210–20.

Gemes, K. 1992. 'Nietzsche's Critique of Truth', in *Philosophy and Phenomenological Research*, 52/1: 47–65. Reprinted in Richardson, J. and Leiter, B. (eds.), *Oxford Readings in Philosophy: Nietzsche* (New York and Oxford: Oxford University Press): 40–58.

Gemes, K. 2008. 'Nihilism and the Affirmation of Life: A Review of and Dialogue with Bernard Reginster's *The Affirmation of Life: Nietzsche on Overcoming Nihilism*', in *The European Journal of Philosophy*, 16/3: 459–66.

Hampshire, S. 1954. 'Logic and Appreciation', in Elton, W. (ed.), *Aesthetics and Language* (Oxford: Oxford University Press): 161–9.

Leiter, B. 2002. *The Routledge Philosophy Guidebook to Nietzsche on Morality* (London: Routledge).

Leiter, B. and Sinhababu, S. 2007. 'Introduction', in Leiter, B. and Sinhababu, N. (eds.), *Nietzsche and Morality* (New York and Oxford: Oxford University Press).

May, S. 2002. *Nietzsche's Ethics and his War on 'Morality'* (New York and Oxford: Oxford University Press).

Nietzsche, F. 1993. *The Birth of Tragedy*, Tanner, M. (ed.), Whiteside, S. (trans.) (Harmondsworth: Penguin).

Nietzsche, F. 1998. *On the Genealogy of Morality*, Clark, M. and Swensen, A. (trans.) (Indianapolis: Hackett).

Nietzsche, F. 2001. *The Gay Science*, Williams, B. (ed.), Nauckhoff, J. and del Caro, A. (trans.) (Cambridge: Cambridge University Press).

Nietzsche, F. 2002. *Beyond Good and Evil*, Horstmann, R. and Norman, J. (eds.), Norman, J. (trans.) (Cambridge: Cambridge University Press).

Nietzsche, F. 2005. *Ecce Homo*, in *The Anti-Christ, Ecce Homo, Twilight of the Idols, and Other Writings*, Ridley, A. (ed.), Norman, J. (trans.) (Cambridge: Cambridge University Press).

Nietzsche, F. 2005. *Twilight of the Idols*, in *The Anti-Christ, Ecce Homo, Twilight of the Idols, and Other Writings*, Ridley, A. (ed.), Norman, J. (trans.) (Cambridge: Cambridge University Press).

Reginster, B. 2009. *The Affirmation of Life: Nietzsche on Overcoming Nihilism* (Cambridge, MA: Harvard University Press).

Santayana, G. 1955. *The Sense of Beauty* (New York: Dover Publications Inc.).

1

Art and Affirmation

Bernard Reginster

There is no such thing as pessimistic art—Art affirms.

The Will to Power, §821

Throughout his productive life, Nietzsche repeatedly offers the suggestion that affirming life is coming to see it as *beautiful*—that is to say, that the affirmation of life is essentially an aesthetic or artistic stance. The suggestion is made explicitly in Nietzsche's earliest book, *The Birth of Tragedy*, where he memorably claims that 'it is only as an *aesthetic phenomenon* that existence and the world are eternally *justified*' (*BT*, 5, 24). It is found again in *The Gay Science*, in which '*amor fati*' or being 'a Yes-sayer' is made to rest on the ability 'to see as beautiful what is necessary in things' (*GS*, 276; cf. 107). *On the Genealogy of Morals* presents art as 'fundamentally opposed to the ascetic ideal', the idealization of life-denial (*GM*, III, 25). And *Twilight of the Idols*, along with a substantial number of unpublished notes, claims that 'art is the great stimulus to life' (*TI*, IX, 24; cf. *WP*, 802, 821–2, 852–3), and that 'beauty incites' to a continued engagement with it (*TI*, IX, 22).

For all its tantalizing appeal, however, the precise meaning of this suggestion is elusive. This is in part, as I shall argue, because Nietzsche's conception of the manner in which seeing it as beautiful underwrites an affirmation of life undergoes a dramatic, if subtle, shift. I shall here attempt to describe this shift. Even though it might seem ambitious enough, my purpose will remain limited to what we can learn about the affirmation of life from its connection to the experience of it as beautiful. I shall say nothing about the conditions of the possibility, the desirability, and the prospects, of this affirmation.

1 AFFIRMATION AND ILLUSION

The suggestion that affirming life is seeing it as beautiful is first offered in *The Birth of Tragedy*, of which it is arguably the guiding theme, and in which it receives one of its most sustained developments. I shall therefore begin here. The 'justification' of existence is a problem in this book because Nietzsche has essentially appropriated, under the guise of 'Dionysian insight', Schopenhauer's 'pessimism':

> the Dionysian man resembles Hamlet: both have once looked truly into the essence of things, they have *gained knowledge*, and nausea inhibits action; for their action could not change anything into the eternal nature of things... Knowledge kills action; action requires the veils of illusion.
>
> (*BT*, 7; cf. *WP*, 853)

This short summary alludes to Schopenhauer's view that suffering is an essential, and therefore a necessary, feature of life (*WWR*, I, 56; II, xlvi, 573). Suffering, for Schopenhauer, is the experience of resistance to the satisfaction of our desires (*WWR*, I, 56, 309; 65, 363); his demonstration of its inevitability implies the impossibility of *fulfillment*, a condition in which nothing is left to be desired. This, in turn, accounts for the inhibition of action, which figures prominently in Nietzsche's summary: if fulfillment is impossible, there is no point in striving for it. He who has recognized such facts is 'in danger of longing for a Buddhistic negation of the will' (*BT*, 7), a negation of life.

Nietzsche observes that such a negation is far from inevitable. Indeed, it is rather rare, thanks to the hold various forms of *illusion* have over us:

> It is an eternal phenomenon: the insatiable will always find a way to detain its creatures in life and compel them to live on, by means of an illusion [*Illusion*] spread over things. One is chained by the Socratic love of knowledge and the delusion [*Wahn*] of being able thereby to heal the eternal wound of existence; another is ensnared by art's seductive veil of beauty fluttering before his eyes; still another by the metaphysical comfort that beneath the whirl of phenomena [*Erscheinungen*] eternal life flows on indestructibly—to say nothing of the more vulgar and almost more powerful illusions which the will always has at hand. These three stages of illusion are actually designed only for the more nobly formed natures, who actually feel profoundly the weight and burden of existence, and must be deluded by exquisite stimulants into forgetfulness of their displeasure.
>
> (*BT*, 18)

The central message of *The Birth of Tragedy* is that the affirmation of life requires 'illusion [*Illusion*]', which allows us to 'forget' the displeasure caused by 'the weight and burden of existence'. Not every kind of illusion is equally capable of underwriting a true affirmation of existence, however, and Nietzsche undertakes to distinguish among 'three stages of illusion' in order to show that only one of them, the illusion created by Greek tragedy, can produce a genuine affirmation.

The first kind of affirmation is the optimistic 'cheerfulness' of the 'theoretical man', who believes that everything in existence admits of a causal explanation, which, through the appropriate technological applications, can be used to correct its defects—'the unshakable faith that thought, using the thread of causality, can penetrate the deepest abysses of being, and that thought is capable not only of knowing being but even of *correcting* it' (*BT*, 15). Nietzsche characterizes the hallmark of this cheerfulness, which he associates with the figure of Socrates, in the following terms:

> it substitutes for a metaphysical comfort an earthly consonance, in fact, a *deus ex machina* of its own, the god of machines and crucibles, that is, the powers of the spirits of nature recognized and employed in the service of a higher egoism; it believes that it can correct the world by knowledge, guide life by science, and actually confine the individual within a limited sphere of solvable problems, from which it can cheerfully say to life: 'I desire you; you are worth knowing'.
>
> (*BT*, 17)

Nietzsche dismisses this kind of illusion as a 'delusion [*Wahn*]' apparently for two main reasons. First, its effectiveness in producing and sustaining an affirmative stance toward existence depends on its *not* being recognized as illusion, that is to say, on its inducing false belief. Second, the illusion that motivates the 'theoretical man' also happens to contain within itself the seeds of its own demise. For the pursuit of scientific knowledge, which it advocates, necessarily leads to the discovery of the limits of science: it is, as Nietzsche never tires of repeating, the very will to truth of the 'scientific spirit' that led to the discovery, especially in the philosophies of Kant and Schopenhauer, that science gives us knowledge only of 'phenomena', and not of things as they are in themselves (*BT*, 18). This inevitable discovery eventually shatters the 'delusion of limitless power' of theoretical optimism (ibid.), by raising the possibility, established as actual fact by Schopenhauer, that suffering is not a metaphysically contingent but a necessary—and therefore incorrigible—feature of our existence.[1]

The second kind of affirmation is made possible by a purely Apollonian culture, in which it assumes the form of 'the splendid "naïveté" of the earlier Greeks, which,

[1] Nietzsche's rejection of Schopenhauerian metaphysical dogmatism in his so-called 'positivistic' period led him to a brief dalliance with 'theoretical optimism' and the rejection of the 'metaphysical comforts' of *The Birth of Tragedy*, on the grounds that they 'hinder men from working for a real improvement in their condition by suspending and discharging in a palliative way the very passion which impels the discontented to action' (*HH*, I, 148; cf. 108). For a critical discussion, see Young (1992), chapter 3.

according to the characterization given above, must be conceived ... as the victory which the Hellenic will, through its mirroring of beauty, obtains over suffering and the wisdom of suffering' (*BT*, 17). In a purely Apollonian culture, that is to say, in a culture in which Apollonian arts have not been combined with Dionysian arts, the affirmation of existence is made possible by draping a 'veil of beautiful appearances' over its true character. Nietzsche defines this 'naïve' stance as 'a consummate immersion in the beauty of appearance [*in der Schönheit des Scheines*]', which therefore 'can be understood only as the complete victory of Apollonian illusion [*apollinische Illusion*]' (*BT*, 3).

Crucial to this kind of affirmation is a proper understanding of the notion of a 'beautiful appearance'. The not infrequent terminological association of 'appearance [*Schein*]' with 'deception [*Täuschung*]' makes it tempting to regard it as a simple deception, the production of comforting false *beliefs* about the character of our existence. But Nietzsche denies this from the outset: he insists that 'we must also include in our image of Apollo that delicate boundary which the dream image must not overstep lest it have a pathological effect—in which case mere appearance would deceive us as if it were crude reality' (*BT*, 1). Being seduced by the beautiful appearance of purely Apollonian art is not being deceived in the way the 'theoretical man' proves to be, but we shall see that it still involves a greater measure of deception than the illusion created by the Dionysian arts. The Apollonian subject is 'dreaming', as Nietzsche says, but he is also conscious that he is dreaming and deliberately chooses to keep on dreaming (ibid.). Although he knows that the true character of his existence may well differ from the beautiful appearance it assumes in his 'dream-images', he does not know whether, or how, it so differs. His indulgence in 'beautiful appearances' is therefore not a response to knowledge so much as an avoidance of it.[2]

[2] In *The Birth of Tragedy*, the relation between Apollonian art and the knowledge of the terrible character of existence is left somewhat ambiguous. On the one hand, Nietzsche suggests that this knowledge actually motivated the creation of a 'veil of beautiful appearance': 'The Greek knew and felt the terror and horror of existence. That he might endure this terror at all, he had to interpose between himself and life the radiant dream-birth of the Olympians' (*BT*, 3). This in turn would explain why the encounter with a Dionysian outlook aroused in the Apollonian Greek 'the shuddering suspicion that all this was actually not so very alien to him after all' (*BT*, 2). On the other hand, Apollonian affirmation cannot assume the form of a 'splendid "naïveté"' unless Apollonian illusion has achieved a 'complete victory', by which Nietzsche seems to suggest that the knowledge of the terrible character of our existence has been thoroughly suppressed. On this view, although such knowledge did originally motivate the creation of Apollonian illusion, it would not persist as what motivates its perpetuation. For if it did, the contrast between a purely Apollonian and a 'tragic' culture would become unclear. We might therefore plausibly suppose that those who participate in a purely Apollonian culture deliberately refrain from looking behind its beautiful appearances not because they have maintained a determinate knowledge of what they conceal, but

The illusions produced by Apollonian art differ from those under which the theoretical man labors in virtue of their *resilience*, by which I mean their ability to survive the revelation of their character as illusions. Several possible factors might explain the resilience of illusions. First, illusions might be resilient by virtue of their *psychological inertia*: sensory illusions, transcendental conditions of experience, or even entrenched prejudices are resilient in that way. Second, the resilience of an illusion might rest on the fact that it never owed its effectiveness to the presumption of veracity it managed to create. On the contrary, some illusions come packaged with a *presumption of falsity*, by wearing, so to speak, their character as illusions on their sleeves. Such is the case, for instance, of pretense or make-believe: the little girl who pretends to be a princess will not be deterred from her pretense by the revelation that she is, in fact, not a princess, presumably because her representation of herself as a princess never *aimed at the truth* in the way ordinary belief does, and so is not vulnerable to the knowledge of it.[3] Third, the resilience of an illusion may depend on the fact that it represents a wish as fulfilled: the distinctive Apollonian creation, the 'radiant dream-birth of the Olympians', for instance, depicts a world in which human beings are represented as intimately related with immortal and powerful god-like figures, capable of overcoming suffering (*BT*, 3).

But none of these three factors explains the resilience of *artistic* illusions. Such illusions presumably owe their resilience to their distinctively *aesthetic appeal*, specifically their *beauty* or, more precisely, to the peculiar *pleasure* the experience of beauty affords. Thus, Nietzsche reminds us that the essential business of Apollonian arts is to produce 'the rapturous vision, the pleasurable illusion [*die entzückende Vision, den lustvollen Schein*]' (*BT*, 4).

In *The Birth of Tragedy*, the nature of this aesthetic pleasure is ambiguous. On the one hand, it is the sensual pleasure we take from certain sensible qualities of works, such as their formal harmony or their brilliance.[4] By virtue of causing a *positive* sensual pleasure of this sort, beauty is also bound to *arouse desire* (for its perpetuation or reproduction). On the other hand, Nietzsche also understands aesthetic pleasure *negatively* as Schopenhauer did, that is to say, as the experience

simply because they do not wish to risk threatening the comfort and pleasure they take in them. On this distinction, see Stern (1983).

[3] See Gendler (2003; 2007). It is worth noting that Gendler (2007) herself points out that pretense may vary in vivacity and motivational force, suggesting that some forms of pretense might invite a presumption of veracity while others might come packaged with a presumption of falsity. I ignore these complications here.

[4] The German '*Schein*' designates not only 'appearance' but also brilliance, or the character of 'shining', a connotation of which Nietzsche makes explicit use in his description of Apollo as 'the shining one [*der "Scheinende"*]' (*BT*, 1). I owe this point to Gudrun von Tevenar.

of the *absence* of the pain it is in the very nature of desires to cause. The experience of an object's beauty produces such pleasure precisely by disarming the subject's desires and offering it to his 'pure' or 'disinterested' contemplation (*WWR*, I, 38, 197).

This relation of pure contemplation is one of *detachment*, as Schopenhauer makes clear in his characterization of the artistic genius: 'there floats before the mind of the genius, in its objective apprehension, the phenomenon of the world as something foreign to him, as an object of contemplation, expelling his willing from consciousness' (*WWR*, II xxxi, 387). The genius absorbed in contemplation 'loses himself' in it, insofar as he no longer *identifies* with anything or anyone in the world, which accordingly 'floats before' his mind, and has become 'foreign' to him.[5] Nietzsche evidently draws on these ideas in passages like the following: 'So extraordinary is the power of the epic-Apollonian that before our eyes it transforms the most terrible things by the joy in mere appearance and in redemption through mere appearance. The poet of the dramatized epos cannot blend completely with his images any more than the epic rhapsodist can. He is still that calm, unmoved contemplation which sees the images before its wide-open eyes.' (*BT*, 12; cf. 5: 'The plastic artist, like the epic poet who is related to him, is absorbed in the pure contemplation of images.... Thus, by this mirror of illusion, he is protected against becoming one and fused with his figures.')

There are some significant differences between the effects of the experience of beauty in these two conceptions: the sensual pleasure taken in beautiful forms diverts attention away from the terrible aspects of our existence, which are thus 'veiled and withdrawn from sight' (*BT*, 3), whereas pure contemplation can very well keep attention focused on these aspects, but in a way that leaves the contemplating subject uninvolved in, and therefore unconcerned by, them.[6]

[5] While the ordinary subject's interested consciousness of the world is the consciousness of a world in which he finds *himself* engaged in a particular way, the disinterested consciousness achieved in aesthetic experience is of a world from which the subject is somehow absent: for example, his body may continue to figure in that world, but only as 'an object among objects', that is to say, as *a* body, but not as *his* body. Since this lack of identification is the defining feature of aesthetic contemplation, Schopenhauer appears to overreach when he insists that to a disinterested consciousness the world can no longer be a world of particular individuals bearing particular relations to each other, but must be universals considered in their 'absolute essence and existence', that is to say, 'Ideas'. On this and related issues, see Janaway (1996).

[6] See Schopenhauer's description of this phenomenon: 'Every state or condition, every person, every scene of life, needs to be apprehended only purely objectively, and made the object of a description or sketch, whether with brush or with words, in order to appear interesting, delightful, and enviable.... Therefore Goethe says: "What in life does us annoy,/We in picture do enjoy." There was a period in the years of my youth when I was constantly at pains to see myself and my actions from outside, and to picture them to myself; probably in order to make them enjoyable to me' (*WWR*, I xxx, 372). On this and other related issues, see Reginster (2008).

Whether by generating sensual pleasure or disinterested contemplation, the purpose of the 'beautiful appearance' is to distract or detach, and so to release or liberate us, from the suffering that is essential to our existence—to achieve what Nietzsche repeatedly calls a 'redemption through pure appearance [*Erlösung durch den Schein*]' (*BT*, 4). Apparently, the main shortcoming of an affirmation based on a purely Apollonian 'beautiful appearance' is that it remains avoidance or evasion, a deliberate ignorance of the true character of existence, or a disengagement from it. The Apollonian subject, to be sure, is open to the suspicion that things might not be as appealing as he represents them to be, but this is a suspicion he carefully leaves unexplored. And no genuine *affirmation* can be based on the ignorance of the true character of what is to be affirmed. As Julian Young puts it,

> what the solution offers as a way of overcoming pessimism, of avoiding the pessimist's judgment on life, is self-deception, telling oneself 'lies'. But this implies that in the fullness of knowledge one would *not* affirm life as worth living. It implies, more briefly, that life is not worth living.[7]

The distinctive mark of tragic art, by contrast, is that it rests on an insight into the terrible character of our existence: in tragedy, 'the contemplative Aryan is not inclined to interpret away... the misfortune in the nature of things' (*BT*, 9). The distinctive character of tragedy is to combine Dionysian insight with Apollonian arts—more specifically, to articulate this insight in Apollonian symbols and images.[8] I shall leave aside the contentious exegetical—and philosophical—issue of whether Dionysian art is possible without recourse to Apollonian representational resources, or on the contrary requires them, and I shall concentrate on the incontrovertible fact that, when they are combined with Dionysian insight in tragedy, the significance of Apollonian appearances is dramatically altered.

The Apollonian appearance is now marshaled to reveal, rather than conceal, the truth, even if negatively, by being an appearance that 'denies itself and its Apollonian visibility' (*BT*, 21). Furthermore, a tragic representation invites

7 Young (1992, 48).

8 This claim is repeated time and again in the book: for instance, 'we must understand Greek tragedy as the Dionysian chorus which ever anew discharges itself in an Apollonian world of images' (*BT*, 8). It is a matter of scholarly controversy whether there could be 'pure' Dionysian arts, that is to say, arts that do not have to resort to Apollonian representational resources (e.g., *BT*, 2, 5), or whether there actually are pure Dionysian arts (e.g., *BT*, 6), but they require the accompaniment of Apollonian images and symbols to be tolerated (e.g., *BT*, 21). *The Birth of Tragedy* is not devoid of ambiguity on this score, and some scholars have argued that the ambiguity is inevitable, perhaps even deliberate (see, in particular, Pautrat, 1971).

identification rather than disengagement—the subject exposed to it sees himself as implicated in what he contemplates: 'The image . . . now shows him his identity with the heart of the world' (*BT*, 5). Even tragic art, however, continues to deal in illusion. If tragic illusion is to represent a higher 'stage' of illusion than purely Apollonian illusion, it cannot simply conceal under a veil of beautiful appearances 'these nauseous thoughts about the horror and absurdity of existence', but it must manage to turn them 'into notions with which one can live' (*BT*, 7). And therein lies the very paradox of tragedy that so intrigued Nietzsche, as it had Schopenhauer before him: how can the tragic representation of the terrible character of our existence produce *pleasure?*

Nietzsche rejects Schopenhauer's view that the *objectification* of the true character of existence *disengages* us from it, and that the pleasure we take at the representation of a tragedy lies in this disengagement (a view he associates with purely Apollonian illusion). His own answer is that the true character of existence is kept in full view in tragedy, and the pleasure we take at this representation is made possible by the manner in which it is *interpreted* or *seen*. This is where the element of illusion lies. The 'tragic myth', which is exemplified in all the tragedies, is a certain kind of illusion, which does not conceal, but interprets in symbols, and 'transfigures', the true character of our existence; and it does not detach, but on the contrary invites an identification with what it so represents:

> The tragic myth, too, insofar as it belongs to art at all, participates fully in this metaphysical intention of art to transfigure. But what does it transfigure when it presents the world of appearance in the image of the suffering hero? . . . It is precisely the tragic myth that has to convince us that even the ugly and disharmonic are part of an artistic game that the will in the eternal amplitude of its pleasure plays with itself. . . . again and again it reveals to us the playful construction and destruction of the individual world as the overflow of a primordial delight. Thus the dark Heraclitus compares the world-building force to a playing child that places stones here and there and builds sand hills only to overthrow them again.
>
> (*BT*, 24)

Unlike the delusion of the theoretical man, or the 'beautiful appearance' created by the purely Apollonian artist, the tragic myth does not conceal the terrible aspects of our existence, such as the unavoidable suffering and the constant passing away, but it offers a particular interpretation of it, which is supposed to be comforting. The comforting thought tragedy induces in its spectators is, as Nietzsche sees it, 'that we are merely images and artistic projections for the true author, and that we have our highest dignity in our significance as works of art'

(*BT*, 5).[9] But such indifference to our own individual fate requires that we identify *exclusively* with the 'true author' of the world, the 'primordial Oneness' or the 'child' engaged in a perpetual play of creation and destruction (see *BT*, 6). In other words, it requires us to see ourselves as other than we empirically are: it requires us to see ourselves 'metaphysically'. The comfort tragedy provides is a 'metaphysical comfort', and, to that extent, it remains a form of diversion or disengagement, possible only, in the final analysis, through a kind of deception or detachment. Raymond Geuss puts the point succinctly:

> What looks just fine from the point of view of the Child—Raymond dying painfully in a highly interesting and dramatic way—won't be nearly so satisfactory to me as the empirical person I am. The function of art is to give me a proper glimpse of *one* side of the relation between the Child and me—the side of our 'identity', while at the same time hiding the other side from me, *deceiving me* about the non-identity that exists between myself and the Child, and the possible implications that has for my ability to see my life as worthwhile.[10]

Nietzsche himself expresses misgivings along such lines about this view of tragedy in his 'Attempt at Self-Criticism'. Recalling a question he had raised, all but rhetorically, in *The Birth of Tragedy*—'*would it not be necessary* for the tragic man of such a culture, in view of his self-education for seriousness and terror, to desire a new art, the *art of metaphysical comfort*...?' (*BT*, 18)—he now answers:

> No, thrice no! O you young romantics: it would *not* be necessary! But it is highly probable that it will *end* that way, that *you* end that way—namely, 'comforted', as it is written, in spite of all self-education for seriousness and terror, 'comforted metaphysically'—in sum, as romantics end, as *Christians*. No! You ought to learn the art of *this-worldly* comfort first: you ought to learn to laugh, my young friends, if you are hell-bent on remaining pessimists.
>
> (*BT*, 'Attempt', 7)

In the 'Attempt', Nietzsche comes to identify the real opponent to the tragic stance he advocates as not Socratism, but Christianity. This is, presumably, because Christianity acknowledges the inevitability of suffering in this life no less than does tragedy, and produces an interpretation of it that is also supposed to be comforting. The Christian interpretation is comforting by virtue of being 'metaphysical', that is to say, of invoking 'another world', in which the sufferings of 'this world' are absent. What disturbs Nietzsche about his own youthful enthusiasm for the tragic myth is its metaphysical character, its invitation to

[9] This picture, which Nietzsche calls in the 'Attempt' an 'artist's metaphysics', is discussed in detail by Gardner (2013).

[10] Geuss (1999, 107–8). Young (1992, 51–4) raises a similar objection.

discount, or altogether ignore, 'this', the empirical, world in favor of a mythical 'other' world. In the final analysis, it passes off what is in reality a 'negation of life' for an affirmation of it, just as much as the Christian myth does. For it still implicitly claims that the justification of our existence in this (empirical) world cannot be found in it and must be sought *outside* of it, in a world beyond or behind it.

Nietzsche's misgivings about the ability of beauty—understood as illusion, as a 'veil' draped over the otherwise intolerable truth concerning the character of our existence—to underwrite a genuine affirmation grow in later works. In the first four books of *The Gay Science*, the '*good* will to appearance', which remains there conceived as deception or falsification (see *GS*, 78, 299) and is supposed to counter the '*honesty*' that would 'lead to nausea and suicide', now only allows us to cope or to endure: 'As an aesthetic phenomenon existence is still *bearable* for us [*erträglich*], and art furnishes us with eyes and hands and above all the good conscience to be *able* to turn ourselves into such a phenomenon' (*GS*, 107). As Nietzsche eventually makes clear, however, to affirm life must be more than 'bearing' it or 'concealing' its true character: '*amor fati*:... [n]ot merely bear [*ertragen*] what is necessary, still less conceal it... but *love* it' (*EH*, II, 10; see *WP*, 1041).

In fact, Nietzsche goes so far as to suggest that the very need for 'beautifying' illusions is a 'revenge on life':

> let nobody doubt that whoever stands that much in *need* of the cult of surfaces must at some time have reached *beneath* them with disastrous results. Perhaps there even exists an order of rank among these burnt children, these born artists who can find the enjoyment of life only in the intention of *falsifying* its image (as it were, in a longwinded revenge on life): the degree to which life has been spoiled for them might be inferred from the degree to which they wish to see its image falsified, thinned down, transcendentalized, deified.
>
> (*BGE*, 59; cf. 39)

It is now 'the suffering, desperate, self-mistrustful, in a word the sick [who] have at all times had need of entrancing *visions* to endure life', and it is now 'the artists of decadence, who fundamentally have a *nihilistic* attitude toward life, [who] take refuge in the *beauty of form*' (*WP*, 852).

2 TWO POINTS OF VIEW: 'SPECTATOR' VS. 'CREATOR'

An important line of thought left undeveloped in *The Birth of Tragedy* points to a different approach. It bears on the 'comfort' the tragic myth is supposed to provide. This myth, remember, invites us to identify with an entirely reckless and amoral artist-god who wants to experience, whether he is building or destroying, in the good and in the bad, his own joy and glory—one who, creating worlds, frees himself from the *distress* of fullness and *overfullness* and from the *afflictions* of the contradictions compressed in his soul.

(*BT*, 'Attempt', 5)

I observed earlier that this identification *could be* comforting only if we discounted or ignored our empirical nature. But it remains to be asked why, assuming we managed to do so, such identification *could be* a source of comfort at all. Presumably, we find this symbolic representation of the character of our existence attractive *only because the activity of the creative artist evoked here appeals to us in the first place.*

This largely implicit line of thought announces a fundamental shift in the approach to the 'aesthetic problem' Nietzsche was eventually to advocate explicitly. While his dispute with Schopenhauer initially concerns the nature of the effect the contemplation of beauty is supposed to have on its spectator, it comes to focus on the assumption that the aesthetic problem should be approached from the point of view of the *spectator* in the first place. Schopenhauer, Nietzsche remarks, 'instead of envisaging the aesthetic problem from the point of view of the artist (the creator), considered art and the beautiful purely from that of the "spectator"' (*GM*, III, 6; see *Z*, II, 15). The fundamental assumption of Schopenhauerian aesthetics is that the purpose of art is to induce a certain *view* of things. And while in *The Birth of Tragedy* Nietzsche disagrees with his predecessor on the question of whether the aesthetic view of things is meant to *calm* rather than to *arouse*, he still largely subscribes to that assumption: the artist apparently creates only in order to be 'entertained' as the spectator of his own creations (*BT*, 5).

A simple observation appears to motivate Nietzsche's shift from an *aesthetic* to an *artistic* approach: if the purpose of a work of art is to convey to its spectators, or to awaken in them, a certain view of its object, then the creative artist must have this view *already* to guide his production of the work; but what reasons would the artist have then to produce such a work? If we dismiss as implausible the suggestion that all artists are motivated by an altruistic concern for the well-being of their spectators, we are left without a clear answer to this question, and it becomes tempting to follow Nietzsche in moving away from the point of view of the spectator in our approach to art.[11]

[11] This line of argument against a 'spectator's view' of the creative artist is developed by Soll (1998, 109), who offers the following conclusion: 'He does not create a work just in order to be able to be a spectator of it. The joys of creation consist not just in one's enjoyment of the results . . . , but

The shift to the point of view of the creator is an invitation to consider art and its effects from the perspective of the creative artist. It suggests, in particular, that the significance of art is to be found less in its *products* than in the *creative activity* by which they are produced. And the proper effect of art, accordingly, is less to produce a certain comforting view of things than to incite to a certain kind of activity: 'the effect of works of art is to excite *the state that creates art*' (*WP*, 821; see *TI*, IX, 22: 'all beauty incites to procreation—that precisely this is the *proprium* of its effect'). It presumably follows that the affirmative dimension of art—particularly, its ability to produce an affirmation of suffering—will now have to be sought in the very activity of creation.

3 TWO PARADOXES OF AFFIRMATION

The failure of illusion to produce a genuine affirmation of life leads Nietzsche to maintain that affirming life requires affirming it in its very 'terrifying and questionable character'. And to affirm the terrifying and questionable character of life is not simply to acknowledge and endure it, indeed not even to find it conditionally valuable—it is

> to perceive not merely the necessity of those sides of existence hitherto denied, but their desirability; and not their desirability merely in relation to the sides of existence hitherto affirmed (perhaps as their complement or precondition), but for their own sake.
>
> (*WP*, 1041; cf. *EH*, II, 10)

This is the first paradox of affirmation: existence must be affirmed not merely *in spite* of what seems most deniable about it—its terrifying and questionable character—but (at least in part) *because* of it. Nietzsche characterizes affirmation as standing 'in a Dionysian relationship to existence' (ibid.), which he had already described in *The Birth of Tragedy* as the paradoxical phenomenon of taking joy at suffering itself (*BT*, 2). For Nietzsche, merely to accept the inevitability of what is terrible or problematic in existence (such as, primarily, suffering), or to recognize its desirability only as a (contingent) by-product or enabling condition of something one affirms, is not to affirm it. This is presumably because someone who merely accepts the terrible or questionable character of existence, or even

also in the enjoyment of the process of creation—of creation as such. Nietzsche is surely right to insist that theories attempting to ground the value of artistic creation in that of disengaged aesthetic contemplation are inadequate.' Young (1992, 118–25) also emphasizes this contrast. However, both Soll and Young conflate the objection to a 'spectator's view' of the significance of art with the objection to the claim that aesthetic contemplation is essentially disinterested.

recognizes its contingent desirability, can still coherently deplore it and aspire to a different life.

Nietzsche's revaluation of values is intended to offer a resolution of this paradox, particularly the revaluation of suffering in terms of an ethical outlook based on his concept of the will to power. Specifically, he shows that suffering is an essential ingredient of the good he calls 'power', which he defines as the activity of confronting and overcoming resistance in the pursuit of some determinate end.[12] If this activity of overcoming resistance is a good, indeed *the* source of happiness (*A*, 2), and if this activity constitutively involves the experience of resistance, or suffering, then suffering is a constituent of happiness, and of the 'pleasure' it involves: 'Thus, all pleasure includes pain' (*WP*, 658; 657, 699).[13]

It is tempting to infer from what we have seen so far that the affirmation of life is, or is based on, a judgment that it is *good*, and that, since in reality it is not, such a judgment could be made possible only by the illusions produced by art. Now that we have determined that illusion is unable to ground a genuine affirmation of life, it seems as though this affirmation would then require establishing the judgment that life, including what is terrifying and questionable in it, is good. And it is also tempting to regard Nietzsche's revaluation of values, particularly his revaluation of the role and significance of suffering in human existence, as aiming to establish precisely that judgment.

But Nietzsche notoriously declares that '*the value of life cannot be estimated*' (*TI*, II, 2), a claim he justifies on essentially epistemic grounds:

> One would have to be situated *outside* life, and on the other hand to know it as thoroughly as any, as many, as all who have experienced it, to be permitted to touch on the problem of the *value* of life at all: sufficient reason for understanding that this problem is for us an inaccessible problem.
>
> (*TI*, V, 5)

[12] Soll (1998) recognizes the significance of the concept of will to power for the revaluation of suffering in ways that anticipate my own view in Reginster (2006), but he curiously continues to insist, without explanation, that even once suffering has been so re-evaluated, we still require illusion to affirm it. Andrew Huddleston has suggested to me that illusion might remain necessary to affirmation—not as what allows us to see life as good, but as a motivational booster to continue our engagement in it. The illusion would not be about the value of suffering as such, but in the manner in which the value of suffering is represented (e.g., set to beautiful music)—although why it would remain an *illusion* in that case is unclear. We might take this suggestion to be that there is a distinction between the (theoretical) judgment that life has value and the affirmation (in the form of a practical engagement) of life—which would presumably be analogous to the distinction between judging that someone is worthy of trust and actually trusting her—and that the latter would require the seductions of artistic 'transfiguration'. This is an interesting suggestion, though not one that is, to my knowledge, explicitly taken up by Nietzsche.

[13] I examine this paradoxical idea in detail in Reginster (2005).

The heart of the argument is the claim that one can never 'know' enough about life to be 'permitted' to judge its value.

This alone, it must be noted, already represents a significant departure from the conception found in *The Birth of Tragedy*:

> The conception of the work that one encounters in this book is singularly gloomy and unpleasant: ... there is only *one* world, and this is false, cruel, contradictory, seductive, without meaning—A world thus constituted is the real world. We *have need of lies* in order to conquer this reality, this 'truth', that is, in order to *live*.... One will see that in this book pessimism, or to speak more clearly, nihilism, counts as 'truth'.
>
> (*WP*, 853)

In other words, Nietzsche evidently believed in that book that the value of life *could* be estimated. And his estimation of it followed Schopenhauer: life is essentially suffering; suffering is evil; life itself is therefore evil and should be denied. A momentous change must have taken place for Nietzsche to come to the view that 'the value of life cannot be estimated'.

We might be inclined to attribute this change to a repudiation of the Schopenhauerian metaphysical dogmatism that stills dominates *The Birth of Tragedy*: since we lack complete knowledge of the nature of life, particularly of its character 'in itself', we cannot pass a legitimate judgment on its value. But most of Schopenhauer's metaphysical arguments for the inevitability of suffering have an explicitly *empirical* basis: they do not look objectionably dogmatic and Nietzsche never rejects the conclusion they are intended to support.[14]

This suggests that his change of mind should rather be attributed to the revaluation of values he develops throughout his later works. This is perplexing since, as I noted earlier, it is tempting to regard this revaluation as aiming to establish that life is good (at least in part) because of the suffering in it, and so worthy of affirmation. However, considered closely, Nietzsche's revaluation of suffering does *not* show that it is always good, but only that a life cannot be considered objectionable simply in virtue of including suffering. In other words, the revaluation of suffering only debunks the pessimistic devaluation of life that forms the background of *The Birth of Tragedy* (which Nietzsche eventually calls 'nihilism'). But it does not establish that life actually is good, or even that its value can be estimated. For even though suffering *as such* is no longer seen as objectionable, particular sufferings in particular circumstances may still prove to be deplorable. Whether particular sufferings in particular circumstances will

[14] On the empirical character of Schopenhauer's metaphysics, see Reginster (2006, 106–7); see also Hannan (2009, 16–7, 44–51); and on Nietzsche's appropriation of Schopenhauer's arguments for the inevitability of suffering, see Reginster (2006, 124–6).

contribute to, or detract from, the value of an individual's life, or indeed from the value of life in general, conceived as the aggregation of the lives of all individuals, is for Nietzsche an entirely contingent and unpredictable matter (see *TI*, V, 5). This is why he may conclude that, his revaluation of suffering notwithstanding, 'the value of life cannot be estimated'.[15]

In Nietzsche's considered view, then, the affirmation of life cannot be, or be based on, a judgment of its value. This has led a number of scholars to characterize affirmation as a positive attitude that involves or entails no judgment concerning its value. Daniel Came, for instance, proposes to think of it as a positive *affective* attitude, and observes that 'to have an affectively positive attitude toward X need not entail having any beliefs about the objective value of X, or even the belief that X has an objective value.'[16] And Ken Gemes regards affirmation as an essentially *non-reflective* attitude, and takes the very reflective concern with the value of life to evince already a problematic, 'negative' attitude toward it.[17]

However, I remain inclined to regard the affirmation of life as being, or involving, some sort of positive *evaluative* stance toward it, if only for two reasons. First, the strongly evaluative terminology of the early works ('justification [*Rechtfertigung*]') can still be found in the late works: 'an ecstatic affirmation of the total character of existence... sanctifies and *calls good* even the most terrible and questionable qualities of life' (*WP*, 1050; my emphasis). Second, Nietzsche insists on the role played by the 'revaluation of values' in making possible the affirmation of life: it is 'a higher order of values... that say Yes to life' (*EH*, III, *CW*, 2). This view of affirmation as valuation has one troubling consequence, however: it brings in full view the second paradox of the affirmation

[15] Although I did acknowledge some of the limitations of this revaluation for the affirmation of life in Reginster (2006, 187–9, 266–7), I failed to conclude explicitly that this revaluation forms only a necessary condition of affirmation, not doing enough to discourage the suggestion that it is *sufficient* for it.

[16] Came (2005, 47). Note that Came only rejects the idea of affirmation as a conferral of 'objective value' to life. It is otherwise doubtful that Nietzsche would accept the sharp contrast between affect and value on which his suggestion depends. If, as many scholars believe, Nietzsche endorses one or another kind of subjectivism about value, then 'to have an affectively positive attitude toward X' could not so neatly be divorced from having an *evaluative* attitude toward it.

[17] See Gemes (2015). It should be noted, however, that an unreflective attitude could nevertheless be an *evaluative* one. From the fact that an *explicit* judgment of value would indeed require reflection, it does not follow that an unreflective stance of affirmation is not, if only implicitly, evaluative itself. In suggesting that one affirms life to the extent that one manages to eschew the concern to justify it, Simon May (2011) appears to aim at divorcing affirmation from any sort of evaluation.

of life. How could Nietzsche declare, on the one hand, that the value of life cannot be estimated and advocate, on the other, its affirmation, if that involves some sort of positive valuation of it? How is the affirmation of life even possible if it consists in adopting some sort of positive valuation of it, while continuing to recognize that its value cannot be estimated? The answer to this question, I now want to suggest, lies in a reconsideration of the concept of beauty.

4 THE CONCEPT OF BEAUTY

Alexander Nehamas[18] has recently argued that the judgment that something is beautiful is distinctive in that it does not settle anything about one's evaluation of it, it is not a final 'verdict', but merely an inducement to deepen one's acquaintance or to continue one's engagement with it. In matters of beauty, as Nehamas puts it, '[e]valuation settles nothing. It is a commitment to the future' (53). Crucially, on this view, the desire to pursue one's engagement with the beautiful object is not predicated upon the guarantee that such an engagement will be a source of enjoyment or benefit. And this is because the judgment that something is beautiful 'does not look back at what I have learned and experienced so far, but at what—without knowing exactly what it is—I hope to learn and experience in the future' (55). There is an essential element of risk and uncertainty—beauty can always turn out to be a siren's song that leads to shipwreck—but this very element of risk and uncertainty is (at least partially) *constitutive* of the value I acknowledge when I judge something beautiful:[19] 'Beauty always remains a bit of a mystery, forever a step beyond anything I can say about it, more like something calling me without showing me exactly what it is calling me to' (78).

This characterization suggests a way in which the judgment of beauty, though in some sense a positive valuation of its object, is nevertheless compatible with the claim that the value of this object cannot be estimated once and for all. In fact, an object the value of which has been so estimated *could not* be judged beautiful:

[18] In his wonderful 2007 book. Parenthetical page numbers in the text refer to this edition.

[19] When Nehamas declares that 'as long as we find something beautiful we feel certain that it can still yield something of value, despite the fact that we don't know what that is' (76), he only presents it as a *necessary* condition of the thing's beauty. For we can have the very same experience—i.e., the sense that there is something good there, although we do not know what—about things we do not necessarily find beautiful. For example, an obscure and complicated philosophical paper might arouse that sense and persuade us to go on reading, without (necessarily) eliciting the experience that the article is 'beautiful'. As Nehamas suggests, the experience of beauty requires that this element of uncertainty be *itself* seen as appealing, which is presumably not necessarily the case with the obscure but intriguing article.

> That forward-looking element and the risks that attend it are essential to beauty, which withers when it can promise nothing it has not given already, and signals the fading of love. For love, as Proust wrote... 'is born, it lives, only for so long as there is something left to conquer. We love only that which we do not wholly possess.' Beauty points to the future, and we pursue it without knowing what it will yield.
>
> (62)

Insofar as affirming life is finding it beautiful, it is not, or is not based on, the judgment that it actually *is* good, or that it will turn out well. It certainly inspires the hope for these things, but it also inspires this hope in a peculiarly ambivalent way. I have in mind here two forms of ambivalence. There is, in the first place, the ambivalence characteristic of hope itself: hope motivates, but insofar as it cannot guarantee against disappointment, it also inhibits, it makes us hesitate to pursue its object. But there is also, in the second place, the ambivalence created by the fact that (part of) what is enjoyed in the experience of beauty is the element of mystery and uncertainty, or, so to speak, hopefulness itself. The hope beauty arouses is thus a hope that seeks to have only enough of the things hoped for to sustain itself, but also apprehends fulfillment as what would put an end to the joy of hopefulness.

In both of these respects, then, while the beauty of an object incites the desire to know or to engage further with it, it also arouses a certain reluctance to do so. This peculiar ambivalence, it turns out, characterizes the very attitude *The Birth of Tragedy* attributes to the tragic subject, once we remove from it those metaphysical *accoutrements* Nietzsche himself eventually repudiated. It characterizes specifically a modification the Apollonian 'beautiful appearance' undergoes when it is combined with Dionysian insight:

> To be sure, the Apollonian projection that is thus illuminated from inside by music does not achieve the peculiar effect of the weaker degrees of Apollonian art. What the epic or the animated stone can do, compelling the contemplative eye to find calm delight in the world of individuation, that could not be attained here, in spite of a higher animation and clarity. We looked at the drama and with penetrating eye reached its inner world of motives—and yet we felt as if only a parable passed us by, whose most profound meaning we almost thought we could guess and that we wished to draw away like a curtain in order to behold the primordial image behind it. The brightest clarity of the image did not suffice us, for this seemed to wish just as much to reveal something as to conceal something. Its revelation, being like a parable, seemed to summon us to tear the veil and to uncover the mysterious background; but at the same time this all-illuminated total visibility cast a spell over the eyes and prevented them from penetrating deeper.
>
> (*BT*, 24)

When it takes on a Dionysian dimension, the beautiful appearance arouses a curiously paradoxical attitude, characterized by a mixture of desire to find out more about the beautiful object and of reluctance to do so.

Despite some half-hearted references to the Schopenhauerian view of beauty as the property by which an object invites disinterested contemplation, and ultimately resignation, Nietzsche favors already in *The Birth of Tragedy*, and unequivocally after it, the opposite view of beauty as a property by which an object arouses desire and interest: beautiful appearances 'at every moment make life worth living at all and prompt the desire to live on in order to experience the next moment' (*BT*, 25; see *GM*, III, 6; *TI*, IX, 22). And although he relies there on a classical view of beauty as referring to sensual properties such as formal harmony and brilliance, suggesting that the desire it arouses and the pleasure it gives are themselves sensual, his conception of beauty and of the attitude it produces in those who encounter it soon gains in breadth and complexity: 'all beauty incites to procreation', Nietzsche writes later on, but immediately specifies 'that precisely this is the *proprium* of its effect, from the most sensual regions *up into the most spiritual*' (*TI*, IX, 22; my emphasis). Beauty cannot simply be the property of what arouses *sensual* desires since things we would not judge beautiful can have this effect, and things we would judge beautiful can lack it. Beautiful things incite desire, but the desire they incite must be of a distinctive sort.

If beauty is conceived as referring to sensible properties such as formal harmony, proportion, or brilliance, the desire beauty inspires is essentially a desire for the reproduction of the pleasure produced by the contemplation of such harmony and brilliance. It is therefore a desire to *remain* with the beautiful appearance that produces such pleasure, and not to move beyond it—'It is a dream! I will dream on!' (*BT*, 1) This may explain why, in *The Birth of Tragedy*, Nietzsche is not that concerned to distinguish between this conception and the Schopenhauerian conception of beauty. In both cases, the contemplation of beauty induces the spectator to go no further, either by causing 'will-lessness', or by producing a desire to perpetuate, or reproduce, the beautiful appearance. On the alternative conception of beauty that emerges in Nietzsche's later works, by contrast, beauty is now thought to inspire a desire for *new artistic creation*—that is to say, a desire to *go beyond* the beautiful appearance that produces this desire, by engaging more deeply with the object that appears under such a beautiful guise.

The change in Nietzsche's view of the relation between beauty and affirmation is as dramatic as it is subtle. Existence continues to be justified as an 'aesthetic phenomenon', as a 'veil of beautiful appearances', but the meaning of the beautiful appearance is fundamentally altered. In *The Birth of Tragedy*, for the most part, the veil of beautiful appearances was supposed to derive its power from the fact that it was a veil that *concealed*; it seduced the beholder to go no further than its appearances, by beguiling and mesmerizing him, and appealing to his need for comfort and security. Now, it is supposed to derive its power from the fact that it is a veil that summons and reveals; it invites the beholder to look further, to engage more deeply, arousing his spirit of 'adventure' or, as we shall see shortly, his will to power. Something is thought to lie 'behind' the appearances in both cases: it is the 'true world'—'there is only *one* world, and this is false, cruel, contradictory, seductive, without meaning' (*WP*, 853)—in Nietzsche's early metaphysical dogmatism, whereas it later ceases to be the 'true world', as opposed to the merely 'apparent' world (see *TI*, IV, 6), to become simply the world we do not know yet, or with which we have yet to engage, as opposed to those parts of the world that are 'apparent' to us simply insofar as they are already known.

On this modified view, beauty remains the quality of an 'appearance' or a 'veil', which one is still advised not simply to tear in order to uncover what it conceals:

> one will hardly find us again on the paths of those Egyptian youths who endanger temples by night, embrace statues, and want by all means to unveil, uncover, and put into a bright light whatever is kept concealed for good reasons.... We no longer believe that truth remains truth when the veils are withdrawn; we have lived too much to believe this. Today we consider it a matter of decency not to wish to see everything naked, or to be present at everything, or to understand and 'know' everything.
>
> (*GS*, P, 4)

But the recommendation not simply to tear the veil is no longer justified, as Nietzsche retrospectively notes it was in *The Birth of Tragedy*, by the need to conceal the metaphysical necessity of suffering, and to make use of artistic illusion to restore or buttress '*faith* in life': '"Life *ought* to inspire trust [*Vertrauen*]": the task thus imposed is tremendous. To solve it, man must be a liar by nature, he must be above all an *artist*' (*WP*, 853). In that book, subscribing as it still was to 'moral' (Schopenhauerian) values, the recognition that suffering is inevitable was intolerable, and required a veil of beautiful appearances to restore trust in life. In the wake of the revaluation of suffering, the experience of pain still undermines trust in life but to a very different effect:

> The trust [*Vertrauen*] in life is gone: life itself has become a *problem*. Yet one should not jump to the conclusion that this necessarily makes one gloomy. Even love of life is still possible, one loves life differently. It is the love for a woman that causes doubt in us.
>
> The attraction of everything problematic, the delight in an *x*, however, is so great in such more spiritual, more spiritualized men that this delight flares up again and again like a bright blaze over all the distress of what is problematic, over all the danger of uncertainty, and even over the jealousy of the lover. We know a new happiness.
>
> (*GS*, P, 3)

While the 'veil of beautiful appearance' was earlier seen as a 'shroud', a 'sweetener', or an 'illusion' that represents life as good and trustworthy (*BGE*, 39), it is now meant to make it appear 'profound', mysterious, or 'problematic'. But the very problematic character of life, the fact that it cannot be 'trusted', is now (part of) what makes it appealing or seductive, by arousing our spirit of 'adventure'. From this perspective, to 'know everything', or to 'see everything naked' would be indecent, not because things are bound to prove disappointing once we know them completely, although they certainly could, but because complete knowledge is itself disappointing, insofar as it deprives things of their problematic character, of their mysterious allure, and puts an end to the adventure which their encounter had promised.[20]

This idea echoes a curious passage from *The Birth of Tragedy*, in which Nietzsche attributes to Lessing a crucial insight about the true motivation of the seeker after truth: 'Therefore Lessing, the most honest theoretical man, dared to announce that he cared more for the search after truth than for truth itself—and thus revealed the most fundamental secret of science' (*BT*, 15). Read carefully, this passage places the seeker after truth in a peculiarly ambivalent position: he must both want and not want to find the truth. He cannot be a genuine seeker after truth unless he wants to find it, but actually finding it would deprive him of what he cares most about, the *search* after it, and so he must also want not to find it. It is the *unveiling* of the truth, not the 'naked' truth, which the seeker after truth enjoys.

Seen as a matter of finding beauty in life, the affirmation of life thus requires the ability to enjoy its 'problematic' character or, as Nietzsche says, the ability to take 'joy no longer in certainty but in uncertainty' (*WP*, 1059; 1060). Uncertainty has its dangers, to be sure: upon further acquaintance, the beautiful object might prove disappointing, harmful, perhaps even destructive. But therein lies its distinctive value: 'For believe me: the secret for harvesting from existence the greatest fruitfulness and the greatest enjoyment is—to *live dangerously!*' (*GS*, 283).

5 THE MEANING OF TRAGEDY

Tragedy fascinates Nietzsche because it manages to represent the most terrifying and questionable aspects of our existence in a way that incites us to affirm, rather than deny, it. And the terrifying and questionable aspect of existence on which

[20] All this should invite caution in interpreting the end of *GS*, P, 4, as a simple return to an Apollonian cult of 'surfaces' and 'appearances'.

Nietzsche focuses most persistently is the inevitability of suffering, understood as the experience of resistance to the satisfaction of our desires. In *The Birth of Tragedy*, he had argued that tragedy could make such suffering tolerable only by producing a comforting *view* of it by resorting to certain sorts of illusion. As he considers the issue again in his late works, Nietzsche proposes a different answer:

> One question remains: art also brings to light much that is ugly, hard, questionable in life—does it not thereby seem to suffer from life?—And there have indeed been philosophers who lent it this meaning: Schopenhauer taught that the whole object of art was to 'liberate from the will', and he revered tragedy because its greatest function was to 'dispose one to resignation'.... *What does the tragic artist communicate of himself?* Does he not display precisely the condition of *fearlessness* in the face of the terrifying and questionable?... Bravery and composure in the face of a powerful enemy, great hardship, a problem that arouses aversion—it is this *victorious* condition which the tragic artist singles out, which he glorifies. In the face of tragedy the warlike in our souls celebrates its Saturnalias; whoever is accustomed to suffering, whoever seeks out suffering, the *heroic* man extols his existence by means of tragedy.
>
> (*TI*, IX, 24)

Nietzsche's new answer rests on a fundamental shift of perspective: he considers the tragic effect no longer from the perspective of the 'spectator' but from that of the 'artist'. It is no longer a question of producing a deceptive but comforting *view* of life, but of inciting a distinctive sort of *active* engagement with it.[21] The tragic artist invites its audience to respond to 'the terrifying and the questionable' in our existence as he does—as so many challenges, calls to adventure, or opportunities for overcoming. His distinctive achievement is to represent 'a powerful enemy, great hardship, a problem that arouses aversion' in such a way as to awaken 'the warlike in our souls'—that is to say, our spirit of adventure, our will to power, which welcomes and 'seeks out suffering' precisely insofar as it is recognized as an essential ingredient of the pursuit of power.

The effect of tragedy is thus, like that of other works of art, 'to excite *the state that creates art*'. And once we appreciate its value, this creative *activity* itself, rather than some comforting *view* of the world it might produce, redeems suffering: 'Creation—that is the great redemption from all suffering, and life's growing light. But that the creator may be, suffering is needed and much change'

[21] In spite of his emphasis on the contrast between 'passivity' and 'activity' in describing the proper effect of art, Young (1992, 128–9) continues to think of art as producing or inducing a certain *view* of things rather than as inciting a certain kind of *activity*. And since he continues to regard an artistic view of things as involving essentially illusion, he is led to the conclusion, which I have been disputing, that 'life, real life, is unaffirmable' (139).

(*Z*, II, 2). Suffering is 'redeemed' not insofar as it is eliminated, or simply concealed, but insofar as it is an essential 'ingredient' of such creative activity.[22]

But the incitement to pursue and deepen our engagement with an existence that includes such terrifying and questionable aspects by representing them as challenges or calls to 'adventure' offers no guarantee that something good will come out of it. On the contrary, it pointedly provides no assurance that those terrible and questionable aspects will be redeemed or even that they are redeemable at all. Tragic art does not make such aspects appealing by demonstrating their actual goodness, anymore than it does by concealing their evil character under a veil of illusion. It does so by making them appear 'problematic'—by suggesting, for example, that the suffering they involve is only problematic, and not necessarily an objection against them. Stendhal, Nietzsche remarks approvingly, 'once called the beautiful *une promesse de bonheur* [a promise of happiness]' (*GM*, III, 6). And happiness lies, in Nietzsche's view, in the taking up of challenges, the activity of confronting and overcoming resistance (see *GM*, I, 10), the paradigm of which is *creative* activity. Since the value of such an activity lies (in part) in its being challenging, and since it would not be challenging if its outcome were certain, then its value must lie (in part) in the very uncertainty of its outcome. Thus, the beautiful appearance of a thing arouses love for it, a desire to engage with it that is predicated, however, not upon the conviction that it will prove good or beneficial, but upon doubt and uncertainty about it: 'It is the love for a woman that causes doubt in us'.

Nietzsche recognizes that it takes a certain type of individual to recognize and appreciate beauty so understood. It takes, as he likes to put it, an individual with 'strength':

> It is a question of *strength*... *whether* and *where* the judgment "beautiful" is applied.... the feeling of *power* applies the judgment "beautiful" even to things and conditions that the feeling of impotence could only find *hateful* and 'ugly'. The nose for what we could still barely deal with if it confronted us in the flesh—as danger, problem, temptation—this determines even our aesthetic Yes.
>
> (*WP*, 852; cf. *Z*, II, 7)

By contrast, the enjoyment of beautiful appearance, in the sense of a comforting vision assumed by this notion in *The Birth of Tragedy*, is now explicitly denounced as 'nihilistic' and belonging to 'weakness':

[22] I distinguish Nietzsche's view of the relationship between suffering and creativity from other views with which it has often been confused in Reginster (2006, 193–4). I also suggest that there is a way in which Nietzsche may have come to see the 'tragic failure' of characters such as Oedipus as a necessary consequence of the good life as he conceives of it (see 248–50).

the artists of decadence, who fundamentally have a *nihilistic* attitude toward life, take *refuge* in the *beauty of form*.... ("Love of beauty" can therefore be something other than the *ability to see* the beautiful, *create* the beautiful; it can be an expression of the very *inability* to do so).

(*WP*, 852)

Nietzsche is *not* here making a claim about the relativity of the *concept* of beauty—for instance, that it designates the lure of what is dangerous and problematic to some, and the comfort of harmonious forms to others. The parenthetical comment indicates that he is rather making a claim about the relativity of the *ability to apply* this concept correctly: it takes 'strength' to recognize beauty.

The concept of strength assumes a variety of guises in Nietzsche's philosophy. But it is often closely associated with his concept of will to power. The will to power is the desire for the confrontation and overcoming of resistance in the pursuit of some determinate project—in other words, it is a desire for *challenges*. Although 'strength' is sometimes used as a synonym for 'will to power' (see, e.g., *GM*, I, 13), it is more plausibly defined as the characteristic of those individuals whose *ability* to satisfy their will to power is great enough that they have not been induced to suppress it by the repeated experience, or simply the prospect, of its frustration, as typically do those who are crippled by a sense of 'impotence' (ibid.). From the point of view of those 'strong individuals' who deliberately seek out challenges, the appeal of the beautiful veil of appearances would lie precisely in its character of 'danger, problem, temptation'.[23]

Affirmation is an essentially 'tragic' attitude, for Nietzsche, for tragic art is essentially the enterprise of showing that life could be beautiful because it essentially involves the confrontation of suffering, and because the outcome of this confrontation is essentially uncertain—and indeed that beauty itself is the characteristic of that which promises the 'adventure' of such an uncertain confrontation. In making the affirmation of life a matter of seeing it as beautiful, then, Nietzsche suggests that what makes it worth living is, at least in part, the

[23] Beauty cannot simply be the quality of that the value of which is uncertain, since, presumably not every object the value of which is uncertain will appear beautiful. Those objects we find beautiful must therefore possess some further characteristic in virtue of which they appear pregnant with at least 'a promise of happiness'. Nehamas (2007) does not address this problem explicitly, although we might suppose he would follow Nietzsche in acknowledging a certain kind of relativity in judgments of beauty (*WP*, 804). Beauty, in Nietzsche's view, is the quality of what incites to creative activity. Whether a particular object is taken to have this quality will presumably depend upon the particular configuration of 'strengths' of the individual who makes the judgment. Unfortunately, I cannot pursue this important issue here.

very uncertainty about whether or not it is worth living.[24] And this is why he believes that it is possible to affirm life without being able to estimate its value. Indeed, on this view, the inestimability of the value of life is a condition of the very possibility of its affirmation.[25]

REFERENCES

Came, D. 2005. 'The Aesthetic Justification of Existence', in Ansell Pearson, K. (ed.), *A Companion to Nietzsche* (Oxford: Blackwell Publishing): 41–57.

Gardner, S. 2013. 'Nietzsche's Philosophical Aestheticism', in Gemes, K. and Richardson, J. (eds.), *The Oxford Handbook of Nietzsche* (New York and Oxford: Oxford University Press): 599–628.

Gemes, K. 2015. 'Nietzsche, Nihilism, and the Paradox of Affirmation', in Came, D. (ed.), *Nietzsche on Morality and the Affirmation of Life* (New York and Oxford: Oxford University Press).

Gendler, T. 2003. 'On the Relation between Pretense and Belief', in Kieran, M. and Lopes, D. (eds.), *Imagination, Philosophy and the Arts* (New York: Routledge): 125–41.

Gendler, T. 2007. 'Self-Deception as Pretense', *Philosophical Perspectives: Philosophy of Mind*, 21/1: 231–58.

Geuss, R. 1999. 'Art and Theodicy', *Morality, Culture, and History* (Cambridge: Cambridge University Press): 78–115.

Hannan, B. 2009. *The Riddle of the World* (New York and Oxford: Oxford University Press).

Janaway, C. 1996. 'Knowledge and Tranquility: Schopenhauer on the Value of Art', in Jacquette, D. (ed.), *Schopenhauer, Philosophy, and the Arts* (Cambridge: Cambridge University Press): 39–61.

May, S. 2011. 'Why Nietzsche is Still in the Morality Game', in May, S. (ed.), *Nietzsche's* On the Genealogy of Morality: *A Critical Guide* (Cambridge: Cambridge University Press): 78–100.

Nehamas, A. 2007. *Only a Promise of Happiness: The Place of Beauty in a World of Art* (Princeton: Princeton University Press).

Nietzsche, F. 1969. *Ecce Homo*, Kaufmann, W. (trans.) (New York: Random House).

[24] There is potential for paradox in the claim that (part of) what makes life worth living is uncertainty over whether it will have been worth living. For the very presence of uncertainty over whether or not life will have been worth living would make it certain that life will have been worth living. The paradox rests on an equivocation between two senses of 'worth living', which should be distinguished. It designates, on the one hand, the 'beauty' of life, the lure of its mysterious and problematic character: for example, will the 'adventures' it promises prove exhilarating? Will they involve the successful overcoming of resistance? It might also refer, on the other hand, to the 'success' of life—the fact that one's engagement with it and its challenges has actually been exhilarating or enjoyable.

[25] I would like to thank an audience at the Institute of Philosophy of the University of London for their useful responses to an earlier version of this chapter, and Andrew Huddleston for reading and commenting helpfully on it.

Nietzsche, F. 1968. *The Twilight of the Idols*, Hollingdale, R. J. (trans.) (Harmondsworth: Penguin).

Nietzsche, F. 1968. *The Will to Power*, Kaufmann, W. and Hollingdale, R. J. (trans.) (New York: Random House).

Nietzsche, F. 1969. *On the Genealogy of Morals*, Kaufmann, W. (trans.) (New York: Random House).

Nietzsche, F. 1971. *The Birth of Tragedy*, Kaufmann, W. (trans.) (New York: Vintage).

Nietzsche, F. 1974. *The Gay Science*, Kaufmann, W. (trans.) (New York: Random House).

Nietzsche, F. 1978. *Thus Spoke Zarathustra*, Kaufmann, W. (trans.) (Harmondsworth: Penguin).

Nietzsche, F. 1986. *Human, All Too Human*, Hollingdale, R. J. (trans.) (Cambridge: Cambridge University Press).

Nietzsche, F. 1988. *Sämtliche Werke. Kritische Studienausgabe in 15 Einzelbänden*, Colli, G. and Montinari, M. (eds.) (Berlin: de Gruyter).

Nietzsche, F. 1990. *Beyond Good and Evil*, Hollingdale, R. (trans.) (Harmondsworth: Penguin).

Pautrat, B. 1971. *Les Versions du Soleil. Figures et Système de Nietzsche* (Paris: Seuil).

Reginster, B. 2005. 'Nietzsche on Pleasure and Power', *Philosophical Topics*, 33/2: 161–91.

Reginster, B. 2006. *The Affirmation of Life: Nietzsche on Overcoming Nihilism* (Cambridge, MA: Harvard University Press).

Reginster, B. 2008. 'Knowledge and Selflessness: Schopenhauer and the Paradox of Reflection', *The European Journal of Philosophy*, 16/2: 251–72.

Schopenhauer, A. 1969. *The World as Will and Representation*, Vols. I and II, Payne, E. F. J. (trans.) (New York: Dover).

Soll, I. 1998. 'Schopenhauer, Nietzsche, and the Redemption of Life Through Art', in Janaway, C. (ed.), *Willing and Nothingness: Schopenhauer as Nietzsche's Educator* (Oxford: Clarendon Press): 79–115.

Stern, D. 1983. 'Unformulated Experience: From Familiar Chaos to Creative Disorder', *Contemporary Psychoanalysis*, 19/1: 71–99.

Young, J. 1992. *Nietzsche's Philosophy of Art* (Cambridge: Cambridge University Press).

2

Beauty is False, Truth Ugly: Nietzsche on Art and Life

Christopher Janaway

1 ART, INSIGHT, AND ILLUSION

In John Keats' 'Ode on a Grecian Urn' the poet contemplates and idealizes an ancient piece of pottery that speaks the famous words 'Beauty is truth, truth beauty'. A few short quotations from Nietzsche may cast some light on my title, suggesting as they do Nietzsche's wholehearted disagreement with the urn's message:

> What means do we have for making things beautiful, attractive and desirable when they are not? And in themselves I think they never are!
>
> (*GS*, 299)[1]

> Truth is ugly: *we possess art* lest we perish of the truth.[2]

> Art, in which precisely the *lie* hallows itself, in which *the will to deception* has good conscience on its side.
>
> (*GM*, III, 25)

These passages, written in mid- or late career, give the clear impression that for Nietzsche art is the production of beauty that deceives, and that truth is not only ugly, but so ugly that we could not live without obliterating it by falsifications of some kind. In *The Gay Science* he also writes:

> *Honesty* would lead to nausea and suicide. But now our honesty has a counterforce that helps us avoid such consequences: art, as the *good* will to appearance.... As an aesthetic

[1] In referring to Nietzsche's works I cite from the translations listed at the end of this essay (with a few exceptions to which I alert the reader in context).

[2] Note from 1888, *KSA*, 13, 500.

phenomenon existence is still *bearable* to us, and art furnishes us with the eye and hand and above all the good conscience to be *able* to make such a phenomenon of ourselves.

(*GS*, 107)

Here, as in the much discussed passage in the same book about 'giving style to one's character' (*GS*, 290), Nietzsche invites us to take the falsifying, distorting, and beautifying that occurs in the activity by which an artist produces an art work and transpose it to the case of the self: we are the 'artists' who make a falsifying 'work' out of the raw material that is also ourselves—and without such falsification of ourselves by ourselves, it seems, existence could neither be borne nor even continued. But if we are to learn this from art proper, art proper must also be concerned essentially with making false appearances.

In a recent book Bernard Reginster contrasts the later phase of Nietzsche's career with his position in the earlier work *The Birth of Tragedy*, in which Nietzsche has not yet developed the doctrine of will to power and has only the illusions of art to prescribe as an antidote for those who have 'looked boldly into the terrible destructiveness of so-called world history as well as the cruelty of nature, and [are] in danger of longing for a Buddhistic negation of the will', that is to say, those who have achieved 'Dionysian wisdom' (*BT*, 7). Tragic wisdom, at that early stage, thus prescribes eschewing the Dionysian depths and remaining at the Apollonian surface with its beautiful appearances—being, in other words, 'superficial—out of profundity' (*GS*, P, 4). In his later works, by contrast, tragic wisdom ceases to be (partly) Apollonian and becomes a fully Dionysian wisdom. The affirmation of life no longer requires that we avoid what *The Birth of Tragedy* characterizes as the 'insight into the horrible truth' of our condition (*BT*, 7). We are now capable of contemplating this truth without being driven to nihilistic despair by it because the revaluation made possible by the doctrine of the will to power actually enables us to welcome and affirm it (Reginster, 2006, 248–9). Reginster is using this contrast with *The Birth of Tragedy* primarily to portray and make plausible a central element in the later Nietzsche's position, which can be described—in a brief sketch—as follows. Will to power is to be the new criterion of value in human life, and if we understand will to power rightly, we see that many things that we tend to evaluate in strongly negative terms must instead be valued positively. Coming to see this is, for Reginster, what Nietzsche means by revaluing values. Thus:

if... we take power—the overcoming of resistance—to be a value, then we can see easily how it can be the principle behind a revaluation of suffering. Indeed, if we value the overcoming of resistance, then we must also value the resistance that is an ingredient of it. Since suffering is defined by resistance, we must also value suffering.

(Reginster, 2006, 177)

In Reginster's illuminating account, will to power has a paradoxical structure: in willing some end, we will to overcome obstacles or hindrances that stand in our way; but that implies that in some sense we will to encounter hindrances. What we will is not straightforward satisfaction or pleasure, but the existence of obstacles for our willing to test itself against and overcome, and this has the consequence that 'its satisfaction brings about its own dissatisfaction . . . it is a kind of desire that does not allow for *permanent* (once-and-for-all) satisfaction' (247). However, rather than finding in this a reason for despair, as Schopenhauer does, Nietzsche urges that to find value in the very '*activity* of confronting and overcoming resistance' without that activity's reaching any ultimate resting place where desire ceases, is to have discovered a 'new happiness'.[3] Nietzsche associates this attitude with Dionysus, and, Reginster suggests, 'the distinctive characteristics of Dionysus' life are the characteristics of the *creative life*' (242). If one comes to value this creative life, there are certain implications for what else one values. Valuing creativity implies a positive evaluation of suffering, of loss, of impermanence (or becoming), and of one's own ultimate personal failure.[4]

Reginster articulates an important and central strand in Nietzsche's later thought about value in human life, and for present purposes I shall not question what he says about the will to power and its role in revaluing values. But before contrasting Nietzsche's later views with those of *The Birth of Tragedy*, we should probe in more detail the statement that his earlier view 'has only the illusions of art to prescribe as an antidote for . . . those who have achieved "Dionysian wisdom"'.[5] I shall argue that if we separate out the tragic artist from the purely Apollonian artist, and from the Socratic 'theoretical man' whose particular preoccupations allegedly gained hegemony over art at a later stage, we shall find a triangle of different attitudes to truth, from which it will emerge that tragic art in particular is not limited to superficial or beautifying illusion. This is not a new thought, as Michael Tanner, for one, has written that 'Beauty, in Nietzsche's early view, is both an intimation of the horror of life and a consolation for it. . . . Art, at its greatest, tells the truth and makes it possible to bear it' (Tanner, 1993, xxix).

[3] Reginster (2006, 247) citing *GS*, P, 3. [4] See Reginster (2006, 243–8).

[5] Having read Reginster's Chapter 1 in this volume, I am pleased to find a good measure of agreement between his detailed reading of *The Birth of Tragedy* and mine.

2 TRUTH AND ILLUSION IN APOLLONIAN ART

The premise that provides the framework for the whole of *The Birth of Tragedy* is that Apollo and Dionysus stand for two contrasting creative forces that exist in nature, in the psychology of artists and their audiences, and in cultural movements, trends, and periods. Nietzsche uses a swarm of different expressions to characterize art that is driven by the Apollonian (or Apolline)[6] creative force, and there can be no very precise way of summing it up. Especially important notions seem to be 'dream', 'image', 'illusion', 'beauty', 'form', and 'individuation'. Although Nietzsche begins by associating Apollo with the visual arts, and speaks of sculptural images of the Olympian gods as its pinnacle, he finds the purest poetic manifestation of the Apollonian in the Homeric epics. In his heroes, but especially in his gods, Homer portrays glorious individuals of overwhelming beauty, prowess, and resistance to death, enabling us to delight in the surface texture of what is, for Nietzsche, a dream world:

> *Homer*... is related to that Apolline folk culture as the individual dream artist is related to the dream faculties of the people and of nature in general. The Homeric *naïveté* can only be understood as the complete triumph of Apolline illusion... Amongst the Greeks the 'will' wished to contemplate itself, in the transfiguration of genius and the world of art; in order to glorify themselves, its creations had to feel themselves worthy of glorification; they had to see themselves in a higher sphere... It was in this sphere of beauty that they saw reflections of themselves, the Olympians.
>
> (*BT*, 3)

Nietzsche is also clear about what gave the Greeks reason to relish the beauty of this illusory realm of great individuals, to indulge in such a dream world from which they would rather not wake up. They were motivated by a 'tremendous need', namely that of requiring a 'justification for the life of man'; to fulfil this need their artistic talent battled with their 'talent... for suffering and the wisdom of suffering'[7] and overcame it. To see why creating the image-world of the Olympian gods was a triumph, we must therefore see what it was a triumph over—and Nietzsche presents this more plainly than anything else in his book, in the passage on the folk tale of the daemon Silenus, whose voice proclaims:

> Miserable, ephemeral race, children of hazard and hardship, why do you force me to say what it would be much more fruitful for you not to hear? The best of all things is

[6] Nietzsche's word is *apollinisch*: the Whiteside translation renders this as 'Apolline', which I retain (along with 'Dionysiac') in quotations.

[7] These quotations and all others in this paragraph are from *BT*, 3.

something entirely outside your grasp: not to be born, not to *be*, to be *nothing*. But the second-best thing for you—is to die soon.

(*BT*, 3)

The Greeks must believe this pronouncement to be true, or at least to be plausible or a part of the truth, since otherwise it would not give rise to the need, the battle, or the victory that Apollonian art provided them with. Nietzsche confirms that the Greek 'knew and felt the fears and horrors of existence'. The relation of Apollonian artistic illusion to the truth the Greeks thus recognized is described as follows: they veiled or concealed the truth with illusion, they 'had to interpose the radiant dream-birth of the Olympians between themselves and those horrors'. The reason for this action, and the outcome of it, is that this 'artistic *middle world*'—a screen between themselves and reality—enabled the Greeks to regard human existence as justified. Existence had no value and could not be affirmed in reality, but in a substitute dream-reality, made sufficiently radiant and engaging, it could.

Thus, the statement above from Reginster about 'remaining at the surface with its beautiful appearances' seems to apply particularly well to Apollonian art. Yet even here, as we have said, the creator, audience, and wider culture of Apollonian art must have had *some access to the truth* they triumph over. A culture or an individual who was not tormented to any degree by the knowledge or feeling of the horrors of existence would feel no 'ardent longing for illusion and for redemption by illusion' (*BT*, 4): they might enjoy illusion for other reasons, but unless some intimation of the horrors of existence, such as they are, exerted a force somewhere upon the psyche, the incentive behind Apollonian art would have disappeared. The relation between the façade and the force that motivates it must be a matter of some speculation. Nietzsche does nothing to locate this activity of 'veiling' or 'interposing' anywhere concrete. It is really no use asking whether it occurs in the mind of the individual poet or audience member, in the communal enactment of a public recitation, or in the general outlook of a whole culture whose members habitually learn and repeat the poems—these are not questions to which we should expect precise answers. However, alternative methods of 'veiling' or 'concealing' seem to be: (1) that one participates in a deliberate pretence or make-believe that the truth is other than it is; (2) that one practises a kind of self-distraction, occupying the mind with something fictional so that it gives little or no thought to the truth; (3) that one engages in some form of self-deception and successfully conceals the truth from oneself; and (4) that one undergoes something like a repression outside of one's own conscious control, and becomes unaware of the truth and of one's need to veil it, although still under its influence. In all these cases—even the last—mere lack of awareness of the horrors of existence is not what is required. Thus even at the height of Apollonian artistic dream-world creation, there cannot be sheer ignorance of the horrible truth. Art is here driven by some original, pre-artistic awareness of truth, and gains its point by blunting or wholly disarming the effect of that truth upon the psyche.

3 TRAGIC ART AND TRUTH

However, Greek culture moves beyond this predominantly Apollonian stage. The familiar central claim of *The Birth of Tragedy* is that tragedy, the highest art form, combines the genius of both Apollo and Dionysus.[8] The most down-to-earth and unequivocal contrast between Apollo and Dionysus lies in their linkage with the different formal parts of Attic tragedy, the dialogue and chorus respectively. In the dialogue we have once more a represented world, the images of individuals, clearly drawn, distinct, and splendid—larger than life. But the chorus is non-individuating and non-representational. Born out of music and communal movement, and stating its lyrical message always through these media, its essence is not to present images. It originates, according to Nietzsche, in the wild intoxication of ecstatic group revelry, and stands for a loss of the sense of individuality, for the individual's merging with a joyful release into something greater. It is this non-imagistic, anti-individual, primordially musical element that characterizes the Dionysian in art.

Now, what Nietzsche describes in section 7 of *The Birth of Tragedy*—full of obscurity though it is—is a state in which a knowledge of truth has been attained, but where Apollonian illusion no longer suffices as a means for surviving it. The Dionysian man, says Nietzsche, resembles Hamlet: 'both have truly seen to the essence of things, they have *gained knowledge* [*erkannt*] ... true knowledge [*wahre Erkenntniss*], insight into the terrible truth outweighs every motive for action, for Hamlet and Dionysiac man alike' (*BT*, 7).[9] For the Hamlet-like Dionysian man this knowledge cannot be banished from his consciousness, or veiled by purely Apollonian means:

> Now no comfort avails any more; longing transcends a world after death, even the gods; existence is negated along with its glittering reflection in the gods or in an immortal beyond. Conscious of the truth he has once seen, man now sees everywhere only the

[8] See, e.g., the beginning of *BT*, 5.

[9] Whiteside's translation slightly modified.

horror or absurdity of existence; ... now he comes to know the wisdom of the sylvan god, Silenus: it nauseates him.[10]

(*BT*, 7)

So when Nietzsche follows this up by saying that art approaches as 'a redeeming, healing enchantress. She alone can turn these nauseous thoughts at the horror or absurdity of existence into ideas compatible with life',[11] he cannot mean Apollonian art. Apollonian art provided comfort, but comfort no longer avails. Apollonian art created the glittering reflection of the gods, but that too is now negated along with the world. Apollonian art protected its adherents from nausea at the truth because it prevented them from properly coming to know it: but what about those who have become properly acquainted with that truth so that it sticks resolutely in their consciousness and nauseates? It is the Dionysian element in tragedy that Nietzsche leans upon at the end of this passage: 'The satyr chorus of the dithyramb is the salvation of Greek art'.

Tragedy provides what Nietzsche now calls a 'metaphysical consolation', namely 'that whatever superficial changes may occur, life is at bottom indestructibly powerful and joyful' (*BT*, 7). Nietzsche's description of the way tragedy does this is diffused through the pages of sections 7–10. Hard though the description is to grasp, a vital central thought is that tragedy enables one to *live with* the truth by confronting it in an affirmative frame of mind, not to live *in spite of* the truth by veiling it over. Tragic art can 'turn these nauseous thoughts at the horror and absurdity of existence into ideas that one can live with' (*BT*, 7)—where the verb *umbiegen*, to turn around, bend, or divert, seems a significantly different metaphor from that of veiling or interposing.[12] In the latter case, horrific thoughts are blocked out and something beautiful put in their place. Now, in tragedy, the thoughts remain in consciousness but are encountered differently and put to a different use. The Dionysian effect of tragedy is its alleged ability to dissolve the sense of individuality and merge the participant or spectator into a 'primal oneness' or 'primal being' (*das Ur-Eine* or *Ursein*). From the consciousness that characterizes this wider standpoint it is possible to rejoice in the destructiveness of life towards the individual. But for this to occur it must be

[10] Here, exceptionally, I use Kaufmann's translation (in *The Birth of Tragedy and The Case of Wagner* (New York: Vintage Books, 1967)), slightly modified.

[11] *BT*, 7, Whiteside's translation slightly modified.

[12] In an earlier version of this passage in the essay 'Die dionysische Weltanschauung' (1870) Nietzsche uses the verb *umwandeln*, to transform ('transform these nauseous thoughts ... into ideas one can live with'). He uses *umbiegen* (*KSA*, 1, 567) a few sentences earlier, saying that through tragic art the Hellenic will operated to 'turn around that mood of negation again' (*jene verneinende Stimmung wieder umzubiegen*, ibid., 566, my translation).

the case that, in addition to being absorbed into the non-individuated state, one has before one the representation of the individual in whose destruction one rejoices—whence the unique power of the union between Apollonian image and Dionysian intoxication:

> we must see Greek tragedy as the Dionysiac chorus, continuously discharging itself in an Apolline world of images . . . this primal ground of tragedy radiates that vision of the drama which is entirely a dream phenomenon and thus epic in nature, but on the other hand, as the objectification of a Dionysiac state, it is not Apolline redemption through illusion, but rather a representation of the fragmentation of the individual and his unification with primal being. Thus the drama is the Apolline symbol of Dionysiac knowledge and Dionysiac effects, and consequently separated from the epic as by a tremendous chasm.
>
> (*BT*, 8)

Tragedy, then, uses the beautiful imagery of the grand individual character, not as a means by which to escape from or veil the horrific truth of life, but to serve in full view as the symbolic victim of life's true horrors, now seen in an extraordinarily heightened mood from a viewpoint in which one can rejoice at life's very merciless destruction.[13]

So does the early Nietzsche prescribe the illusions of art as the only antidote for those who have looked boldly into the terrible destructiveness of world history and the cruelty of nature? Yes and No. Tragic art incorporates illusion in its character portrayal and scenes of dialogue, and without that illusion it could not function; but it is emphatically not Apollonian 'redemption through illusion'—rather an Apollonian *Versinnlichung*, or making sensible, of Dionysian *Erkenntnisse*—Dionysian insights, cognitions, knowledge. Thus it is not from the use of illusion alone that tragedy gains its value. It gains it rather from the combination of illusion and an emotional involvement in a deeper unity that happily consigns the symbolic individual human life to oblivion, and so enables its audience to reach a cognitive awareness of a terrible truth—at least about life's suffering, loss, impermanence, and failure—and leaves them in a position to embrace that truth.

[13] In 'Die dionysische Weltanschauung' Nietzsche gives (perhaps clearer) emphasis to the notion of the *symbol*, which he distinguishes from *truth*. The art that unites Dionysus and Apollo is 'a veiling of the truth which though more transparent than beauty, is still a veiling [*Umschleierung*]'; the Dionysian human being here 'goes beyond beauty and yet does not seek truth. He stays suspended in the middle between the two. He strives not for beautiful illusion, but yet for illusion [*Schein*], not for truth [*Wahrheit*], but for *verisimilitude* [*Wahrscheinlichkeit*]. (Symbol. Sign of truth)' (*KSA*, 1, 567). Still, this form of art 'rested on a view of gods and world different from the older view of beautiful illusion'. Tragedy stands symbolically for the horrific truth. Apollonian art shuns truth in favour of false beauty.

4 ART, TRUTH, AND SOCRATISM

The idea that tragedy is concerned with knowledge or recognition of truth might seem odd given the contrast Nietzsche draws between tragedy and the force of Socratism, which is not only opposed to tragedy and uncomprehending of it, but brings about its death. Socrates is the 'prototype of *theoretical man*' who delights in the process of uncovering truth, 'who, in his faith in the explicability of the nature of things, attributes the power of a panacea to knowledge and science, and sees error as the embodiment of evil' (*BT*, 15). If tragedy does what we have said it does, how could truth-obsessed Socrates be the fatal opposite of the tragic poet?

In Nietzsche's critique of Socratism we may see an early version of what became his call to question the will to truth in *On the Genealogy of Morality* (III, 23–7). There, in the passage we cited above, Nietzsche sets art against the will to truth: 'art, in which precisely the *lie* hallows itself, in which the *will to deception* has good conscience on its side, is much more fundamentally opposed to the ascetic ideal than is science' (*GM*, III, 25). Nietzsche seems to invite reminiscence of his earlier discussion of Socrates, and of the aesthetic Socratism that allegedly transformed Greek art for the worse, when he typifies the antagonism of art and ascetic ideal as 'Plato *contra* Homer', and laments that an artist's subservience to the ascetic ideal is the truest corruption of the artist there can be. Nietzsche speaks here as though uncovering truth were in itself something antithetical to art. But we need not assume that there is only one way to encounter the truth. Socrates, as portrayed in *The Birth of Tragedy*, is wedded to explanation, rational grounding, theory, and dialectic—'to be beautiful everything must first be intelligible' (*BT*, 12). When unaffected by Socratism, tragedy was a potent collaboration between dream-image and delighted dissolution of individuality, which combined intuition (*Anschauung*) and ecstasy (*Entzückung*); art infused by Socratism is a counterfeit of this which replaces intuition with conceptual thoughts (*Gedanken*), and ecstasy with mere 'affects' (*Affecte*; see *BT*, 12). Socratism's mission is to subordinate both image and intoxication to the *rational*. So once Socratism takes hold and becomes entrenched, we (as its heirs) are prone to assume that argument and explanation are the sole or primary means to access truth. But when it was uninfected by Socratism, the story goes, tragedy enabled a uniquely powerful *aesthetic* confrontation with truth. Before the over-concern for rational explanation became dominant in Greek culture, participants in tragedy could be brought to a Dionysian form of cognition (*Erkentniss*), an encounter with truth made sensible through the beautiful image.

When the later Nietzsche recommends that 'the value of truth is for once to be experimentally *called into question*' (*GM*, III, 24) it is fairly clear that his target is a particular manner in which truth is valued, the 'overestimation of truth . . . belief in the *in*assessability, the *un*criticizability of truth' (*GM*, III, 25), the idea that seeking and being in possession of the truth in the ways that science privileges, is something whose value is unconditional.[14] Moreover, to call the value of truth into question experimentally is not to say that we must be content *solely* with illusions, or that there is *no* value in pursuing truth. Rather, it opens up the thought that turning away from the Socratic rational examination of life, and embarking upon works of artistic illusion, fiction, imagination, or dreams may sometimes be necessary in the service of life. But even if one lies with a good conscience, it does not prevent one from believing in and wanting at least some of the truth.

5 ART AND TRUTH IN THE LATER NIETZSCHE

What, then, can we find in the way of continuities and discontinuities between Nietzsche's earlier and later views of the relation between art and truth? In later writings Nietzsche abandons the crypto-Schopenhauerian relic of '*das Ur-Eine* and, as he says in his 1886 Preface to *The Birth of Tragedy*, he can now regard the book's whole 'artist's metaphysic' as 'arbitrary, idle and fantastic' (*BT*, 'Attempt', 5). But what has essentially altered as regards the question of art's relation to truth? Superficially at least, the picture of art as an essentially untruthful and deceiving activity pervades the rhetoric of the later writings. A plethora of passages in *The Gay Science*, *Beyond Good and Evil*, the *Genealogy*, and *Twilight of the Idols* present the role of art and artists variously as that of lying, simplifying, glorifying, selecting, rounding out, hiding and reinterpreting the ugly, seeing things from a distance, round a corner, cut out of context, distorted, through coloured glass, or covered with not fully transparent skin, telling tall tales, playing tricks, taking pleasure in life only by falsifying its image, showing us falsehood with a good conscience, and helping us embrace the good will to illusion, the cult of the untrue, the cult of surface, the transformation of things so that they mirror one's power, the will to invert the truth, the will to deception, and the will to untruth at any price.[15] Nietzsche rejoices in art's not seeing things for what they *are*, that latter being, he says, 'anti-artistic' (*TI*, IX, 7). It should be noted once again that Nietzsche's preoccupation in many of these passages is not with art as

[14] See Janaway (2007, 229–39).
[15] See *GS*, 85, 107, 290, 299, 361; *BGE*, 59, 192; *GM*, III, 25; *TI*, IX, 9.

such, but with learning from artists how to interpret and value oneself: we wish to be wiser than artists, he says, 'For usually in their case this delicate power stops where art ends and life begins: *we*, however, want to be poets of our lives, starting with the smallest and most commonplace details' (*GS*, 299). But, as we said above, if what we learn from poets comprises all these forms of lying and distorting, surely that can only be because poets as such, in their art, lie and distort. Even if Nietzsche is questioning or ambivalent about the value of seeking truth, he need not be indecisive as to whether or not art functions as truth-teller or falsifier. From the many passages cited above, it looks on the surface as if art tends consistently towards the opposite of truth-telling in the period we are discussing: if it is truth you want, do not go to art, but if something other than truth is valued, art may be uniquely placed to help.

However, I want to suggest that remaining at this surface alone may miss some subtleties to be found in Nietzsche's position. For one thing, 'perishing from the truth' is an alternative to 'Not facing the truth'; but it is equally opposed to 'Facing the truth and not perishing from it'. So that late note 'Truth is ugly: *we possess art* lest we perish of the truth' could be read with an Apollonian or a tragic inflection, or perhaps both. An apprehension of the ugly may be something we must shield ourselves from by a compensating illusion; it may also be something which we can be enabled to tolerate and even rejoice in. In the last year of his creative life Nietzsche wrote some words, destined for publication in two works, that convey something of what he was trying to say about the tragic experience from the start:

> Saying Yes to life in its strangest and hardest problems; the will to life rejoicing over its own inexhaustibility even in the very sacrifice of its highest types—that is what I called Dionysian, that is what I guessed to be the bridge to the psychology of the tragic poet.... to be oneself the eternal joy of becoming, beyond all terror and pity—that joy which includes even joy in destroying.[16]
>
> (*TI*, X, 5)

The point of 'Saying Yes to life in its strangest and hardest problems' seems to be the acceptance of the kind of truth that, with Reginster, we saw involved in a revaluation of values—the truth that, because of the nature of will to power,

[16] Nietzsche also quotes this passage again in *EH*, III, *BT*, 3. Note the lexical reversion to the Schopenhauerian 'will to life', and the past tense in 'what I called', 'what I guessed'. There is some retrieval of *The Birth of Tragedy* at work in these late passages.

suffering, loss, impermanence, and failure must be encompassed within what we value in life—and Nietzsche is still prepared to link this insight with the psychology of the tragic *poet*. So a tension persists between art as comforting deception and art as medium for a joyous confrontation with terrible truth.

Prominent concerns in *The Gay Science* of 1882 are the intellectual conscience and the virtue of honesty. Alongside them are the repeated recommendations to look to the activities of artists to learn creative attitudes towards oneself. Aaron Ridley finds these seemingly conflicting preoccupations unified in the following way:

> The artist's 'intellectual conscience', which insists on honesty, drives him—once he has honestly recognized the character of his and our most fundamental needs—to cultivate and value the false, but to do so to the minimum extent necessary to ward off 'nausea and suicide'... The creative spirit envisaged in *The Gay Science* is... one who, first, faces the truth as honestly as possible; second, tries to see as beautiful as much as possible of 'what is necessary in things' [see *GS*, 276]... and then, finally, falsifies those conditions that defeat this attempt—that is, turns 'existence' into an 'aesthetic phenomenon'—to the least possible degree consistent with making life 'bearable'.
>
> (Ridley, 2007, 82–4)

On this reading, when Nietzsche talks of art as a counterforce to honesty, he has in mind not a total or permanent self-deception or screening off of the truth, but instead a subtle finessing of the truth, as in his comments that 'we do not always keep our eyes from rounding off, from finishing off the poem;... At times we need to have a rest from ourselves by looking at and down at ourselves and, from an artistic distance, laughing *at* [*over*] ourselves or crying *at* [*over*] ourselves' (*GS*, 107). Thus, for Ridley: 'it is a condition of the kind of creativity that Nietzsche is interested in that one first face the truth, and only then embark upon one's (modest) falsifications and rounding off of it' (2007, 83). One needs to falsify to some degree—and to which degree is a test of the limits of one's 'strength', as Nietzsche says in *Beyond Good and Evil*:

> so that the strength of a spirit would be proportionate to how much of the 'truth' he could withstand—or, to put it more clearly, to what extent he needs it to be thinned out, veiled over, sweetened up, dumbed down, or lied about.
>
> (*BGE*, 39)

But on this reading the ideal towards which art provides a helping hand is that of facing up to the truth of life as honestly as one can. Art's falsifications are no self-subsistent exercise in escaping from truth, but rather an employment of illusion in the service of the intellectual conscience, with its project of confronting the truth—a change of tactic when all other means take us to the limit of what we can bear.

Such an amicable settlement between the values of truth-telling and of producing illusions displays a Nietzsche apparently comfortable with himself. However, I think that for that very reason we should question Ridley's reading. Elsewhere Nietzsche paints the value of truth as poignantly troubling and problematic, as in 'what meaning would *our* entire being have if not this, that in us this will to truth has come to a consciousness of itself *as a problem*?' (*GM*, III, 27), and this remark from his notebooks: 'About the relation of art to truth I became serious at the earliest time: and even now I stand before this dichotomy [*Zwiespalt*] with a holy terror' (*KSA*, 13, 550). Nietzsche is troubled, rather than settled, about the possibility of reconciling art with truth. And the unease increases with some of his later additions to *The Gay Science*, in Book Five and the second edition Preface, which, as we shall see, raise more radical questions about the very nature of truth and the value of our pursuing it.

6 UNEASE ABOUT THE NATURE AND VALUE OF TRUTH

Nietzsche manifests ambivalence about the desirability of seeking truth at all, in or out of art. Disturbed by the idea of truth posited as an unconditionally valuable goal before which we must sacrifice our personal interests and, in a sense, ourselves—truth 'posited as being, as God, as highest authority', along with 'a certain *impoverishment of life*' (*GM*, III, 24–5)—Nietzsche does not recommend ceasing to value truth, but merely calling the value of truth into question experimentally. Why? The answer is in his question 'What meaning would *our* entire being have if not this, that in us this will to truth has come to a consciousness of itself *as a problem*?' (*GM*, III, 27). By the time of the *Genealogy* Nietzsche is where he is, he is what he is, as an investigator into the value of our values, because he has been guided by a commitment to truthfulness. But he has come along the way to recognize this as a distinctly moral commitment, as the 'Christian truthfulness' that has undermined the belief in God, and is in the process of undermining morality.[17] At the same time the questionable status of truthfulness as a value keeps resurfacing throughout his work:

[17] See also *GS*, 344.

We do not consider the falsity of a judgment as itself an objection to a judgment; this is perhaps where our new language will sound most foreign. The question is how far the judgment promotes and preserves life, how well it preserves, and perhaps even cultivates, the type... To acknowledge untruth as a condition of life: this clearly means resisting the usual value feelings in a dangerous manner.

(*BGE*, 4)

So there are other values that can trump those of seeking and holding true beliefs. Yet at times, Nietzsche envisages an ideal that seems to involve apprehending as much truth as one can about life: 'the ideal of the most high-spirited, vital, world-affirming individual, who has learned not just to accept and go along with what was and is, but who wants it again and again *just as it was and is* through all eternity' (*BGE*, 56), or someone who does not want 'anything to be different, not forwards, not backwards, not for all eternity. Not just to tolerate necessity, still less to conceal it..., but to *love* it' (*EH*, II, 10). In a similar vein is the most famous passage (*GS*, 341) in which he imagines someone becoming so well disposed to themselves and to life that they would rejoice at the prospect of that life's endlessly recurring. In these places the ideal appears to be that of a tragic wisdom in which the horrors can be seen for what they are and borne with exceptional strength, even assigned a positive value. This appears to involve confronting life truthfully, loving or saying yes to a life that is unalterably what it is, not blurring, concealing, or falsifying it into an illusory version that one can like or affirm. But then again, also in *The Gay Science*, the one thing that 'is needful' is 'that a human being should *attain* satisfaction with himself—be it through this or that poetry or art' (*GS*, 290). Nietzsche is after an attitude of positive self-evaluation, but seems unsettled as to whether the form it should take is that of fictionalizing or confronting the truth about oneself.[18] His 'holy terror [*Entsetzen*]' before the dichotomy 'art and truth'[19] may be evidence that his own attitude here is dichotomous.

Section 344 of *The Gay Science* contains an important argument that illuminates Nietzsche's later concerns about what he calls 'science'. Here is how Nietzsche poses the problem:

We see that science, too, rests on a faith; there is simply no 'presuppositionless' science. The question whether *truth* is necessary must get an answer in advance, the answer 'yes', and moreover this answer must be so firm that it takes the form of the statement, the

[18] On the tension between self-affirmation and aesthetic self-satisfaction, see Janaway (2007, 254–64).

[19] *KSA*, 13, S. 550 (16 (40): my translation).

belief, the conviction: '*Nothing is more* necessary than truth; and in relation to it, everything else has only secondary value.' This unconditional will to truth—what is it?

Science (including the historical, interpretive disciplines practised by Nietzsche himself) not only seeks truth, but bases itself on a prior conviction or faith that seeking and attaining truth has a value that is not conditional upon anything else. 'Will to truth', as Nietzsche explains by paraphrase later in the section, is an attitude of desiring 'truth at any price'. So Nietzsche wants to know the nature of this demand that enquiry makes upon itself. Is it unconditionally valuable to hold true rather than false beliefs, unconditionally valuable 'not to let oneself be deceived'? Nietzsche suggests not. True beliefs could be regarded as unconditionally more valuable only if there were some guarantee that they brought greater benefit than false beliefs, but for Nietzsche this is not a safe assumption:

Is it really less harmful, dangerous, disastrous not to want to let oneself be deceived? What do you know in advance about the character of existence to be able to decide whether the greater advantage is on the side of the unconditionally distrustful or the unconditionally trusting? But should both be necessary... then where might science get the unconditional belief or conviction on which it rests, that truth is more important than anything else, than every other conviction? Precisely this conviction could never have originated if truth *and* untruth had constantly made it clear that they were both useful, as they are.

The explanation Nietzsche offers instead is that, as 'scientific' enquirers, we unconditionally demand of ourselves *truthfulness*—that is, the virtue of not being deceitful, even to ourselves. But this means, he argues, that the ground of our faith in truth is *moral*. Since the crafty flexibility and deceitfulness of an Odysseus[20] have at least as good a case for being useful strategies, where could the unconditional demand for truthfulness come from, other than from morality itself? So, Nietzsche contends that (unwittingly) we find ourselves morally bound into our unquestioning valuation of the pursuit of truth.

What, then, is Nietzsche's alternative? Not the abandonment of all pursuit of truth, let alone the abandonment of the concept of truth. Rather, an attempt to see the value of truth-acquisition as conditional—on the values of health, strength, affirmation, or the degree of viability, bearability, and self-satisfaction we can sustain. Can we put life first, and sacrifice truth-seeking to life if need be? The attempt (or experiment)[21] to do so will mean stepping away from the demand to seek truths at all costs, in two related senses: one is to embrace the deliberate artistic reshaping of our experience as a way of enhancing it for

[20] Alluded to in *GS*, 344, by the word *polytropoi*: Odysseus is described as *polytropos* in the opening line of the *Odyssey*.

[21] See *GM*, III, 24.

ourselves; the other is to accept superficial appearances and see ourselves as under no constraint to delve beneath them. A resonant and much quoted passage ends the Preface to *The Gay Science*, combining the related themes of artistic reshaping and the abandonment of any search for a hidden truth:

> Oh those Greeks! They knew how to live: what is needed for that is to stop bravely at the surface, the fold, the skin; to worship appearance, to believe in shapes, tones, words—in the whole Olympus of appearance! Those Greeks were superficial—*out of profundity*! And is not this precisely what we are coming back to, we daredevils of the spirit... Are we not just in this respect—Greeks? Worshippers of shapes, tones, words?
>
> (*GS*, P, 4)

One further aspect of the (in the broad sense) scientific conception of truth-seeking enquiry that Nietzsche is out to undermine, is its commitment to an ideal of selfless objectivity:

> The lack of personality always takes its revenge: a weakened, thin, extinguished personality, one that denies itself and its own existence, is no longer good for anything good—least of all for philosophy. 'Selflessness' has no value in heaven or on earth; all great problems demand *great love*, and only strong, round, secure minds who have a firm grip on themselves are capable of that. It makes the most telling difference whether a thinker has a personal relationship to his problems and finds in them his destiny, his distress, and his greatest happiness, or an 'impersonal' one, meaning he is only able to touch and grasp them with the antennae of cold, curious thought. In the latter case nothing will come of it, that much can be promised.
>
> (*GS*, 345)

Opposed to this is Nietzsche's model of interpretation through the affects, a model in which intellectual insight increases through multiplying affects as far as possible. In the *Genealogy* he speaks of

> the capacity to have one's pro and contra *in one's power*, and to shift them in and out: so that one knows how to make precisely the *difference* in perspectives and affective interpretations useful for knowledge... *the more* affects we allow to speak about a matter, *the more* eyes, different eyes, we know how to bring to bear on one and the same matter, that much more complete will our 'concept' of this matter, our 'objectivity' be.
>
> (*GM*, III, 12)

Nietzsche here urges 'philosophers' to practise a form of enquiry that engages as many personal feelings as possible, and understands its subject matter more fully as a result. His own affectively engaged and rhetorically provocative investigation of the origins of our values stands as a good exemplar of such enquiry.[22]

[22] See Janaway (2007) on this theme.

For Nietzsche the best investigator is not a dispassionate 'pure subject', the object of investigation is not something mysterious and unattainable lurking behind our many experiences, and the exercise of investigation is not self-validating. Truth is multiple, located on the surfaces of things, best found through keeping alive our feelings, and best sought in the service of some values external to the activity of truth-seeking itself, values of health, flourishing, and life-affirmation. So the hard-and-fast distinction between something's being a falsification and something's being an insight into truth is now removed. When Nietzsche returns to the tragic artist proper in *Twilight of the Idols*, art re-emerges as the conveyor of stark truth: 'art also presents a lot that is ugly, harsh, questionable in life,—doesn't this seem to spoil life for us?' (*TI*, IX, 24). On the other hand, 'artists have valued appearance more highly than reality' (*TI*, III, 6)—but now the interesting twist: '"appearance" here means reality *once again*, only selected, strengthened, corrected... The tragic artist is not a pessimist,—he says *yes* to the very things that are questionable and terrible, he is *Dionysian*' (*TI*, III, 6).

So while art reveals ugly truths to be faced and affirmed, at the same time any absolute distinction between 'reality' (the 'true world') and the realm of appearance or illusion can be seen as unstable or bogus.[23] It emerges now that those artist's procedures of simplifying, correcting, and selecting are ways of opening up other perspectives upon oneself, not deceptions but ways of gaining access to something that one genuinely is. Already in *The Gay Science* Nietzsche says that artists

> have taught us to value the hero that is hidden in each of these everyday characters and taught the art of regarding oneself as a hero, from a distance and as it were simplified and transfigured—the art of 'putting oneself on stage' before oneself. Only thus can we get over certain lowly details in ourselves. Without this art we would be under the spell of that perspective which makes the nearest and most vulgar appear tremendously big and as reality itself.
>
> (*GS*, 78)

Artists then seem to be adept at doing what all seekers after improved understanding would need to do anyway, namely engaging their diverse feelings, finding new interpretations, and moving between them.[24] Hence gaining truth about oneself would in the end *be* a skilful process of selecting, simplifying, seeing from a distance, and so on. Selecting and simplifying our view of ourselves is

[23] See also the much discussed section of *Twilight of the Idols* entitled 'How the "True World" finally became a Fable' and the influential discussion of it in Clark (1990, 109–17).

[24] See Janaway (2007, 202–22) for an account of this.

something we must do anyway: artists are simply experts at doing so. In that case, what we gain from all the artistic distorting and styling Nietzsche recommends is, after all, a better insight into the truth.[25]

REFERENCES

Clark, M. 1990. *Nietzsche on Truth and Philosophy* (Cambridge: Cambridge University Press).

Janaway, C. 2007. *Beyond Selflessness: Reading Nietzsche's* Genealogy (New York and Oxford: Oxford University Press).

Nietzsche, F. 1988. *Sämtliche Werke. Kritische Studienausgabe in 15 Einzelbänden*, Colli, G. and Montinari, M. (eds.) (Berlin: de Gruyter).

Nietzsche, F. 1993. *The Birth of Tragedy*, Tanner, M. (ed.), Whiteside, S. (trans.) (Harmondsworth: Penguin).

Nietzsche, F. 1998. *On the Genealogy of Morality*, Clark, M. and Swensen, A. (trans.) (Indianapolis: Hackett).

Nietzsche, F. 2001. *The Gay Science*, Williams, B. (ed.), Nauckhoff, J. and del Caro, A. (trans.) (Cambridge: Cambridge University Press).

Nietzsche, F. 2002. *Beyond Good and Evil*, Horstmann, R. and Norman J. (ed.), Norman, J. (trans.) (Cambridge: Cambridge University Press).

Nietzsche, F. 2005. *Ecce Homo*, in *The Anti-Christ, Ecce Homo, Twilight of the Idols, and Other Writings*, Ridley, A. (ed.), Norman, J. (trans.) (Cambridge: Cambridge University Press).

Nietzsche, F. 2005. *Twilight of the Idols*, in *The Anti-Christ, Ecce Homo, Twilight of the Idols, and Other Writings*, Ridley, A. (ed.), Norman, J. (trans.) (Cambridge: Cambridge University Press).

Reginster, B. 2006. *The Affirmation of Life: Nietzsche on Overcoming Nihilism* (Cambridge, MA: Harvard University Press).

Ridley, A. 2007. *Routledge Philosophy Guidebook to Nietzsche on Art* (London: Routledge).

Tanner, M. 1993. 'Introduction', in Nietzsche, *The Birth of Tragedy*, Whiteside, S. (trans.) (Harmondsworth: Penguin): vii–xxx.

[25] Earlier versions of this chapter, or parts of it, were delivered as talks at the universities of Freiburg, Calgary, Sussex, Ghent, and London. I am grateful to my hosts, audiences, and co-presenters on all these occasions. For their comments on written versions, I especially thank Ken Gemes, Simon May, Mark Migotti, David Owen, Bernard Reginster, Aaron Ridley, and Bart Vandenabeele.

3

Nietzsche on Tragedy and Morality

Christopher C. Raymond

1 INTRODUCTION

In the final book of Plato's *Republic*, Socrates challenges the lovers of tragic poetry to show 'that it is not only pleasurable, but also beneficial to political systems and to human life'.[1] The history of philosophical interpretations of tragedy can be read, in large part, as a series of attempts to answer his challenge. This chapter aims to shed light on Nietzsche's unique place within this tradition.

From Socrates' point of view, an adequate defence of tragedy would have to explain its *moral* value—that is, how it makes its audience more virtuous and wise. While there are some who deflect the challenge, claiming that the pleasure we get from tragedy is morally neutral Nietzsche takes a far more radical approach.[2] He maintains that the distinctive value of tragedy as an art form depends on its *conflict* with morality. This thesis is central to all his major writings on tragedy, although my focus here will be its pivotal role in *The Birth of Tragedy*.

I want to begin, however, by exploring the background to Nietzsche's theory. After briefly reviewing the critique of tragedy in the *Republic*, I shall compare two ways of trying to reconcile tragedy and morality, drawn from Aristotle's *Poetics* and Schiller's theoretical essays. I shall then consider Nietzsche's repudiation of this project, and his own attempt to explain the value of tragedy in non-moral

[1] 607d9–10. The 'it' actually refers to 'mimetic' poetry, which includes comedy. But tragedy is Socrates' primary concern.

[2] For an example of the former approach, see Goethe's essay 'On Interpreting Aristotle's *Poetics*': 'Once the poet has fulfilled his duty, has tied significant knots and unravelled them appropriately, the same will happen in the spectator's mind. The complications will confuse him, the solution will enlighten him, but he will not go home a better person. Rather, he would be amazed at himself—if he were unusually observant—for coming back home just as frivolous or stubborn, as aggressive or meek, as kind or unkind as he was when he left' (*Essays on Art and Literature*, 199).

terms. I conclude by asking whether Nietzsche provides a more useful framework for thinking about tragedy than his predecessors, as some have contended.

Of course, any general claim about tragedy raises the question of scope. Nietzsche does not intend his theory to account for all, or even many, of the works that historically have been considered tragedies. An important part of his aim is to draw a boundary around the concept of tragedy, and so his use of the term is always heavily normative. At the same time, his view must not be wholly revisionary. Unless it helps us understand some works that already are part of the canon, and whose greatness is evident, it is unclear why we should pay much attention to what Nietzsche thinks about 'tragedy'. And in fact, Nietzsche *does* claim that his theory applies to some central cases: Sophocles' *Oedipus* plays and Euripides' *Bacchae*; Shakespeare's *Hamlet* and *Macbeth*; and, most problematically, Wagner's *Tristan* and *Ring*. If it can illuminate just one of these examples, it will be worth taking seriously.

2 TRAGEDY, MORALITY, AND HAPPINESS: SOCRATES' CHALLENGE

In the summer semester of 1870, Nietzsche taught a course on Sophoclean tragedy at the University of Basel, where he had been made Professor of Greek at the age of 24.[3] His lecture notes begin with a discussion of the *Oedipus Tyrannus* and the problems it poses for modern aesthetics. According to the principle of poetic justice, a tragedy should display an 'exact proportion' between guilt and suffering, and virtue must be rewarded in the end. But where, Nietzsche asks, is the guilt in the case of Sophocles' Oedipus, who suffers like no other figure of the stage? He was *fated* to kill his father and marry his mother; his crimes, moreover, were committed in ignorance.[4] And yet, Aristotle treats the play as a paradigm of tragic drama.

The modern critic is faced with an embarrassing choice: he must either find some flaw in Oedipus' character that could make his suffering seem justified (e.g., 'hubris'), or else judge Sophocles' play a failure and Aristotle a fool. In Nietzsche's view, this only proves how impoverished the modern idea of tragedy has become.

[3] *KGW*, II, 3: 1–57. Translations from the Sophocles lectures are my own.

[4] Some versions of the myth explain Oedipus' fate through the inheritance of sin. In the *Septem* of Aeschylus, for example, the curse on the house of Thebes is the result of an original 'transgression': Laius was warned three times by Apollo not to have any children, yet through 'mindless madness' he defied the god and 'begot his own death' (743–57). In another version, Laius is cursed by Pelops for the rape of his son Chrysippus. Nietzsche points out that Sophocles' play mentions none of this; in his view, the family curse is an 'Aeschylean' device (*KGW*, II, 3: 10).

For the Greeks, the meaning of tragedy lay in the '*undeservedness*' of Oedipus' fate: 'unconscious guilt, unmerited suffering, in short, the true terror of human existence [*das wahrhaft Schreckliche des Menschenlebens*] was their tragic muse' (10).[5]

According to Nietzsche, the reason why modern critics misunderstand works like the *Oedipus Tyrannus* is that they evaluate art from a 'moral' rather than an 'aesthetic' standpoint. His immediate target, as we have seen, is the principle of poetic justice—a term coined by the seventeenth-century English poet and critic Thomas Rymer, and familiar to Nietzsche through Georg Gottfried Gervinus' studies of Shakespeare (1849–1852).[6] In defence of the principle, Gervinus writes: 'if the encroachments of passion are glorified in poetry, if unmerited sufferings remain unexpiated, if the moral comes not forth victorious out of the ruin of vice, and the face of eternal justice remains veiled, then the work of art excites only pain and vexation instead of satisfaction'.[7]

As far as Nietzsche is concerned, this notion of what a poet must do to please his audience is merely a modern prejudice. The Greeks at the theatre of Dionysus were not shown 'the face of eternal justice', nor were they repulsed by the horrors on the stage. Through tragedy, they experienced a joy that transcends the narrow outlook of morality and communes with the divine.

[5] Nietzsche's view on the innocence of Oedipus dates back at least to his final semester at Schulpforta (spring 1864), when he wrote a study of the first chorus of the *Oedipus Tyrannus* in Latin, German, and ancient Greek. However, his early interpretation of the play is overtly moralizing: 'The idea of tragedy is as follows: "the divine often imposes suffering on mankind without his being guilty; not in an arbitrary manner, but for the maintenance of a moral world-order"' (see Henrichs, 2005, 447–8). As Brobjer (2005) has pointed out, Nietzsche's reading borrows heavily from Gustav Dronke's *Die religiösen und sittlichen Vorstellungen des Aeschylos und Sophocles* (1861)—often to the point of plagiarism.

[6] For Rymer, see the excerpt from *The Tragedies of the Last Age* (1677) in Sidnell (1991, 291–5). The following quote is representative: 'besides the purging of the passions, something must stick [for the spectator] by observing that constant order, that harmony and beauty of Providence, that necessary relation and chain, whereby the causes and effects, the virtues and rewards, the Vices and their punishments are proportioned and linked together; how deep and dark so ever are laid the springs and however intricate and involved their operation' (294). Rymer's polemics helped inspire Nahum Tate's infamous revision of *King Lear*, in which Cordelia is rescued from death and married off to Edgar.

[7] In *Shakespeare Commentaries*, II, 613, Gervinus (1853) explains that poetic justice, as exemplified by Shakespeare, does not mean that 'for a fixed crime a fixed punishment is assigned, and for this or that virtue a reward' (ibid.). Rather, virtue is seen to be its own reward: 'Death indeed in Lear befalls the many without distinction, but Cordelia dies in the glory of a blessed deliverer, Lear in expiation, Gloucester smiling, Kent with joy, the others lie caught in their own snares, robbed of their aims, the worldly souls forfeiting the world, which was all to them.... And the sublime moral lesson which lies in the exercise of this justice, is this, that death is in itself no evil, that life is in itself no blessing, that outward prosperity is no happiness, but that inner consciousness alone; that the greatest reward of virtue is virtue itself, and the greatest punishment of vice is vice itself' (616–17).

In the Basel lectures, Nietzsche offers only a basic sketch of the theory that will appear a year and a half later in *The Birth of Tragedy* (1872).[8] But already he is emphatic that tragedy does not have a *moral* purpose or effect. In making this claim, Nietzsche takes sides in a debate that stretches back to antiquity. Before I go on to consider the details of his theory, it will be useful to review some of the key developments within this tradition.

The tradition begins, of course, with Socrates' argument for banning the tragic poets from the ideally just city. The critique of tragedy in the *Republic* should be read in light of the dialogue's broad 'eudaimonistic' framework. Socrates is asked by his friends to explain the value of justice (*dikaiosunê*). He has to persuade them that being just is not only instrumentally good (because it brings honours and rewards, and helps one avoid the pain of punishment), but also valuable in its own right. In response, Socrates leads them through a long and complex argument designed to show that moral virtue (which includes justice as an essential part) is the cause of *eudaimonia*, or 'happiness', for those who have it, and that without it our lives are not worth living. Central to the argument is a theoretical account of virtue as the rule of reason in the soul. The result is a revolutionary picture of the human condition, on which happiness is not subject to the vicissitudes of fortune, since whether or not we choose to be good is, in principle, up to us.[9]

Socrates' fundamental objection to tragedy is that it repudiates this picture, and encourages a false and destructive view of the relationship between morality and happiness.[10] The critique divides roughly into two main parts, relating to the content of tragedy and to its psychological effect. In books 2 and 3, Socrates recites examples of tragic poetry (chiefly from Homer) that portray human beings as living in an unjust and inhospitable world, where death is an irredeemable evil, and the good are made to suffer through powers beyond their control—

[8] 'The *tragic idea* is that of the cult of Dionysus: the resolution of the *individuatio* into another world-order: invitation to the belief in transcendence through the fears and terrors of existence [*die furchtbaren Schreckmittel des Daseins*] ... tragedy surely did not offer any hope for a world after death. But for a moment a view of an entirely transfigured order of things opened up to the Greek: the same feeling we have when watching a Shakespearean tragedy' (12–13). Nietzsche inherits the then-common 'diptych' view of Sophocles' *Oedipus* plays, and claims that in the *Oedipus at Colonus* the dissonances of the earlier work are resolved, the suffering of the hero transfigured and redeemed. '*Katharsis* enters as a necessary feeling of consonance in a world of dissonance. In Sophocles, *suffering*, the origin of tragedy, wins its transfiguration: it is understood as something holy' (39).

[9] This picture of the human condition is given mythical form in the story of Er that concludes the dialogue. There are important questions as to how far moral virtue and therefore happiness, on the *Republic*'s own terms, is really 'up to us', but I cannot explore them here.

[10] See Halliwell (2002).

chance, necessity, and the whims of pitiless gods.[11] His concern is that if the ideal city's young guardians are exposed to such a pessimistic vision of life, their commitment to moral virtue will be undermined. Consider some famous lines the *Republic* does not mention, sung by the chorus of the *Oedipus Tyrannus* just after the truth about their ruler has come to light:

> Oh, what a wretched breed
> We mortals are:
> Our lives add up to nothing.
> Does anyone, anyone at all
> Harvest more of happiness
> Than a vacant image,
> And from that image fall away?
> You are my pattern,
> Your fortune is mine,
> You, Oedipus, your misery teaches me
> To call no mortal blessed.[12]

The chorus of elders interprets Oedipus' fortune (*daimôn*) as a pattern for the race of mortals: happiness, for creatures like us, is a mere illusion. If that is the truth about our condition, what reason is there to be virtuous?

One can see why Socrates would be concerned about the influence of tragedy on the young, who are liable to accept what they hear uncritically. But what about the rest of society? Why should mature adults not be allowed to attend the Dionysia or listen to Homer? The answer comes in book 10, where Socrates returns to the topic of poetry in order to show that it corrupts even the best of us. His argument draws on the psychological theory developed in earlier parts of the dialogue. The key stretch begins at 603e, when Socrates claims that if a 'good man' meets with misfortune, such as the death of a son, his soul is divided.[13] He has a natural impulse to grieve, to weep and wail and curse the gods, but his sense of shame restrains him. Custom (*nomos*) says that he ought to stay composed, since human events are not worthy of great concern; and grief impairs our ability 'to deliberate about what has happened and, as with the fall of the dice, to arrange our affairs, given what has befallen us, in whatever way reason determines would

[11] To take one example, Socrates quotes a pair of lines from a lost play by Aeschylus: 'A god makes mortals guilty, when he wants to destroy a house utterly' (380a, trans. Reeve). See also 392a–b: 'poets and prose writers get the most important things about human beings wrong. They say that many unjust people are happy and many just ones wretched, that doing justice is profitable if it escapes detection, and that justice is another's good but one's own loss'.

[12] 1186–96, trans. Meineck and Woodruff.

[13] I take it that the 'good man' (*epieikês anêr*, see 605c) ought to be distinguished from the person of complete virtue, who would not be at all tempted to succumb to grief.

be best' (604b–c). But when disaster strikes the heroes of tragedy, the desire to grieve overwhelms them and they flood the stage with tears. (Again, think of the final scenes of the *Oedipus Tyrannus*, where Oedipus bewails his fate for nearly 200 lines, and rebukes the chorus for wondering if he 'deliberated wisely' in choosing to blind himself rather than take his own life (1367).) In the throng of the tragic festival, we are invited to abandon our shame and weep along in sympathy. Socrates explains:

> When even the best of us hear Homer, or some other tragic poet, imitating one of the heroes in a state of grief and making a long speech of lamentation, or even chanting and beating his breast, you know we enjoy it and give ourselves over to it. We suffer along with [*sumpaschontes*] the hero and take his sufferings seriously. And we praise the one who affects us most in this way as a good poet.[14]

Through sympathy, the poet aims to satisfy the 'natural appetite' for grieving that all human beings share, but which ought to be restrained and starved. Although it may appear to be a harmless indulgence, over time, Socrates says, tragic poetry nourishes and strengthens this desire, undermining the rule of reason in our souls.[15]

The objection is not that tragedy gives pleasure or arouses emotion per se. The point, rather, is that the emotions elicited by tragedy have a particular *evaluative content*: they imply judgments about what really matters.[16] The hero's outpouring of grief is based on the perception that something essential to his happiness has been lost. In so far as we 'suffer along with' him, we accept that his perception is accurate and that his grief is an appropriate response. But then we also tacitly accept that happiness and moral virtue can come apart. So whether or not we would affirm upon reflection that virtue is all that matters, in the theatre, at least, we adopt a radically different view of the world. Socrates thinks that the more often we allow ourselves to inhabit this perspective, the harder it is to bear misfortune in our own lives with fortitude and restraint. Rather than making us 'better and happier', he concludes, tragedy leaves us 'worse and more wretched' (606d).

[14] 605c–d.

[15] See 606a–b: 'what is forcibly kept in check in our personal misfortunes and has an insatiable hunger for weeping and lamenting—since that is what it has a natural appetite for—is the very factor that gets satisfaction and enjoyment from the poets. Second, our naturally best element, since it has not been adequately educated by reason or habit, relaxes its guard over the lamenting one, since it is watching the sufferings of somebody else and thinks there is no shame involved for it in praising and pitying another purportedly good man who grieves excessively. On the contrary, it thinks that to be a clear profit—I mean the pleasure it gets. And it would not want to be deprived of it by despising the whole poem' (606a–b, trans. Reeve).

[16] See Halliwell (2002): 'To lament what is lost or destroyed in suffering is implicitly to cling to a certain sense of what is worth having and preserving in life' (106).

Even if one balks at this last suggestion—that tragedy actually makes us worse—the *Republic* presents a strong case for the view that its purpose is not of a moral or ethical nature. According to the argument, tragedy paints a picture of the world in which some forms of loss matter more than the preservation of virtue, and which, by engaging our sympathy for the suffering hero, invites us to see it as a reflection of reality.

It is not without some regret, however, that Socrates reaches his verdict, and so he asks the lovers of poetry to give an account of why tragedy is not only pleasurable but also beneficial. This challenge sets the agenda for much of the discussion of tragedy within the philosophical tradition, whether or not it is acknowledged. In a moment, we shall see that Nietzsche answers the challenge by rejecting the terms on which it is set. But first I want to consider two attempts to reconcile tragedy and morality, one ancient and one modern, in order to bring out what is unique in his response.

3 'NOT ONLY FOR PLEASURE': THE MORAL VIEW OF TRAGEDY

The first attempt to defend tragedy from the *Republic*'s critique is usually credited to Aristotle. The definition of tragedy in *Poetics* 6 ends with the clause: 'and through pity and fear accomplishing the *katharsis* of such emotions'.[17]

The notion of *katharsis* has inspired a diverse range of interpretations, many (but not all) of which give it a moral significance.[18] According to the standard neo-classical reading, Aristotle believes that the aim of tragedy is to *purge* the spectator of his emotions, leaving him better equipped to deal rationally with life's misfortunes.[19] The audience sees that emotional weakness itself is the cause of the hero's suffering, and learns by example to control its passions. Aristotle's disagreement with the *Republic*, then, is primarily over an empirical matter—that is, whether tragedy leaves its audience more or less susceptible to harmful emotions.[20] But this account of *katharsis* saddles Aristotle with a strange view of the spectator's psychology. Surely we think that Oedipus gives into his grief *because he*

[17] 1149b24, trans. Halliwell in the Loeb Classical Library.

[18] For a survey of the major interpretations, see Appendix 5 in Halliwell (1998). Scott (2003) argues that the mention of *katharsis* is a later interpolation.

[19] Nietzsche seems to subscribe to the 'pathological' reading defended by Jacob Bernays, according to which *katharsis* is 'a harmlessly pleasurable means of expending pent-up or excessive emotions' (Halliwell, 1998, 353). Although Bernays denied that Aristotelian *katharsis* is a moral notion, Nietzsche tends to lump his reading together with the neo-classical view. (See the reference in *BT*, 22 to *katharsis* as a 'pathological-moral process'.)

[20] At *HH*, I, 212 Nietzsche sides with Plato over Aristotle.

is wretched, not that he is wretched because of his grief. It is difficult to see how one could have the latter response without already viewing the emotions as harmful. But an audience like that would not need to be purged.[21]

A more nuanced and persuasive reading of the *Poetics* as an answer to Plato has been defended by Martha Nussbaum. On her interpretation, *katharsis* is a matter not of purging the spectator's passions, but of 'clearing them up'.[22] Aristotle's theory depends on a more positive view of the tragic emotions, which is in turn grounded in a competing account of virtue's relation to *eudaimonia*.

For Aristotle, happiness requires more than the possession of good character; it consists in a life of virtuous *actions*. But a person's capacity to act virtuously is not wholly determined by the state of his soul. It may require external goods like health, wealth, citizenship, family, and friendship. Moreover, a person of good character might be faced with situations in which it is impossible to avoid doing wrong.

According to Nussbaum, Aristotle recognized that 'the tragic genre is built around an acceptance of the ethical significance of uncontrolled reversals, the existence of a gap between being good and living a flourishing life.'[23] In Sophocles' *Philoctetes*, Neoptolemus faces the choice of deceiving Philoctetes and disgracing his character, or preserving his honour and failing to help the Greek army achieve victory. Motivated by love for his supposed parents, Oedipus leaves Corinth and brings pollution to the people of Thebes. The emotions elicited by tragedy, in Aristotle's view, imply true judgments about *eudaimonia* and its vulnerability to fortune. Through its reminders of human fragility, tragedy 'clears up' our understanding of the good life, and leaves us better attuned to the reality of our ethical condition.

Does this adequately address Socrates' main objection? Importantly, for Aristotle, the perspective on the world opened up by tragedy is compatible with the belief that moral virtue is essential to happiness, even if not sufficient for it. We may pity Philoctetes because he is in monstrous pain and cut off from human society. At the same time, what ultimately justifies our pity is that he is unable to lead a life of virtuous action.

But one might wonder whether this insight is available to us only upon reflection. Tragedy focuses our attention on what is vulnerable to fortune, not on the value of what is stable and in our control. If the audience sees that everything a person cares about can be destroyed by chance and necessity, why should it suppose that virtue counts for much? This goes to the heart of Socrates' complaint. The question is how much *weight* a tragedy (or a performance of tragedy) gives to

[21] The neo-classical notion of *katharsis* is closely akin to Stoic views of tragedy, which face the same basic objection. See Halliwell (2005, 405–9).

[22] Nussbaum (1992, 143–7). [23] Ibid., 111–12.

virtue in the balance of values, and what we should say about a work that gives it little or none.[24]

In this connection, it is worth comparing Friedrich Schiller's attempt to reconcile tragedy and morality. Schiller develops his theory within the framework of Kant's transcendental idealism, which rejects the eudaimonistic approach to ethics. Kant attributes the desire for happiness (and the avoidance of pain and suffering) to the empirical or sensuous side of human nature. Because empirical motives are subject to physical laws, they cannot be used to ground the value of moral virtue: an action done for the sake of the agent's own happiness has no greater inherent worth than any other event in nature—for example, a pine cone falling from a tree. In his view, an action has genuine value only if it stems from a separate, non-empirical motive of duty or obedience to the moral law, which is binding on all rational beings and the source of human freedom and dignity. Given this picture, tragedy's exposure of a gap between goodness and happiness does not, by itself, threaten to undermine the authority of moral demands. On the contrary, Schiller argues, tragedy represents the triumph of the moral will in the face of extreme suffering.

In the essay 'On the Art of Tragedy' (1792), Schiller echoes Plato's Socrates in defining tragedy as the 'art that establishes the pleasure of sympathy as its purpose'.[25] Yet his analysis of this pleasure is radically different from what we find in the *Republic*, where it is explained by a universal human desire to grieve. For Schiller, the pleasure of sympathy is an expression of our moral natures. In the first instance, our sympathy for the suffering hero gives us pain; but our reflective awareness of this pain brings with it a feeling of sublime pleasure. For we recognize our power as rational beings to transcend the desires of the ego and freely obey the moral law.[26]

[24] Nussbaum (ibid.) claims that in spite of his horrible suffering, Oedipus's unshaken nobility of character 'shines through'. Nussbaum admits that these are 'judgment calls' (157), and says that Euripidean tragedy might be more difficult for Aristotle to accommodate: 'even where virtue is retained it does not seem to count for as much, in a world where its due expression is curtailed' (158).

[25] Schiller (1993, 6).

[26] Ibid., 4: 'Now, we are not acquainted with more than two sorts of sources of pleasure: the satisfaction of the urge to be happy and the fulfilment of moral laws. Hence, a pleasure proven not to have sprung from the first source must have its origin necessarily in the second source. It is from our moral nature, then, that the pleasure emanates by means of which painful emotions captivate us when we hear of them and in certain cases, even when they are originally felt, still touch us in a pleasurable way'. A bit further on, Schiller adds: 'the very assault on our sensuous life is the condition for igniting that power of mind, whose activity produces the pleasure that we take in sympathetic suffering. Now, this power is none other than reason' (5).

Schiller thinks the poet must be careful, however, not to overwhelm his audience with the painful side of sympathy, or else a play might simply cause revulsion. The 'incongruity' (*Zweckwidrigkeit*) in nature that brings about the hero's misfortune must give way to a higher sense of 'purposiveness' (*Zweckmäßigkeit*)—that is, a sense of the harmony between humanity's deepest interests and the world at large.[27] The most effective means of arousing the spectator's sympathy, according to Schiller, is for the hero to fall into disaster through necessity or blind fate. On the other hand, it is also the most liable to provoke disgust, since being subject to fate is 'always humiliating and debilitating for entities that are free and self-determining'.[28] But when moral freedom overcomes even the harshest necessity, tragedy achieves its ultimate goal:

> This happens when even that dissatisfaction with fate falls to the wayside, losing itself in the presentiment or rather in a distinct consciousness of a teleological connection among things, a sublime order, a benevolent will.... Its apparent violation, which in a single case caused pain, becomes simply a goad to our reason to search out general laws for a justification of this particular case and to resolve the isolated dissonance within the grand harmony.[29]

Schiller claims that 'the most splendid pieces of the Greek stage leave something to be desired' because the hero's humiliation and suffering are left unredeemed. In his view, the ancient Greeks never realized the full potential of the art form they created. He attributes this failing to their primitive religious and philosophical outlook, and suggests that tragedy is the one area of art where modern man could surpass the Greek achievement.[30]

[27] Ibid., 7. In an essay from the following year, Schiller writes: 'in order for human *intelligence* to reveal itself as a force independent of nature, it is necessary for nature first to demonstrate all its might before our eyes. The *sensuous being* must *suffer* deeply and vehemently, the pathos must be present, so that the rational being can testify to its independence' ('On the Pathetic', *Essays*, 45). The hero must suffer 'vehemently', according to Schiller, because otherwise the audience cannot be sure if his heroic actions stem from the desire for happiness or the motive of duty. But the pathos of the drama must not be too great for the moral will to be overcome.

[28] Ibid., 9. [29] Ibid.

[30] Schopenhauer's account of tragedy owes an obvious debt to Schiller. In *The World as Will and Representation*, Schopenhauer argues that the purpose of tragedy is to show us that the only path to transcendence is through resignation of the will-to-live. The pleasure of watching tragedy consists in the awareness that there is a part of our nature that is not subject to the Will—our noumenal self, or the thing that is metaphysically identical with the world beyond appearance. Tragedy's proper effect is realized only when our compassion for the suffering hero is eclipsed by 'the knowledge that the world and life can afford us no true satisfaction, and are therefore not worth our attachment to them' (*WWR*, II, 433–4). On both accounts, the pain of sympathy is a means to a higher form of consciousness. Schopenhauer also adopts Schiller's progressivism, claiming that tragedy reaches its apotheosis in the modern period, when the spectator's 'resigned exaltation of the mind' is displayed by the tragic hero himself (434). (He cites *Hamlet* and Bellini's *Norma* as examples (*WWR*, I, 253; II, 435), and quotes the conclusion of Schiller's *The Bride of Messina*, 'Life is not

Although Schiller denies that the *justification* of morality depends on its connection to happiness, he recognizes that, from a psychological standpoint, a significant enough gap can prevent tragedy from fulfilling its purpose. In the ideal case, our sense of the 'sublime order' of things will eclipse any lingering pain over what the hero has suffered. It will seem that he has lost nothing of deep significance, as long as his moral integrity remains intact.[31] The dissonances of the drama are resolved into a 'grander harmony'.

Schiller's ideal ends up looking very much like the demand for poetic justice. It is telling that he regards Greek tragedy as a defective form of the genre because it fails to display the triumph of the moral will. One might think that his attempt to reconcile tragedy and morality succeeds at too high a price, if it forces him to exclude the Greeks from the centre of his conception of tragedy.

It could be argued that both Aristotle and Schiller fail to meet Socrates' challenge head on. Whereas Aristotle's theory gives insufficient weight to the pessimism of a play like the *Oedipus Tyrannus*, its sense of insurmountable ruin and loss, Schiller simply reshapes the concept of tragedy to guarantee it a morally beneficial effect. Both assume, like Socrates, that whatever value tragedy does have must be understood in moral or ethical terms. Nietzsche flatly rejects this assumption, and defends the value of tragedy on the ground that it does *not* have a moral aim.

4 NIETZSCHE AND THE REVALUATION OF TRAGEDY

At several points in *The Birth of Tragedy*, Nietzsche emphasizes his unique position within the history of aesthetics:

the greatest good'. But he pointedly omits the second half of the couplet: 'But the greatest evil is guilt.') In Greek tragedy, by contrast, Schopenhauer finds the 'spirit of resignation' to be lacking: 'Almost all [ancient tragedies] show the human race under the dreadful dominion of chance and error, but not the resignation these bring about which redeems us from them' (434–5). The reason, he explains, is that the Greeks 'had not yet reached the summit and goal of tragedy, or indeed of the view of life generally'.

[31] Here it is worth noting Schelling's strained attempt to read the *Oedipus Tyrannus* along Kantian lines: 'in order not to allow necessity to overcome him without simultaneously overcoming it, the protagonist also had to atone voluntarily for this guilt—guilt imposed by fate itself. This is the most sublime idea and the greatest victory of freedom: voluntarily to bear the punishment for an unavoidable transgression in order to manifest his freedom precisely in the loss of that very same freedom, and to perish amid a declaration of free will' (253–4). Schelling continues: '[H]ow can one in any sense call an ending unfortunate in which, for example, the protagonist voluntarily gives his own life, which he can no longer conduct with dignity or in which he brings down upon himself other consequences of his unmerited guilt—as does Sophocles' Oedipus, who cannot rest until he himself has disclosed the entire, terrible entanglement and that entire, frightful fate itself?'

Never since Aristotle have we been given an account of the tragic effect from which we might infer any artistic states or aesthetic activity on the part of the listener. Now the grave events are supposed to be leading pity and terror inexorably towards the relief of discharge; now we are supposed to feel elevated and inspired by the triumph of good and noble principles, by the sacrifice of the hero in the interest of a moral view of the world. I am certain that for many people precisely this, and this alone, is the effect of tragedy, but it is equally clear that none of them, nor any of the aestheticians who interpret on their behalf, has ever experienced tragedy as a supreme *art*.

(*BT*, 22)[32]

In a later section, he remarks: 'no one seeking to deduce the effect of the tragic from moral sources alone, as has been customary in aesthetics for far too long, should believe that he has done any kind of service to art, which must insist on purity in its sphere above all else' (*BT*, 24). As in the Sophocles lectures, Nietzsche contrasts his own 'aesthetic' account of the effect of tragedy with the 'moral' views of his predecessors.[33] It would be a mistake, however, to take him to be advocating a doctrine of 'art for art's sake', or subscribing to anything like a 'cult of beauty'. To see this, we need to take a look at the larger project within which his theory of tragedy is developed.

The Birth of Tragedy is ostensibly, in the first place, an account of the origin of Attic tragedy, and of its death at the hands of Socrates and Euripides. When read carefully, however, it becomes clear that this historical narrative is at the service of a far more ambitious goal. The overarching aim of the book is to address what Nietzsche sees as a crisis in modern culture. Among its central theses is the claim that all cultures depend upon *illusions*—indeed, that we need illusions in order to find life bearable at all.[34] Nietzsche believes that Western civilization has been sustained for more than 2,000 years by a single, dominant illusion: that human reason is capable not only of understanding existence, but 'even of *correcting* it' (*BT*, 15). This optimism finds its archetypical expression in Socrates' doctrine that knowledge is the cause of virtue, and virtue the cause of happiness (*BT*, 14). According to Nietzsche, the influence of this 'Socratic' illusion (or simply 'Socratism') is apparent in all aspects of modern life—the relentless pursuit of scientific knowledge and technological progress, political revolutions and movements for social reform, the Enlightenment image of man as an autonomous moral subject, and the Christian view of the world as the creation of a just and

32 Translations are from Whiteside, with some minor modifications.

33 For a helpful discussion of Nietzsche's contrast between 'moral' and 'aesthetic' modes of evaluation, see Came (2004).

34 *BT*, 18. See also *WP*, 853.

rational God. What unites these phenomena is the belief that suffering is due to our own irrationality and injustice, and that reason and virtue can therefore secure our happiness. And it is because of this belief, Nietzsche thinks, that tragedy has been repeatedly misunderstood.

Another central thesis of *The Birth of Tragedy*, however, is that the Socratic illusion is inherently unsustainable. Spurred on by his own desire for knowledge, modern man is being forced to recognize that illusion and error are the very conditions of human;[35] that reason is just a tool of irrational forces or 'drives', which bring us into the world only so that we may strive, suffer, and die; that the ordinary conception we have of ourselves, as stable individuals with real goals and purposes, is just nature's means of perpetuating our futile existence; and that the problem the problem of suffering has no rational solution (*BT*, 15). Confronted with this reality, modern man finds his life terrifying and absurd, and looks for a way to escape or transcend it. Religion offers no consolation, because it asks him to believe in a metaphysical realm that he knows he cannot accept. This is the crisis of modernity as *The Birth of Tragedy* envisions it: once modern man has seen through the illusion of Enlightenment, how will he be protected from despair?

'From the Greeks', Nietzsche writes in a notebook from 1871, 'we can learn what we ourselves are going through'.[36] The opening narrative of *The Birth of Tragedy* describes a parallel crisis in ancient Greek culture. Rejecting the ideal of 'Greek serenity' made popular by Winckelmann, Nietzsche claims that the early Greeks 'knew and felt the fears and horrors of existence' (*BT*, 3), but *overcame* this knowledge through the illusions of art.[37] At first they were saved by the

[35] On this point, Nietzsche was strongly influenced by his reading of F. A. Lange's monumental *History of Materialism* (1925 (1866)). The following quote from Lange is representative: 'a reality such as man imagines to himself, and as he yearns after when this imagination is dispelled, an existence absolutely fixed and independent of us while it is yet known by us—such a reality does not exist and cannot exist, because the synthetic creative factor of our knowledge extends, in fact, into the very first sense-impressions and even into the elements of logic' (II, 336). Nietzsche suggests that even the rules of logical inference do not correspond to any mind-independent reality (*BT*, 18). I cannot comment here on the coherence of his view.

[36] *KSA*, 7, 13[2].

[37] Nietzsche's picture of the Greeks also challenges Schopenhauer, who had claimed that Greek culture was naïvely optimistic, but that tragedy provided an outlet for their pessimistic tendencies. See *WWR*, II, 585: 'remote as the Greeks were from the Christian and lofty Asiatic worldview, and although they were decidedly at the standpoint of the affirmation of the will, they were nevertheless deeply affected by the wretchedness of existence. The invention of tragedy, which belongs to them, is evidence of this.' Later on he remarks: 'existence is certainly to be regarded as an error or mistake, to return from which is salvation; it bears this character throughout. Therefore it is conceived in this sense by the ancient Samana religions, and also by real and original Christianity, although in a roundabout way. Even Judaism itself contains the germ of such a view, at any rate in the Fall of man; this is its redeeming feature. Only Greek paganism and Islam are wholly optimistic; therefore in the former the opposite tendency had to find expression at least in tragedy' (605).

Apollonian arts of sculpture and epic poetry, in whose beautiful images of gods and heroes they saw the harsh features of their own lives transfigured. With the introduction of the cults of Dionysus, however, these images began to lose their persuasive power. In the wild frenzy of the Bacchic orgy, with its earth-shattering music, the Greek felt an intoxicating sense of oneness with the 'primal ground of being' (*BT*, 1). But it also left him overexposed to the nullity of mankind.

Descending from his ecstatic heights, he was repulsed by the thought of having to carry on living, knowing that 'action can change nothing in the eternal essence of things' (*BT*, 7).[38] Like modern Socratic man, he had seen the truth and needed a new life-affirming illusion. According to Nietzsche, tragedy was created in order to fulfil this need. At the tragic festival, the Greeks were confronted with the truth about their condition in a way that allowed them to endure and even *celebrate* it. Nietzsche's account of how tragedy achieved this miracle is incredibly intricate, and I cannot hope do it full justice here. But it is important to see how radically it departs from earlier models, especially in regard to the role of the drama. Nietzsche claims that tragedy evolved out of the choral dithyramb, itself a sublimation of the Bacchic orgy. In the communal dance, the members of the chorus surrendered their identities and received the 'metaphysical consolation... that whatever superficial changes may occur, life is at bottom indestructibly powerful and joyful' (*BT*, 7).

The dithyramb gives birth to tragic drama when the chorus-leader (under Apollo's inspiration) separates himself from the throng and interprets the Dionysian state through an act of mimesis.[39] Nietzsche speculates that the original tragic subject was the myth of Dionysus 'Zagreus', who was torn apart at the hands of his brothers the Titans (*BT*, 10). The god's dismemberment represents the Schopenhauerian truth that individuation itself is a curse, and the mystery that the highest bliss is achieved only through annihilation.

All of the earliest tragic heroes, Nietzsche says, were merely masks of Dionysus, their stories all variations on this single *Ur*-myth. The purpose of the drama is to create a realm of Apollonian 'semblance' (*Schein*), which protects the chorus from the terrifying aspect of the Dionysian. The tragic hero appears as a striving and suffering individual, while the chorus-member now becomes a *spectator*, pitying and fearing for the image on the stage, and forgetting that its fate is also his own. At the moment of the hero's destruction, however, the veil is torn,

[38] Nietzsche likens the Dionysian reveller to Hamlet: 'True understanding, insight into the terrible truth, outweigh every motive for action.... Aware of truth from a single glimpse of it, all man can now see is the horror and absurdity of existence'.

[39] Nietzsche's chronological account reflects the *atemporal* priority of the Dionysian over the Apollonian in his view of the tragic effect.

revealing the true Dionysian significance of the drama. But rather than devastate the audience, the sacrifice of the hero produces an overwhelming joy. In a key passage, Nietzsche describes the spectator's experience as a 'schism within the self':

> He beholds the transfigured world of the stage and yet negates it. He sees the tragic hero before him, in epic clarity and beauty, and yet rejoices in his destruction. He understands the dramatic events to their very depths, yet he is happy to escape into incomprehension. He feels that the hero's acts are justified, and yet is all the more uplifted when those acts destroy their originator. He trembles at the sufferings which will befall the hero, and yet they give him a higher, much more powerful pleasure.
>
> (*BT*, 22)

Through the hero's sacrifice, the audience achieves the transcendence of the Dionysian state without feeling the full weight of its terror.

Given this picture, it is clear why Nietzsche thinks the pleasure of tragedy cannot be derived from any moral source. The tragic myth represents humanity's subjection to nature, the futility of reason and virtue against chance and misfortune. We are not simply devastated by the sight of this, however, because the chorus' music transports us to a divine perspective, from which it appears that 'even ugliness and discord are an artistic game which the Will plays with itself in the eternal abundance of its delight' (*BT*, 24).[40]

Nietzsche thinks that the feeling of moral triumph *precludes* this effect. In the central sections of *The Birth of Tragedy*, he describes how Greek tragedy was destroyed by the Socratic drive for knowledge. From an Enlightenment standpoint, the pessimistic myths and lyrical expressivism of the earliest tragedies made no sense. The Athenians started to demand that their experience at the tragic festival cohere with the worldview they brought with them to the law courts and the agora. The poets would eventually give in, relegating the Dionysian chorus to a subsidiary role and making plot and dialogue the soul of the drama. Irresolvable conflicts were replaced by denouements in which good triumphed over evil. As a result of these innovations, tragedy was no longer able to perform its redemptive function.

[40] In one of his less obscure descriptions of the effect of tragedy, Nietzsche writes:

> Only from the spirit of music can we understand delight in the destruction of the individual. For only in single instances of such destruction can we clearly see the eternal phenomenon of Dionysian art, which expresses the will in its omnipotence, behind the *principium individuationis*, the eternal life that lies beyond the phenomenal world, regardless of all destruction. Metaphysical delight in the tragic is a translation of the image: the hero, the supreme manifestation of the will, is negated to our gratification, because he is only a phenomenon, and the eternal life of the will is left untouched by his destruction.
>
> (*BT*, 16)

It is only now, Nietzsche claims, since the Socratic drive has finally undermined itself and modern man's faith in reason has been shattered, that tragedy can be reborn.

In Nietzsche's view, then, Socrates was right to suspect that tragedy did not morally improve the Athenians or teach them how to live. But he was wrong to think that tragedy did not benefit them. He failed to understand the true purpose of the tragic festival, regarding it as nothing more than a socially sanctioned way for them to indulge their irrational desires. He was blind to the fact that the audience's pleasure was based on a deeper wisdom—on their subconscious knowledge that there is no escape from suffering, even for the best of us. Likewise, those who tried to answer Socrates' challenge wrongly assumed that tragedy, in order to have genuine value, must uphold a vision of the world where reason and virtue triumph over the greatest misfortunes. On the contrary, Nietzsche thinks, tragedy is meant for those (like himself) who have already *seen through* this illusion.[41]

The question then arises regarding how tragedy is supposed to make life seem worth living once we step outside of the theatre. It may provide us with a moment of affirmation, but how do we incorporate this experience into the rest of our lives? I do not believe Nietzsche has a clear answer to this question. On his account, tragedy gives the audience a way of seeing the world, but it does not offer any solution for how to live in it.[42] This is an important part of what he means, I take it, when he says that tragedy has an 'aesthetic' effect, and that it demands 'purity in its sphere'. There is a fissure between the Dionysian perspective on existence and the standpoint of practical reason. Nietzsche appears to regard taking part in the tragic festival as like participating in a religious ritual: the process must be endlessly repeated, and there are no possible substitutes. But unlike in a ritual such as the Christian Eucharist, there is no connection between the experience of tragedy and the *praxis* of everyday life.[43] This follows from Nietzsche's denial that art has a cognitive function. Its aim is not to engender any

[41] Schacht (2001) is especially good on this point.

[42] I am not persuaded by the efforts of commentators to derive any sort of positive ethic from Nietzsche's theory of tragedy. Han-Pile (2006) offers numerous insights into *The Birth of Tragedy*, but I disagree with her view that tragedy provides a *solution* to the problem of suffering. On her reading, Nietzsche's claim is that the tragic artist 'gives us in his work a way... to *understand* that through [the] creative process, suffering is redeemed and life becomes worthwhile' (387). In the subsequent paragraph she writes: 'in the *Birth* true salvation lies in our willingly accepting pain and finding the strength, not only to bear it passively, but to actively transmute it into pleasure through artistic creation' (388). But this suggests that the value of tragedy is *cognitive*, whereas Nietzsche is emphatic that art deals in illusions.

[43] I owe this point to Matthew O'Brien.

beliefs or knowledge, but to relieve the burden of knowledge. How, then, does the spectator carry on living? Perhaps the best answer Nietzsche can give is that he goes on being seduced by the same illusions as before. He may leave the theatre feeling renewed and strangely reconciled to existence, but he does not have any more *reason* to live.[44]

5 NIETZSCHE'S LEGACY RECONSIDERED

Nietzsche would later find much to object to in *The Birth of Tragedy*'s portrayal of tragedy—above all, the ideal of 'metaphysical consolation', which he blames on the unhealthy influence of Schopenhauer and Wagner. But his denial that tragedy has a moral purpose or effect remains a cornerstone of his revised account.[45] The development of Nietzsche's conception of tragedy can be seen to reflect a more basic change in his understanding of pessimism. Beginning with *Human, All Too Human* (1878), the need for metaphysical transcendence is no longer treated as a given, as an ineluctable part of human nature, but as something to be interrogated, critiqued, and explained.[46] Suffering and existence, Nietzsche comes to think, are not *objectively* undesirable; they only appear so when viewed from a particular *evaluative perspective*. In later works, he labels this the perspective of 'morality', and argues that it is an artefact of physical and psychological weakness. The mistake he made in *The Birth of Tragedy* was to suggest that tragic affirmation requires transcending the human condition and viewing the hero's suffering from a divine standpoint. The later Nietzsche ascribes this affirmative stance to the *tragic poet*, who communicates his own godlike vision: 'The tragic man says Yes

[44] In *BT*, 21, Nietzsche says that tragedy functioned as a 'restorative draught' for the Greeks who fought in the Persian Wars. He is likely drawing on Plato's *Laws*: 'The gods... took pity on the human race, born to suffer as it was, and gave it relief in the form of religious festivals to serve as periods of rest from its labours. They gave us the Muses, with Apollo their leader, and Dionysus; by having these gods to share their holidays, men were to be made whole again, and thanks to them, we find refreshment in the celebration of these festivals' (2004, 653c–d, trans. Saunders).

[45] See, e.g., *D*, 72, 240; *TI*, IX, 24, X, 5; *WP*, 821, 851–3.

[46] See *HH*, I, 27: 'But in the end one also has to understand that the needs which religion has satisfied and philosophy is now supposed to satisfy are not immutable; they can be *weakened* and *exterminated*. Consider, for example, that Christian distress of mind that comes from sighing over one's inner depravity and care for one's salvation—all conceptions originating in nothing but errors of reason and deserving, not satisfaction, but obliteration. A philosophy can be employed either to *satisfy* such needs or to *set them aside*; for they are acquired, time-bound needs resting on presuppositions that contradict those of science.' See also *HH*, I, 9, 26, 37, 110; and *WEN*, 221–2 (19[85]): 'The so-called metaphysical need proves nothing about any reality corresponding to that need: on the contrary, because we have this need we hear the language of the will, not that of the intellect, and we go astray if we believe this language. We would have to accept a god if he were demonstrable *without* being made to appear necessary to us by a need'.

to even the bitterest suffering: he is strong, full, deifying enough to do so.'[47] The value of tragedy is not that it offers redemption from the world, but that it holds out the possibility of taking an attitude to life that transcends the moral perspective, thereby obviating the need for redemption.

In spite of this significant change in Nietzsche's thinking, his insistence on the conflict between tragedy and morality provides a continuous thread from the Basel lectures to the last published works. It also has had an influence on contemporary philosophical approaches to tragedy. Bernard Williams and Sebastian Gardner, for example, both have defended broadly 'Nietzschean' views of the relationship between tragedy and morality. Gardner writes:

> Fundamental to tragedy is the sense of an opposition between human beings and the world at large, this 'other' of humanity assuming various determinate forms (the gods, Necessity, Fate or Fortune, Nature etc.), but in all cases presenting itself as antagonistic to humanity: the world is regarded not as furthering but rather as negating, and as lacking any inner accord with, the attempts of human beings to realize value.[48]

Since practical reason views the demands of morality as supreme and well founded, and tragedy represents the world as hostile to our deepest ends, Gardner argues, appreciating tragedy requires that we abandon the perspective of moral agency. In a similar vein, Williams contrasts the 'moral' conception of the world with the patterns of 'stark fiction', for which Sophoclean tragedy (especially the *Trachiniae*) serves as a paradigm. Stark fictions offer valuable reminders of what moral philosophy, in his view, tends to forget: 'the very plain fact that everything that an agent most cares about typically comes from, and can be ruined by, uncontrollable necessity and chance'.[49] As rational agents trying to get on in the world, we have to forget; as theorists, however, we should be more honest with ourselves. By representing 'undeserved and uncompensated suffering' with such power and directness, Sophoclean tragedy allows us to confront and better understand the 'horrors' that underlie our practical self-conception.[50]

Williams believes that tragedy provides a more truthful picture than morality, while Gardner does not privilege one perspective over the other, but attempts to show only that the two are incompatible.[51] Nietzsche, as we have seen, would

[47] *WLN*, 14[89] (249–50). This is already to a certain extent prefigured in *The Birth of Tragedy*: 'we can imagine the tragic artist himself as he creates his characters, like a prolific deity of individuation . . . and the way his tremendous Dionysian impulse then devours this whole world of phenomena, in order, behind it and through its destruction, to give a sense of the supreme artistic primal joy within the womb of the primal Oneness' (*BT*, 22).

[48] Gardner (2003, 229–30). [49] Williams (2006, 54). [50] Ibid., 56, 59.

[51] Gardner claims only that they conflict 'at the first level of reflection' (presumably he means our state of consciousness as spectators in the theatre), and leaves open the possibility of a 'reconciliation'

agree with Williams, though he would deny that the value of tragedy is mainly cognitive. Setting that issue to one side, the question of their compatibility strikes me as highly significant. If it is true that tragedy conflicts with the view of the world we adopt as moral agents, and we value tragedy in part because it gives us insight into our lives, then perhaps we should consider that worldview a sham. On the other hand, we might follow Plato's Socrates and doubt that tragedy paints a truthful picture of life. Another alternative, of course, is to keep honouring both perspectives, and hope that the inconsistency does not trouble us.[52]

I want to conclude by briefly considering whether the Nietzschean view is plausible. To decide this, we would have to see if it helps illuminate actual examples of tragedy. But it is striking how few examples Nietzsche even mentions, much less analyses in any detail. In *The Birth of Tragedy*, he discusses Sophocles' *Oedipus* plays, the *Prometheus Bound*, and Euripides' *Bacchae*, yet in each case he is clearly more interested in the background myth than in what the poet does with it.[53] In section 17, he goes so far as to suggest that *none* of the surviving Greek plays supports his account, since the musical element has been lost (and even if we did have the music, it could never have the significance for us that it did for the Greeks). This is a consequence of his view that the drama is only a beautiful veil, whose main purpose is to protect the audience from total submersion in the Dionysian depths.

Nietzsche thinks that if we read a Greek tragedy, or see it performed without the music, it is bound to seem much shallower than it is. One might be tempted to write this off as an idiosyncrasy of his early devotion to Wagner, but in the later works he is even less interested in discussing examples. After *Daybreak* (1881), which contains a fascinating—although not wholly convincing—passage on *Macbeth* (with a brief reference to Sophocles), not a single work of tragedy is mentioned. In a couple of places, he indicates that it would be futile to support his claims with evidence, because we moderns will always interpret tragedy in a way

at a 'higher, speculative philosophical level' (245). I do not find this distinction persuasive, as will become clear below.

[52] Interestingly, Gardner doubts that tragic experience—even if it were more truthful—*could* have any bearing on our practical lives: '[T]hough tragedy may allow us, as spectators, to 'see' beyond morality, it does not take us, as *agents*, beyond morality. This is part of the reason why we need to repeat the experience: the perspective opened up by tragedy is one that we, as beings with lives to lead, cannot occupy' (240). A bit further on he adds: 'when we reflect on tragedy at a remove from the original experience, restored to the perspective of morality, we then reinterpret our experience—as morality requires us to do—in morally congenial terms, thereby arriving at a moral interpretation of tragic suffering and affirmation' (241).

[53] Moreover, his readings of Sophocles and Aeschylus in section 9 are infused with Wagnerian allusions—so much so, that at times one might think he is really talking about the *Ring*.

that satisfies our moral prejudices.[54] But unless his view can shed light on actual examples, we should wonder whether he is writing about real human practices, or just constructing an ideal of his own. As we have seen, Nietzsche himself tries to motivate his theory by appealing to the failure of other approaches to understand particular tragedies. So it is reasonable to ask whether his approach can do a better job. The kind of close reading which that would require is not something I can embark on here. I would instead like to put forward two general reasons for scepticism about the Nietzschean view.

First, it strikes me that the Nietzschean view depends on an overly restrictive conception of morality.[55] It is certainly true that many great tragedies make a mockery of poetic justice: the gods inflict suffering beyond measure, the lives of blameless men and women are destroyed, and the most sincere attempts to be wise and good bring about disaster. But it is a further step to say that morality makes no difference in the scheme of things. This does seem to be what the chorus in the *Oedipus Tyrannus* concludes, when it sings, 'Our lives add up to nothing.' Perhaps we cannot be a good audience, and share in the chorus' grief, unless we see the world in the same way at that moment. But the chorus does not have the last word. A good audience will also think it genuinely *matters* whether Oedipus acts brutally towards Tiresias; or whether he chooses to blind himself; or whether Creon takes pity on Oedipus' daughters/sisters, instead of casting them out. As far as Nietzsche is concerned, these decisions and actions all belong to the realm of Apollonian semblance, and in the 'total effect' of tragedy they cease to matter. But it seems to me to be an open question whether the horror of Oedipus' suffering should eclipse all other concerns—a lot will depend on the particulars of the performance. The play clearly does not have a moral purpose, if one assumes that moral demands are only intelligible in a world where the good always triumph. The Greek poets seem to uniformly

[54] *D*, 240: 'we need first to *adjust* and *justify* the goal of a Shakespearean drama, that is to say, not to understand it'. See also *WP*, 852.

[55] For example, Gardner (2003) claims that 'there is an inherent tendency for moral consciousness, by virtue of its internal rationality rather than as a merely psychological matter, to conceive the world in terms that secure the objective purposiveness and well-foundedness of moral action, and that at the extreme, moral consciousness will conceive the world as having morality as its essence, and nature as having the facilitation of the moral will as its ultimate purpose' (229). He defends this Kantian assumption on the grounds that on 'any conception of morality intelligible to us, moral value is regarded as supreme (absolute, unconditional). Consequently morality must represent itself as able to *make up for* tragic loss and suffering. What sort of value would moral value be, if it could not do this?' (235). As we have seen, this is the basis for the *Republic*'s critique of tragedy, but Aristotle seems to have disagreed. Gardner's argument is helped by the fact that it takes Schiller and not Aristotle to be representative of the moral view. One could argue that he dismisses Nussbaum's Aristotelian approach too quickly: 'the import of tragedy is reduced to the knowledge that the world can fail to be positively instrumental in relation to our aim of flourishing' (234, n. 48).

reject that assumption. It is, however, an important part of Nietzsche's inheritance, and one could argue that it left him blind to the diverse ways in which tragedy could have ethical import. The lesson might not be that we have to choose between tragedy and morality, but that we have to revise our expectations about the moral life.[56]

The second reason for scepticism is related to the first. The Nietzschean view tends to reduce the experience of tragedy to a single perspective (e.g., of the chorus, or of the hero), or even a single moment of 'tragic affirmation'. Such an approach fails to give sufficient weight to the polyphonous, multi-perspectival nature of tragedy, and the possibilities for irony and ambiguity this produces.[57] Tragedies do not simply show human beings meeting disaster, but responding to their misfortune, interpreting and trying to make sense of their situation. We are invited to engage critically with what is being portrayed, and to avoid making facile moral judgments. This reflective quality enables us to respond to Oedipus' self-blinding with pity and horror, but also ask ourselves whether he acted wisely (as does the chorus). Again, Nietzsche would say that such questions are irrelevant to the play's true Dionysian significance. But practical reflection seems to be integral to the aesthetic appreciation of tragedy, which, I would argue, is much more cognitively complex than he allows.

This is not to deny that certain tragedies may be best interpreted through a Nietzschean lens. But I suspect that by starting with his framework, we are more likely to constrain the possibilities of what tragedy can achieve. At the same time, I think Nietzsche does illuminate, perhaps more powerfully than any thinker before or since, an important function of art—its capacity to represent situations and events in life that defy any practical response. These are moments when, as

[56] This seems to be Williams' view in *Shame and Necessity* (1993), which is still very much in the Enlightenment tradition and to that extent only superficially Nietzschean. The later essay on the *Trachiniae* is far more pessimistic about our ethical condition.

[57] For example, Williams' reading of the *Trachiniae* leans heavily on Hyllus's final speech: 'All the force of the play is directed toward leaving in the starkest relief its extreme, undeserved, and uncompensated suffering.... "There is nothing here that is not Zeus" is not a comforting or explanatory remark: it registers only inexplicable necessity, a necessity which may indeed be ascribed to the activities of the gods, but if so, to gods who do not explain themselves or take any notice of the suffering that they bring about'. But the role of 'necessity' is often not transparent. Williams chooses the *Trachiniae* because it is a 'simple' play, but he fails to consider the extent to which Hyllus's suffering is the responsibility of his father Heracles. Nussbaum (2009) raises apt criticisms of Williams' reading but does not go far enough. On the question of Deianeira's innocence, see Hall (2009). In general, there is a danger in isolating a single speech from its context and taking it to be the play's definitive statement. Kitto (2002) puts the point sharply: 'Take life at its worst, as Sophocles does in this play, with Hyllus protesting against the gods: we can still see that human wrongdoing is a major cause of human suffering' (298).

Wittgenstein puts it, 'the tree, instead of bending, breaks'.[58] The demands of reason are silenced, because there is nothing to be done. Art offers us a way to face such moments, comprehend them, and ideally find meaning in them. But this strikes me as a function more proper to lyric poetry or certain types of music than to tragic drama—for the reasons I have sketched above.[59] I would also suggest that the response such art tends to evoke is not joy, or even affirmation, but something more like awe.[60]

REFERENCES

Brobjer, T. H. 2005. 'Sources of and Influences on Nietzsche's *The Birth of Tragedy*', *Nietzsche-Studien*, 34: 277–98.

Came, D. 2004. 'Nietzsche's Attempt at a Self-Criticism: Art and Morality in *The Birth of Tragedy*', *Nietzsche-Studien*, 33: 37–67.

Gardner, S. 2003. 'Tragedy, Morality and Metaphysics', in Bermúdez, J. L. and Gardner, S. (eds.), *Art and Morality* (London: Routledge): 218–59.

Gervinus, G. G. 1863. *Shakespeare: Commentaries* (2 vols.), Bunnett, F. E. (trans.) (London: Smith, Elder and co.).

Goethe, J. W. von. 1994. *Essays on Art and Literature*, Geary, J. (ed.), von Nardoff, E. and von Nardoff, E. H. (trans.) (Princeton: Princeton University Press).

Hall, E. 2009. 'Deianeira Deliberates: Precipitate Decision-making and *Trachiniae*', in Goldhill, S. and Hall, E. (eds.), *Sophocles and the Greek Tragic Tradition* (Cambridge: Cambridge University Press): 69–96.

Halliwell, S. 1998. *Aristotle's Poetics* (Chicago: University of Chicago Press; 2nd edition).

Halliwell, S. 2002. 'Mimesis and the Best Life: Plato's Repudiation of the Tragic', reprinted in *The Aesthetics of Mimesis: Ancient Texts and Modern Problems* (Princeton: Princeton University Press): 98–117.

Halliwell, S. 2005. 'Learning from Suffering: Ancient Responses to Tragedy', in Gregory, J. (ed.), *A Companion to Greek Tragedy* (Malden, MA, and Oxford: Blackwell): 394–412.

Han-Pile, B. 2006. 'Nietzsche's Metaphysics in the *Birth of Tragedy*', *The European Journal of Philosophy*, 14/3: 373–403.

Henrichs, A. 2005. 'Nietzsche on Greek Tragedy and the Tragic', in Gregory, J. (ed.), *A Companion to Greek Tragedy* (New York and Oxford: Oxford University Press): 444–58.

[58] 1984, 1.

[59] Recall Nietzsche's claim that tragedy is much closer to lyric (and the choral dithyramb) than to epic. Yeats and Rilke provide a number of instances of the kind of poetry I have in mind. Consider these lines from Yeats, written a couple of years before he discovered Nietzsche: 'I wander by the edge/Of this desolate lake/Where wind cries in the sedge:/*Until the axle break/That keeps the stars in their round,/And hands hurl in the deep/The banners of East and West,/And the girdle of light is unbound,/Your breast will not lie by the breast/Of your beloved in sleep.*'

[60] Among the many people with whom I discussed this chapter during its long genesis, I would especially like to thank Charles H. Cecil, Chris Sykes, and Paul Woodruff, for their extensive conversations and comments on earlier drafts. I am also very grateful to Daniel Came for his suggestions, patience, and encouragement.

Kitto, H. D. F. 2002. *Greek Tragedy* (London: Routledge; 6th edition).
Lange, F. A. 1925 (1866). *The History of Materialism*, Thomas, E. C. (trans.) (London: Routledge; 3rd edition).
Nietzsche, F. 1967. *The Will to Power*, Kaufmann, W. and Hollingdale, R. (trans.), Kaufmann, W. (ed.) (New York: Random House).
Nietzsche, F. 1968. *The Twilight of the Idols*, Hollingdale, R. J. (trans.) (Harmondsworth: Penguin).
Nietzsche, F. 1993. *The Birth of Tragedy*, Whiteside, S. (trans.), Tanner, M. (ed.) (London: Penguin).
Nietzsche, F. 1997. *Daybreak: Thoughts on the Prejudices of Morality*, Clark, M. and Leiter, B. (eds.) (Cambridge: Cambridge University Press).
Nietzsche, F. 1997. *Human, All Too Human: A Book for Free Spirits*, Hollingdale, R. (trans.) (Cambridge: Cambridge University Press; 2nd edition).
Nietzsche, F. 1997. *Selected Letters of Friedrich Nietzsche*, Middleton, C. (trans. and ed.) (Indianapolis: Hackett, 1997; 2nd edition).
Nietzsche, F. 2003. *Writings from the Late Notebooks*, Bittner, R. (ed.) (Cambridge: Cambridge University Press).
Nietzsche, F. 2005. *The Anti-Christ, Ecce Homo, Twilight of the Idols, and Other Writings*, Ridley, A. and Norman, J. (eds.) (Cambridge: Cambridge University Press).
Nietzsche, F. 2009. *Writings from the Early Notebooks*, Löb, L. (trans.), Geuss, R. and Nehamas, A. (eds.) (Cambridge: Cambridge University Press).
Nussbaum, M. C. 1992. 'Tragedy and Self-Sufficiency: Plato and Aristotle on Fear and Pity', *Oxford Studies in Ancient Philosophy*, Vol. X (New York and Oxford: Oxford University Press): 107–59.
Nussbaum, M. C. 2009. 'Bernard Williams: Tragedies, Hope, Justice', in D. Calcutt (ed.), *Reading Bernard Williams* (Oxford: Routledge): 213–41.
Plato. 2004. *Laws*, Saunders, T. J. (trans.) (London: Penguin).
Plato. 2004. *Republic*, Reeve, C. D. C. (trans.) (Indianapolis: Hackett).
Schacht, R. 2001. 'Making Life Worth Living: Nietzsche on Art in *The Birth of Tragedy*', in Richardson, J. and Leiter, B. (eds.), *Nietzsche: Oxford Readings in Philosophy* (New York and Oxford: Oxford University Press): 186–209.
Schelling, F. W. J. 1989. *The Philosophy of Art*, Stott, D. W. (trans.) (Minneapolis: University of Minnesota Press).
Schiller, F. 1993. *Essays*, Hinderer, W. and Dahlstrom, D. O. (eds.) (New York: Continuum).
Schopenhauer, A., 1966. *The World as Will and Representation* (2 vols.), Payne, E. F. J. (trans.) (New York: Dover).
Scott, G. 2003. 'Purging the *Poetics*', *Oxford Studies in Ancient Philosophy*, Vol. XXV (Oxford: Oxford University Press): 233–64.
Sidnell, M. J. (ed.) 1991. *Sources of Dramatic Theory, Vol. 1: Plato to Congreve* (Cambridge: Cambridge University Press).
Sophocles. 2003. *The Theban Plays*, Meineck, P. and Woodruff, P. (trans.) (Indianapolis: Hackett).
Williams, B. 1993. *Shame and Necessity* (Berkeley: University of California Press, 1993).
Williams, B. 2006. '*The Women of Trachis*: Fictions, Pessimism, Ethics', reprinted in *The Sense of the Past: Essays in the History of Philosophy*, Burnyeat, M. (ed.) (Princeton: Princeton University Press): 49–59.
Wittgenstein, L. 1984. *Culture and Value*, Winch, P. (trans.) (Chicago: University of Chicago Press).

4

Nietzsche's Illusion

Ken Gemes and Chris Sykes

1 INTRODUCTION

It is no longer controversial to argue, as Nietzsche himself did in his 'Attempt at Self-Criticism', that the early Nietzsche of *The Birth of Tragedy*[1] and the *Untimely Meditations* is thematically continuous with the later, and now more canonical, Nietzsche of *Beyond Good and Evil* and *On the Genealogy of Morality*.[2] Daniel Came (2005), for instance, argues that the normative projects of both the early and later Nietzsche focus on the problem of creating a 'secular theodicy'; that is, showing how to reconcile Schopenhauer's descriptive claim that the world is inevitably full of suffering with the normative claim that life is worthy of affirmation. While Nietzsche was apologetic about certain naïve Schopenhauerian metaphysical formulations in *The Birth of Tragedy*, recent scholarship supports the view that at the time of composing *The Birth of Tragedy* he was already suspicious of such metaphysics.[3] Basically, as we shall see below, he included them in *The Birth of Tragedy* for largely rhetorical and polemical purposes. The central thesis of this essay is in line with the claim that there is a deep continuity throughout Nietzsche's intellectual career and the claim that Nietzsche was never seriously wedded to Schopenhauer's metaphysics of the will as thing-in-itself. The received wisdom it puts in play is the claim that Nietzsche's primary focus was on the problem of suffering. Against this it will be

[1] *The Birth of Tragedy* was first published in 1872. In the edition of 1886 Nietzsche added the 'Attempt at a Self-Criticism' as a new preface while keeping the original preface dedicated to Wagner.

[2] Special thanks are due to Gudrun Von Tevenar for detailed criticisms of an earlier draft, and to Simon May and Christopher C. Raymond for discussions about some of the central themes of this paper.

[3] Christopher Janaway's essay 'Nietzsche as Schopenhauer's Educator' in Janaway (1998) and Appendix I of Janaway (1998), being Janaway's translation of Nietzsche' unpublished essay of 1868, 'On Schopenhauer', also published in *Writings from the Early Notebooks* (*WEN*, 1–9), clearly demonstrate Nietzsche's early scepticism towards Schopenhauer's metaphysics of the will as the thing-in-itself. See also Staten (1990), Poellner (1998), and Ridley (2007).

argued that his focus was on the existential lack of meaning which he took to be particular apposite to modern times.

This is not to say that Nietzsche was not at all concerned with the problem of suffering, but that, in contrast to Schopenhauer, suffering per se was never the fundamental objection to life. While it is true that to some extent the meaninglessness of suffering was also an important issue for Schopenhauer, Schopenhauer saw this as a strictly atemporal problem. For Nietzsche, in the wake of Wagner, this lack of meaning was the particular challenge facing modernity. Not suffering, but the meaninglessness of life, and the subsequent nihilism it heralds, is the fundamental threat for modernity. As Nietzsche says in the third essay of the *Genealogy*:

> he [man] did not know how to justify, explain, affirm himself: *he suffered from the problem of his meaning* [emphasis ours]. He suffered otherwise as ill, he was for the most part a *diseased* animal; but *the suffering itself was not his problem* [emphasis ours], rather that the answer was missing to the scream of his question: '*to what end* suffering?' Man, the bravest of animals and the one most accustomed to suffering, does *not* negate suffering, he wants it, he even seeks it out, provided one shows him a meaning for it, a to-this-end of suffering. *The meaninglessness of suffering, not suffering itself, was the curse thus far stretched over humanity* [emphasis ours].
>
> (*GM*, III, 28)

The argument of this paper is that this position of the third essay of the *Genealogy* is basically the position of *The Birth of Tragedy*. The continuity between early and later Nietzsche is constituted in the import he gives to the question of meaning. An interpretive offshoot of this analysis is that Wagner is a fundamental inspiration and foil for Nietzsche's thought. While, arguably, the problem of suffering was Schopenhauer's central concern, for Wagner, as we shall see below, the problem of meaning was his central concern.[4]

What is particular to the early Nietzsche of *The Birth of Tragedy* and the *Untimely Meditations* is the overt emphasis on the need for mythologizing in the construction of meaning. The early Nietzsche, like Wagner, bears a direct connection to that prominent strain of German Romanticism which emphasized the essential link between mythology and culture. This line of romanticism contrasts the naïve mythology, which allegedly gave unity to Attic culture, with the modern need for a self-consciously constructed mythology. No longer capable of naïve belief in myth, we moderns need to self-consciously construct myths in order to provide the unity necessary for a new cultural flourishing.[5]

[4] Soll (1990) and Came (2005) both take Nietzsche to be responding to the problem of affirming life in the face of Schopenhauer's claim that life is inevitably full of suffering.

[5] For more on this, see Williamson (2004).

The later Nietzsche was much more nuanced on the importance of mythology, tending to emphasize the more general need for illusions (*Wahn*, but see Section 8 for more on Nietzsche's idiosyncratic use of this term). More importantly, the later Nietzsche is decidedly more pessimistic about the very possibility of the rebirth of a higher general culture.[6] Where Schopenhauer extolled breaking through the veil of Maya (illusion) in order to realize that life must be denied, Nietzsche followed Wagner in insisting that we need to create *Wahn* in order to affirm life.

2 MYTHICAL NARRATIVES AND NARRATIVES OF MYTH

Nietzsche's early project of the period 1870–1876 is best viewed as a project of understanding the ways in which cultures are able to perpetuate myths which allow their members to affirm life despite its horrors. Both the 'artiste's metaphysics' (*BT*, 'Attempt', 2) of *The Birth of Tragedy* and the narrative of culture in the *Untimely Meditations* are self-consciously written as mythic narratives which aim to make existence bearable.

These works move between the perspectives of a metanarrative which outlines the overarching framework of illusion required in order to find life meaningful, and various first-order narratives which seek to provide such illusions.[7] In the first 18 sections of *The Birth of Tragedy* there is a first-order narrative of metaphysical redemption as experienced by the Attic Greeks. In the later sections of *The Birth of Tragedy* and in the *Untimely Meditations* there is a first-order narrative of culture and genius, conceived of as an analogue of the myths of Attic Greece serviceable for contemporary culture. Both of these first-order narratives offer the 'metaphysical solace' which Nietzsche in the early works takes as a necessary condition for the affirmation of existence. Myth is not only that which can seduce us back to life in spite of its horrors, it is a prerequisite for cultural flourishing, since

> without myth every culture loses the healthy natural power of its creativity: only a horizon defined by myths completes and unifies a whole cultural movement.
>
> (*BT*, 24)

While Nietzsche never actually gives an account of what he means by 'myth', his usage suggests the following as a serviceable definition of his core notion: myth is

[6] *Thus Spoke Zarathustra* sees Nietzsche return to the project of creating a self-conscious mythical narrative. However, this narrative is clearly aimed at cultivating and inspiring a gifted few, rather than aiming to foster a general rebirth of culture (the aim of the early works *The Birth of Tragedy* and *Untimely Meditations*).

[7] For more on the different levels of narrative, see the excellent discussion in Poellner (1998).

a literally fictive narrative encompassing symbolical archetypes that help provide a structural unity to experience.[8]

The need for solace which myth serves is contingent on a particularly pessimistic way of understanding empirical reality as comprised of instrumental, self-serving desire; an endless flux devoid of higher ideals. The natural world does not contain the kind of values which we take to be necessary to give meaning to our lives. Nietzsche's solution to this existential problem is that '[t]he individual must be consecrated to something higher than himself' (*UM*, IV). Participation in the greater whole is the essence of the '*sense for the tragic*' (*UM*, IV), and he furthermore claims that 'all the ennoblement of mankind is enclosed in this supreme task ... There is only one hope and one guarantee for the future of humanity: it consists in his *retention of the sense for the tragic*' (*UM*, IV). Unlike the earlier culture of the Attic Greeks, whose sense for the tragic is expressed in overtly metaphysical or mystical terms, the modern rebirth of the tragic must be based on a non-metaphysical footing, which nevertheless offers the same metaphysical solace which the Greek found in tragedy. This is the myth of the genius. According to this myth, the individual must live for the sake of the highest exemplars or specimens that the human race is capable of producing.[9] It is these individuals who collectively redeem the individual's experience of life as otherwise meaningless and insignificant.[10] Stripped of its more overtly Schopenhauer-inspired metaphysical trappings, the tragic myth offers a relatively simple message: from the perspective of the individual, life appears capricious and without meaning. Tragedy provides a supra-individual perspective which mitigates this by supplying a narrative that allows the individual to reinterpret his seeming insignificance; his seemingly insignificant life is seen to play a part in a story of great significance.

The early works, seen through this prism, reveal a degree of coherence not always apparent in the secondary literature. Nietzsche identifies in *The Birth of Tragedy* the nature of the illusion which allows the Greeks to go on living. He finds this metaphysical solace to offer a workable alternative to the predominant

[8] Poellner (1998) identifies three senses of 'myth' which are operative in the early Nietzsche: Myth as a narrative which connects day-to-day reality with an underlying atemporal metaphysical ground in an oblique fashion not fully discursively interrogable; myth as a narrative that juxtaposes transient human life to this ground in a manner which allows this life to be viewed 'in a certain sense, *sub specie aeterni*' (Poellner, 1998, 64); and, finally, myth as a false story.

[9] For Nietzsche this modern myth of the genius is still a tragic myth in that it acknowledges the inevitable suffering of life.

[10] A variant of this theme reoccurs in *Thus Spoke Zarathustra* where the prophet Zarathustra continually inveighs his disciples to seek meaning through consecrating their lives towards the future coming of the *Übermensch*.

illusion of modern Socratic culture, and attempts in the *Untimely Meditations* to propagate this alternative secular myth through his mythologizing depictions of Schopenhauer (*UM*, III) and Wagner respectively (*UM*, IV). These depictions are close analogues of what he calls in the second of the *Untimely Meditations*, 'monumental history', and are attempts to inspire an attachment to a new, consoling myth that will unify German culture.

In what follows, we first lay out some of the background assumptions Nietzsche is operating with; what he takes to be necessary attributes of experience for reality to be bearable, and why he takes it that reality lacks the relevant attributes. We then lay out Nietzsche's account of the various illusions which serve to make life bearable. As we shall see, cultures exhibit predominantly Apollonian, Dionysian, or Socratic characteristics which determine the form their cultural illusion takes.

3 METAPHYSICS AND PESSIMISM

A unifying theme in the early works (1870–1876) is a certain kind of pessimism which leads Nietzsche to the conclusion that 'illusion', 'deception', and 'myth' are necessary to make bearable one's experience of the world. The pessimism of *The Birth of Tragedy* is manifested in the claim that philosophical theodicy—the enterprise of offering a *rational* justification for existence—is impossible.[11] This pessimism is to be overcome through artistic illusion:

> The only possibility of life: art. Otherwise a turning away from life. The complete annihilation of illusion is the drive of the sciences: it would be followed by quietism—were it not for art.
>
> (*WEN*, 22)

> My philosophy is an *inverted Platonism*: the further something is from true being, the purer, the more beautiful, the better it is. Living in illusion as the goal.
>
> (*WEN*, 52)

> Absolute knowledge leads to *pessimism*; art is the remedy against it.
>
> (*WEN*, 110)

It is this line of thinking that is behind Nietzsche's famous dictum that 'it is only as an *aesthetic phenomena* that existence and the world are eternally *justified*' (*BT*, 5).

[11] There is a distinction to be made between an epistemically rational justification and the kind of prudential justification predicated on the necessity of illusion that Nietzsche recommends. Deliberate use of illusion can only be part of a prudential, not epistemic, justification. We may be prudentially justified in accepting illusions which are evidentially unwarranted, but we cannot be epistemically justified in accepting such illusions.

Nietzsche suggests that the most common form of falsification in modern culture concerns our relationship to the natural world. Modern Socratic culture is predicated on the illusion that reason can ameliorate, even eradicate, the suffering of worldly existence. Where the horrible nature of empirical reality presses itself so insistently that deluding oneself about the possibility of escaping suffering becomes impossible, Nietzsche is interested in what other kinds of illusion might still make existence bearable, and even an object of affirmation. Such a case is presented in the Attic Greeks, who 'knew and felt the terrors and horrors of existence', and that it is only thanks to art, that they were in some way able to 'overcome' this knowledge (*BT*, 3).[12] The falsification they engaged in, and in which their art played a central role, was one which left their knowledge of empirical reality's horrible nature untouched. This awareness of life's horrors is captured in the 'wisdom of Silenus':

> Wretched, ephemeral race, children of chance and tribulation, why do you force me to tell you the very thing which it would be most profitable for you *not* to hear? The very best thing is utterly beyond your reach: not to be born, not to *be*, to be *nothing*. However, the second best thing for you is: to die soon.
>
> (*BT*, 3)

4 NIETZSCHE VERSUS SCHOPENHAUER ON THE PROBLEM OF PESSIMISM

Before examining how, according to Nietzsche, art is capable of 'mediating' this knowledge, and what he takes to be distinctive about the Greek case, we need to consider Nietzsche's relation to Schopenhauer. Nietzsche's early admiration for Schopenhauer is well known, and is clearly demonstrated by the 'Schopenhauerian formulations' (*BT*, 'Attempt', 6) in which much of *The Birth of Tragedy* is couched. This has led some to claim that in *The Birth of Tragedy* Nietzsche helps himself to Schopenhauer's metaphysics.[13] It appears that the 'wisdom of Silenus' is Schopenhauer's pessimistic conception of reality as a manifestation of a raging and unquenchable will expressed in terms of 'folk wisdom', rather than in terms of transcendental metaphysics. Schopenhauer conceives of empirical reality as the expression of the metaphysical Will's endless 'blind striving'. To will is to

[12] '[A]ll this [knowledge] was constantly and repeatedly overcome by the Greeks, or at least veiled and partly withdrawn from view, by means of the artistic *middle world* of the Olympians. In order to be able to live, the Greeks were obliged, by the most profound compulsion, to create these gods' (*BT*, 3).

[13] See Soll (1990, 109) and Young (1992, 26).

suffer; so, being essentially creatures of will, we necessarily suffer. Satisfaction can only be conceived of negatively, which is to say, as the absence of such striving. This Schopenhauer takes to be impossible, so long as we exist as empirical selves (that is, as striving beings). His evaluative hedonism leads him from the assessment that pain *necessarily* predominates over pleasure, to the conclusion that life is worthless.

Ivan Soll (1990) has given a representative and illuminating reading of this kind. Nietzsche, according to Soll, holds the same descriptive account of reality as Schopenhauer; pain necessarily predominates over pleasure. Nietzsche's task in *The Birth of Tragedy* is to find different evaluative criteria by which to measure life, such that the pessimistic conclusion that 'life is worthless and should be denied' can be resisted (Soll 1988: 122).[14] The problem with such readings is their assumption that Nietzsche takes suffering per se to be problematic in the manner which Schopenhauer so clearly does. Throughout Nietzsche's works, suffering in and of itself is never intrinsically problematic. The case is no different in *The Birth of Tragedy*. The real problem is that individuals of a particularly introspective or 'noble' type (*BT*, 15) suffer from a feeling that their existence is groundless. This is the intimation that human striving, despite what we might tell ourselves, amounts to nothing. Nietzsche champions myth as the necessary means of overcoming such nihilistic feelings. Myth offers a way of addressing this existential need by providing narratives which link up an otherwise insignificant life to an overarching metaphysical worldview. Hence it is not the suffering that human beings have to endure which causes people to despair of life, but its insignificance:

> a people—or for that matter, a human being—only has value to the extent that it is able to put the stamp of the eternal on its experiences; for in doing so it sheds, one might say, its worldliness and reveals its unconscious, inner conviction that time is relative and that the true meaning of life is metaphysical.
>
> (*BT*, 23)

Note that Nietzsche does not here assert that the meaning of life is metaphysical. He merely highlights the function of the conviction that the meaning of life is metaphysical. The Greeks are Nietzsche's paradigm of a people saturated in myth who were 'compelled to connect everything they experienced, immediately and involuntarily, to their myths ... thereby even the most immediate present was

[14] As Soll puts the point, '[Nietzsche's] solution does not depend upon allowing for a limited amount of variation in an inescapably dismal existence, but upon radically changing the criteria of what makes an existence dismal or not' (1990, 122). Julian Young (1992) similarly suggests that the fundamental problem of *The Birth of Tragedy* is that 'we stand in need of a 'solution' to the suffering and absurdity of life' (Young, 1992, 25).

bound to appear to them straight away *sub specie aeterni* and, in a certain sense, as timeless' (*BT*, 23).

This paean to myth is certainly not limited to *The Birth of Tragedy*. It occurs repeatedly in the early works. Only by internalizing a narrative, which gives one a sense of significance over and above everyday reality, can the individual succeed in overcoming their existential malaise:

> All living things require an atmosphere around them, a mysterious misty vapor; if they are deprived of this envelope, if a religion, an art, a genius is condemned to revolve as a star without an atmosphere, we should no longer be surprised if they quickly wither and grow unfruitful. It is the same with all great things, 'which never succeed without illusion', as Hans Sachs says in the *Meistersinger*.
>
> (*UM*, II, 7)

Myth occupies the central role in the early Nietzsche for fulfilling this distinctive role. In his discussion of Schopenhauer in the third of the *Untimely Meditations* Nietzsche himself indicates that what he learned from Schopenhauer was precisely this feeling of the meaninglessness of existence as the genuine pessimistic challenge, rather than the lack of hedonic satisfaction which life provides:

> [Schopenhauer] teaches us to distinguish between those things that really promote human happiness and those that only appear to do so: how neither riches nor honors nor erudition can lift the individual out of the profound depression he feels at the valuelessness of his existence, and how striving after these valued things acquires meaning only through an exalted and transfiguring overall goal: to acquire power so as to aid the evolution of the *physis* and to be for a while the corrector of its follies and ineptitudes. At first only for yourself, to be sure; but through yourself in the end for everyone.
>
> (*UM*, III, 142)

5 THE CONSOLATION OF ILLUSION VERSUS THE CONSOLATION OF METAPHYSICAL INSIGHT

According to a common reading of *The Birth of Tragedy*, art consoles us by providing us with metaphysical knowledge (see, for instance Young, 1992, and Ridley, 2007). On this view, art supplements our knowledge of the horrors of reality; alongside our experience of the empirical world we intuit a consoling metaphysical knowledge. We are able to see the world as justified from this cognitively privileged perspective available to us through certain kinds of art (see for example Young, 1992, 37, and Ridley, 2007, 32–3). While some recent commentators who take this line (e.g., Ridley) have pointed out that the 'artiste's metaphysics' of *The Birth of Tragedy* does not rely on Schopenhauer's metaphysics of the Will as thing-in-itself, they still take Nietzsche as offering a substantive metaphysics. For such accounts the success of his putative theodicy is dependent on this metaphysics' truth. We hold that Nietzsche does not propound any speculative metaphysic as true. Nietzsche took Kant's *Critique of Pure Reason* to render all such speculation pointless.[15] The Greeks were not consoled on account of having special *knowledge*, but rather by dint of *believing* a first-order mythical narrative of the underlying unity of all things. This consoling narrative of the Greeks is nevertheless simply a *myth* (hence not knowledge). Nietzsche's point is to bring out the way in which belief in myths consoles. He is interested, to borrow his phrase, in the 'utility for life' of these beliefs, not their veracity. The main argument of *The Birth of Tragedy* is not parasitic on a substantive metaphysics (the three most substantive claims he makes about the nature of reality in *The Birth of Tragedy*—namely that life is full of suffering, that nature reveals itself to be amoral, and that human reason cannot ameliorate or change these facts—are more empirical than metaphysical).

To develop the claim that the consolation comes from myth it helps to further contrast this view with the claim that it is metaphysical knowledge that provides consolation. To begin with it is worth pointing out that the 'artiste's metaphysics' which Nietzsche occasionally appears to adopt in *The Birth of Tragedy* is clearly not Schopenhauer's metaphysics of the Will.[16] On the one hand, Nietzsche describes the 'will' of *The Birth of Tragedy* (repeatedly in inverted commas) as intentional, 'creating the world' out of itself.[17] In the 'Attempt at a Self-Criticism', he goes further, describing the creative agency depicted in the 'artiste's metaphysics' as

[15] Nietzsche's references to the 'hardest fought victory' (*BT*, 18) won by Kant and Schopenhauer in *The Birth of Tragedy* are somewhat ambiguous. Nietzsche's claim in *The Birth of Tragedy* seems to be that Kant demonstrates that we cannot have access to metaphysical knowledge through the *empirical sciences*. This leaves open the possibility that we can still have access to such knowledge through other means—for example, music (see *BT*, 16). However, this reading is made problematic by numerous notebook entries which make clear that Nietzsche is a neo-Kantian sceptic about metaphysical knowledge, along the lines of Lange.

[16] For discussion of this, see Staten (1990), Poellner (1998), and Ridley (2007).

[17] See the 'Appendix' to Staten (1990), where the point is made that throughout *The Birth of Tragedy*, Nietzsche repeatedly places references to the 'Will' in inverted commas (for example in *BT*, 3), as well as alternating between this term and others such as 'primal oneness' (*das Ur-Eine*) (1990, 192). Moreover, he repeatedly adds such qualifiers as in *The Birth of Tragedy*, 1, where 'in an *eccentric sense*, one could apply to Apollo what Schopenhauer says about human beings trapped in the veil of maya...' (*BT*, 1; emphasis ours)'. One eminently plausible explanation for this is that Nietzsche is describing a particular *worldview* on the one hand, and *psychological phenomenology* on the other, using terminology borrowed from Schopenhauer. This idiosyncrasy is not surprising if one considers that at the time of writing *The Birth of Tragedy* Nietzsche is a philology professor whose extremely limited exposure to modern philosophy extended to Schopenhauer, German materialism, and a little smattering of Kant. Strange as it may now seem, dressing up his psychological observations in terminology borrowed from Schopenhauer probably seemed to him to lend legitimacy to his project. In this respect *The Birth of Tragedy* mirrors Wagner's own theoretical prose works which also borrowed from Schopenhauer in order to gain philosophical legitimacy. Section 6

an utterly unscrupulous and amoral artist-god who frees himself from the dire pressure of fullness and *over-fullness*, from suffering the oppositions packed within him, and who wishes to become conscious of his autarchic power and constant delight and desire, whether he is building or destroying, whether acting benevolently or malevolently.

(*BT*, 'Attempt', 5)

He calls the world 'the release and redemption of god, *achieved* at each and every moment, as the eternally changing, eternally new vision of the most suffering being of all' (ibid.). Although later on we claim that *this* metaphysics itself has the status of a myth—that is, a false depiction of reality—here it is sufficient to note that this is certainly not the Will as Schopenhauer understands it. The Will in Schopenhauer's transcendental system is atemporal, non-purposive, and non-causal. Furthermore, as noted above, Nietzsche himself already in 1868 categorically rejects Schopenhauer's arguments for the noumenal status of the Will.[18] He argues there that Schopenhauer helps himself to metaphors which can only have any sense if predicated of the phenomenal world of space-time, and fallaciously applies them to the world as it is in-itself (that is, abstracted from the categories of the understanding).[19] Moreover, Schopenhauer 'puts in place of the Kantian X, the will, [which] is created only with the help of a poetic intuition, while his attempted logical proofs can satisfy neither Schopenhauer nor us' (*WEN*, 3). All Schopenhauer succeeds in demonstrating is that 'there may be a thing-in-itself, albeit in no other sense than that in the realm of transcendence anything is *possible* that is ever hatched out in the mind of a philosopher' (*WEN*, 3–4). In the 1878 edition of *Human, All Too Human* Nietzsche again clearly rejects the possibility of any knowledge of the thing-in-itself.[20] So those who claim that in *The Birth of Tragedy* Nietzsche is committed to Schopenhauer's metaphysics of the thing-in-itself as Will are committed to the implausible claim that Nietzsche, having rejected

of the 'Attempt' supports this reading, as Nietzsche bemoans that at the time of *The Birth of Tragedy* he lacked 'a *language of my very own* for such personal views and acts of daring, labouring instead to express strange and new evaluations in Schopenhauerian and Kantian formulations'.

18 Cf. *WEN*, 1–8, especially 3–4.

19 Nietzsche notes that 'we are obliged to protest against the predicates attributed by Schopenhauer to his will, which sound far too definite for something absolutely unthinkable and which are gained throughout from their opposition to the world of representation; while between the thing-in-itself and the appearance even the concept of opposition is meaningless' (*WEN*, 3). He goes on: 'all the predicates of the will . . . are borrowed from the world of appearance . . . [despite the fact that] it is extremely doubtful that they have any meaning at all outside the sphere of human knowledge' (*WEN*, 5–6).

20 See for example *HH*, 9, 10. Notes from late 1886 make it clear that Nietzsche was at the time unsympathetic to the idea of the thing-in-itself as Will (cf. *KSA*, 8, 350).

Schopenhauer's posit of thing-in-itself as Will in 1868, was repersuaded of it in 1870 when writing *The Birth of Tragedy*, and thereafter abandoned it again.

One reason why one might be tempted to impute Schopenhauer's metaphysics to Nietzsche in *The Birth of Tragedy* is his discussion of aesthetics. In particular, Nietzsche makes a great deal of the supposed 'metaphysical' nature of music as revelatory of the Dionysian ground underlying appearance. This is music's alleged ability to intuit a 'direct copy of the will'. As Henry Staten notes though, this seems to owe much to Nietzsche's wish to elevate Wagner's music to the significance which he takes the composer to expect (see Staten, 1990, 192–3). Schopenhauer's aesthetics of music is deployed in *The Birth of Tragedy* in a somewhat 'off the peg' fashion. It is used in a rather hasty attempt to locate music within the narrative.[21]

Schopenhauer argues for the cognitive value of art, claiming that in art we grasp the Platonic forms. He claims that music is 'an objectification and copy of the whole *will* as the world itself is' (*WWR*, II, 257).[22] For Schopenhauer, as well as giving us metaphysical knowledge, art has hedonic and prudential value.[23] First, in the act of aesthetic contemplation the individual is 'lifted out' of his individual self as willing being, and perceives the world as a 'pure subject of knowing'. In this will-less state, the individual is free from desire and the suffering which attends it. Second, in perceiving the true nature of reality as Will, the individual gains the understanding that 'denial of the Will-to-live' is the only rational course of action. Nietzsche makes clear that art functions, in direct contrast, 'as a saving sorceress with the power to heal. Art alone can redirect those repulsive thoughts about the terrible or absurd nature of existence into representations with which man can live' (*BT*, 7). Art is a 'supplement' which we place beside life, colouring it in a way that makes it possible to affirm life despite all its sufferings. The Apollonian, in particular, is clearly described as offering 'beautiful *illusions*'. This notion of art is clearly foreign to Schopenhauer. Again, this line of thought is continuous with that of the third essay of

[21] This is not to say though that Nietzsche doesn't take music to have a special status amongst the arts, or indeed in the functioning of tragedy. He clearly takes the powers of rhythm to play a key role in inducing a particular phenomenology of a Dionysian orgiastic unity that is unique to tragedy. This though is a claim on the psychological level, rather than the metaphysical.

[22] Schopenhauer goes on to state: 'music is by no means like the other arts, namely a copy of the Ideas, but a *copy of the will itself*' (*WWR*, II, 257).

[23] It is worth noting the extremely puzzling ontological status of both the neo-Platonic 'forms', and the character of the 'Will' which is revealed in music. If the Will *still* appears to us as representation in music, in what sense can this be said to be a more 'immediate' copy of the Will? Furthermore, such an assertion seems to presuppose that we *know* the nature of the Will, in order to have a correct criterion of assessment. For a general discussion of Schopenhauer's aesthetics, and the problems associated with this, see Gardiner (1963), Janaway (1996).

the *Genealogy*, where Nietzsche explicitly rejects the Kantian and Schopenhauerian accounts of aesthetic experience as providing an escape from interestedness, and favours Stendhal's formulation of the beautiful as '*une promesse de bonheur*' and as 'an *excitement of the will* ("of interest")' (*GM*, III, 7). For the Nietzsche of *The Birth of Tragedy*, in Attic Greece the wisdom of Silenus is overcome by the Apollonian 'middle world' of artistic glorification; by representing existence as 'suffused with a higher glory' (*BT*, 3). Art for Schopenhauer offers us the promise of redemption, first from pain (through temporary suspension of the will in aesthetic contemplation) and, second, and more profoundly, through fostering denial of the will itself through our understanding the true, horrible nature of existence as Will. In contrast, Nietzsche clearly sees art as a *means* which the Will itself uses to retain our interest in empirical existence. Apollonian art is a means of glorifying the empirical world, holding it up as something worthy of our affirmation.

One might try to argue for the cognitive role of art in *The Birth of Tragedy* by ascribing cognitive value to Dionysian, as opposed to Apollonian, art, arguing that Dionysian art allows us to see the true nature of existence beyond the veil of appearances. Initially this may seem plausible, particularly when Nietzsche says that 'the Dionysian artist has become entirely at one with the primal unity, with its pain and contradiction, and he produces a copy of this primal unity as music' (*BT*, 5); and again, 'music refers symbolically to the original contradiction and original pain at the heart of the primal unity, and thus symbolises a sphere which lies above and beyond all appearance' (*BT*, 6).

There are three things to say about this. First, if Dionysian man really does intuit metaphysical knowledge, and this is the knowledge of the Schopenhauerian Will, why would this be consoling, given the terrible nature of the Will as Schopenhauer portrays it? Second, taking the Dionysian as a cognitively privileged position, whose value is *derived* from this position, seems deeply 'un-Nietzschean'. Nietzsche repeatedly stresses the 'ascetic', or 'life-hating' character of philosophical agendas which champion truth for its own sake, or as a panacea for life's problems. This theme is certainly not limited to late Nietzsche; for instance, it is central to the second of the *Untimely Meditations*. Furthermore, in *The Birth of Tragedy* itself Nietzsche critiques the naïvety of Socratic man for thinking that the depths of reality can be fathomed and *knowledge* can heal all ills. Yet the metaphysical reading of the Dionysian attributes this same naïvety to Nietzsche. It is incorrect to infer from the fact that music 'symbolises' a realm behind appearance that this symbolism corresponds to anything in reality. Music's 'mythic' role is precisely to provide the psychological intimation of another realm. It is this intimation, not any actual existence, that consoles the Dionysian reveller.[24] In saying that music imbues art with metaphysical significance Nietzsche is explaining the phenomenology of the aesthetic experience; it provides the intimation of a great underlying unity. He is not thereby committing himself to any substantive metaphysical claim about an underlying reality which the phenomenology might track. Third, and perhaps most probatively, Nietzsche is quite explicit in *The Birth of Tragedy* that such a Dionysian way of conceiving the world is just another form of illusion, on a par with the Socratic illusion that through knowledge life is correctable, or the Apollonian illusion of beauty that veils the horrors of existence:

> It is an eternal phenomenon: *by means of an illusion* [*Illusion*; emphasis ours] spread over things, the greedy Will always finds some way of detaining its creatures in life and forcing them to carry on living. One person is held fast by the Socratic pleasure in understanding and by the delusion [*Wahn*] that he can thereby heal the eternal wound of existence; another is ensnared by art's seductive veil of beauty fluttering before his eyes; a third by the metaphysical solace that eternal life flows on indestructibly beneath the turmoil of appearances—to say nothing of the commoner and almost more powerful illusions [*Illusionen*] which the Will constantly holds in readiness. Indeed, *these three levels of illusion* [*Illusionenstufen*; emphasis ours] are only for those equipped with nobler natures, who generally feel the burden and heaviness of being with more profound aversion and who have been tricked by exquisite stimulants into ignoring their aversion. Everything we call culture consists of such stimulants; depending on the proportion of the mixture, we have a culture which is predominately *Socratic* or *artistic* or *tragic*; or, if historical illustrations are permitted, a culture is either Alexandrian or Hellenic or Buddhistic.[25]
>
> (*BT*, 18)

The fact that Nietzsche describes the metaphysical solace provided by the Schopenhauerian thought that eternal life flows beneath the turmoil of appearances as one of three levels of illusion, and, more generally, the fact that he takes illusion as the means by which life is made bearable, surely puts paid to the

[24] Note the consolation here is not in *any knowledge* of the existence of another world of primal unity, because in fact there is no such world. The consolation lies in the illusion that the pain of individuation can be overcome. Of course, the question of how illusions can provide solace here remains. Part of the answer seems to be that through Dionysian intoxication rationality is overcome, and the border between illusion and reality is put in abeyance.

[25] In a similar vein Nietzsche says, 'if one construes a delusion as such, the will—*if* it wants us to continue to exist—must create a *new* one. *Culture* is the continuous replacement of delusions with more noble ones; i.e. the "motives" of our thinking rise higher and higher above the material and assume a greater universality. The goal of "humanity" is the most that the will can offer us as a phantom. Basically, nothing changes. The will does what it has to do and the representation tries to reach the universally concerned essence of the will. Culture lies in the thinking of the good of organisms that are greater than the individual' (*WEN*, 29).

notion that it is metaphysical *knowledge* that provides the consolation that seduces one back to life.

6 THREE TYPES OF COMFORTING ILLUSION

Nietzsche analyses three distinct types of illusion which work at the level of culture as 'exquisite stimulants' (*BT*, 18), by which the individual is 'tricked' into believing life has meaning, and is thus worth living. He concludes that '[e]verything we call culture consists in such stimulants' (*BT*, 18). The Socratic illusion works by propagating the false belief that 'the depths of nature can be fathomed and knowledge can heal all ills' (*BT*, 17). An artistic (or Apollonian) culture diverts our attention away from the objectionable nature of life by focusing our energies on the adoration of beautiful form.[26] The tragic works by the illusion of a 'metaphysical solace'. It fosters the belief in a unity which underlies the apparent world, and offers the myth that in death, the individual will find redemption and reunification with the reality beneath appearance. The Dionysian man lives through a different kind of falsification, which is nevertheless still illusory. The Dionysian myth acknowledges that the empirical world is a thoroughly wretched place. The metaphysical myth of a 'Primordial Oneness' or 'Artist-god', with whom we are reunited in death, is the result of this recognition. It is worth pointing out that Nietzsche explicitly aligns the Dionysian with 'Buddhistic' culture (*BT*, 18). This is clearly not accidental, and elsewhere in the book we are told that the Dionysian's principal effect is 'lethargy' and 'a mood of ascetic resignation'—traits Nietzsche commonly associates with Buddhism. 'The orgiastic experience leads a people in just one direction, along the road towards Indian Buddhism' (*BT*, 21).

This might seem extremely surprising, especially given the strong association between the Dionysian and intoxication and frenzy. However, Nietzsche does have grounds for this claim. Whereas Socratism and Apollonian art console through a falsification or a veiling of elements of reality, the Dionysian offers a 'metaphysical solace'. What this means is that the consoling illusion of the Dionysian pertains not to the empirical world, but a metaphysically distinct reality, with which the empirical world has a derivative relation. Empirical life

[26] See Wagner's own thoughts on art's essentially affirmative nature: 'Art is pleasure in itself, in existence, in community' (*RA*, 36). See also (*AP*, 155–6, 161) and (*RA*, 32, 34–5).

is so horrible that we need the myth of a metaphysically distinct world. The narrative of the 'primal One' from which we spring, and with which in death we are later reconstituted, is a means of alleviating this condition. The problem with such solace is that it can work too well. In the case of extreme religious asceticism, we become so enraptured with the idea of other-worldly unity that we have little incentive to remain engaged with the empirical world.

It may appear surprising, given Nietzsche's strident polemics against 'other-worldly' metaphysics in his later writing, that he apparently advocates a form of metaphysical escapism, and furthermore to suggest that such escapism is 'Dionysian'. The important point to note is that Attic Greek culture is valued as a successful *mediation* of the Dionysian; Nietzsche does not extol Attic culture as purely Dionysian. Nietzsche in *The Birth of Tragedy* is not advocating a return to a pure Dionysian stance. The tragic is a subspecies of metaphysical solace, one that presents the content of the Buddhist worldview in an affectively positive fashion. Nietzsche's admiration for the Attic Greeks is founded precisely on this mediation, which he takes them to have attained. What is often missed is that a pure Dionysian culture taken to its limits is potentially enervating.

Homeric Greece appears to be Nietzsche's paradigm of Apollonian culture. In Apollonian culture, art functions to 'seduce' the individual to life through the repeated representation of the world as beautiful:

> Apollo overcomes the individual's suffering by his luminous glorification of the *eternity of appearance*; here beauty gains victory over the suffering inherent in life; in a certain sense, a lie is told which causes pain to disappear from the features of nature.
>
> (*BT*, 16)

Apollonian culture depends on the continual falsification of nature, both by omitting or misrepresenting elements which are questionable, and by presenting empirical reality in such a way that lends it an air of permanence and fixity which it in fact lacks.[27]

In contrast to Attic tragic culture, with its admixture of the Apollonian and the Dionysian, Socratic culture rests on the belief that reality is correctable through

[27] Nietzsche describes the 'glorious "naïveté"...the flower of Apollonian culture' as 'a victory which the Hellenic will gains over suffering and the wisdom of suffering through the image of beauty shown in its mirror' (*BT*, 17). The 'naïveté' is 'glorious' in contradistinction to the 'cheerfulness' of the later Greeks, which is described as a 'senile, unproductive pleasure in existence' (*BT*, 17). Nietzsche's point seems to be that the 'naïve' Apollonian artist was constantly faced with reminders that life was *not* in fact the way he chose to represent it. Compare the later preface to *The Gay Science* 'Oh, those Greeks! They knew how to live. What is required for that is to stop courageously at the surface, the fold, the skin, to adore appearance, to believe in forms, tones, words, in the whole Olympus of appearance! Those Greeks were superficial—out of profundity!' (*GS*, P, 4).

the application of knowledge. Suffering is interpreted as the result of a contingent state of ignorance that reason has the power to overcome. It expresses 'a profound *delusion* [*Wahnvorstellung*] ... that thought ... is capable not simply of understanding existence, but even of *correcting* it' (*BT*, 15). As Nietzsche describes,

> it puts in the place of a metaphysical solace a form of earthly harmony, indeed its very own *deus ex machina*, namely the god of machines and smelting furnaces, i.e. the energies of the spirit of nature, understood and applied in the service of higher egotism; it believes in correcting the world through knowledge, in life led by science; and it is truly capable of confining the individual within the smallest circle of solvable tasks, in the midst of which he cheerfully says to life: 'I will you, you are worth understanding.
>
> (*BT*, 17)

Socratism is clearly a form of mystification, a false narrative which nevertheless gives a sense of meaning and purpose to existence. 'Even then that metaphysical drive still attempts to create for itself a kind of transfiguration, albeit in a much weaker form, in the Socratism of science' (*BT*, 23).

Nietzsche offers two main reasons why Socratism is declining, and why any new myth which would replace it cannot be parasitic on its central elements. Socratism valorizes the pursuit of truth as one of life's most valuable activities. But pursuing truth has the side effect of uncovering the falsity of the very presuppositions on which the Socratic high estimation of truth is built. As we come to understand the true nature of life we realize the inevitability of suffering and thus uncover the lie of Socratic optimism.[28] Nietzsche also claims that Socratism is socially and politically unstable. Its 'optimism' gives rise to unrealistic social aspirations on the part of the disaffected members of society, or 'slave' class. Socratism's characteristic 'optimism'—the belief that earthly harmony and happiness are attainable goals—expresses belief in a worldly '*deus ex machina*'. Whereas religion typically consoles through the belief that a god will right wrongs in a life to come, the Socratic worldview hopes for restitution and justice in the here and now. The empirical world is felt to operate according to moral principles, such that through the passage of time and the application of human endeavour, 'things will turn out for the best.' This widely held belief, when manifested at the local level of the socially disaffected and politically ostracized 'slave class', breeds the false belief that 'earthly happiness for all' (*BT*, 18) is a

[28] This foreshadows Nietzsche's later understanding of the will to truth as a sublimated form of self-cruelty: 'Has not man's self-deprecation, his *will* to self-deprecation, been unstoppably on the increase since Copernicus?' (*GM*, III, 25). The will to truth eventually uncovers its own mendacious roots, for while it presents itself as a will to objectively understand it is eventually exposed as a highly subjective manifestation of the life-denying ascetic ideal.

viable political goal. This, however, is a myth. Society requires, according to Nietzsche's draconian view, a slave class for its continuation. This class has until now been held in check by ideological false beliefs which reinforce the existing social order; for example, the belief in the 'dignity of work'. As this illusion collapses, the slave class demands a reconfiguration of society, which is in fact impossible.

> [T]he fruits of this optimism ripen, when the acid of this kind of culture trickles down to the very lowest levels of our society, so that it gradually begins to tremble from burgeoning surges and desires, when the belief in the earthly happiness of all, when the belief that such a general culture of knowledge is possible, gradually transforms itself into the menacing demand for such Alexandrian happiness on earth, into the invocation of a Euripidean *deus ex machina*! It should be noted that Alexandrian culture needs a slave-class in order to exist in the long term; as it views existence optimistically however, it denies the necessity of such a class and is therefore heading towards horrifying extinction when the effects of its fire words of seduction and pacification, such as 'human dignity' and 'the dignity of labour', are exhausted.
>
> (*BT*, 18)

This early foray of Nietzsche's into social commentary may strike the reader as somewhat naïve. He does not sufficiently explain why such a slave class is necessary for the continuation of modern culture, or indeed why the demands of this class are irreconcilable with the interests of the wider culture. In an unpublished work of 1871, 'The Greek State: Preface', he partially fleshes this out, intimating that a slave class is required in order to provide for men of culture.[29] Here Nietzsche fails to distinguish between society's goal by his lights (the propagation of geniuses), and the goals internal to late Socratic culture (broad based mediocrity). Socratism need not fall apart from internal contradiction and political strife. Indeed, the realization of the deep robustness of modern philistine, Socratic—that is, scientific—culture is a fundamental source of the later Nietzsche's profound pessimism about the possibility of a general cultural renewal.

7 SCHOPENHAUER, WAGNER, AND NIETZSCHE ON THE FUNCTION OF ILLUSION

In order to grasp the role which Nietzsche envisions for art, in providing illusions which sustain the individual, it is helpful to isolate Schopenhauer's notion of 'delusion' (*Wahn*) as developed in the section titled 'On the Metaphysics of Sexual Love' (*WWR* II). The sex drive is the most direct presentation of the

[29] Note from 1888: *KSA*, 1, 765–77.

will-to-live: 'the ultimate goal of almost all human effort' (*WWR* II, 533). Furthermore, 'instinct' is the means by which the 'will of the species' succeeds in subverting the individual's own egotistically driven ends, towards the ends of the species:

> nature can attain her end only by implanting in the individual a certain *delusion* [*Wahn*], and by virtue of this, that which in truth is merely a good thing for the species seems to him to be a good thing for himself, so that he serves the species, whereas he is under the delusion that he is serving himself. In this process a mere chimera, which vanishes immediately afterwards, floats before him, and, as motive, takes the place of a reality. This *delusion* is *instinct*. In the great majority of cases, instinct is to be regarded as the sense of the *species* which presents to the will what is useful to *it*.
>
> (*WWR*, II, 538)

This drive is 'a delusion that conceals the service of the species under the mask of an egotistical end' (*WWR*, II, 541). Putting aside the question of how a 'blind striving' such as the Will could manifest such seeming intentionality, the interesting import of this is the notion that the species acts through the individual, deluding him into acts which serve its perpetuation. The species' 'interest' is straightforwardly its continuation.[30] This is a repeated theme in Schopenhauer. It is built into our nature as creatures with desires that we are not simply deluded about the possibility of the satisfaction of desire. We are also deluded about the relation between our desires and our interests. Our genuine interests, claims Schopenhauer, are not served by pursuing our desires; in fact, they are only achieved through the cessation of desire.

Wagner was clearly struck by the Schopenhauerian conception of *Wahn*, most famously in *Die Meistersinger von Nürnberg*. The '*Wahn* monologue' of the protagonist Hans Sachs declares that life is permeated by *Wahn*. Sachs' challenge is to attempt to 'guide the *Wahn* subtly to perform a nobler task'.[31] The crucial difference between Wagner's and Schopenhauer's conception of *Wahn* is that for Wagner *Wahn* is not unambiguously pernicious.[32] Indeed Wagner, in extolling

[30] Nietzsche seems to allude to a mechanism similar to this in numerous places both in *The Birth of Tragedy* and *Untimely Meditations*. Similarly, in his later work as well there is the repeated notion that '[the Will] would rather will nothingness than not will' (*GM*, III, 1). What appear to be life-denying actions are in fact deeply sublimated forms of willing that allow individuals to go on living.

[31] 'Jetzt schaun wir, wie Hans Sachs es macht dass er den Wahn fein lenken kann, ein edler Werk zu tun' (Warrack, 1994, 156)—Now we show how Hans Sachs can delicately control illusion so as to make a precious work (translation ours).

[32] This perversion of Schopenhauer is perhaps most conspicuous in *Tristan and Isolde*. There, the lovers find redemption precisely through the *Wahn* of sexual love, whereas King Marke, in resisting this illusion, is denied the possibility of metaphysical redemption. See Borchmeyer (1991, 365–6).

the redemptive power of illusion, even goes so far as to coin the striking expression '*wahrster Wahn*' [truest illusion].[33]

In the theoretical work 'On State and Religion', which Nietzsche read at the time of writing *The Birth of Tragedy*, Wagner attempts to explain this strange notion of useful *Wahn*. He draws distinctions both between creative and destructive forms of *Wahn* (in particular in the political sphere), and between two forms of *Wahn* which differ in the scope of their mystification. On the one hand is 'worldly' *Wahn*. In the example of patriotism, the individual sacrifices himself for an object over and above his immediate interests. He is deluded into identifying his egoistic ends with the ends of the state. His delusion is twofold: first, he believes that his real interests are identical with those of the state; second, he shares the general delusion that a final satisfaction of desire is possible. On the other hand, Wagner identifies a different kind of *Wahn* which he associates with religion. Unlike worldly *Wahn*, which remains entirely submerged in desires concerning everyday reality, religion attains a perspective from which it sees the fleeting, and ultimately futile, nature of earthly desires. Religion displays an awareness that all such goals cannot touch on the problem of existence:

> [Religion's] basis is a feeling of the unblessedness of human being, of the State's profound inadequacy to still the purely-human need. Its inmost kernel is denial of the world—i.e. recognition of the world as a fleeting and dreamlike state reposing merely on illusion (*auf einer Täuschung*)—and struggle for Redemption from it, prepared-for by renunciation, attained by Faith.
>
> (*AP*, 23–4)

This seems to be simply an iteration of Schopenhauer's assessment of revelation; the capacity to pierce the veil of individuation, and see the nature of reality as Will. The 'religious eye' (*der religiösen Vorstellung*) comprehends that satisfaction cannot be attained in this world 'and hence requires another world for its redemption' (*AP*, 24).

Crucially, Wagner poses the question: given what the religious man knows about earthly existence, how is he able to continue to live? That is to say, why should he have any interest in the empirical world? Wagner apparently discounts the standard argument that one acts morally in this life so as to be rewarded in the world to come. Instead, prefiguring Nietzsche, he argues that art produces a

[33] In *BT*, 1, Nietzsche gives a full quotation of the passage from *Die Meistersinger* which contains this unusual phrase. For more on Wagner, Nietzsche, and *Wahn*, see the interesting account in Shaw (1960).

specific kind of *Wahn*, which makes life bearable. Just as the more simple individual's existence requires the consolations of patriotism, so the noble individual needs an illusion worthy of his powers. It is thus the

> work of that man-redeeming *Wahn* which spreads its wonders wherever the individual's normal mode of view can help itself no farther. But in this instance the *Wahn* must be entirely candid; it must confess itself in advance for an illusion, if it is to be willingly embraced by the man who really longs for distraction and illusion in the high and correct sense we mean. The *Wahn*-picture brought before him must never afford a loop-hole for re-summoning the earnestness of life through any possible dispute about its actuality and provable foundation upon fact, as religious Dogma does: no, it must exercise its specific virtue through its very setting of the conscious *Wahn* in place of the reality. This office is fulfilled by *Art*; and in conclusion... Art [is] the kindly life-saviour who does not really and wholly lead us out beyond this life, but, within it, lifts us up above it and shows it as itself a game of play, a game that, take it ne'er so terrible and earnest an appearance, yet here again is shown us as a mere *Wahn*-picture, as which it comforts us and wafts us from the common truth of our distress (*Noth*).
>
> (*AP*, 33)

It is art's job to provide the illusions by which we are able to find the world bearable. Despite the 'common truth of our distress' we perceive life as a 'game of play'. We thus still recognize the nature of life, but apprehend this fact in a fashion which somehow makes it bearable.[34] For Wagner, and Nietzsche following him, art has the role of offering solace to the individual who has grasped a 'terrible truth'. This solace is not through any putative knowledge of a metaphysical reality. Our strivings in the empirical world ultimately appear insignificant, lacking the necessary gravitas we desire. We need *metaphysical* illusion, as this is a supplement which lends the empirical world the necessary 'colouring'. Nietzsche uses Schopenhauerian language to engage with Wagner, rather than Schopenhauer. The immediate significance of Wagner's piece for *The Birth of Tragedy* is the idea that art affords the most sophisticated illusion of the will, which seduces us back to life even when we are fully cognizant of the world's lack of fit with our desires. A *metaphysical* illusion, not metaphysical knowledge as per Schopenhauer, enables us to cope with the nature of *empirical* reality.[35]

[34] Wagner highlights the paradoxical nature of the claim that a certain kind of illusion actually enables us to grasp an otherwise unbearable truth; 'The nothingness of the world, here it is harmless, avowed as though in smiling: for our willing purpose to deceive ourselves had led us on to recognise the world's real state without a shadow of illusion' (*AP*, 34).

[35] See *WEN*, 36–7.

Art is clearly subservient to the 'will' for both Wagner and Nietzsche. As Nietzsche puts it

Homeric 'naïveté' can be understood only as the complete victory of Apollonian illusion; it is an illusion of the kind so frequently employed by nature to achieve its aims. The true goal is obscured by a deluding image; we stretch out our hands towards the image, and nature achieves its goals by means of this deception. In the Greeks the 'Will' wanted to gaze on a vision of itself as transfigured by genius and the world of art.

(*BT*, 3)

So art in fact serves the will. This is clearly a considerable departure from Schopenhauer. Wagner is surely the main source of inspiration for this view of art as essentially affirmative of empirical reality; art as an artefact which celebrates willing existence rather than facilitating its negation.

The Hellene, by nature profound and uniquely capable of the most exquisite and most severe suffering... has gazed with keen eye into the midst of the fearful, destructive havoc of so-called world history, and has seen the cruelty of nature, and is in danger of longing to deny the will as the Buddhist does. Art saves him, and through art life saves him—for itself.

(*BT*, 7)

When comparing Wagner to Schopenhauer on the value of art and illusion, one is struck by the affirmative character that Wagner gives them. Schopenhauer takes art to provide a means to at least temporary release from the bondage of the Will, and he takes this to be good. For Wagner art and illusion lead one to affirm life and hence willing, and he takes this to be good. In this essential point Nietzsche is a follower of Wagner not Schopenhauer. Relatedly, Nietzsche's idiosyncratic use of the term '*Wahn*' follows that of Wagner rather than Schopenhauer. For Nietzsche and Wagner there is a positive sense of *Wahn*. This is most strikingly demonstrated in Wagner's coinage of the very odd phrase '*wahrster Wahn*' (literally this could be translated as 'truest delusion'). For Nietzsche, following Wagner, it is through *Wahn* that art performs the positive task of wooing us back to life. In ordinary German, and in Schopenhauer's usage, '*Wahn*' has strongly negative connotations of falsity, and thus it is most aptly translated as 'delusion'.[36]

Nietzsche and Wagner are in a certain sense local thinkers. While Schopenhauer was concerned with the eternal problem of suffering, Wagner and

[36] English editions of *The Birth of Tragedy* consistently translate '*Wahn*' as 'illusion' rather than 'delusion'. In keeping with what is said above about the positive nature of *Wahn* for Nietzsche this translation is perfectly justified. However, this means that the English text fails to duplicate the oddity that Nietzsche's use of '*Wahn*' presents to German readers.

Nietzsche were very much concerned with a cultural malaise they took to be endemic to their current times.[37] This was part of their shared romantic inheritance. Nietzsche took over Wagner's obsession with the perceived degeneration of current culture, and followed Wagner in attempting to revitalize that culture through the deliberate constructions of new life affirming myths. However, Nietzsche eventually came to see Wagner as a sign of, rather than answer to, degenerate culture. Wagner sought in his operas, especially his *Ring* cycle, to provide a new mythology which could lead to cultural renewal. However, Nietzsche, after initially endorsing Wagner in *The Birth of Tragedy* as the elect agent of cultural renewal, came to see Wagner, especially the Wagner of *Parsifal*, as falling into the life-denying solace of religious consolation. This goes some way to explaining Nietzsche's puzzling insistence that *Thus Spoke Zarathustra* is his key work, and that those of us who are not touched by it (including the present authors) have not understood him. Nietzsche, well before that book, had already dismissed Wagner as a possible provider of a new mythology that would allow for a Dionysian revival of high culture. We may surmise that Nietzsche himself took up this task with *Thus Spoke Zarathustra*.[38] One gets a sense of his trajectory from the last lines of *Twilight of the Idols*:

[37] Of course, Nietzsche does make claims about past cultures, for instance in *The Birth of Tragedy*, the *Untimely Meditations*, and the *Genealogy*. But his primary purpose in doing so is to sharpen the focus on what he perceives to be our current cultural malaise. For more on this theme, see Gemes (2006).

[38] Here we are interpreting both Wagner's *Ring* cycle and Nietzsche's *Zarathustra* in light of Schelling's claim that 'the modern world has no real epic, and that, since mythology becomes established only in the epic as such, it also has no self-enclosed mythology' (Schelling, 1989, 71). This is not to say that Nietzsche was directly aware of Schelling's claim. Nietzsche's understanding of the need for a modern epic came from his engagement with Wagner and Hölderlin. In 1861, while still at high school, Nietzsche had written an essay in praise of Hölderlin. Defining his mission, Zarathustra says:

> when my eyes flee from the present to the past, it always discovers the same thing: fragments and limbs and dreadful chances—but no men!...I walk among men as among fragments of the future: of the future which I scan. And it is my art and aim, to compose into one and bring together what is fragment and riddle and dreadful chance.
>
> (Z, II, 21)

Here Nietzsche almost certainly had in mind the following passage in Hölderlin's *Hyperion*, itself a self-conscious attempt at creating a mythologizing epic poem:

> I can think of no people more at odds with themselves than the Germans. You see artisans, but no men, thinkers, but no men...is this not like a battlefield on which hacked-off hands and arms and every other limb scattered about.
>
> (Hölderlin, 1952, 420, translation ours)

I again return to the place from which I set out—the *Birth of Tragedy* was my first revaluation of all values... I again plant myself in the soil out of which I draw all that I will and can—I, the last disciple of Dionysus—I, the teacher of the eternal recurrence.

The eternal recurrence is of course the means by which Zarathustra hopes to reinvigorate his followers and ward of the threat of suicidal nihilism; as such it functions as Nietzsche's grand attempt at a final life affirming myth.

8 CONCLUSION

In a notebook entry of 1878, Nietzsche enters the following observation on his earlier work:

How worm-eaten and full of holes, how well and truly built on deception and dissimulation, human life seemed to me to be. I felt that we owed everything uplifting—illusions, all enjoyment of life—to error and that therefore the origin of such a world must not be sought in a moral being, but perhaps in an artist-creator.[39]

(*WEN*, 239)

On the interpretation advanced here this invocation of an 'artist-creator' should not be taken as a foray in extravagant metaphysical or religious speculation. By 1870, having already critiqued Schopenhauer for having no basis on which to posit the Will as noumenal reality, it would be a truly extraordinary *volte face* on Nietzsche's behalf to be propounding such speculations. Nietzsche in *The Birth of Tragedy* is clearly describing the phenomenology of the tragic reveller; he offers an account of the Attic worldview transcribed into an idiom borrowed from Schopenhauer. Here, as so often in his work, Nietzsche is not as concerned with the *truth* of substantive metaphysical doctrines, as he is with their *utility*. That Nietzsche is already set upon this methodological path is evinced most clearly in the second of the *Untimely Meditations* as is also borne out by numerous fragments from his notebooks of that period. The mythic narrative of *The Birth of Tragedy* informs the narratives which Nietzsche self-consciously propounds in both the third and fourth *Untimely Meditations*. The individual is to be anchored to a quasi-metaphysical entity, 'culture', which the individual can participate in to the extent that he works towards the production of the genius, in whom 'the will comes to its redemption' (*WEN*, 53). This is

[39] 'At that time [of *The Birth of Tragedy* presumably] I believed that from the aesthetic point of view the world was a drama and meant as such by its author, but that as a moral phenomenon it was a *fraud*: therefore I came to the conclusion that the world could be justified only as an aesthetic phenomenon' (*WEN*, 238).

Nietzsche's attempt at a secular variant on the 'tragic myth', the consoling myth which syntheses metaphysical solace with worldly affirmation.

> My religion, if there is anything left that I may call by that name, consists in working for the creation of the genius; education is all that can be hoped for, and all that gives comfort is called art. *Education* is the *love of what has been created*, an excess of love beyond self-love. Religion is '*loving beyond ourselves*'. *The work of art is the image of such a love beyond oneself and a perfect image.*
>
> (*WEN*, 205)

However, this modern tragic myth is framed within a second-order narrative according to which such mythological self-deception is the necessary lot of human beings. Nietzsche himself occupies the perspective of the 'last philosopher', a rather rueful figure who is aware of both the necessity of such narratives, and their falsity.[40] This leaves his early project with a crucial unanswered question. Nietzsche seems to conceive of his audience sometimes as individuals he wishes to internalize a first-order narrative, and at others as individuals who are *aware* of that narrative's function. This prompts the question: what consolation can the second kind of individual (such as Nietzsche) draw given his knowledge that the putative consoling myth is false? Nietzsche takes the function and value of myth to be its ability to distort the nature of the loved object, thus inspiring genuine love, over and above egoistic ends. If one is *aware* that the loved is valued for illusory reasons, how psychologically plausible is it that one can maintain that love?

We have claimed that to understand Nietzsche's wider project it is important to understand his lifelong engagement with Wagner. This stance is surely backed up by the fact that he published one essay and two whole books on Wagner. By contrast, he published only one essay on Schopenhauer.[41] However, it is fair to say that this claim actually embodies a normative stance about how Nietzsche is to be read. Those who see Nietzsche primarily as a philosopher engaging in traditional and perennial philosophical questions of epistemology, metaphysics, and ethics will be prone to emphasize his engagement with Schopenhauer. Those who see Nietzsche primarily as a nineteenth-century *Kulturkritiker* engaged in

[40] 'The last philosopher... proves the necessity of illusion, of art and of the art that dominates *life*... Whether a religion can be built here, into the vacuum, depends on its strength. *We* incline to *culture*: the 'German' element as a *redemptive* force' (*WEN*, 103–4).

[41] Admittedly, he also had an unpublished essay on Schopenhauer, and his 1888 book *Nietzsche Contra Wagner* is a collection of revised aphorisms, and not a new book explicitly devoted to Wagner. Still, the title of that book indicates that as late as 1888 he continued to orientate much of his thinking in relation to Wagner and what he takes Wagner to represent.

questions of the meaning and direction of modernity will be prone to emphasize his relation to Wagner. We believe both interpretations are viable, but in a somewhat Nietzschean spirit we have emphasized the importance of Wagner, since emphasis on the Schopenhauer side of things is now largely the dominant trend.[42]

9 CODA: A NIETZSCHEAN SOLUTION TO THE PARADOX OF TRAGEDY

An interesting corollary which may be drawn from Nietzsche's account of tragedy and illusion in *The Birth of Tragedy* is a solution to the paradox of tragedy. Simply stated, the paradox is allegedly generated by the claims that tragedy involves the depiction of intrinsically unpleasant events (death, murder, betrayals, etc.), yet spectators in some sense enjoy watching tragedies. If Nietzsche is correct that a fundamental problem of human existence is an existential lack of meaning, and that a fundamental function of tragedy is to create the comforting illusion that even if individual lives are wretched they form part of a greater whole imbued with genuine significance, then the appeal of tragedy is understandable. Each of us either has implicit, if not explicit knowledge, or at least fear, that our lives are not only more or less painful but, more importantly, are essentially meaningless. Tragedy recognizes this essential painfulness of existence but holds out the prospect that, even if our individual lives may seem a more or less random series of events that do not hang together as a meaningful whole, they might be part of a wider narrative that exhibits coherence and genuine meaning. Each of us is embedded in their own individual life, hence they cannot see the whole of their life and they cannot see the greater whole of which their whole life forms a part. Tragedy acknowledges the intrinsic painfulness and disappointments of the hero's life, but from a distanced perspective that puts the tragic hero's life in a context of a clearly significant greater narrative. That our lives, as insignificant as they seem from our very partial viewpoints, might themselves be part of a greater meaningful whole is the great solace and pleasure tragedy can offer us.

As noted above, Nietzsche maintains that '[t]he meaninglessness of suffering, not suffering itself, was the curse thus far stretched over humanity'—in which

[42] Further complicating these issues is the fact that Wagner often presented his work as a response to Schopenhauer. The accuracy of this presentation is itself a controversial matter. When it comes to theoretical matters Wagner was not an especially gifted writer or reader.

case tragedy, by showing suffering within a meaningful coherent narrative, is another of those comforting illusions that are the core subject of Nietzsche's *The Birth of Tragedy*.[43]

REFERENCES

Borchmeyer, D. 1991. *Richard Wagner: Theory and Theatre* (New York and Oxford: Oxford University Press).

Came, D. 2005. 'The Aesthetic Justification of Existence', in Ansell Pearson, K. (ed.), *A Companion to Nietzsche* (Oxford: Blackwell Publishing): 41–58.

Gardiner, P. 1963. *Schopenhauer* (London: Penguin).

Gemes, K. 2001. 'Post-Modernism's Use and Abuse of Nietzsche', *Philosophy and Phenomenological Research*, 62/2: 337–60.

Gemes, K. 2006. 'We Remain of Necessity Stranger to Ourselves: The Key Message of Nietzsche's *Genealogy* Davis Acampora, C. (ed.), *Nietzsche's* On the Genealogy of Morals: *Critical Essays* (Lanham, MD: Rowman & Littlefield Publishers): 191–208.

Gemes, K. 2009. 'Freud and Nietzsche on Sublimation', *Journal of Nietzsche Studies*, 38: 38–59.

Hölderlin, F. 1952. *Dichtungen und Briefe* (Munich: Winkler-Verlag).

Janaway, C. 1996. 'Knowledge and Tranquillity: Schopenhauer on the Value of Art', in Jacquette, D. (ed.), *Schopenhauer, Philosophy, and the Arts* (Cambridge: Cambridge University Press): 39–61.

Janaway, C. (ed.) 1998. *Willingness and Nothingness: Schopenhauer as Nietzsche's Educator*, (Oxford: Clarenden Press).

Nietzsche, F. 1977. *Nietzsche Contra Wagner*, in Kaufmann, Walter (ed. and trans.), *The Portable Nietzsche* (Harmondsworth: Penguin).

Nietzsche, F. 1986. *Untimely Meditations*, Hollingdale, R. J. (trans.) (Cambridge: Cambridge University Press).

Nietzsche, F. 1988. *Sämtliche Werke: Kritische Studienausgabe in 15 Einzelbänden*, Colli, G. and Montinari, M. (eds.) (Berlin: de Gruyter).

Nietzsche, F. 1996. *Human, All Too Human*, Schacht, R. (ed.), Hollingdale, R. J. (trans.) (Cambridge: Cambridge University Press).

Nietzsche, F. 1998. *On the Genealogy of Morality*, Clark, M. and Swensen, A. (trans.) (Indianapolis: Hackett).

Nietzsche, F. 1999. *The Birth of Tragedy*, Geuss, R. and Speirs, R. (eds.), Speirs, R. (trans.) (Cambridge, Cambridge University Press).

Nietzsche, F. 2001. *The Gay Science*, Bernard Williams (ed.), Nauckhoff, J. and del Caro, A. (trans.) (Cambridge: Cambridge University Press).

Nietzsche, F. 2002. *Beyond Good and Evil*, Horstmann, R. and Norman, J. (eds.), Norman, J. (trans.) (Cambridge: Cambridge University Press).

[43] While here the stress is on a coherence that can provide meaning, Gemes (2001; 2009) argues that the related notion of unity is central to Nietzsche's ideal for both genuine culture and genuine individuals.

Nietzsche, F. 2009. *Writings from the Early Notebooks*, Geuss, R. and Nehamas, A. (eds.) (Cambridge: Cambridge University Press).

Poellner, P. 1998. 'Myth, Art and Illusion in Nietzsche', in Bell, M. and Poellner, P. (eds.), *Myth and the Making of Modernity: The Problem of Grounding in Early Twentieth-Century Literature* (Amsterdam-Atlanta: Rodopi).

Ridley, A. 2007. *Routledge Philosophy Guidebook to Nietzsche on Art* (Oxford: Routledge).

Schelling, F. 1989. *The Philosophy of Art*, Scott, D. (ed. and trans.) (Minneapolis: University of Minneapolis Press).

Schopenhauer, A., 1969. *The World as Will and Representation*, Vols. I & II, Payne, E. F. J. (trans.) (New York: Dover).

Shaw, L. 1960. 'The Noble Deception: "*Wahn*", Wagner, and "Die Meistersinger von Nürnberg"', *Monatshefte*, 52: 97–112.

Soll, I. 1990. 'Pessimism and the Tragic View of Life: Reconsiderations of Nietzsche's *Birth of Tragedy*', in Solomon, R. and Higgins, K. (eds.), *Reading Nietzsche*, (New York and Oxford: Oxford University Press): 104–32.

Staten, H. 1990. *Nietzsche's Voice* (Ithaca, NY: Cornell University Press).

Wagner, R. 1994. *Religion and Art* (London: University of Nebraska Press).

Wagner, R. 1995. *Art and Politics* (London: University of Nebraska Press).

Warrack, J. (ed.) 1994. *Die Meistersinger Von Nűrnberg* (Cambridge: Cambridge University Press).

Williamson, G. 2004. *The Longing for Myth in Germany: Religion and Aesthetic Culture from Romanticism to Nietzsche* (Chicago: University of Chicago Press).

Young, J. 1992. *Nietzsche's Philosophy of Art* (Cambridge: Cambridge University Press).

5

Orchestral Metaphysics: *The Birth of Tragedy* between Drama, Opera, and Philosophy

Stephen Mulhall

Although it can hardly be denied that *The Birth of Tragedy* is—as its first paragraph declares—centrally concerned to advance the science of aesthetics by coming to grips with the essence of Attic tragedy, it should not be forgotten that its author also characterizes the book (in his foreword to it) as being in constant conversation with Richard Wagner, and hence as a continuation of their joint struggle properly to grasp the true purpose and full value of Wagnerian opera, understood as aspiring to the status of a *Gesamtkunstwerk*. One might say that *The Birth of Tragedy* is an attempt to make sense of the Wagner circle's habit of referring to their leader as Aeschylus—to ground Nietzsche's intuition that the work of both men embodies an enigmatic sublimity of a distinctive kind, one that can properly be individuated only by placing each in the light cast by the other. To christen Wagner as Aeschylus reborn is to say not just that Wagnerian opera can only be rightly understood as a transfiguration of Attic tragic drama, but also that Attic tragic drama can only be rightly understood if seen as essentially capable of such transfiguration. The genealogical narrative that Nietzsche unfolds, with Aeschylus as the origin and Wagner as its present culmination, is thus a way of rendering perspicuous aspects of the essence of each body of work that might otherwise remain occluded, whilst recognizing that their distinctive sublimity would be lost if its enigmatic quality were ever (*per impossibile*) entirely dissipated.

It is not surprising that a young philologist of exceptional gifts, encountering works of art of whose excellence he is immediately convinced, but who cannot as immediately articulate the grounds of that conviction to his own satisfaction (any more than can the creator of those works), should turn for illumination to the unchallenged exemplars of artistic excellence with which he has been so much preoccupied. But this particular philologist was also a philosopher—someone whose formation included immersion in Schopenhauer, and thereby in Kant's world-historical transfiguration of the metaphysical impulse that first found its distinctively philosophical expression in Plato. Consequently, the conversation between Wagner and Aeschylus that informs *The Birth of Tragedy* in fact involves a third party—call him Schopenhauer as Educator, the teacher who makes it possible to read Kant as a culminating, subversive transfiguration of Socrates, the exemplary philosopher.

Suppose we regard the author of *The Birth of Tragedy* as the site or vessel of this three-cornered conversation. What form of writing might he forge to embody such an exchange—one in which each contributor might retain his individuality without denying his internal relatedness to the others? Can there be a mode of discourse that makes equal, and equally essential, reference to opera, tragic drama, and philosophy, tapping into the distinctive powers of each without corrupting the fruitfulness of all? Just what kind of text is *The Birth of Tragedy?*

1 THE SATYR'S VISION: TRAGIC DRAMA

Nietzsche's vision of Attic tragedy is crystallized in section 8 of *The Birth of Tragedy*, and the following paragraphs summarize its main elements:

> Enchantment is the precondition of all dramatic art. In this enchanted state the Dionysiac enthusiast sees himself as a satyr, and *as a satyr he in turn sees the god*, i.e., in his transformed state he sees a new vision which is the Apolline perfection of his state. With this new vision the drama is complete.
>
> This insight leads us to understand Greek tragedy as a Dionysian chorus which discharges itself over and over again in an Apolline world of images. Thus the choral passages which are interwoven with the tragedy are, to a certain extent, the womb of the entire so-called dialogue, i.e., of the whole world on stage, the drama proper. This primal ground of tragedy radiates, in a succession of discharges, that vision of drama which is entirely a dream-appearance, and thus epic in nature; on the other hand, as the objectification of a Dionysiac state, the vision represents not Apolline release and redemption in semblance, but rather the breaking-asunder of the individual and its becoming one with the primal being itself. Thus drama is the Apolline embodiment of Dionysiac insights and effects.
>
> (*BT*, 8)

The basic claim here is that the tragic chorus is the artistic imitation of a more primitive, more explicitly religious phenomenon—that of the agitated mass of

Dionysus's servants shouting in jubilation as they are seized by moods and insights so powerful that they transform themselves before their own eyes, making them think that they are seeing themselves restored to what they regard as the fundamental spirit of nature—the satyrs (hybrids of the human and the equine, emblems of the omnipotent life-force). In that transfigured state, they undergo a vision of their god, Dionysus, as the underlying truth of things, a revelation of reality in comparison to which 'real' experience is mere appearance. Following his methodological principle that origins manifest essence, Nietzsche invites us to understand the chorus in Attic tragedy as an artistic reconstitution of the satyr chorus, and as itself the primal ground or heart of the tragic drama it helps constitute.

In this way, he finds aesthetic and metaphysical significance in an architectural fact about Attic tragedy—that the place of the chorus in Greek theatres was the orchestra, a semicircular area in front of the stage. The scene of their singing and dancing was thus essentially liminal with respect to both drama and spectators, internally related to both and so not exclusively identifiable with either. The chorus was Janus-faced—it was capable of engaging with the characters in the drama in ways not available to mere spectators, and yet its distinctive theatrical space makes it the innermost of the concentric circles of terraces on which those spectators sat (taking in both the drama as a whole and the cultural world of which it was the expression), inviting them not only to view but to identify with the chorus, and thereby to overcome their metaphysical distance from the drama in which that chorus is involved. The chorus's function as participant-observers thus allows the audience to experience the drama as if they too were participants in it.

The dramatic action on stage is then to be understood as a vision of the chorus, and so of the audience—a vision of their suffering, glorified master, Dionysus. As Nietzsche puts it: '[R]ight down to Euripedes, Dionysus never ceased to be the tragic hero, and ... all the tragic figures of the Greek stage, Prometheus, Oedipus, etc., are merely masks of that original hero, Dionysus' (*BT*, 10). By this, Nietzsche means (at least) that these tragic figures are not so much individuals as individualities, mythic archetypes rather than particular embodied souls; that they are no more absolutely distinguishable from the chorus and so from the audience than they are from one another or from the god they body forth; and that their vicissitudes reveal the vulnerability of our moral status to unfathomable contingency (as Oedipus is polluted by deeds whose nature and consequences exceed the reach of his intentions), the ultimate unintelligibility of reality (with Oedipus' mastery of the Sphinx's riddle being shown to be both catastrophic in consequence and yet merely apparent, since he cannot utilize his ability to define human beings in general in order to comprehend himself or his human others), and the origin of human suffering as lying in the fate or condition of individuality as such, rather than anything that specific individuals happen to do or suffer.

But Nietzsche's claim is that these Dionysian insights and effects (of both content and form) are given Apolline embodiment—in his terms, that the dramatic vision the chorus discharges is essentially a dream-appearance. By this, he means (at least) that it discloses a divine power that is independent of those to whom it is made manifest; that the god manifests himself as a sequence of erring, striving protagonists; that those protagonists participate in a representation of release and redemption, even if not release and redemption *by* representation—by means of semblance or image-making; and that while the distinctions between character, chorus, and audience are problematized or weakened, they are not entirely deconstructed. In short, the womb of Dionysian ecstasy does and must discharge itself in structured, ordered words and deeds: its prodigious episodes of collectively declaimed words interwoven with music and dance engender modes of speech that incarnate a form of aesthetic and dramatic fulfilment in the absence of dance and music, and in the mouths of recognizably individual speakers.

By thus understanding the tragic chorus as an aesthetic transfiguration of the satyr chorus, and viewing the dramatic whole of which that chorus is a part in the terms provided by his interpretation of that part, Nietzsche makes good on his opening claim—that Attic tragedy not only presents miraculous events (such as Oedipus' redemptive transfiguration at Colonus) but is itself a metaphysical miracle, a work of art that is Apolline and Dionysian in equal measure, an unprecedented pairing of two conflictual but productive artistic drives that Nietzsche names after the two Greek deities of art—Apollo standing for image-making and sculpture, and Dionysus for the imageless art of music.

Attic tragedy therefore establishes that the complementarity of Apollo and Dionysus is at least as important as their conflict. For while the culture which first acknowledged them initially understood them as essentially oppositional, hence as primarily revealing fundamental differences between individual art forms (as well as divisions within the impulses which give rise to artistic creation, and rifts in the underlying reality from which those creations emerge and into which they aspire to penetrate), the genealogical productivity of their mutual antagonism ultimately revealed an enigmatic but undeniable mutual dependence: a realization that each found its highest expression within the highest expression of the other. To regard each as essentially sunderable from the other would be to occlude the capacity of each to break itself asunder, overcoming its initial absolute individuality or distinctness in order to become more than it could otherwise be, and thereby more itself. And in so doing, it discloses the mysterious primal unity of being.

Nietzsche's opening, summary articulation of this central point—about the pairing of Dionysus and Apollo—depicts it in terms of a productive mutual provocation, at once akin to and different from that of reproduction by sexual difference. First, the stimulation of each by the other induces each to produce ever more vigorous offspring of its own (each being thereby the womb for its own progeny). Then an artistic form is established that is equally indebted to both—in which the Dionysian element forms the womb for the Apolline, but the Apolline perfects the Dionysian, so that its divine vision might be externalized and so rendered viewable, and a coherent embodiment for the womb which is compelled to discharge or project that vision might be engendered. This artistic progeny is thus a hybrid: it both contains and constitutes an aesthetic and metaphysical centaur.

Can one say the same of *The Birth of Tragedy* itself? Since it presents Attic tragedy as a centaur, it certainly contains one; can it also be said to constitute one? According to its account of the centaur it contains, the essence of that hybrid resides in a transfiguration of the satyr chorus, in which state or condition the Dionysiac enthusiast sees himself as a satyr, and as such suffers a vision of his god which perfects the state in which he suffers it. Can this characterization be applied to the author of that account?

Suppose we begin with that author's vision—in this case, a vision of Attic tragedy. It is certainly one which regards the constituent elements of that genre as various, internally related manifestations or masks of a divine duality, godheads engaged in a drama of conflict and redemption in which their distinctive identities are provisionally and miraculously overcome, and so in which the vicissitudes of that archetypal pairing make darkly visible the primal unity of all things. To this extent, *The Birth of Tragedy* plainly reproduces the basic structure of the phenomenon its opening sections depict.

That depiction more specifically claims that the visions with which it is concerned take the form of tragic mythical dramas; can the depiction itself be said to manifest (inflections of) the same three formal features? The broader historical narrative that contextualizes Nietzsche's account of Attic tragedy suggests an affirmative answer. The tragic dimension of that narrative lies in its basic structure of birth, death (or suicide), and prophesied, transfiguring rebirth. Furthermore, its mythic status is reinforced by the fact that the narrative is genealogical in form: for each succeeding episode thereby appears as a further manifestation of the fate of the divine duality of Apollo and Dionysus.

The key characteristic of mythic logic central to Nietzsche's reading of Attic tragedy—its conviction that apparently diverse and distinct phenomena are in truth metamorphoses of one or two timeless, underlying principles or powers—is thereby generalized, so that the whole of human history in the West is dramatized as a series of masks or manifestations of these dual divinities, each a more or less productive variation upon the original stock (an effect of their mutual excitation, whether irritable or arousing, and of exogenous shocks or graftings). Many of Nietzsche's own remarks about myth prepare us for the thought that the remarks themselves should be seen as being as much mythological in status as exercises of historical scholarship. He defines myth as 'the most significant example', and tragic myth as 'myth which speaks of Dionysiac knowledge in symbols'—both definitions patently possessed of reflexive application, given *The Birth of Tragedy*'s deployments of Apollo and Dionysus as infinitely suggestive exemplars of the primal unity of being. He further associates myth with the basic structure of genealogical narrative when he attributes to myths a 'natural tendency to go on living and to throw out new shoots' (*BT*, 10), as well as a vulnerability to intellectual scepticism whose pressures result in the transformation of myth into a finished sum of historical events whose credibility wanes in proportion to the extent to which they are dogmatically asserted, until the myth then wilts, discolours, and finds that its blossoms and leaves are scattered to the four winds.

What, then, of the idea that *The Birth of Tragedy* exemplifies an essentially dramatic mode of vision? Nietzsche specifies the category of the dramatic, understood in comparison with that of the poetic, in the following way:

> [W]hat makes a poet a poet is the fact that he sees himself surrounded by figures who live and act before him, and into whose innermost essence he gazes... For the genuine poet metaphor is no rhetorical figure, but an image which takes the place of something else, something he can really see before him as a substitute for a concept.... [O]ne only has to have the ability to watch a living play continuously and to live constantly surrounded by crowds of spirits, then one is a poet; if one feels the impulse to transform oneself and to speak out of other bodies and souls, then one is a dramatist.
>
> Dionysiac excitement is able to transmit to an entire mass of people this artistic gift of seeing themselves surrounded by just such a crowd of spirits with which they know themselves to be inwardly one. This process of the tragic chorus is the original phenomenon of *drama*—this experience of seeing oneself transformed before one's eyes and acting as if one had really entered another body, another character.
>
> (*BT*, 8)

The thought that, in these terms, Nietzsche envisions his own work as going beyond the poetic to the dramatic helps to account for his use of a literary technique that Silk and Stern rightly describe as pervasive in *The Birth of Tragedy*, and which they label 'metalepsis' (that is, metonymy, but of a double, complicated or indirect kind). What they have in mind is Nietzsche's tendency to depict the character and vicissitudes of a phenomenon in terms provided by aspects or elements of the phenomenon itself—as when Apolline culture is depicted in terms appropriate to Apolline art ('the glorious Olympian figures... stand on the gable of this structure'), or Attic tragedy is equated with two tragic characters ('at once Antigone and Cassandra'), or the power of a myth is described in terms of the powers belonging to a mythological character ('it rises once more like a wounded hero'), or the passing of tragedy is characterized in terms of the lamented death of a mythic god ('Great Pan is dead!').[1]

Our discussion suggests a way of understanding why this technique is so appropriate and so effective: for it amounts to Nietzsche's writing not just as if the mythical figures of Greek tragic drama were living incarnations of concepts (so that his thinking is, as it were, poetic—literally figurative), but as if he had really entered into their body and soul, and thereby into the view of the world that they incarnate. He sees everything through their eyes, articulating his experience in the terms they embody, as if the texture of their world has become that of his own subjectivity—as if he is possessed by them, transformed into these various manifestations of the dual godhead, one more mask for the divinities he divines everywhere.

In part, this metaleptic strategy follows from the liminal position appropriate to any author who understands himself as aspiring to occupy the orchestral position of the tragic chorus. For it enacts a provisional subversion of the supposedly absolute division between the spectator and the characters of Attic tragedy—as if Nietzsche is re-enacting his experience of utter identification with those mythic figures in order to invite his reader not only to undergo that experience with him, but also to experience Nietzsche's own transfiguration of tragic mythic drama in a similar way (by thinking and acting as if one had really entered—by way of Nietzsche's ensouled body of choric writing—into the body and soul of Nietzsche's Apollo and Dionysus). But one might equally well view metalepsis not merely as a strategy adopted within the book, but also as the basic principle of its construction. For if *The Birth of Tragedy* does invite an understanding of itself as structured overall in the terms it posits for understanding the structure of one phenomenon it analyses, then that part of the book stands for

[1] For a much longer list of examples, and their textual locations, see Silk and Stern (1981, 198–204).

(substitutes or goes proxy for, incarnates or exemplifies the living spirit of) the whole—an essentially metonymic effect.

2 INTERLUDE: THE OPERATIC TRANSFIGURATION OF VOICE, BODY, AND WORDS

I suggested earlier that another part of *The Birth of Tragedy* might have a metonymic function: the account offered, in its concluding sections, of Wagnerian opera. More specifically, my claim was that Nietzsche is not only as much concerned to illuminate Attic tragedy by reference to Wagner as to illuminate Wagner by reference to Attic tragedy, but also wants us to understand his own text in the terms provided by his analysis of both.

The mythic principle of genealogical substitution and displacement we have already encountered would suggest that Wagner's relation to Aeschylean drama is given in the metamorphosis of the term 'orchestra', from naming the site of the chorus to that of the players of musical instruments. On Nietzsche's understanding, this linguistic displacement marks and effects both change and continuity, signifying a transfiguring recurrence or recreation: the Wagnerian orchestra is a mask of the tragic chorus, which was itself a mask of the satyr chorus.

The envisaged architecture of Bayreuth emphasizes one central continuity by placing every seat in the audience at exactly the same level, thus echoing the egalitarianism implicit in the encircling terraces of the original Greek theatre. In both dispositions, matters of social distinction recede in the face of an essentially communal identification with the drama about to unfold—the expression of an existing or passionately desired sense of unity with one another, and with the truth dramatized on stage. The central discontinuity lies in the fact that the location whose liminality serves to effect this transcendence of individuation is occupied not by singing and dancing seers, and thus by words interwoven with music and action, but by makers of music alone. If the pairing of Attic tragedy and Wagnerian opera allows each to illuminate the other, this (un)masking tells us that music is the often-occluded essence of the phenomenon of Greek tragic drama, and that Wagner's way of rearticulating that aesthetic original nevertheless gives an unprecedented dominance to the role of music within the envisaged totality of the *Gesamtkunstwerk*. The key feature of music in this context—its Dionysian essence—has primarily to do with the fact that Nietzsche views it as imageless, essentially non-representational. More precisely, the distinction between representation and that which is represented, between symbolic form and symbolic content, has no application to music: it refuses that mode of articulating and hence individuating its meaning, because it *is* its meaning—it means itself. Since its mode of signification is not that of semblance-making, it is particularly suited to articulating the underlying truth of things, with which we and all existing things are ultimately one.

Viewing myth and music as each other's other allows Nietzsche to see that Wagner's most recent thoughts about opera—according to which music was ultimately more important than the words and deeds dramatized on stage—provide an unprecedentedly deep acknowledgement of the extent to which the womb-like Dionysian enchantment out of which the tragic chorus speaks is an essentially musical mood or mode of attunement. Since no one in Nietzsche's era (or indeed our own) was in a position to experience the musical element of the tragic chorus, his experience of Wagner's transfigured version of it was an indispensable means of disclosing its true significance. And to those who point out that, since Nietzsche had, at the time of composing *The Birth of Tragedy*, never experienced a Wagner opera in performance, and had probably only ever heard piano reductions of their scores, his sense of the priority of the musical element in such operatic work was, to say the least of it, potentially overdetermined, Nietzsche might reply that it was precisely his ecstatic apprehension of the unrealized totality of those works by means of an experience of their scores that confirmed him in his sense of the distinctive physiognomy of both Wagnerian opera and Attic tragedy. One might say that, just as the striking presence of the musical element in Wagnerian opera revealed to Nietzsche the nature and significance of the missing element in our experience of Attic tragedy, so the striking dramatic element of Attic tragedy helped to flesh out the nature and significance of the as-yet missing element in his experience of Wagnerian opera.

But the displacement of the ancient chorus by the modern symphonic orchestra invites the question: where is that chorus displaced to? In the context of opera, the answer must surely be: fully onto the stage—to the dramatized, lyrical words and deeds of the singers. And since this displacement reshapes the distinction between the chorus and the individual protagonists of these tragic mythological dramas, the original significance of the tragic chorus will inevitably be redistributed between those two kinds of dramatic-operatic being.

One possible implication of this redistribution emerges if we pair a remark of Nietzsche's with one from Stanley Cavell's discussion of opera. Nietzsche's remark comes from a scathing critique of the prevailing, non-Wagnerian forms of operatic work:

What will become of the Dionysiac and the Apolline where there is such a mixture of styles as I have shown to lie at the heart of the *stilo rappresentativo*?—where music is regarded as the servant and the libretto as master, where music is compared to the body and the words to the soul?

(*BT*, 19)

Cavell's discussion recasts Nietzsche's familiar metaphor of the body from a rather different perspective, that of a commentary on the conjunction of opera's founding with the advent of Cartesian scepticism in modern philosophy, during which he attempts to specify opera's distinctive conception of the relation between the human being and her body:

[A] relation in which not this character and this actor are embodied in each other, but in which this voice is located in—one might say disembodied within—this figure, this double, this person, this persona, this singer, whose voice is essentially unaffected by the role.

A Cartesian intuition of the absolute metaphysical difference between mind and body, together with the twin Cartesian intuition of an undefined intimacy between just this body and only this spirit, appears to describe conditions of the possibility of opera...

[S]urely the operatic voice is the grandest realization of having a signature, of an abandonment to your words, hence of your mortal immortality.

(Cavell, 1994, 137, 144)

Nietzsche wishes to revive the idea of music as the Dionysian soul and words as the Apolline body of Wagnerian opera; he thereby inverts the evaluative hierarchy written into the essentially representational style of current operatic forms, but leaves unquestioned the assumption that the relation between soul and body is inevitably both oppositional and hierarchical. Cavell transfigures the issue by considering the individual figure of the opera singer, and by viewing her as essentially individuated in that medium by her voice. Her voice is a manifestation or incarnation of her spirit or signature, rather than of her soul—or rather, the terms 'spirit' and 'signature' here substitute for or displace the term 'soul', retaining its function of referring to a person's essence or identity, but distancing themselves from the assumption that that essence is simply immortal, and so essentially opposed to its body; for the opera singer's voice is enigmatically intimate with her body, hence her mode of immortality is distinctively mortal. And her voice both realizes and is realized by an abandonment to her words, not an abandonment of them. Cavell thereby rejects the idea that words are a mere vessel for or servant of the voice—hence essentially opposed to or other than it, and so the human being who voices them. What the opera singer's voice is truly dislocated from or disembodied within is neither her words nor her body, but rather (as Cavell's prose, with its rapid sequence of terms for it—each no sooner deployed than displaced—positively enacts) her persona or mask: that is, her role as an actor in lyric drama as such, and her specific character in this particular opera (whoever it may be). Her voice thereby reveals music and words as essentially unified aspects of the identity that survives any maskings or unmaskings it undergoes—a duality whose productive conflict and complementarity reveal an underlying individuality.

Looking back on *The Birth of Tragedy* 15 years later, Nietzsche declares that its author, this new soul, stammering in a strange tongue, 'ought to have sung . . . and not talked!' (*BT*, 'Attempt', 4). Cavell's transfiguration of one of that author's key figures in the light of one of his key points of metonymic reference suggests that this attempt at self-criticism is not so much an external critique as a deployment of that same strange tongue, only without the stammer. At the very least, it suggests that the guidance Nietzsche hesitantly wished to take from his impressions of Wagnerian opera will be found in the specific modulations of his authorial voice; and since its capacity for song must be more dependent upon language alone than any opera to which it adverts, its signature or spirit must be realized primarily in the specific mode of Nietzsche's abandonment to words, his willingness to be ecstatically possessed by *their* individual spirit or signature, their mortal immortality.

That mortal immortality is most generally realized in the genealogical vicissitudes of words from Aeschylus' days to Wagner's and now our own—that is, by the endlessly reconfigured orchestrations of their individual and collective histories to which *The Birth of Tragedy* is so obsessively attuned. And the specifically Wagnerian music of Nietzsche's voice is not audible outside or beside itself in opera, as if *The Birth of Tragedy* is an alternative libretto for *Tristan and Isolde*. It is rather realized in that text's becoming increasingly possessed by those libretti: for its concluding sections begin to deploy the register of Wagnerian myth in the metaleptic way in which it employs Aeschylean and Sophoclean myth throughout—shifting from citation (as in 'the fire-magic of music' (from act III of *The Valkyrie*), or 'the wide space of the world's night' (from act III of *Tristan*)) to straightforward use (as when describing the German yearning for the 'blissfully enticing call of the Dionysiac bird which is on the wing, hovering above his head, and which wants to show him the way' (just like the forest-bird in *Siegfried* that leads the hero to the rock on which Brünnhilde is sleeping) (*BT*, 20, 21, 23). Here, then, is a second way in which this book invites an understanding of itself in the terms it offers for an understanding of one specific phenomenon it aspires to comprehend—a second instance of structural metonymy.

3 THEORETICAL MAN: SOCRATES AS A MASK OF APOLLO

Even if one accepts *The Birth of Tragedy*'s analysis of Attic tragedy and Wagnerian opera as having such metonymic significance, however, there is one specific difference between the vision analysed and the analytical vision. Whereas the tragic chorus discharges a spectacle of Dionysus alone, Nietzsche's dramatic, tragic myth of Western culture envisions a dual godhead, a conflictual partnership between Apollo and Dionysus as the primal ground of all things. This suggests that Nietzsche is as much a servant of Apollo as he is of Dionysus, or at least a worshipper of their union or pairing. After all, his more purely textual counterpoint to Aeschylean rebirth in Wagner cannot call upon music in any literal sense; it must draw more extensively and systematically upon the Apolline dimension of these creative drives. Furthermore, Nietzsche's struggle to understand the enigmatic sublimity of Attic tragedy and Wagnerian opera is informed throughout by his inheritance of Kant and Schopenhauer, and so by an indebtedness (however troubled) to the tradition of philosophy. Phrased in mythic terms, this poses the question: how does the presence of both Apollo and Socrates inflect or transfigure the exemplary significance of Dionysus in the Nietzschean metaphysical vision of Western culture?

So formulated, this query makes a questionable assumption—that Apollo and Socrates are two essentially distinct figures in Nietzsche's dramatic mythology. This assumption might seem to be confirmed by Nietzsche's way of introducing Socrates to his narrative of Attic tragedy's suicidal embodiment in the work of Euripides: 'In a certain sense Euripides, too, was merely a mask; the deity who spoke out of him was not Dionysus, nor Apollo, but an altogether newborn daemon called *Socrates*' (*BT*, 12). But this remark will be misunderstood unless we take seriously the work of the words 'daemon' and 'mask' within it.

Talk of Socrates as a daemon is doubly metaleptic: it exploits Socrates' characterization of himself as possessed of an attendant or indwelling spirit in order to characterize the link between Euripides and Socrates, and it invokes a flavour of malignity now attending post-Christian uses of the term. But a 'daemon' is, in this context, not straightforwardly identifiable with a divinity: in Greek mythology, a daemon was a being whose nature lay somewhere between that of gods and men, hence at best a divinity of an inferior kind. The term certainly doesn't make Socrates sound like a third amongst equals in Nietzsche's theology.

Might we then, consider him instead as a mask of Apollo (and so consider Euripides in the same terms)? A masking relation allows for both continuity and discontinuity: what lies beneath the mask is both distinguishable from the mask itself and yet its underlying truth. The suggestion is not that Socrates has no independent mythic significance at all; it is that this significance is ultimately to be understood as an inflection of that of Apollo—more specifically, an inflection of Apollo that aspires to repress or deny rather than to honour or even to accommodate Dionysus (in the manner that Nietzsche envisages Apollo making room for this foreign, barbarous deity upon his initial arrival on Attic shores, before their brief and passionate union in Attic tragedy). Socrates represents the aspect of Apollo that regrets that accommodation, that cannot comprehend why he entered into the marriage that resulted from it, and that desperately desires a divorce.

Nietzsche himself encapsulates Socrates' mythic significance as follows: he is the archetype of theoretical man. Theoretical man is optimistic, both morally and more generally. Morally, he believes that 'virtue is knowledge; sin is only committed out of ignorance; and the virtuous man is a happy man'; in other words, being moral is simply a matter of implementing practical reason. In the theoretical domain, optimism is equally central: here, the key Socratic belief is that not only can reason grasp the uttermost depths of being, but it can correct it (improve it, engender progress). Hence the mythical resonance of the dying Socrates, rendered immune to the fear of death by reason and knowledge; it declares that a fully comprehended individual life is the only justifiable one, but that it is humanly available.

The moral and metaphysical content of this archetype utterly contradicts that of Oedipus or Antigone, those embodiments of the reality of moral luck and of the ultimate incomprehensibility of being. But from the Socratic perspective, nothing else should be expected from a medium and a genre that conflates illusion and reality—that addresses the chaotic and opaque energies of the emotions rather than the mind, and that gives itself over to inspiration rather than comprehensible bodies of creative principle. Theoretical man thus distinguishes art sharply from knowledge, as well as distinguishing within the realm of knowledge between science and metaphysics, which (as the name suggests) incorporates and goes beyond scientific knowledge, involving what one might call knowledge of knowledge. And as the various aspects of human engagement with reality are distinguished from one another, so a hierarchy of their value is simultaneously established, with art at the bottom and philosophy at the top.

From the perspective of the modern philosophical tradition (call it that of Kantian Enlightenment), Socratic theoretical optimism thus appears as a commitment to a multifaceted principle of autonomy. Its moral ideal for the individual is mirrored at the level of culture by a conception of its various dimensions as logically distinct and self-sufficient intellectual enterprises; at both levels, individual flourishing and fulfilment resides in a proper recognition of their autonomy in relation to their equally autonomous others.

Even this brief account suggests that the key connection between Socrates and Apollo lies in the former's hyperbolic incarnation of the latter's governing *principium individuationis*. The media of sculpture and dreams are Apolline because they are populated with sharply delineated human and divine figures, hence a kind of celebration of the individual; but the world of dream-experience, so often hard to distinguish from that of real experience, more generally exhibits 'the logical causality of line and outline, colour and grouping' (*BT*, 2). For if subjective experience (whether real or illusory) is to convey or represent a world, two things are required. It must present a multiplicity of discriminable entities, entities that can only be grouped or linked to one another in causal (or any other) relations if they can be recognized as distinct, individual entities; and what is thereby represented must be distinguishable from the representation of it—that is, the individual subject of the experience must be distinguishable from its objects (and of course from other subjects of experience). Genuinely cognitive representation must balance the competing demands of identity and relation, multiplicity and oneness: objects can only make a world (as opposed to a chaos or plenum) if they stand in relations with one another, and individuals can only recognize themselves as such in relation to a world of independently existing objects with which to contrast the course of their subjective experience.

I have phrased these claims about individuation in Kantian terms precisely because Nietzsche himself is necessarily interpreting the genealogical development of theoretical man in the terms bequeathed to him from Kant via Schopenhauer. But of course, Nietzsche also reads Kant as the first philosopher to disclose the delusion at the heart of the Socratic inflection of this Apolline principle:

> Whereas this optimism once believed in our ability to grasp and solve . . . all the puzzles of the universe, and treated space, time and causality as entirely unconditional laws of the most general validity, Kant showed that these things actually only served to raise mere appearance, the work of maya, to the status of the sole and supreme reality and to put this in the place of the innermost and true essence of things, thereby making it impossible really to understand this essence—to put the dreamer even more deeply to sleep.
>
> (*BT*, 18)

On this reading, the Socratic project is given a tragic inflection by a philosopher whose aim was to further or complete it. The critique of pure reason employs the very tools of the understanding that Socrates held to be capable of grasping the whole of reality; but when applied to the understanding itself (as they must be, given that human understanding is part of reality), they reveal it to be essentially limited, conditioned, and unsatisfiable. For Kant's Transcendental Analytic grounds the very possibility of knowledge about reality by showing that the mind's basic categories necessarily apply to the world of our experience; but it does so only on the assumption that we first receive something for those categories to synthesize—a body of intuition from whose marriage with the mind's activity a world will emerge, but whose brute givenness points to a reality that lies *ex hypothesi* beyond our categorial grasp: call it the realm of things-in-themselves. At these limits, therefore (one might think of them as the threshold of modernity), Socratic logic finally curls up around itself and 'bites its own tail' (*BT*, 15). Kant stands for an embryonic form of tragic knowledge about knowledge—a mournful vision of the necessary disappointment to which all theoretical optimism is fated.

His work thus reveals the groundlessness of the Socratic privileging of metaphysics. To be sure that such knowledge is to be valued above all other modes of human engagement with reality, we must be sure that it is (however partial or incomplete in fact) completable in principle—that is, capable of grasping the whole of reality. But our best attempt to achieve that certainty—to show that reality and our cognitive powers really are as if made for one another—in fact forces us to acknowledge the enigmatic existence of an aspect of reality that necessarily transcends those powers. And if we cannot coherently think of theoretical knowledge as total, then we cannot justifiably devalue artistic modes of engagement with reality by comparison with it. In this way, the Socratic project finds itself acknowledging in its own metaphysical terms the very thing that it originally criticized Attic tragedy for endorsing (and would certainly criticize Wagnerian opera for recovering) in its distinctive terms—the Dionysian idea that no account of reality is complete, which does not acknowledge both its underlying affinity with, and its inherent transcendence of, the human capacity to make sense of it.

To subvert the Socratic inflection of metaphysics is thus not to condemn the metaphysical enterprise as such: on the contrary, the Kantian transfiguration or unmasking of Socratic metaphysics makes possible a mode of metaphysical thinking that is no less insightful or valuable than other forms of human engagement with reality, because it too acknowledges the essential complementarity of Apollo and Dionysus. But in thereby locating Kant's achievement as one episode in a genealogical story that pivots upon dramatic and operatic stagings of the intimate strife between Apollo and Dionysus, Nietzsche does mean to put in question the Socratic perception of an absolute distinction between metaphysics and every other mode of human culture, and in particular between metaphysics and art. The point is not to counter-claim (in the same absolutizing spirit) that there is absolutely no difference between these ways of engaging with reality. The point is rather to affirm their internal relatedness—not only by confirming Nietzsche's perception of a metaphysical dimension in Attic tragedy and Wagnerian opera, but also by inviting us to perceive the dramatic and mythological dimensions of Kantian metaphysics. Seen through the lens of Attic tragedy, Kant's fundamental duality of concept and intuition, theoretical form and sensory content, appears as an epistemological restaging of the underlying structure of a tragic drama. The dark Dionysian womb of givenness engenders a sublime marriage of concept and intuition that discloses the world and the knowing subject as if made for one another, thereby presenting itself as if given for just such a purpose—as if fated to discharge itself in the Apolline synthetic activity it suffers. That synthetic activity's attempts to grasp its own nature inexorably engender an intuition of a realm necessarily beyond its own grasp, an undifferentiatable, Dionysian reality from which it first emerged and towards which it endlessly, impossibly aspires. And it is to this tantalizing intuition of a unity underlying Kant's apparently binary critical system that post-Kantian philosophers from Fichte through Hegel to Schopenhauer are each, in their differing ways, responsive.

What Nietzsche also detects in the apparently abstract content of Kant's texts, is the transposition into a cognitive key of the utterly primordial mythic theme of individuation as a fate or condition to which we are condemned, and condemned to deny. For Kant's vision of us as finite knowers stages a crucifixion scene—portraying us as crucified by the burden of understanding (our conditioned capacity for cognizing reality necessarily sundering us from the world and our fellow-knowers of it), and as in turn crucifying that understanding (for according to the Transcendental Dialectic, human reason has an ineradicable tendency to construct ideas of total or unconditioned knowledge, and to present them to the understanding as attainable ideals rather than purely regulative incitements to endless incremental improvements in knowledge). And if this fantasy of overcoming our limits is no less a part of our rational nature than the limits themselves, then the process of succumbing to, overcoming, and then succumbing once again to that impulse to transcend our finitude promises to be unending.

As if to confirm this, Kant's own depiction of this primordial oscillation between the acceptance and rejection of finitude itself exemplifies it. On the one hand, his account of knowledge as finite or conditioned presents itself as giving us an assurance that we can have genuine knowledge of the way things are, and indeed of anything and everything knowable. On the other hand, in doing so, he projects a distinction between things as they appear to us and things in themselves, assigning the latter to a domain beyond our grasp; and he also projects an origin for the content of our concepts that precedes any of the distinctions imposed by the synthetic activity of the mind. In other words, Kant finds himself invoking a conception of reality as essentially beyond our grasp, to which the discriminations which supposedly make knowledge possible do not apply; and in so doing, he violates the very limits of knowledge that these invocations are intended to support—thereby succumbing to the very same tendency to deny our finitude that he wants to correct.

Can Nietzsche, unlike Kant, find a way of acknowledging the reality of that transgressive impulse and its intuition of beyondness, but without succumbing to it? Or must we see his deployment of the mythical duality of Apollo and Dionysus as just such a transgression, insofar as the figure of Dionysus appears to represent what—on Nietzsche's own Kantian and Schopenhauerian understanding—must be essentially beyond our representational grasp? If we are to understand Nietzsche's metaphysical vision at all, we cannot make do with Apollo alone (that way Socratic imbalance lies)—the reality and significance of Dionysus must be conveyed, and so must be represented, somehow; but any representation of him seems fated, simply by virtue of being a representation of the unrepresentable—to betray the insight it purports to convey.

There is, however, a difference between unwittingly betraying one's own insight, and a dramatic staging of that inevitable betrayal (one whose very theatricality is intended to invite acknowledgement of its nature). By recasting Schopenhauer's metaphysical vision of *The World as Will and Representation* (itself a recasting of Kant's vision of knowledge as a cursed marriage of concepts and intuitions) as a mythic drama of Apollo and Dionysus, Nietzsche underlines the non-literal status of his own discourse, and thereby problematizes the relation between such hyberbolically fictional figures and the reality they purportedly represent. He then reinforces the point by multiplying the ways in which Dionysus appears in his genealogical narrative—as if disarticulating or dismembering him: the god has so many different manifestations in *The Birth of Tragedy* that no particular one (whether religious, artistic, or metaphysical) can be taken as truly representing him. Rather, each is presented as one of his masks, and thus invites the inference that even this re-membering or re-presentation (construed as an attempt to identify what lies behind them all) can only amount to the construction of one more mask—one more inevitable failure to grasp the god himself. The book is, one might say, a mask composed of masks, or perhaps a masque of masks, the nature of whose constituent elements declares its own necessary distance from its object.

Dionysus is thus not one element in a Nietzschean master-narrative of Western culture presenting the work of Aeschylus, Wagner, Kant, and endless others as mere symptoms or instances of an underlying duality that has at last been captured in *The Birth of Tragedy*. Dionysus is primarily present in the elusive, dissonant rhythm or pulse—at once synchronic and diachronic—orchestrated by Nietzsche's animated collage or frieze of various attempts to represent him (and to deny him). Each is thereby disclosed as at once similar to and yet different from every other, both individual and typical, with strengths and limitations all of its own; hence each makes an indispensable contribution to the overall display. But neither any individual element nor some conjunction of them—not even their reincorporation into the larger representation that is *The Birth of Tragedy*—can constitute a complete or total image of Dionysus. It is rather in the book's ragged edges and internal seams, its overt refusal to cohere as a single, totalizing representation, and its openness to further insertions or extensions (a Frankenstein's monster of ecstatic scholarship), that its real attempt to present the god of the unrepresentable is to be found.

One might regard this as an attempt to acknowledge the centrality of the principle of individuation in any human attempt to grasp the essence of reality (given the inevitably structured, differentiating, and individuating nature of representation), while denying its absoluteness or self-sufficiency. The duality of Nietzsche's godhead is thus not so much the introduction of another deity into Apollo's temple, but rather an attempt to worship Apollo non-idolatrously—to acknowledge that we can only grasp reality in terms of some particular way of organizing it, but that any such way could never fuse with the reality it represents, and will inevitably be limited or conditioned by its organizing principles. So we cannot avoid committing ourselves to some such representation (or mode of representation); but we can allow that commitment to be informed by the awareness that—being possessed of limits—it will be open to supplementation, contestation, and displacement by other representations, each of which will itself be vulnerable to the same process of overcoming. And Dionysus does not lie behind any or all of these visions, but is rather dispersed between them—manifest in the recurring impulse to re-member him that generates such endlessly shifting family resemblances.

The Birth of Tragedy certainly questions the absoluteness of any principles of individuation at the disciplinary or cultural level, while acknowledging their necessity in some form or other. For its multiple metonymic structure problematizes prevailing conceptions of the distinctions between different art forms, between art and philosophy, and between art, politics, religion, science, and philosophy. A form of philosophical writing that thinks of itself as internally related to both Attic tragedy and Wagnerian opera, and of both these art forms as themselves internally related (as masks, displacements or transfigurations of one another), does not deny the differences between art and philosophy. It rather questions the prevailing ways of characterizing and evaluating those differences, and suggests rather different terms in which to conceive them. It thereby invites the culture as a whole to rethink the way in which it has conceived of metaphysics, art, politics, and religion as essentially autonomous enterprises, but again without denying their differences or suggesting that they should be regarded as an undifferentiated whole.

So Nietzsche doesn't dismiss his inheritance of metaphysical aspirations or responsibilities; he rather suggests that they be shouldered in rather different ways, even by philosophers, and in particular that the metaphysical project can only benefit from exploiting the fullest possible range of representational modes, while acknowledging the fatedness of any representational project, even a philosophical *Gesamtkunstwerk*, to partiality (call it particularity of perspective). This is why he presents his own metaphysical vision as the present culmination of the long genealogical narrative that is its dramatic content, a narrative in which prior visions endlessly engender variously inflected displacements or transfigurations of themselves, only to be transfigured in their turn.

The Birth of Tragedy is thus both a narrative of, and one more narrative in, an unending sequence of self-overcoming narratives, each revising the limits of its predecessors before being in turn revised, but all thereby amounting to versions of the same vision of human reality as a matter of endlessly constructing, transgressing, and reconstructing the limits of our present representations of reality. Nietzsche thereby declares the natality of his own vision (its otherness to absolute originality or self-origination), and foretells its future overcoming; and by thus indicating the conditions and limitations of his own work, as if underling the inevitable failure of its inevitably Apolline endeavour, he hopes to conjure the absent presence of Dionysus.

This suggests an interpretation of the genealogical sequence of texts that makes up Nietzsche's own body of writing. We might see each as a new mask of its author—one formed by critically evaluating its predecessor (call it a process of unmasking), which necessarily results in a new mask or remasking, one which exceeds or transgresses the form or structure of its predecessor without ever distinguishing itself absolutely from it. In this sense, the Nietzsche texts that follow *The Birth of Tragedy* might be thought of as a sequence of displacements or transfigurations of its tragic, dramatic myth of Western culture; so that, for example, one might wish to explore the dialectic of slave and master in *On the Genealogy of Morality* as a mask of the original duality of Apollo and Dionysus—each a metonym of the individual text that activates it and of the process of transition from each such text to the next in the unfolding sequence of Nietzsche's writing life (their mode of textual becoming).

And this line of thought further suggests that the conflictual complementarity of Apollo and Dionysus might be thought of as Nietzsche's first attempt to represent the dynamics of self-identity as a process of endless self-overcoming. From this perspective (call it perfectionist), Apollo stands for the self's need for individuation, for a stable outline or provisional structure of values and affects, and Dionysus stands for the self's impulse endlessly to overcome any such structure, even if necessarily in the name of another, as yet only prophetically grasped, restructuring of itself. And if this is a point of view on *The Birth of Tragedy* that only becomes available much later in the unfolding unmaskings and remaskings of the text by its author, and so amounts to a critical reconstruction or re-membering of it, then that is exactly what, from the point of view at issue, one would expect.

REFERENCES

Cavell, S. 1994. *A Pitch of Philosophy: Autobiographical Exercises* (Cambridge, MA: Harvard University Press).

Nietzsche, F. 1999. *The Birth of Tragedy*, Geuss, R. and Speirs, R. (eds.), Speirs, R. (trans.) (Cambridge: Cambridge University Press).

Silk, M. S. and Stern, J. P. 1981. *Nietzsche on Tragedy* (Cambridge: Cambridge University Press).

6

Nietzsche on the Aesthetics of Character and Virtue

Daniel Came

1

This essay addresses the question of the relation of aesthetic to ethical value in Nietzsche's early and later writings.[1] My central contention is that Nietzsche wanted to effect a *rapprochement* between aesthetics and ethics, to extend the structure of aesthetic judgment into the ethical domain, and, indeed, to effect the substitution of aesthetic for ethical concepts when dealing with such typically ethical domains as action, motivation, and character, and their adoption as the predominant terms in practical reasoning. The paper explores the development and transformations of this theme from its introduction in *The Birth of Tragedy* to Nietzsche's imperative in *The Gay Science* to give 'style' to one's character and thereby 'turn oneself into a work of art' (*GS*, 290). In particular I am interested in what is distinctive about Nietzsche's aestheticist approach to ethical questions, and in what respects, and to what degree, he extends the norms of aesthetic judgment and practice into the realm of ethical appraisal and practical reason.

2

'Aestheticism', in the sense that concerns me here, may be understood as a revisionist approach to ethics. Someone who wants to effect a *rapprochement* between ethics and aesthetics—assuming that he wishes to retain the core features of at least one of these kinds of judgment—may do so in a way that favours either the former or the latter. That is, he may wish to extend the structure of ethical

[1] I thank Christa Davis Acampora for comments on an earlier draft.

judgment (roughly as we now practise it) into the aesthetic domain; or, conversely, he may seek to change the way we make ethical judgments to bring them into line with modes of aesthetic valuation, to adjust the ethical/aesthetic borderline in favour of the latter domain.[2] This second strategy characterizes Nietzsche's position. The hallmark of Nietzsche's 'positive' ethics is a tendency to make ethical (-sounding) judgments that behave like aesthetic ones.

In opposition to those philosophers who would view ethical and aesthetic judgment as radically dissimilar systems of thought and feeling, the denial of a strict separation of the two kinds of judgment might be said to represent the workings of enlightened common sense on these matters. Works of art, including those which make no attempt at the realistic depiction of human life, are regularly subject to ethical assessment, and there is a lively debate as to the relevance of these evaluations to their aesthetic status.[3] Less obviously, conduct and character can be judged aesthetically—when we praise an action for its gracefulness, or a person for their wit or charm.

However, none of this is to say, with Wittgenstein, that 'ethics and aesthetics are one',[4] however that might be understood; for the above cases are exceptions to the rule in that they involve the ascription of what we feel to be aesthetic properties, such as charm or grace, to the typical subjects of ethical assessment, and vice versa. The two kinds of judgment are usually quite distinct: the zones of ambiguity and continuity are restricted, and the respects in which they differ—in their logic, their social function and their place in individual lives—are numerous.

But here, as elsewhere, the majority or mainstream mode of judgment is not everything. 'Assimilationist' (and 'separatist') accounts of ethics and aesthetics need not present themselves as schemata for ordinary evaluative practice. Someone might accept that the two kinds of judgment are usually distinct, and yet point out that boundaries in this area are not forever fixed by what most people accept, that within certain limits of intelligibility there is room for individuals and communities to negotiate the ethics/aesthetics divide on their own terms; and thus for arguments in favour of a revision in our ordinary practice.[5] Perhaps most

[2] Or, of course, he may pursue some combination of the two strategies. For simplicity's sake, we may say that an ethic is aestheticist *to the extent that* it imports features of aesthetic judgment into the ethical sphere, without seeking any general account of what balance of revisions is required for aestheticism *tout court*.

[3] For recent interventions in this perennial dispute, see, in defence of the aesthetic relevance of ethical judgments in the arts, Carroll (1996) and Gaut (1998); and in the opposite camp, Anderson and Dean (1998).

[4] *Tractatus Logico-Philosophicus*, Proposition 6.421.

[5] Compare in this respect the relation of ethical judgment to religious faith: 400 years ago, the common sense position may have been one of wholesale dependence of the former on the latter; the intellectuals of the Enlightenment made an ultimately successful case for the autonomy of the former, a situation which persists today; yet religious conservatives may still intelligibly call for a

of us do tend to keep our ethical and aesthetic faculties in separate boxes, and perhaps we do usually take the deliverances of the former more seriously; but, revisionists like Nietzsche will suggest, perhaps we shouldn't—either, on realist grounds, because this practice misrepresents the true nature of the respective values, or because it would be more rewarding, or just more interesting, or in some other pragmatic sense more valuable, to do things differently.

3

The idea that aesthetic and ethical value, the beautiful and the good, must in some deep sense be akin or even identical, may be traced back in Western philosophy at least as far as Plato. In the *Symposium*, Diotima makes the connection by means of her famous *scala amoris*. Love, *erōs*, takes as its immediate object 'giving birth in beauty' (206a–b).[6] Being the desire 'to possess the good forever', it naturally seeks satisfaction in an immortal object; and thus in procreation, since for mortal creatures such as ourselves, the nearest approach to immortality is through the creation of forms which will in turn propagate themselves *ad infinitum*. All men are thus, by divine dispensation, 'pregnant . . . both in body and soul' (206c).

Being divinely ordained, the ensuing 'birth' must come about by means that are 'harmonious with the divine'—that is, by means of the *beautiful*, so that beauty in others becomes the immediate object of erotic desire. At the lowest, bodily level, this desire is manifested in ordinary heterosexual love, whose aim is biological procreation, the continuance of the goods realized in a person's life in that of his offspring. But in some cases, the soul too is pregnant, and seeks to propagate itself in the form of lasting ideas about the good, in poetry and politics and philosophy, and in the flourishing of the souls of others.

This love too seeks beautiful occasions—first in the bodily beauty and charm of individual friends or *erōmenoi*, and then, ascending, to their beauty (that is, goodness) of soul, and thus to intellectual beauty in general as instantiated in good institutions and sciences; never at any time losing sight of its former objects, but rather forming an ever more general conception of them, until the lover is ready for the final revelation, that of 'the Beautiful itself, absolute, pure, unmixed,

reversion to the *status quo ante*. Some of the 'aesthetes' discussed below, most obviously Nietzsche in his more philhellenic moments, exhibit this kind of nostalgic-reactionary strain with respect to the supposedly more beauty-friendly ethic of the classical world.

[6] Plato (1997).

not polluted by human flesh or colours or any other great nonsense of mortality... the divine Beauty itself in its one form' (210e). Only in communion with this Form of the Beautiful (which, it is suggested, may be identical with the Form of the Good) can the philosophic soul give birth to ideas that are truly beautiful, and to traits (in itself and others) that are truly virtuous and good.

4

It might seem strange that a Platonist doctrine should have been invoked as part of a naturalizing account of virtue, but this does indeed seem to have been Nietzsche's intention. The Platonic equation of beauty with goodness, whereby (roughly speaking) the beautiful is the good as it features as the object of *erōs*, and may be predicated not only of sensible objects and bodies but also of the individual *psuche*, soul or character is reflected, for example, in Nietzsche's claim that a preference for higher or lower individuals 'is at bottom a question of taste and aesthetics' (*WP*, 353), and in his imperative to give 'style' to one's character and thereby 'turn oneself into a work of art' (*GS*, 290).

Indeed, for Nietzsche, the life-enhancing effects of beauty and the depressing effects of ugliness are such central and universal features of human nature as to provide our chief impetus towards the cultivation of virtue, as well as our strongest defence against life-denying pessimism: 'the sight of what is ugly makes one bad and gloomy' (*GS*, 290). As naturally self-reflective creatures, the ethical qualities brought most often and most vividly to our attention are our own, so that if an exalted pleasure is to be derived from the contemplation of virtue, and a depressing effect from surveying what is vicious, each of us has excellent reason to ensure that his own life and soul are in good ethical-aesthetic shape. Virtue therefore is both partly constituted by the capacity to feel this pleasure and, as one of the natural affections, it is one of the objects in which pleasure is found.

On Nietzsche's view of the person, as in the Platonic original,[7] the self or psyche is not a monadic unity, but is composed of several elements—the various instincts, drives, and passions—which may be more or less unified depending on their interrelations. These relations are determined by the relative proportions of

[7] See *Republic*, bk. IV. The correct relationship between the soul's three elements that is constitutive of justice and the other virtues is often described by Plato in terms that suggest its aesthetic appeal: 'once he [sc. the just man] has treated the three factors as if they were literally the three defining notes of an octave—low, high and middle—and has created a harmony out of them and however many notes there may be in between; once he has bound all the factors together and made himself a perfect unity instead of a plurality, self-disciplined and internally attuned: then and then only does he act' (Plato, 1998, 443d–e).

the parts, and by their conflict or harmony with one another (the degree to which the exercise or satisfaction of one frustrates the operations of another, and the affective by-products generated by such interference). Presumably, certain configurations of these elements will be simply pleasing in themselves, much as certain colours are. Furthermore, just as our tastes are gratified by certain compositional aspects of parts of the external world—a delicate musical cadence, the fine proportions of a statue—so our inner sense relays to the mind aspects of its own composition that please or displease.

5

The general picture here is clear: as self-conscious beings, each of us must endure the review of his own mind and actions just as much as that of his immediate surroundings, and the aesthetic sense is just as keen in its appraisal of the objects and relationships it finds within as it is of those in its environment. If the furniture of my house has the power to depress my spirits, then I have excellent eudaimonic reasons to change it if I can; likewise, if what I see of the furniture of my mind fills me with loathing and despair, I should require no further motivation towards reform.

But will this reform be ethical as well as aesthetic? That is to say, does an inwardly pleasing and harmonious character express itself in noble affect and action in respect of self and others? One might argue, as Shaftesbury did, for a strict correspondence between the two realms, between virtue and beauty of character:[8] On this view, a mind is beautiful to the extent that it embodies virtue, and ugly or deformed just insofar as it displays vice. We should thus understand 'virtue' and 'ethical beauty' as names for the very same property, meaning that ethical and aesthetic evaluations of character are exactly isomorphic, and that questions concerning the good life could be viewed under either an ethical or an aesthetic aspect.

On this view, the aesthetic aspects of the good life are intimately bound up with their ethical correlates. An aestheticist like Nietzsche, by contrast, requires no such connection. His is an 'immoralist' doctrine that proposes an outright replacement of traditional morality, seeking to devote himself exclusively, not necessarily to aesthetic goals, but to practical-existential criteria which are best served by aesthetic devices, and to regard all conventional normative considerations as potentially matters of indifference, suspicion, or magnificent contempt.

[8] Shaftesbury's favoured term for that in which ethical beauty resides is 'mind', although on occasion he also uses 'soul', 'temper', or 'character', and often simply speaks of the 'inward constitution' or of what is 'within', in opposition to 'outward' bodily features. 'Beauty' is his catch-all term for whatever qualities of mind are aesthetically desirable, but he clearly does not regard it as a monolithic property without sub-types, any more than 'virtue' names a single, unitary state of character, as opposed to picking out any of a number of quite diverse forms of goodness.

6

Nietzsche's attempt to redraw the boundaries between aesthetics and ethics is part of his general aesthetic approach to life, inaugurated in *The Birth of Tragedy*, a work that is framed by two of Nietzsche's most famous, and most perplexing, pronouncements concerning the ethics/aesthetics relationship. In his original 'Foreword to Richard Wagner', Nietzsche informs us that 'art is the highest task and real metaphysical activity of this life' (*BT*, 17, 18); a remark somewhat amplified in the brilliant 'Attempt at a Self Criticism', with which he prefaced the 1886 edition of *The Birth of Tragedy*: 'art—and not morality—is... the real metaphysical activity of man' (*BT*, 8). The work closes with a reiteration of the claim, originally canvassed early on, that 'existence and the world appear justified only as an aesthetic phenomenon' (*BT*, 5, cf. 25).

Regarding the first remark, it is clear from the original context that Nietzsche chiefly intends it as a rebuttal of those who have little respect for aesthetic activity and experience, who 'see in art nothing more than an amusing sideshow, a readily dispensable tinkling of bells to accompany the seriousness of existence' (*BT*, 'Foreword'). For such people, art could hardly have the function that he wishes to ascribe to it in *The Birth of Tragedy*—that of transforming and sustaining an entire culture's sense of itself in relation to the world, of calibrating its members' various impulses so as to enable them to achieve both individual fulfilment and authentic political community.

This role, 'metaphysical' in the sense that it facilitates man's most general understanding of the world and his place in it, found its paradigm in the culture of the early Attic tragedies. The works of Aeschylus and Sophocles, if Nietzsche is to be believed, effect a unique synthesis of the two elements in human nature and experience that he labels 'Apollonian' and 'Dionysian': the first joyful and serene, associated with beauty, formal clarity, moderation, and the life of the individual, the second ecstatic and frenzied, linked to barbarity, chaos, excess, and the blending of persons into the 'mysterious primordial Unity' (*das Ur-Eine*) (*BT*, 1).[9]

The precise origin of these drives is not clear. At some points, it appears that Dionysus alone represents raw nature, the terrible reality against which Apollo stands for 'mere appearance', a fragile human construct built upon a 'hidden substratum of suffering and knowledge' (*BT*, 4); at other times, both seem to 'burst forth from nature itself, without the mediation of the human artist' (*BT*, 2).

[9] Nietzsche's Dionysus and Apollo ostensibly correspond to the Schopenhauerian metaphysics of 'Will' and 'representation', in which the world appears both as raw primal unity (Will) and, in its phenomenal aspect, as a realm of individuated things (representation). Behind this, of course, lies Kant's noumenon/phenomenon distinction.

Whatever their source, both urges find expression in the arts, the Apollonian in sculpture and epic poetry, the Dionysian in music and lyric poetry. Tragedy unites the two poetic forms, in the pleasing imagery of the stage and the fluid unity of the chorus respectively.[10] Each consoles the spectator for the incompleteness of the other: Apollo with the emergence of formal beauty out of the 'fearful swirling compulsive process of annihilation' (*BT*, 7), Dionysus with the promise that behind all the barriers of culture 'life is indestructibly powerful and pleasurable' (*BT*, 7). From this 'metaphysical comfort' emerges a 'pessimism of strength', the capacity to accept the full reality of suffering, including one's own, and yet to rejoice in life.

The ethical aspect of all this emerges when Nietzsche turns to what he saw as the nemesis of Attic tragedy: the philosophical discourse of Socrates. The 'noble' Greeks, schooled in tragic acceptance of their terrible heroic world, required neither explanations of why things were as they were, nor explicit justifications for acting as they did. This unquestioning confidence in the order of things eventually eroded, however, and the result was the 'anti-Dionysian' art of Euripidean tragedy and Socratic dialectic.

Socrates, constitutionally unable to experience the Dionysian communion that bound his fellow citizens to one another, looked upon contemporary life and its apotheosis in tragic theatre and saw 'something utterly unreasonable, where causes appear to lack effects and effects appear to lack causes; and moreover the whole so colourful and diverse that it could only repel a balanced constitution' (*BT*, 14). In place of their fatalism he demanded reasons, an intelligible accounting for facts and actions—a demand which proved lethal to a culture utterly reliant on mysticism and instinct.[11] Out of its demise were born the realism of Euripidean (and modern) drama, and the reductive rationalism of Western philosophy.

The Athenians 'justified' their world aesthetically, by finding beauty and energy even in its most terrible depredations;[12] we moderns, the heirs of Socrates, can accept only reasoned justifications, typified by the empirical generalizations of science and the universal norms of morality. But it seems that we are wrong, and they were right: rationalism in art and in ethics is doomed to fail even on its

[10] This division is not quite accurate: Sophoclean tragedy is always, for Nietzsche, more the creation of Dionysus than of Apollo. Even the 'Apollonian dream-world of the stage' emerges directly out of, and is but a mask for, the 'terrifying inner world' of the Dionysian (*BT*, 9).

[11] See Havas (2002) for a somewhat Wittgensteinian exposition of this contrast between tragic rule-following and Socratic reason-giving.

[12] As Richard Schacht points out, this is the respect in which, in Nietzsche's words, it is always 'art's metaphysical intention to transfigure' (*BT*, 24), that is, to alchemize the meaningless sufferings of mere natural 'existence' into the (aesthetically) magnificent struggle that is human 'life'. See Schacht (1977). See also the essay by A. E. Denham in this volume.

own terms, and only an aestheticized conception of life can ultimately reconcile us to the conditions of our existence.

Here, then, is the philosophical core of *The Birth of Tragedy*, which shares with Nietzsche's later position, as we shall see, an attempt to supplant the Judaeo-Christian moral mode of evaluation with an aesthetic one. It goes beyond it in two key respects, however: first, the focus of aesthetic attention is deeper, from human lives and experiences to the whole of 'existence and the world'; and second, the range of targets is broader, taking in not just traditional morality, but with it the very idea of rationality, and the whole spectrum of practices that depend on it.

For both the early and later Nietzsche, in the throes of Schopenhauerian pessimism, the dreadful aspects of both the human and natural worlds call for something like a theodicy—some mode of 'justification' that would allow the troubled soul to accept its place in them.[13] The cult of intelligibility embodied in morals, in science, in contemporary philosophy and realistic art, fails to offer such a justification.[14] The consolations of Apollo and Dionysus, by which we are enabled to view the world as we do the objects of our aesthetic attention, with serene detachment or self-negating bliss, provide the only viable alternative. The individual agent resembles the artist, not so much as author of his own life, but more as one who surrenders himself to creative impulses that transcend and transfigure him. He cannot be a work of art in his own right, but he can try to see himself as a single figure making its contribution to the all-encompassing *Gesamtkunstwerk* that is the tragic world.

7

According to Alexander Nehamas's influential reading of Nietzsche's mature philosophy, a version of this tendency to view life and the world as a work of art survives as a dominant influence on his later work. This view, says Nehamas, is one by which Nietzsche

> looks at the world in general ... as if it were a literary text ... he arrives at many of his views of the world and the things within it, including his views of human beings, by generalising to them ideas that apply almost intuitively to the literary situation, to the creation and interpretation of literary texts and characters.
>
> (Nehamas, 1985, 3)

This 'overarching metaphor' (164) of the literary text informs, we are told, such diverse doctrines as: the 'will to power' (construed as a theory of substance and causation whereby objects, much like literary characters, exist only as complex

[13] For a fuller discussion of this theme, see Came (2005; 2013).
[14] I discuss Nietzsche's critique of Socratic rationalism at length in Came (2004).

bundles of interdefined properties, no one more 'essential' than any other, so that their apparent possession of causal efficacy in their own right is but an illusion); the 'eternal recurrence' (understood not as a piece of a priori cosmology, but as the view that because we are—again like literary characters—simply the sum of our experiences and actions, one can only will a change in one's past at the cost of willing one's own non-being, so that our lives must be 'justified' *in toto* or not at all); and 'perspectivism' (a methodological pluralism resulting from the view that the world 'can be interpreted equally well in vastly different and deeply incompatible ways' (99), a feature it shares—or so says Nehamas—with literary texts).

Nehamas has been criticized[15] (rightly in my view) for the extravagance of his central claim, given the paucity of direct textual evidence for it. The claim that the later Nietzsche saw the whole world as a literary work, and viewed individual inhabitants merely as characters subservient to some greater 'text', seems too close to *The Birth of Tragedy*'s conception of nature itself as a work of art shaped by creative forces that transcend the human, and thus to extend the anti-individualism of that early work beyond actual lifespan. It also relies very heavily on an exclusively literary model, a reliance which sits ill with Nietzsche's enthusiasm for, and frequent allusions to, the plastic and performing arts. Nevertheless, if we put aside his overall theoretical apparatus, many of Nehamas's most valuable insights can be preserved in the framework of a less single-minded aestheticism that may be found in Nietzsche's later works.

8

One important theme with obvious artistic analogues is that of *creativity*. Once dubiously located in the 'primordial Unity', creativity has, by this later period, come back within the sphere of human culture, but it remains the one source of hope that the world might be redeemed for (at least some of) its inhabitants. This need for redemption has also been reassigned to a human origin. It is no longer the well of pain at the heart of things (the mature Nietzsche had ceased to believe in a 'heart of things'), but the insufferable mediocrity and lifelessness of our civilisation, from which mankind needs to be relieved; the symptom has become the disease. Here is a typically hyperbolical passage from *Thus Spoke Zarathustra*:

> I call it the state where everyone, good and bad, is a poison-drinker: the state where everyone, good and bad, loses himself: the state where universal slow suicide is called—life. Just look at these superfluous people! They steal for themselves the works of inventors and the treasures of the wise: they call their theft culture—and they turn everything to sickness and calamity...

[15] For example in Leiter (1992).

> Only where the state ceases, does the man who is not superfluous begin: does the song of the necessary man, the unique and irreplaceable melody, begin.
>
> (*Z*, I, 11)

The *Übermensch* of *Zarathustra* is one of a series of ideal types that permeates Nietzsche's writing, beginning with the noble Hellene of *The Birth of Tragedy*, and developing into the 'higher man' of the mature philosophy. As Philippa Foot (1973) has pointed out, the reasons we are given for preferring these higher individuals to the 'herd' are chiefly aesthetic ones, albeit of a quite sophisticated kind.

The masses, the 'many-too-many', are not just 'poison-drinkers', 'apes', dwellers in 'the mud and the abyss'; they are mere imitators. They are proud of their 'culture', as if it were their own creation, but it is not: it has been created by others, by real 'inventors', and merely appropriated by them for their own petty purposes. Even the state, the 'new idol' which they venerate, was not invented by them but *for* them, in order to 'lure them' out of their condition as a 'people' and turn them into a 'state', by those who are both creators and, just as potently, 'destroyers', iconoclasts.

Compared with the superfluous, the higher man has the great aesthetic virtue of *originality*: he is 'solitary', his 'song' is 'unique'—and it is uniquely his, for he possesses 'greatness, that is to say, creativeness' (ibid.). It is 'necessary' precisely because it has the gratuitousness of true art, born not in the vulgar 'marketplace' of practical life, but in self-imposed seclusion of spiritual inwardness.

What, in his 'creativeness', does this splendid individual create? The most obvious answer is, 'himself'. This is to an extent right: the higher men are those who, in the words of section 335 of *The Gay Science*, 'are new, unique, incomparable, who give themselves laws, who create themselves'. But in fact the originality of the higher man goes further yet, extending beyond mere self-creation, and into the domain of value itself.

Here is another very typical passage, this time with a more explicit stress on creativity:

> Evaluation is creation: hear it, you creative men! Valuating is itself the value and jewel of all valued things.
>
> Only through evaluation is there value: and without evaluation the nut of existence would be hollow. Hear it, you creative men!
>
> A change in values—that means a change in the creators of values. He who has to be creator always has to destroy.
>
> (*Z*, I, 15)

Over and above the process of self-creation, the higher man is urged to exercise what we may call (although Nietzsche would not) *ethical creativity*.[16] It is not merely the lives and souls of the superfluous that are awry, but the very values they have been given and adhere to. For the creators of those values—and under the latter heading Nietzsche certainly means to include the norms of conduct, routes of feeling, and ideals of character that constitute what he understands by 'morality'—Zarathustra reserves a certain horrified respect for fellow artists, albeit of a peculiarly degenerate school, who have produced 'a device of Hell . . . a horse of death jingling with the trappings of divine honours'.

By contrast, he whose life tends towards the *Übermensch*, in creating himself, becomes the creator of the very values he lives by. He invents himself by rejecting, through sheer force of will, the values of the many, and then—much more difficult—by finding the values by which he as an individual may flourish, and living up to them.[17] And if someone can really manage this, he thereby creates a new domain of good and evil: for the individual, the 'Ego', now has the power, once reserved for whole 'peoples', to turn 'whatever causes it to rule and conquer and glitter, to the dread and envy of its neighbour' into 'the sublimest, the paramount, the evaluation and meaning of things' (*Z*, I, 15). But in creating new values, he undermines those that he initially rejected. Many powerful acts of ethical creativity will destroy those old values, the values once constitutive of 'morality' itself, altogether.[18]

Nehamas is surely right to see an artistic, if not necessarily a literary, model at work here (Nehamas 1985: 225–34). In Nietzsche's ethical universe, creativity operates much as it does in the more familiar world of the arts, where an individual artist who rejects the prevailing conventions and produces an original and successful work thereby creates a new set of standards, new criteria for aesthetic excellence and deficiency, which others must take account of.[19]

Furthermore, to the extent that his success arises from the deliberate disavowal of some artistic norm, the authority of that norm may be weakened. If others, inspired by his example but not imitating him slavishly, also succeed while rejecting that

[16] I employ this label merely as a less cumbersome alternative to 'evaluative creativity', etc., and not in order to prejudge the issue of whether Nietzsche is really rejecting morality *tout court* or merely offering us a route to a new one.

[17] See the 'three metamorphoses' of the spirit into camel, lion, and child: *Z*, I, 1.

[18] Cf. *Z*, I, 34: he who has the power to be a creator in good and evil, truly, has first to be a destroyer and break values. Thus the greatest evil belongs with the greatest good: this, however, is the creative good . . . And let everything that can break upon our truths—break! There is many a house to build!'

[19] Compare Kant's definition of genius as 'the talent . . . which gives the rule to art': works of genius must 'be models, i.e. be *exemplary*; and, consequently, though not themselves derived from imitation, they must serve that purpose for others' (Kant, 1952, §46).

standard, it will be gradually discredited, until the whole style of art whose practices it codified ceases to be available to us and becomes part of 'cultural history'.

The adoption of this model gives Nietzsche the balance he wants between normativity and individualism. On the one hand, part of what appals him about morality as such is its eagerness to 'level down', to co-opt even the greatest on the same terms as the most spiritually stunted. On the other hand, he has no wish to get rid of value altogether, and realizes that there cannot be values without some degree of interpersonal constraint, operating even on great men. Ethical creativity provides the solution. In a creative practice, the standards set by successful practitioners constrain the activities of others—unless they are themselves imaginative enough to find original ways to get around them, thereby creating new standards for yet others to reckon with, and so on indefinitely. In such a practice, unlike the ethical life as we are familiar with it, rules *are* made to be broken: every success represents a challenge, not so much to emulation as to creative transgression. One is bound by the prevailing norms in inverse proportion to the strength and depth of one's imagination, a conclusion with which Nietzsche should be well satisfied.

The theme of creativity as applied to value is given its fullest development in certain passages in *Beyond Good and Evil.* In this later work, the *übermenschlich* types have become, among other things, the 'new philosophers', who will bring a fresh hope and danger to scholarship as well as to mankind at large. These new philosophers are on no account to be confused with mere 'philosophical workers' who only 'fix and formalize some great existing body of valuations', without contributing anything that is truly their own. The philosophers proper, on the other hand, break free of these norms, however well codified, in order to forge new ones:

> they say: 'Thus it *shall* be!' it is they who determine the Wherefore and Whither of mankind... they reach for the future with creative hand, and everything that is or has been becomes for them a means, an instrument, a hammer. Their 'knowing' is *creating*, their creating is a law-giving, their will to truth is—*will to power.*
>
> (BGE, 211)

Their relationship to their lesser brethren is that of artist to critic; but while every artist must to some extent be a critic, no mere critic is an artist. The new philosophers must possess 'critical discipline, and every habit that conduces to purity and rigour in intellectual matters', much as artists must hone their critical faculties in order to sustain the quality of their work; for 'the critic is the instrument of the philosopher' (*BGE*, 210). But the philosophical worker knows nothing of the facility and daring of the creator, 'that genuinely philosophical combination of a bold exuberant spirituality which runs *presto* and a dialectic severity and necessity which never takes a false step... something easy, divine, and a closest relation of high spirits and the dance'. The mere scholar, who labours under the intellectual yoke of values not of his own making, feels himself thereby constrained, unfree, subject to an external power that he experiences as arbitrary even while he submits to its authority. But the creative moralist, whose values are internal and original to the work that he creates, knows their authority as a 'feeling of freedom, subtlety, fullness of power, creative placing, disposing, shaping': to the artist alone belongs the autonomy of the Kantian subject, for whom 'necessity and 'freedom of will' are ... one' (*BGE*, 213).

9

If what I have said so far is right, Nietzsche saw the individual *qua* agent as an artist, and *qua* bearer of a character and a life as a work of art; but he also saw that this view, if combined with anything like the Romantic conception of the artist, must indeed lead one to embrace a quite different mode of evaluation, and a different understanding of the moral history of mankind.

If in our daily lives we really are something like artists and works of art, then the business of living and of being 'good' or 'noble' will be a creative practice, one whose rules and aims are not fixed in advance, but are subject to alteration, expansion, and wholesale reinvention by determined and imaginative individuals. Those who lack the requisite talents may achieve a sort of secondary goodness, like that of an amateur artist, by conscientiously following the rules by which others have succeeded; but genuine greatness will be different in kind, something available only to a few, not by obedience to any preordained system of rules, but by the selective contravention of existing canons and the invention of new ones.

To assess the continuing health of the practice, one should look not for a general conformity to familiar ethical norms, but for singular transgressions against conventional morality which nevertheless draw our admiration. The very idea of a 'common morality' must be rejected as expressing a cult of the mediocre, and replaced with a discourse of authenticity and originality exalting just what is uncommon, unexpected, revelatory.

With respect to the aesthete's substantive ethical views, the introduction of aesthetic or artistic values into the sphere of ethics may make remarkably little difference—especially if he allows the application of those values to be determined by his moral intuitions, so that there is little possibility of conflict between the two.

On the other hand, a strong sense of spiritual or biographical beauty may bring to view a supplementary realm of values which are quite autonomous *vis-à-vis* morality, and which compete with it for our allegiance. Or, again, a full-blooded aesthetics of character may engender suspicion or outright hostility towards the ideals morality offers, as expressions of a style of valuation now in its degeneracy.

Nietzsche's aestheticism falls into the latter category, and it is in this connection that his attempt to redraw the boundaries between aesthetics and ethics in the name of an 'aesthetic approach to life' slides into his immoralism.

10

In *The Picture of Dorian Gray*, Oscar Wilde touches on a deep contradiction within the aestheticist approach to character and virtue. Dorian lives a beautiful life: one that is rich, varied, delightful, graceful, passionate, and possessed of its own curious integrity. And the wake of ruined lives that he leaves behind him does nothing to lessen the splendour of his own. The story of a person's life can embody aesthetic excellence even when he himself displays the worst moral vices. He whose exclusive aim is to make himself or his life into a work of art attempts a separation between subject matter and execution that leaves him without any apparent reason to be good. The portrait can be magnificent, although its subject is demonic.

For someone like Wilde, an instinctive aesthete who tried also to be good, something not dissimilar to conventional moral rectitude ought to be available within the terms of aestheticism, as a natural consequence not of ascetic self-denial but of beauty in action. But the possibility, realized in Dorian, of a life which is beautiful while at the same time depraved, casts doubt on that prospect. Admittedly, his crimes are productive of great ugliness; but it is his soul, and not his 'life', as the nineteenth-century aesthetic movement understood that term, that he defaces.

In fiction, souls can be as real as we want them to be; but if they are absent from the scientifically respectable world of the nineteenth (or twenty-first) century, how can aestheticism offer a defence against the extremes of immorality which some might use as a means to realize their conception of the beautiful?

This kind of problem arises in relation to Nietzsche's aestheticism, which seems to advocate purely formal aesthetic criteria. If Nietzsche's criteria are purely formal, then there seems to be nothing in his evaluative scheme that precludes a morally repugnant character being deemed praiseworthy. The worry is that Nietzsche's conception of the ideal self is so inclusive as to encompass individuals who are morally repugnant. Indeed, if Nietzsche is commending to us a way of living or a type of character on what appear to be purely aesthetic grounds, then this consequence seems inescapable. Nehamas articulates the problem as follows:

> Nietzsche's emphasis on the aesthetic organizational features of people's lives and characters... brings out a difficulty... that attends [his aesthetic model]. This involves what one may feel compelled to consider a moral dimension. A literary character... may be a perfect character but represent a dreadful person... The uncomfortable feeling exists that someone might achieve Nietzsche's ideal life and still be nothing short of repugnant.
>
> (Nehamas, 1985, 165–7)

It might seem that this objection mistakenly presupposes that Nietzsche is seeking to impose his own idiosyncratic conception of the ideal life or perfect character. This is clearly not the case, but the worry nevertheless remains that if the perfect character is to be specified in purely aesthetic or organizational terms, then it would appear that these terms license the admiration of a monstrous character.

That is not to deny that Nietzsche endorses certain substantive or contentful traits of character that it would not be inappropriate to describe as Nietzschean virtues (e.g., self-mastery, honesty, creativity, politeness, health, courage). But none of these qualities in itself seems sufficient to preclude the extremes of immorality. Nietzsche does not explicitly link his conception of nobility with immoralism. But he is very clear that an honest appraisal of our situation is such that our conduct is never really constrained by moral principles of any kind, and that to suppose that there are external norms or constraints that absolutely prohibit certain actions is to fall into a kind of inauthenticity. Further, given Nietzsche's view that we have a natural instinctual drive to want to hurt others, to take pleasure in the suffering of others, and to oppress those weaker than ourselves, it is difficult to see how the recognition of the non-binding nature of moral norms could remain mere recognition and not lead also to the indulgence of these natural propensities.

In a certain sense, however, the demand for interpersonal norms to be derivable from Nietzsche's aestheticism is to misunderstand the nature of that project as Nietzsche envisages it. As Foot remarks, 'for an artist, rules would indeed be beside the point: the goodness of what he or she makes cannot be the same as the goodness of other artists' work, as if there could be a manual for producing what is good' (Foot, 1994, 6).

The appeal to an 'artistic plan', then, seems to entail an absence of rules given in advance, and it is in this connection that Nietzsche emphasizes that genuine virtue is created by the agent himself, and is elevated to the status of virtue through the individual's investing value in a particular quality or trait of personality. But while such metaphors may enable us to get a handle on at least the structure of a fully realized human life, it does seem to follow from this that a Nietzschean normative ethics is impossible, on the grounds that Nietzsche's understanding of ethical choice and value precludes advocating any particular choices and values.

If a normative theory is understood as a set of principles dictating in advance how one should act in any situation, then Nietzsche cannot (and would not want to) provide one. If Nietzsche's notion of self-artistry is to furnish a practical ethics, this will be on the basis of a notion Nietzsche sketches of the individual engaged in solitary self-cultivation, to the relative exclusion of concern for 'the other'.

Nehamas, as we have seen, would want to argue that the measure of a good or noble life in Nietzsche's work lies in the integrity of a narrative, that to be a self is to constitute a story in which a kind of wholeness prevails. But even interpreted narratively, then, the norm of style remains a purely formal one, and so one cannot tell who is good or noble in Nietzsche's sense by looking at the *content* of their lives. Accordingly, the Nietzschean self may indeed turn immoralist, if he feels that the 'moral' life suppresses traits that are necessary for progress in the art of living.

References

Anderson, J. and Dean, J. 1998. 'Moderate Autonomism', in *British Journal of Aesthetics*, 38/2: 150–66.

Came, D. 2004. 'Nietzsche's Attempt at a Self-Criticism, *Nietzsche-Studien*, 33: 37–67.

Came, D. 2005. 'The Aesthetic Justification of Existence', Ansell-Pearson, K. (ed.), *A Companion to Nietzsche* (London: Blackwells Publishing): 41–57.

Came, D. 2013. 'The Themes of Affirmation and Illusion in *The Birth of Tragedy* and Beyond', in Richardson, J. and Gemes, K. (eds.), *The Oxford Handbook of Nietzsche* (Oxford: Oxford University Press): 209–24.

Carroll, N. 1996. 'Moderate Moralism', *British Journal of Aesthetics*, 36/3: 223–38.

Foot, P. 1973. 'Nietzsche: The Revaluation of Values', in Solomon, R. (ed.), *Nietzsche: A Collection of Critical Essays* (Garden City, NY: Anchor Books): 156–68.

Foot, P. 1994. 'Nietzsche's Immoralism', in Schacht, R. (ed.), *Nietzsche, Genealogy, Morality: Essays on Nietzsche's* 'On the Genealogy of Morals' (Berkeley: University of California Press): 3–13.

Gaut, B. 1998. 'The Ethical Criticism of Art', in Levinson, J. (ed.), *Aesthetics and Ethics* (Cambridge: Cambridge University Press): 183–203.

Havas, R. 2002. 'Socratism and the Question of Aesthetic Justification', in Kemal, S. Gaskell, I. and Conway, D. (eds.), *Nietzsche, Philosophy, and the Arts* (Cambridge: Cambridge University Press): 92–127.

Kant, I. 1952. *The Critique of Judgment*, Meredith, J. (trans.) (Oxford: Clarendon Press).

Leiter, B. 1992. 'Nietzsche and Aestheticism', *Journal of the History of Philosophy*, 30/2: 275–90.

Nehamas, A. 1985. *Nietzsche: Life as Literature* (Cambridge, MA: Harvard University Press).

Nietzsche, F. 1971. *The Birth of Tragedy*, Kaufmann, W. (trans.) (New York: Vintage).

Nietzsche, F. 1978. *Thus Spoke Zarathustra*, Kaufmann, W. (trans.) (Harmondsworth: Penguin).

Nietzsche, F. 1990. *Beyond Good and Evil*, Hollingdale, R. (trans.) (Harmondsworth: Penguin).

Plato. 1997. *Symposium*, Nehamas, A. and Woodruff, P. (trans.), in Cooper, J. (ed.), *Plato: Complete Works* (Indianapolis: Hackett).

Plato. 1998. *Republic*, Waterfield, R. (trans.) (Oxford: Oxford University Press).

Schacht, R. 1977. 'Making Life Worth Living', in Sclafani, R. and Dickie, G. (eds.), *Art and Aesthetics: Theories and Critiques* (New York: St. Martin's Press).

Shaftesbury, A. A. C., Third Earl of. 1999. *Characteristics of Men, Manners, Opinions, Times*, Klein, L. E. (ed.) (Cambridge: Cambridge University Press).

Wilde, O. 2002. *The Picture of Dorian Grey* (London: Wordsworth Classics).

7

Zarathustra vs. Faust, or Anti-Romantic Rivalry among Superhumans

Adrian Del Caro

The question 'What is romantic?' is of relatively little interest to philosophers, but of keen interest to German intellectuals and students of German intellectual history broadly conceived. The debate over classical versus romantic is a major fault line of the modern psyche, helped to prominence by Nietzsche's elevation of the Apollonian/Dionysian dichotomy, then by his career-long insistence that he had invented a new 'Dionysian classicism' in keeping with his 'anti-romantic self-treatment'. Goethe elevated the classical disposition at the expense of the romantic, regardless of how romantic he himself appears in the history of aesthetics, and his stance was adopted by Nietzsche, infused with Dionysian energy and rechristened 'the Dionysian'. In terms of life-affirmation, Germany's two leading figures far and away are Goethe and Nietzsche, a fact borne out by their respective masterpieces *Faust* and *Thus Spoke Zarathustra*. On the world stage the heroes of these works compete beyond good and evil for the honor of 'most life-affirming', each modelling a modernist (read: romantic[1]) vision of the fulfilled, consummated life, yet each

[1] The equation of modernity with romanticism comes as no surprise to any who explore Nietzsche's critique of Rousseau and Wagner, the two romantic figures who tower over all others and are consistently branded as moderns. Rousseau, for example, is referred to in *Twilight of the Idols* as 'this first modern man, idealist and scoundrel in *one* person' (Del Caro 1989, 107), while Wagner in *The Case of Wagner* is ridiculed as 'the Cagliostro of modernity' (Del Caro, 1989, 155). Nietzsche's published works and his notes contain frequent, pointed references to the proximity of romanticism and modernism on the basis of these two leading romantic figures (Del Caro, 1989, 14, 29, 107–9, 125, 155–6, 180). As for the literary and theoretical basis of the equation of modernity with romanticism, as it was conducted by the romantics themselves, see Ernst Behler (1993, 97–8, 103, 141, 300–1) and (1997, 69, 72, 79, 88, 279). Of special interest to the question of romanticism's

rejecting romanticism as a weak, pathological element suggestive of life-denial and nihilism. My essay treats *Zarathustra* as a conversation with Goethe's *Faust*, using the lens of anti-romanticism to distinguish between two modernist heroes. Nietzsche was fond of quoting *Faust* throughout his works, but increasingly he took issue with Faust as an exemplar of humanity, and with *Faust* as tragic material generally. A critical examination of these works approached from the standpoint of anti-romanticism reveals duelling versions of the *Übermensch*, the first literally proposed by Goethe in the context of the earth spirit, the latter posited as an alternative by Nietzsche, who elevated the *Übermensch*-concept to 'the meaning of the earth'.

The theoretical baseline for Nietzsche's lexicon on romanticism stems from Goethe, based on his example as a human being and his own words as spoken to Eckermann:

> The classical I call the healthy, and the romantic the ill. Accordingly the *Nibelungs* are classic like Homer, for both are healthy and hearty. Most of what is modern is not romantic because it is new, but because it is weak, sickly and ill, and what is ancient is not classical because it is ancient, but because it is strong, fresh, cheerful and healthy.
>
> (Eckermann, 1959, 253)

Nietzsche called Eckermann's *Conversations With Goethe* 'the best German book' (*HH*, 'Wanderer', 109), and although he also gave this distinction to Luther's translation of the bible (*BGE*, 247), it is safe to conclude that Nietzsche was serious in elevating the wisdom of Goethe's old age.[2]

What is curious, however, is that Nietzsche did not directly acknowledge Goethe's formulation of classical and romantic (Del Caro, 1989, 92–3), even though his own discussions of romanticism constantly draw on the Goethean juxtaposition (Del Caro, 1989, 40, 60, 77–8, 86, 97). The theoretical opposition of healthy sensuality of strength versus a more or less narcissistic sensuality of weakness generally features Goethe at the expense of Wagner, and eventually the word 'classic' becomes almost synonymous with strength (Politycki, 1989, 281,

contribution to the construction of a modern psyche, Behler observes that Nietzsche's influence was first established in the realm of literature and art, and only migrated to philosophy in the second half of the twentieth century: 'Nietzsche's extraordinary primacy in European intellectual life of the pre-war years was grounded in literature and dealt with the imaginative power of fiction' (Behler, 1997, 279).

[2] All translations from the German are my own, with the exception of citations from *Zarathustra* and *Faust*, where the Cambridge and Norton editions (*Faust*, lines 1113–14, 1334–38, 1766–75), respectively are used. I have also substituted 'superhuman' for 'overman' or 'superman' throughout.

228). I draw attention here to Nietzsche's *silence* in the matter of Goethe's formulation of classical versus romantic, because we will have occasion to ponder this silence when it manifests in important related issues.

The word '*Übermensch*' has its debut, for modern purposes, in Goethe's *Urfaust* of the mid-1770s—the famous decade of *Sturm und Drang* in which Goethe and his peers were young men in their twenties, bombastically expressive, sensible, titanic, brimming with panegyric on Prometheus, and frequently depicting so-called *Kraftmenschen* (power humans) holding forth in *Kraftreden* (power speeches) in the dramas. This was the cultural and intellectual climate in which young Goethe depicted Faust in his study, rejecting the sign of the macrocosm, and longingly declaiming his ambition to grasp nature, to suckle from the breasts of life (*Faust*, l, 455–6). Faust is attracted by the sign of the macrocosm, but he rejects it: 'What a spectacle! But alas! a mere spectacle!' (*Faust*, I, 454). When he leafs to the sign of the earth spirit, he is immediately engaged and invigorated, claiming 'You, spirit of earth, are closer to me', and professing now 'I feel the courage to venture into the world,/To bear the pain and happiness of the earth' (*Faust*, I, 461, 464–5). When he conjures the earth spirit, however, it appears as reddish flame and is so hideous Faust cannot bear its sight, whereupon the earth spirit, apparently relishing Faust's discomfort, exclaims: 'Here I am!—What pitiful horror/Seizes you, superhuman! Where is your soul's call?' (*Faust*, I, 489–90). Although the earth spirit refers to Faust as a 'writhing worm' (*Faust*, I, 498), Faust makes two more attempts to establish a rapport, insisting he is 'a match' for the earth spirit (*deinesgleichen*, *Faust*, I, 499), and that he 'feels so close' to it (*Faust*, I, 511). To this the earth spirit utters its final word before disappearing, leaving Faust shattered: 'You resemble the spirit that you comprehend,/Not me!' (*Faust*, I, 512–13).

The first relevant point here is that Faust, behaving in a titanic storm and stress manner, is ridiculed as a 'superhuman' by the immensely humbling and sublime earth spirit. The second point is that 'superhuman' and 'earth spirit' constitute a juxtaposition; Faust is the state of the art human being, more than human, not satisfied to dwell on the macrocosm and its spectacle, but demanding a direct relationship with nature, with the sources of all life, and he is willing to bear the earth's pain and happiness. This titanic mood extends to his wager with Mephistopheles, such that the ever-striving Faust continues to behave like a superhuman, and what is more, he believes the earth spirit, the 'spirit of deeds' (*Faust*, I, 511), has sent him Mephistopheles as a helper (*Faust*, I, 3217–19, 3244–50). Faust does not feel himself empowered by Mephistopheles, but first of all by the earth spirit, which he continues to believe is closely related to him by virtue of his superhuman striving, whose point of departure is his blasphemous and earth-affirming retranslation of the Gospel of John: 'In the beginning was the Deed!'

(*Faust*, I, 1237). The linkage of 'superhuman' and 'earth' is therefore Goethe's invention. In terms of life-affirmation, Goethe was the first to suggest that humans will need to be superhuman in order to even remotely fathom the meaning of the earth, and only by embracing the earth in the courageous manner indicated by Faust will humans effectively make the transition from the realm of spirit (the macrocosm, the Word/logos, the absolute, the 'spectacle') to the more suitable but also more dangerous and deed-demanding realm of earth spirit.

Conspicuously, Nietzsche was silent on Goethe's use of the term '*Übermensch*', and although he quoted extensively from *Faust* throughout his writings, the only time he referred to the pivotal scene with the earth spirit[3] was in *The Birth of Tragedy*, where he used the earth spirit's words describing itself as 'an eternal sea,/a changeful weaving,/a glowing living' (*Faust*, I, 505–8) to describe Dionysian objectification in Apollonian appearances, similar to the music of the chorus (*BT*, 8). An unattributed quote of *Faust*, peripheral and oblique with respect to both the superhuman and the earth spirit's powerful motivation for Faust's striving—and complicating matters even further, Nietzsche became increasingly critical of Faust as a human being *and* as a tragic hero—as if determined to suppress Goethe's contribution in order to instate his own superhuman. To this day it is Nietzsche's usage of '*Übermensch*' that resonates with readers, and Nietzsche should be credited with popularizing the term, despite its first use in *Faust* (Politycki, 1989, 42). But as I and others have long pointed out, Nietzsche had a way of using sources and authors as masks, and in the case of Goethe in particular, his remarks are 'never fully free of tactical considerations' (Politycki, 1989, 181), and this insight we must extend also to his silence.

Notwithstanding the abundance of sources on which Nietzsche drew for his Zarathustra material, including Zoroaster, Christ, Socrates, Hölderlin's *Hyperion*, Bryon's *Manfred*, and so on, the initial impulse for Zarathustra's teaching maps very closely onto the beginning of Goethe's *Faust*. The scene is of course radically different, because Zarathustra is introduced to us not in a Gothic study crammed with books, but on a mountaintop; still, Zarathustra, like Faust, has reached a point of readiness and will now 'go down' into the world of human beings—he will engage just as Faust begins to engage, the one abandoning his cave, the other abandoning his study and his stale existence as an academic in favor of the sunlit world outside. As a starting point, both heroes also part company with religion, Zarathustra remarking to himself after his encounter with the mountain saint: '"Could it be possible! This old saint in his woods has not yet heard the news that

[3] However, one solid reference to the earth spirit is found in an unpublished note from autumn 1885–autumn 1886: *KSA*, 12, 69, fragment 2 [7].

God is dead!"' (*Z*, P, 2), Faust signalling his departure from God's tutelage by summoning the earth spirit, rewriting John to reflect *deed* in the beginning, and entering into a wager-based pact with Mephistopheles (*Faust*, I, 464–5, 1237, 1692–93). The auspices under which both heroes embark on their quests include denial of God, elevation of the human, and earthly affirmation that promises and purports to be transformative.

What Nietzsche and others ignore at their own peril is that Goethe in his *Faust* invented and then featured this 'earth spirit', a paradoxical concept, even oxymoronic insofar as *earth* and *spirit* do not readily combine.[4] Grammatically and perhaps logically as well, *Erde* is feminine,[5] while *Geist* is masculine, yielding an androgynous being, *der Erdgeist*, to whom Faust feels related and beholden, and by whom he feels empowered. In the earth-affirming context of Faust, it is not a matter of the soul's reconciliation with heaven, but of earth's reconciliation with itself (Kreis, 1995, 80), and Zarathustra has a similar motivation. He knows that the people have allowed God to die, or more dramatically, they have murdered God; what is to prevent them from killing the earth, Kreis asks, since murder of God and murder of the earth are for Zarathustra the complex of a single sacrilege (Kreis, 1995, 83)? Zarathustra so much as says so in the Prologue when he first utters the word '*Übermensch*':

> Behold, I teach you the superhuman!
>
> The superhuman is the meaning of the earth. Let your will say: the superhuman *shall be* the meaning of the earth!
>
> Once the sacrilege against God was the greatest sacrilege, but God died, and then all these desecrators died. Now to desecrate the earth is the most terrible thing, and to esteem the bowels of the unfathomable higher than the meaning of the earth!
>
> (*Z*, P, 3)

Whereas Goethe's Faust *is* a superhuman, in the estimation of the earth spirit and arguably in Faust's own estimation as well, since he claims kinship with and guidance from the earth spirit, Zarathustra 'more modestly' comes only to *teach* the superhuman, and thereby to teach the meaning of the earth. In both cases,

[4] Cf. Eudo Mason: 'One of the chief clues to the true point of the Erdgeist is its actual name, which we have become used to and take for granted, but which was calculated to disconcert Goethe's contemporaries. The metaphysical and emotional associations of the word "earth" (*Erde*) are very different from those of the word "world" (*Welt*), and this distinction is very strongly felt in the German language. The conception of a Spirit of Earth was novel, paradoxical and startling; it could not be seen as simply identical with that of the World Spirit' (1967, 149). See also the many arguments Mason provides for how the earth spirit is an opposite of the macrocosm which Faust rejects; the macrocosm is associated with the life of contemplation, while the earth spirit is clearly associated with the *vita activa* (1967, 124–6, 132, 135, 141–2).

[5] Cf. Gaia, Tellus, Mother Earth, Frau Welt.

however, it is clear that the superhuman represents a new type called for by the absence or disavowal of God, and by the impending vacuum of meaning for the earth. It would be disingenuous for Nietzsche's readers to ignore the previous modelling of the problem by Goethe, just as it would be disingenuous to suggest that Nietzsche did not wish to posit his own version of the superhuman as a rival of Goethe's.

Faust's affirmative achievements will be discussed first, and often enough on Nietzsche's terms, in order to demonstrate both the timeliness and relevant nature of Goethe's thought, as well as to argue that Nietzsche should have acknowledged this contribution instead of adopting a singularly critical stance vis-à-vis the Goethean project of earth-affirmation. Faust clearly sees himself as a man of deeds who rejects the realm of pure spirit and 'the word' in order to engage as fully and as superhumanly as possible with human beings and his environment. While Nietzsche speaks positively of Goethe himself as a free spirit who displayed an admirable emphasis on deeds, he does not carry over this admiration to Faust (Grundlehner, 1986, 156). Yet there is a fundamental affinity between Nietzsche and Goethe on this point, which reveals itself in Nietzsche's adoption of Goethe's Prometheus model from the 1774 poem 'Prometheus', both in *The Birth of Tragedy* and *Zarathustra*; the reason for highlighting this poem is because Prometheus represents the opposite of Schopenhauerian renunciation—Prometheus embodies the fighting spirit that denies *and* creates (Gooding-Williams, 2001, 238). It is simply expedient on Nietzsche's part when he ignores Faust as the 'great' Prometheus, the figure who outlived Goethe's *Sturm und Drang* period and accompanied him at every stage of his life, but elevated the mere poem instead. Faust's wager with Mephistopheles is far more consequential in terms of demonstrating human striving through the titanic spirit. Deeds are bound to emerge in the process of Faust's 'dynamic form of wager', in which the pact becomes 'the co-evolution of organism and environment, body and earth' (Kreis, 1995, 79).

Nietzsche does not tout Zarathustra as a great perpetrator of deeds, and he would be hard pressed to do so given that Zarathustra's 'work' appears to reside in his 'speaking'. But this did not prevent Nietzsche from claiming that *Zarathustra*, as a work, was the greatest *deed* in human history; his concept 'Dionysian' here became 'supreme deed', Goethe and Shakespeare would not be able to breathe for a moment in this 'tremendous passion and altitude' (*EH*, III, *Z*, 6). Goethe's engagement of the Dionysian, itself not insignificant, is ignored along with his invention of the earth spirit. Moreover, what are we to make of this self-referential elevation of 'the deed' of writing *Zarathustra*? There is a mirror relationship at work here; Nietzsche and *Zarathustra* represent writer and deed, while Goethe and *Faust* represent deed and writer. The meaning of this puzzle emerges only when we attribute greater value to the Dionysian as a concept, and infuse it with philosophical meaning as Nietzsche did. By this standard, Goethe and Shakespeare, even Dante for that matter, are mere poets, whereas *Zarathustra* the Nietzschean work is supreme Dionysian (read: philosophical) deed. Goethe—who poured his philosophical self into *Faust*, but never claimed for himself the mantle of philosophy—yields to Nietzsche who poured his philosophical self into *Zarathustra*, and *did indeed* claim the mantle of philosophy, albeit Dionysian philosophy. The extent to which this is a 'deed' remains open to question, especially in the context of Faust's explicit wager never to cease striving, and his explicit alignment with the earth spirit, the 'spirit of deeds'. Nietzsche's appropriation of the concept of the *Übermensch* extends to the repositioning of the earth as the locus of meaning, admittedly something he would have done even without Goethe's example, but it also includes his own version of 'the deed', and instates *Zarathustra* where he claims Faust to be lacking in deeds.

True to his origins in the period of *Sturm und Drang*, Faust is a man of intense *feeling* for whom the passions are existentially validating. Like his cousin Werther, who observed '[t]he things I know, anyone can know—but my heart is mine and mine alone' (9 May 1772), Faust sides with feeling over knowing, but there are important distinctions to be made. Faust has already mastered the realm of knowledge, first off, and he is in mid-life. More significantly, as the superhuman version of a romantic and suicidal Werther, as the anti-Werther if you will, Faust ups the ante on feeling and raises it to titanic proportions, claiming as part of his wager:

> Frenzy I choose, most agonizing lust,
> Enamored enmity, restorative disgust.
> Henceforth my soul, for knowledge sick no more,
> Against no kind of suffering shall be cautioned,
> And what to all of suffering mankind is apportioned
> I mean to savor in my own self's core,
> Grasp with my mind both highest and most low,
> Weigh down my spirit with their weal and woe,
> And thus my selfhood to their own distend,
> And be, as they are, shattered in the end.
>
> (*Faust*, I, 1766–75)

These words are not a mere boast, as they might be if Faust were locked within the 'power speeches' of the brief *Sturm und Drang*. Goethe depicts a Faust who, empowered by the earth spirit and assisted by Mephistopheles, physically embarks on the project embraced here—he sets out to experience in himself 'what to all of suffering mankind is apportioned', and this is the superhuman basis of his striving. A careful analysis of the semantic field here reveals that the condition or state for which Faust strives is in fact *Dionysian*, closely resembling the extremes of emotion, the suspension of the principle of individuation, the embrace of universal suffering, and the inevitable *shattering* (*zerscheitern*), so powerfully depicted by Nietzsche in *The Birth of Tragedy*. Faust is the ultimate sensualist, not because he greedily savors the hedonistic pleasures—that would make him a mere sinner and profligate—but because he aims to *feel* the woe, lust, joy, sorrow, and frenzy of all mankind in his own breast. Nietzsche praised this universalizing capacity of the Greeks in the tragic age, and he praised Goethe for daring to be a sensualist in his own time.

Goethe was criticized in his day for his 'worldliness' and sensuality, qualities Nietzsche openly admired (Del Caro, 1989, 38, 80–1). Thus in his writings Nietzsche frequently came to the defense of Goethe and used his sensual exceptionalism to elevate him beyond his plodding contemporaries. However, the defense of Goethe against the moralizing of his critics did not extend to *Faust*, which was instead subjected to devastating criticism (Politycki, 1989, 16, 281). Goethe the man was not in competition with Nietzsche the man—in no way did Nietzsche enter the agon with Goethe on the biographical field, which would have been futile and ridiculous—but things were different with their respective heroes and superhumans.

Nietzsche's starting point of the 'death of God' repositions humanity and the earth in relation to the search for meaning, but he had two prominent forebears in German intellectual history, namely Hölderlin and Goethe. Hölderlin was the first German novelist to deal with the problem of the loss of the absolute and a cultural center; *Hyperion* is a response to this loss, marking the onset of modernism (Del Caro, 1989, 41–6, 84, 212; Bay, 2003, 25). Behler establishes the onset of modernity in the romantic project of *Poesie*, which saw 'fiction, literature and the arts to be in a process of constant progression and renewal' (Behler, 1993, 72). The distinguishing feature of *Poesie*, moreover, is *irony*, marked by 'alternating denial, affirmation, self-creation, by destruction, expansion and contraction' (Behler, 1993, 88). Nietzsche addresses the problem of the loss of the absolute not as an innovator, but as a continuator of a romantic and modern response launched by Hölderlin in *Hyperion* and Goethe in *Faust*. Of course, Nietzsche's aversion to 'irony', which he associated with Socrates, forced him to resort to a major circumlocution: he worked with classical *dissimulatio*, otherwise known as 'the mask' (Behler, 1993, 252–4). By the time Nietzsche entered the conversation on the death of God, the field was already somewhat crowded by romantic forerunners; where Nietzsche could easily sweep them aside, as in the case of Hölderlin who lived a 'failed' life, he readily did so, but in the notable case of Goethe, a diversified strategy was called for, on the basis of which Goethe the man would be lauded as a worldly, life-affirming 'superhuman' of sorts, while the respective heroes of Hölderlin and Goethe, Hyperion and Faust, are given short shrift.

Highly symbolic and mythologically infused, *Faust* challenges readers in a labyrinthine manner—but more on this later. The pact with Mephistopheles allows Goethe to revisit the Fall on modernist terms, whose contours are spelled out by Kreis. Like Eve's pact with the snake, Faust's trades for wisdom and sensuality, and the first deed he accomplishes is his rejuvenation in the Witch's Kitchen. By the time he leaves that place, Mephistopheles wryly observes in an aside: 'No fear—with this behind your shirt/You'll soon see Helen of Troy in every skirt!' (*Faust*, l, 2603–4). Now the 'broken-down creature of Western rationalism and nihilism', the 'bedeviled creature of reason' Faust becomes young again, and is able to pursue his goal of a unified superhuman self (Kreis, 1995, 79). The fact that this rejuvenation is achieved by magic pales in comparison to the sensual capacities now awakened in Faust—he becomes the opposite of a desiccated scholar sitting in his study pouring over books—he has a body equal to the task of feeling all of mankind's joy and woe in himself. Goethe's design of the wager that ensures ceaseless striving, accompanied by Faust's ambition to be the most life-affirming human possible, are enhanced by the rejuvenation of Faust that soon occurs; from this point onward his body and his senses have the resilience to withstand superhuman impacts, and such impacts are indeed sought by Faust.

It was the sensualist Goethe whom Nietzsche proudly defended in the face of Herder's derisive nickname for him, 'Priap' (Del Caro, 1989, 38; 2011, 235). It has long been understood in Goethe scholarship that both Mephisto and Faust represent dimensions of Goethe, 'and the sensualists have as much right as the idealists to claim him as one of their own' (Mason, 1967, 220). The same holds true for Margarete, the main figure through which Goethe illustrated the 'eternal feminine'; on the surface she is no match for Faust, and Nietzsche found it all too easy to ridicule Goethe for having resorted to such weak tragic material—a young seamstress is seduced by a great scholar and man of the world, who even needs the assistance of the devil in order to perpetrate his vile deed—and this is supposed to be Germany's greatest tragic idea (*HH*, 'Wanderer', 124); Del Caro, 1989, 98)? But Nietzsche knew better. Margarete, like many figures in

Goethe's writings—*Faust* foremost among them—stands for the universal, not the particular, and as the symbol of universal womanhood she obeys what Mason calls 'the innermost laws and needs of her own nature', a nature that is just as capable of sin as of grace, of seeking sensual gratification and maintaining saintly abstinence (Mason, 1967, 240; Del Caro, 2011, 229). The pattern of praising the man while damning his work continues in this example, where Nietzsche picks the low-hanging fruit, makes a very clever point, but refuses to investigate the thoroughly entangling, overpowering, and shattering love experience as it devastates both Faust and Margarete.

Goethe understood that if Faust is to experience all of humanity's woe and joy within himself, it will require him to experience the shattering effect of tragic love, as well as the suffering of woman and man, and for this reason *Faust* Part One dwells as deeply as it does on Faust's relationship with Margarete. Whereas Marlowe's Mephistopheles ensures that Faustus is adequately entertained and tempted by women as the embodiment of *amor carnalis*, Goethe needs his Faust to go much more deeply into the emotion of love. So, for example, when Mephistopheles assists Faust with the seduction of Margarete, it is not, as Nietzsche implies, because Faust cannot seduce her on his own; Mephistopheles helps Faust become rejuvenated and then entangled in order to break him down, or as Mason puts it, Mephistopheles knows that Faust's tender, romantic love 'will degrade him far more effectively and profoundly than any gross liaison with an abandoned woman could do, just because his whole being and not only his physical appetites will be involved in it' (Mason, 1967, 213). Could Nietzsche have remained unaware of the real implications of Faust's profound sensual debacle? Was there nothing in his own life that taught him to respect the power of love, and for that matter the power of woman? In light of his own relationship with Lou Salomé, and in light of his own insistence that he had inherited the Dionysian dowry of being torn to pieces (Del Caro, 2000, 84, 87, 89, 92–3), we should instead suspect that Nietzsche had his own reasons for suppressing the meaning of the bold sensual encounter between Faust and Margarete.

When it came to demonstrating how humanity had to rediscover its potential for embodied, passional existence—which had become increasingly difficult to achieve over the course of millennia of culture devoted to transcendental, metaphysical, and disembodied living in the spirit of Platonism and Christianity—Goethe was the first European to weigh in with a powerful experimental model. Nietzsche's Zarathustra 'speaks' of women and even claims to marry the woman 'eternity' (a personification of the eternal recurrence of the same), but Goethe's Faust is the one who actually engages women in the figures of

Margarete and Helen. As frequently as he quotes *Faust*, one would think that Nietzsche had extraordinary respect for that labyrinthine work—and in many ways he did, despite the gratuitous and sometimes jealous criticism. Nietzsche, we must not forget, is the one who said around the time of composing *Zarathustra*: 'A labyrinthine human being never seeks the truth, but always only his Ariadne—whatever he may say' (*KSA*, 10, 125, 1883). I wrote about the significance of the labyrinth to Nietzsche's writings generally, and to *Zarathustra* and the *Dionysus Dithyrambs* in particular, in order to dispel the facile but stubborn interpretation that Ariadne was Nietzsche's codename for Cosima Wagner, and nothing more (Del Caro, 1988). In fact, so pervasive is the labyrinth metaphor in Nietzsche's writings, applied as it is to notions of seduction, complete abandonment, becoming lost, and eventually finding one's way (one's Ariadne), that I began to conceive of his writings as a deliberate labyrinth constructed by his Dionysian tempter-attempter proclivities. *Zarathustra* as a work is such a labyrinth, and not surprisingly, so is Goethe's *Faust*. While the Ariadne figure in *Zarathustra* is spoken of only in metaphorical terms, most often in some kind of conversation featuring a disguised Dionysus and Ariadne, in *Faust* the Ariadne figure is without doubt Margarete.

Faust in my estimation belongs to those great works of literature referred to as 'labyrinthine' by Penelope Reed Doob, whereby the labyrinth can refer to divine creation, which is impossible to navigate using only reason (Doob, 1990, 67), or to a labyrinth of words represented by difficult and ambiguous works, in which case we share the protagonist's limited point of view, and 'the text itself is a kind of Ariadne's thread extricating us from the maze we all inhabit for the work's duration' (Doob, 1990, 225). The powerful motivation for Goethe to have cast Margarete in the universalizing role of Ariadne is closely related to his concept of the eternal feminine, as well as to Faust's need to span the entirety of human joy and pain; as a male poet depicting a tragic female figure, Goethe (and males generally) 'needs an abandoned woman to inhabit. He also needs to understand the sources from which that figure draws her power' (Lipking, 1988, 29). I submit that Nietzsche was animating his work with Ariadne metaphors for precisely this reason: in order to draw on the Dionysian, universalizing energy that allows access to man and woman in their most tragic state, when they are abandoned, shattered, and ultimately reforged and reborn in the crucible of suffering (Del Caro, 2011). Margarete on this reckoning was a powerful figure in her own right, easily the equal and peer of Faust as a manifestation of the eternal feminine, which Nietzsche refused to dignify as a life-affirming concept (Del Caro, 2011, 226).

What is more, Goethe had an even broader, more encompassing reason to feature the labyrinth in his works. The metaphor of the labyrinth is tied to human striving as discussed in the Prologue in Heaven of *Faust*, but Goethe also uses it frequently 'in the morphological writings as a symbol of inscrutable, complicated nature and its building plans. A resourceful and sagacious mind is needed to unveil nature, one that makes use of the morphological method as the thread of Ariadne' (Müller, 1992, 77; cf. Del Caro, 2011, 231). This observation on the pervasive nature of the labyrinth in Goethe should be considered alongside another motive Nietzsche may have had for not crediting Goethe or Goethe's *Faust* for the exploration of the labyrinth. According to Politycki, Nietzsche's concept of becoming as the prerequisite of all enhancement and higher development is indebted to Goethe's monadological-organic concept of development, which is not based on the will, such that Nietzsche adopts Goethe's concept around 1876 and increasingly uses it to wean himself off Schopenhauer (Politycki, 1989, 52; Del Caro, 1989, 95).[6]

When Mephistopheles first approaches him, Faust demands to know what he is called, giving rise to a witty exchange:

> FAUST: All right—who are you then?
> MEPHISTOPHELES: Part of that force which would
> Do ever evil, and does ever good.
> FAUST: And that conundrum of a phrase implies?
> MEPHISTOPHELES: The spirit which eternally denies!
> (*Faust*, I, 1334–8)

Faust is thus paired with the spirit of denial, of nihilism, which he uses in his titanic striving. If Faust were himself merely a denier, he would be indistinguishable from his nemesis and there would be no striving as such, only hedonistic sampling, as we witness in the case of Marlowe's Faustus. But Mephistopheles is to Faust what the spirit of gravity is to Zarathustra; it helps him rather than destroys him, turning into an affirmative philosophy that overcomes nihilism (Grundlehner, 1986, 184). Zarathustra of course calls the spirit of gravity his 'devil and arch-enemy', and he is personified as a monster, 'half dwarf, half mole, lame, paralyzing, dripping lead into my ear, lead-drop thoughts into my brain' (*Z*, III, 2). This is Mephistopheles' role as long as he is the companion of Faust; he

[6] In fairness to Nietzsche he does at one point refer to Goethe and the labyrinth together, but not in such a way that he credits him for having been the first to problematize the labyrinth in intellectual-historical terms. See, for instance, *GM*, II, 18, where Nietzsche quotes Goethe's 'labyrinth of the breast', which refers not to *Faust* but to the poem 'An den Mond' (To the Moon).

is supposed to wear him down, drag him down ultimately to hell, but Faust is redeemed on the basis of his striving, which he feels is supported by the earth spirit as the 'spirit of deeds'.

Yet another affirmative note is sounded by Goethe in the matter of giving birth. The three most obvious ways in which Faust participates in birthing are his impregnation of Margarete, who is executed as an infanticide; his trip to the realm of the sublime Mothers, which makes it possible for him to conjure Helen; and finally his impregnation of Helen, resulting in the boy-child Euphorion who is born, lives a whole life, and dies a tragic death within a span of mere minutes while his parents watch (*Faust*, I, 9598–900). But Goethe does not limit Faust's role to that of fathering. Faust's love with and for Margarete and Helen, as I have argued is designed to bring him as close as humanly possible to the source of all creativity, 'mystically portrayed as the Mothers, by means of a shattering experience that breaks down the boundary between a man and woman, on the one hand' but also between a man and an infant on the other hand' (Del Caro, 2011, 239). The striking contrasts within Faust, when they are viewed in the light of his striving to embody all human experience, cause him to drift in and out of male individuation, 'even to the point of being reborn and becoming as a child again' (Del Caro, 2011, 239, 243). It does not surprise us to find a concept of the 'male mother' in Nietzsche, where its instrumentality is stronger than in *Faust*, because Zarathustra 'has children' but interacts only symbolically with women. The 'terrible mistress' who speaks voicelessly to Zarathustra in his 'Stillest Hour', reminiscent of Nietzsche's first treatment of the eternal recurrence in section 341 of *The Gay Science*, helps him to give birth to a new, more affirming self: 'You must become a child again and without shame' (*Z*, II, 22).

The birthing metaphors in *Zarathustra* are central to communicating the need to create the superhuman. Wherever there is talk of *Untergang* (perishing, or going under) and *Übergang* (transition, or going over) as Keith Ansell-Pearson writes, '[i]t is a question of giving birth, of child-bearing' (Ansell-Pearson, 1992, 317). The transfiguration called for by Zarathustra is rooted in Nietzsche's understanding that we must practice self-overcoming on the basis of our abysmal experiences and our sickness. 'What Nietzsche is demanding of his readers is nothing less than that they give birth to themselves—the most difficult of all tasks!' (Ansell-Pearson, 1992, 325–6). Indeed, a paradoxical task—and although the female figures are present in *Zarathustra* for the most part only as symbols (cf. Del Caro, 1988), Ansell-Pearson is well within his rights to claim that in Nietzsche's writings there is a celebration of the 'feminine' and of woman conceived as sensuality, the multifaceted body, and passion, an affirmation which stands in marked contrast to the masculinist tradition of Western philosophy which has erected the phallus of Reason in a position of superiority over emotion, desire, and passion.

(Ansell-Pearson, 1992, 327)

This is not the place to detail Nietzsche's masked and veiled treatment of the feminine, which is so often construed only superficially and highlighted for its apparent misogynistic rhetorical flourishes.[7] What is at stake now is that Nietzsche, following in the brilliant example of Goethe, has a vision of a total human being who draws on the feminine and the masculine—Zarathustra is Nietzsche's studied alternative to Faust.

Having illustrated above how Goethe infused *Faust* with a variety of life-affirming qualities that Nietzsche generally chose to ignore or suppress, even though his *Zarathustra* frequently displays its own version of these life-affirming, earth-affirming qualities, I will now focus on his objections to the Goethean project. It will emerge here that despite his admiration for Goethe, which becomes more tenuous in later years, and despite Goethe's formulation of the operative, consequential difference between classical and romantic, Nietzsche will brand *Faust* a romantic work, and Faust himself a romantic figure.

The lifelong elevation of Goethe the man has its purposes in Nietzsche, as we have seen, but clearly one of these was to *delimit* Goethe as a poet. Of course, we know Nietzsche gave highest honors to Heine as a poet (*EH*, II, 4), claiming kinship with him, but in the broadest sense it was Goethe whom Nietzsche held out as the poet, and it is certainly Goethe whom Nietzsche most often criticizes for being a 'mere poet'. This anti-poet dynamic is a labyrinth in Nietzsche, closely related to his status as a Dionysian. In very oversimplified terms, Nietzsche needed to draw on the creativity of the poet, but he also needed to keep his philosophical distance from the fictitious aura of poetry. This split in his nature was by no means academic; Philip Grundlehner describes how Nietzsche parodied *Faust* already in 1860, as a pupil at *Schulpforta*. He referred to *Faust* Part II as obscure, sublime, and euphonious, and he sustained this line of criticism later on in his writings (Grundlehner, 1986, 17, 150). When Goethe writes in the conclusion to *Faust* that 'all that is impermanent/is merely a parable' (*Faust*, I,

[7] Ansell-Pearson does as fine a job as anyone of illustrating Nietzsche's reliance on the feminine, although he insists that Nietzsche is 'postmodernist' in his approach (1992, 328). I tend to agree with Gemes (2001) that Nietzsche parts company with the postmodernists, even though the latter have a valid claim to some of his method. I have treated the feminine in Nietzsche on several occasions, including Nietzsche's suppression of the feminine in Dionysus (Del Caro, 1988; 1990; 1998a; 1998b; 2000).

1214–5), Nietzsche objects to the idealism of this proposition: 'poetry, far from representing an ideal, should seek to manifest an evanescent existence. If poets such as Goethe ignore this principle, they then fail to respond to the real world, which is mutable rather than indestructible' (Grundlehner, 1986, 153–4).

In *Zarathustra*, 'On Poets', Goethe is taken to task directly, 'for all gods are poets' parable, poets' cock and bull!/Indeed, always it lifts us up—namely to the kingdom of the clouds; atop these we set our motley bastards and then call them gods and superhumans' (*Z*, II, 17). Zarathustra implicates himself with this criticism, even as he mocks Goethe's words from the Chorus Mysticus of *Faust*, and the reference to *Übermenschen* here should include Faust and Zarathustra's teachings of the superhuman. This episode is often referred to as Zarathustra's 'lucid moment', i.e., his insight that his own teachings about an authentic habitation of the earth, in which the superhuman becomes the meaning of the earth, could be just another poetic ideal. The decisive difference between Nietzsche and Goethe on poetic idealism is supposed to be that Nietzsche is aware, and that he, unlike Goethe, limits humanity's creativity to that which can be achieved in fact. Gooding-Williams draws the distinction as follows: Zarathustra claims deeper insight than other poets, Goethe in particular, because he does not 'partake in the illusion that the transformation of man into a being beyond man entails the transcendence of our time-bound, earthly, sensual existence'. Moreover, Nietzsche's criticism of Faust is not because Faust is 'too attached to the world of flux and appearance, but because he betokens Goethe's failure to see that an authentic transfiguration of human life is possible without departing our time-bound, earthly existence' (Gooding-Williams, 2001, 191–2).

Tempted as I am to accept the views of Grundlehner and Gooding-Williams, whereby Nietzsche successfully distanced himself from poetry and therefore overcame the poetic idealism of Goethe, there is simply too much evidence in Nietzsche's own writings, including his poetry, pointing to the fact that he not only remained a poet, but elevated poetry to philosophy. Dionysus as Nietzsche purports to have transformed him from art deity to philosopher deity, and the Dionysian as he transformed it from artistic metaphysics to the highest deed of life-affirmation, is quintessential lyrical substance—the very nature of the Dionysian is lyricality, in the sense that life does not speak so much as it sings. What are we to make of the outbreaks and outbursts of lyricality, of song in *Zarathustra*, *Beyond Good and Evil*, and *On the Genealogy of Morality*?[8]

[8] *Zarathustra* is the richest example of lyrical philosophizing, and most would not dispute this. A close examination of *Beyond Good and Evil* reveals how Nietzsche must resort to Dionysian lyricality in the final sections of that book, once he is no longer able to contain the secret that 'gods

Nietzsche seems to use these lyrical intrusions as poetic irony designed to disrupt the appearance of truth and meaningful dialogue, but he could just as well be using them to validate his version of expository, philosophical prose by demonstrating that he will temper its rational bias by using Dionysian lyricality to ward off its smugness and arrogance.

The transcendental solution ascribed to Goethe as romantic idealizing has its most objectionable representation, according to Nietzsche, in the concept of the eternal feminine, and in that principle's agency in liberating Faust from his pact and getting him into heaven. I have already discussed the sensual, life-affirming qualities of the eternal feminine that Nietzsche chose to ignore. Like most readers of *Faust*, he focused mainly or even exclusively on the mere mention of the eternal feminine in the concluding Chorus Mysticus, whereas the eternal feminine spans the entire work, parts one and two, and manifests in Margarete, the Mothers, Helen, Care, and the interceding female penitents of the final scene, only one of whom is Margarete.[9] Grundlehner points out that the poem 'To Goethe' (the first poem of the 'Songs of Prince Vogelfrei' appended to *The Gay Science*) was written around the same time as Zarathustra's rebuff of the eternal feminine in 'On Poets'. Both expressions are a parody of Goethe's concept, whereby the eternal feminine does not lift us up, but instead mixes us in a blend of truth and tricks, or sets our 'motley bastards' atop the clouds. Later, Nietzsche would parody the eternal feminine in a series of aphorisms on woman in *Beyond Good and Evil*, part seven. There Nietzsche claims that Goethe borrowed the concept from Dante and translated it into German. For his part, Nietzsche does not doubt that 'every nobler woman will resist this belief' that the eternal feminine lifts us up, because this is precisely what woman believes of the

also philosophize' (*BGE*, 295). Nietzsche would not have compromised the 'philosophical' tone and validity of his explicitly philosophical book ('Prelude to a Philosophy of the Future') if he shunned poetry, because *BGE*, 295 uses Dionysian lyricality to argue for the legitimacy of Dionysian philosophizing. The same phenomenon occurs in the *Genealogy* in a manner that cannot be overlooked. The Second Treatise concludes with a plea to create a new human being who associates the senses not with asceticism, the evil eye, and bad conscience, but applies these negatives instead to everything that is *unnatural* (*GM*, II, 24). At the point where he begins to become very descriptive of this future human being, he breaks off, creates a new section and explains that at this point he must be silent, because he is about to infringe on the rights of a younger, more future, and stronger individual, namely Zarathustra (*GM*, II, 25). This is not the action of one who disavows poetry, but instead the gesture of one whose supreme Dionysian 'deed' was the creation of *Zarathustra*. Observe, too, that the third essay of the *Genealogy* is preceded by a quote from *Zarathustra*; Nietzsche claims in the Preface that the entire third treatise is an exegesis or commentary of the Zarathustra passage featuring wisdom as a woman (*GM*, P, 8; III, 1).

[9] See Richard Ilgner (2001, 137, 140, 142–5). Of particular interest is how Goethe closes out *Faust* with five female actors, whereas the Prologue in Heaven had featured five males consisting of God, Satan, and the three archangels (142, 145).

Eternal Masculine (*BGE*, 236). Once again a witty and apparently withering blow against Goethe's concept, but in terms of substance it falls short. Recent scholarship on the universalizing tendency of Goethe's writings, which applies first and foremost to his treatment of gender in *Faust*, demonstrates that Goethe drew on sources in classical mythology and Christianity for his architecture of the eternal feminine (Del Caro, 2011)—to dismiss it as readily as he appears to do invites scrutiny of his own conception of the feminine, and I believe Nietzsche did this boldly and deliberately, not merely to discredit Goethe's version but also to elevate the feminine per se.

After all, by giving us his own account of the *Übermensch* Nietzsche was not trying to discredit the concept, but quite clearly to instantiate it as solidly as possible in the wake of Goethe's own conception. He felt that Goethe's Faust was not an adequate model of a superhuman, just as Goethe himself was not an adequate model when it came to illustrating what is classical and tragic (Del Caro, 1989, 98; Politycki, 1989, 228–9). A closer examination of some of his commentaries on Faust as a type are revealing in this regard. The criticism of Faust in 'Schopenhauer as Educator' is some of the strongest anywhere in Nietzsche's writings. Young Goethe, he insists, was enamored of Rousseau's 'gospel of the good nature', and Faust became 'the highest and boldest reflection of Rousseau's human being' (*UM*, III, 4), not exactly high praise when we consider that Nietzsche heaps most of the ills of modernism and romanticism upon Rousseau (Del Caro, 1989, 99–115). Even worse, Goethe's Faust fails as a rebel and liberator even where Rousseau's example is more engaging, such that 'the world liberator Faust becomes only a world traveler, so to speak', and Goethe's human being is 'the contemplative man in high style...he is not the man of action' (*UM*, III, 4). Note that Nietzsche ascribes this Faustian concept to young Goethe, even though Goethe retained the original Faust (*Urfaust*) throughout his life, and worked on the book until his final year of life. And of course most revealing of all is Nietzsche's insistence that Faust fails as a man of deeds, as a man of action; his claim to fame is that he is contemplative and well-traveled. As usual, there is no mention of the earth spirit as the Faust-inspiring and Faust-defining spirit of deeds.

If literary and intellectual history have recognized a divided nature, a divided soul in Faust, Nietzsche is here to dispute even this. Faust laments 'Two souls, alas, are dwelling in my breast,/And either would be severed from its brother' (*Faust*, I, 1113–14), whereupon Nietzsche: 'A German who would have the temerity to claim "two souls, alas, are dwelling in my breast" would seriously violate the truth, or more accurately, fall short of the truth by many souls' (*BGE*, 244). This jibe is aimed at Germans as much as it is aimed at Goethe, because the German soul is not a coherent entity by any means, but a multiplicity of odds and ends: 'The German soul has passages and sub-passages, there are caves in it, hiding places and dungeons; its disorder has much of the charm of the mysterious; the German knows the secret paths to chaos' (*BGE*, 244). With a bit of imagination this would have us thinking of the German soul as a labyrinth, in which case 'two souls, alas' does indeed miss the mark. Compare the 'semi-barbarism' that characterizes the European soul, with its 'access to the labyrinth of incomplete cultures' (*BGE*, 224).[10] German profundity is also interrogated by Nietzsche in this context, since what passes for profundity is nothing more than spiritual indigestion. Still, it is better for a people to be perceived as deep than as Prussian (*BGE*, 244), a remark that to me suggests that Germans are fond of the mask, as are Nietzsche and his masked god Dionysus.

Nietzsche was bound to condemn Faust as a mere romantic hero, speaking of him only in terms that are silent on his superhuman qualities. It has long been recognized by scholars who follow the philosophical thread of Goethe's thought, which is a philosophy of nature, that there is a Faustian dimension to Nietzsche's thought. He seeks a philosophy of nature, according to Alwin Mittasch, that would overcome the opposition of nature and spirit and produce a harmony of human and earth (Mittasch, 1952, 282)—he could not press for the significance of his own superhuman as the meaning of the earth if Goethe had already said all there is to say on the subject. And of course Goethe did not exhaust the subject. Nietzsche insisted that his *Übermensch* was not an ideal, but a proximate reality, the type of human being who has existed throughout history in rare instances, and the type of human being whose existence should be fostered (Del Caro, 2004, 329–35). But the record shows that Goethe's superhuman, ideal or not, and irrespective of the charge that his transfiguration takes places under the aegis of transcendental forces, undertakes the precise mission of earth-affirmation and earth-meaning that Nietzsche reserved for his Zarathustra. And of course Nietzsche did not exhaust the subject, either.

REFERENCES

Ansell-Pearson, K. 1992. 'Who is the *Übermensch*? Time, Truth, and Woman in Nietzsche', *Journal of the History of Ideas*, 53/2: 309–31.

Bay, H. 2003. '*Ohne Rückkehr*', *Utopische Intention und poetischer Prozeß in Hölderlins* Hyperion (München: Wilhelm Fink Verlag).

[10] One might also wish to compare the discussion of the labyrinth in *GM*, III, 24, where the Assassin's motto 'nothing is true, everything is permitted' is referred to as a proposition with 'labyrinthine consequences' and a minotaur.

Behler, E. 1993. *German Romantic Literary Criticism* (Cambridge: Cambridge University Press).

Behler, E. 1997. *Ironie und literarische Moderne* (München: Ferdinand Schöningh).

Del Caro, A. 1988. 'Symbolizing Philosophy: Ariadne and the Labyrinth', *Nietzsche-Studien*, 17: 125–57.

Del Caro, A. 1989. *Nietzsche Contra Nietzsche: Creativity and the Anti-Romantic* (Baton Rouge: Louisiana State University Press).

Del Caro, A. 1990. 'The Pseudoman in Nietzsche, or The Threat of the Neuter', *New German Critique*, 50: 135–56.

Del Caro, A. 1998a. 'Nietzsche, Sacher-Masoch, and the Whip', *German Studies Review*, 21/2: 241–61.

Del Caro, A. 1998b. 'Nietzschean Self-Transformation and the Transformation of the Dionysian', in Kemal, S. Gaskell, I. and Conway, D. W. (eds.), *Nietzsche, Philosophy and the Arts* (Cambridge: Cambridge University Press): 70–91.

Del Caro, A. 2000. 'Andreas-Salomé and Nietzsche: New Perspectives', *Seminar*, 36/1: 79–96.

Del Caro, A. 2004. *Grounding the Nietzsche Rhetoric of Earth* (Berlin: Walter de Gruyter).

Del Caro, A. 2011. 'Margarete-Ariadne: Faust's Labyrinth', *Goethe Yearbook*, 18: 223–43.

Doob, P. 1990. *The Idea of the Labyrinth from Classical Antiquity through the Middle Ages* (Ithaca: Cornell University Press).

Eckermann, J. 1959. *Gespräche mit Goethe in den letzten Jahren seines Lebens*, Houben, H. H. (ed.) (Wiesbaden: Brockhaus).

Gemes, K. 2001. 'Postmodernism's Use and Abuse of Nietzsche', *Philosophy and Phenomenological Research*, 62/2: 337–60.

Goethe, J. W. Von. 1976. *Faust: A Tragedy*, Arndt, W. (trans.), Hamlin, C. (ed.) (New York: W. W. Norton).

Goethe, J. W. Von. 1977. *Faust: Eine Tragödie*, Trunz, E. (ed.) (München: Verlag C. H. Beck).

Goethe, J. W. Von. 1988. 'Prometheus', in *Gedichte* (Berlin and Tübingen: Aufbau-Verlag).

Goethe, J. W. Von. 1989. *The Sorrows of Young Werther*, Hulse, M., (trans.) (London: Penguin).

Gooding-Williams, R. 2001. *Thus Spoke Zarathustra's Dionysian Modernism* (Stanford: Stanford University Press).

Grundlehner, P. 1986. *The Poetry of Friedrich Nietzsche* (New York and Oxford: Oxford University Press).

Ilgner, R. 2001. *Die Ketzermythologie in Goethes Faust* (Herbolzheim: Centaurus Verlag).

Kreis, R. 1995. *Nietzsche, Wagner und die Juden* (Würzburg: Königshausen & Neumann).

Lipking, L. 1988. *Abandoned Women and the Poetic Tradition* (Chicago: University of Chicago Press).

Mason, E. 1967. *Goethe's* Faust: *Its Genesis and Purport* (Berkeley: University of California Press).

Mittasch, A. 1952. *Friedrich Nietzsche als Naturphilosoph* (Stuttgart: Alfred Kröner Verlag).

Müller, I. 1992. 'Der "Ariadneische Faden" in Goethes morphologischen Studien und seine Erscheinung in der "Natürlichen Tochter"', *Acta Historica Leopoldina*, 20: 71–82.

Nietzsche, F. 1988. *Sämtliche Werke: Kritische Studienausgabe in 15 Einzelbänden*, Colli, G. and Montinari, M. (eds.) (Berlin: de Gruyter).

Nietzsche, F. 2006. *Thus Spoke Zarathustra*, Del Caro, A. (trans.), Pippin, R. (ed.) (Cambridge: Cambridge University Press).

Politycki, M. 1989. *Umwertung aller Werte? Deutsche Literatur im Urteil Nietzsches* (Berlin: Walter de Gruyter).

8

Attuned, Transcendent, and Transfigured: Nietzsche's Appropriation of Schopenhauer's Aesthetic Psychology

A. E. Denham

> With regard to all aesthetic values I now avail myself of this principal distinction: I ask in each . . . case 'is it hunger or is it superfluity which has here become creative?'
>
> (*GS*, 370)

> The mother of . . . the fine arts [is] superfluity and abundance. As their father, . . . genius, which is itself a kind of superfluity, that of the power of knowledge beyond the measure required for the service of the will.
>
> (*WWR*, II, 410)

1 SCHOPENHAUER'S LEGACY: THE PROBLEM OF EXISTENCE

1.1

Certainly Schopenhauer, like Nietzsche, regarded 'art from the perspective of life'. 'Not merely philosophy but also the fine arts work at bottom towards the solution of the problem of existence', Schopenhauer observed. The significance of art resides in its ability to articulate and episodically to ameliorate that problem; hence 'the result of every . . . artistic apprehension of things is an expression more of the true nature of life and of existence, more an answer to the question, "What is life?". Every genuine and successful work of art answers this question in its own way' (*WWR*, II, 406). On this point, Schopenhauer and Nietzsche are of one mind: the value of art lies not in *'l'art pour l'art'*, but in the answers it provides to the problem of existence. As Schopenhauer and Nietzsche are standardly read, however, the answers they find in art have little in common. Against that standard reading, I will argue here that Nietzsche's conception of aesthetic experience—and in particular his conception of aesthetic transfiguration—is essentially continuous with Schopenhauer's own. They differ, to be sure, in respect of the normative implications they draw from the nature of aesthetic experience. But while each finds a different moral in the story of art, the story *itself*—the story Nietzsche inherited from Schopenhauer—remains much the same.

1.2

Nietzsche's first published response to Schopenhauer in *The Birth of Tragedy* officially ignores the detail of the latter's aesthetic theory altogether. Instead, Nietzsche there attempts a synthesis of Schopenhauer's idealistic metaphysics with his own aesthetic model in which representation and Will (as Apollonian and Dionysian forces) are fused in the work of art. The result is not a notable success in either literary or philosophical terms: it is a disorderly confusion of inspired phenomenological observation and art criticism, weighed down by a ball-and-chain of second-hand metaphysics. As Nietzsche himself remarked in his 1886 Preface to the re-issue of *The Birth of Tragedy*:

> Is it clear what task I first dared to touch with this book? How I regret now that in those days I still lacked the courage . . . to permit myself in every way an individual language of my own for such individual views and hazards—and that instead I tried laboriously to express by means of Schopenhauerian and Kantian formulas strange and new valuations which were basically at odds with Kant's and Schopenhauer's spirit and taste!
>
> (*BT*, 'Attempt', 6)

Nietzsche also proposes in that Preface, however, that his first essay foreshadows his subsequent philosophical development in that it 'betrays a spirit who will fight at any risk whatever the *moral* interpretation and significance of existence' (*BT*, 'Attempt', 5). Already in *The Birth of Tragedy*, that is, he appreciated that from the standpoint of morality, 'life must continually and inevitably be in the wrong, because life *is* something essentially amoral' (*BT*, 'Attempt', 5). This 'moral perspective' (and the Christian tradition with which it is bound up) Nietzsche condemns as '"a will to negate life", a secret instinct of annihilation, a principle of decay, diminution, and slander . . . the danger of dangers' (*BT*, 'Attempt', 5), and he claims that his hostility to it was already evident in his first published work. This self-portrait of the 1886 Preface seems to me largely accurate; I do not intend to challenge Nietzsche's claim that *The Birth of Tragedy* contained the seeds of his later critique of traditional ethics.[1] But to what extent did Nietzsche's later thought really leave behind Schopenhauer's account of aesthetic experience, as he seems also to suppose?

Schopenhauer's aesthetics are presented in Book III of *The World as Will and Representation* as a theoretical prelude to his ethics; aesthetic experience, Schopenhauer claims, is a kind of finger-exercise preparing one for the ultimate metaphysical feat of transcending individuality, desire, and will. This is one sense in which all art 'works at bottom towards the solution of the problem of existence' (*WWR*, II, 406). At the same time, however, Schopenhauer, like Nietzsche, portrays art as a redemptive activity and a way of *resisting* the standard, pessimistic implications of evaluative nihilism—a reprieve from the bleak condition of *ein unendlich Strebung*. How exactly is aesthetic experience supposed to do that? Schopenhauer's short answer to that question is that in such experience 'knowledge' (our cognitive faculty) 'tears itself free from the service of the will' (*WWR*, I, 178), liberating us from our usual preoccupation with practical ends and aims:

> When . . . an external cause or inward disposition suddenly raises us out of the endless stream of willing, and snatches knowledge from the thralldom of the will, the attention is now no longer directed to the motives of willing, but comprehends things free from their relation to the will. Thus it considers things without interest, with subjectivity.
>
> (*WWR*, I, 196)

Passages such as this have suggested to many readers that, for Schopenhauer, aesthetic experience is a purely cognitive, affect-free affair. This impression is reinforced by Schopenhauer's repeated allusions to the subject of aesthetic experience as a '*pure* knowing subject'. In Books I and II of *The World as Will and Representation*, Schopenhauer sharply distinguishes 'knowledge' as a wholly cognitive faculty from 'will', a wholly conative one, and with this reading in view it is hard to imagine how Nietzsche could *not* abandon Schopenhauer's aesthetic psychology. After all (and setting aside his 'scientistic' middle period in *Human, All Too Human* and *Daybreak*) Nietzsche consistently presents aesthetic experience as an essentially passionate, life-affirming affair—as 'life rejoicing over its own inexhaustibility' (*TI*, X, 5). Schopenhauer, by contrast, plainly does wish to locate aesthetic

[1] Julian Young (1992) dismisses the 1886 Preface as a self-deluding and inauthentic revision of personal history and an early manifestation of Nietzsche's descent into madness. This reading is both tendentious and contrary to best evidence. I am content to take Nietzsche at his word here; the Preface, in fact, seems to me one of Nietzsche's more sober and straightforward evaluations of the significance and genealogy of this own thought.

experience as a preparatory stage-post to the greater project of resignation, and he conceives of aesthetic experience as a vehicle of liberation from the will and desire in *some* sense or other. That experience is, for instance, cast as an intimation of 'how blessed must be the life of a man in whom the will is silenced not for a few moments... but for ever' (*WWR*, I, 390). Nothing, it seems, could be further from Nietzsche's conception of the aesthetic as a state in which 'a man enriches everything from out of his own abundance; what he sees, what he wills, he sees... overladen with power' (*TI*, X, 9). It is thus natural to suppose that Schopenhauer's aesthetic psychology must be as much at odds with Nietzsche's wider agenda as are his ethics. In particular, it seems reasonable to suppose that the account of aesthetic experience developed in Nietzsche's mature work (especially Part V of *The Gay Science*, *Twilight of the Idols*, *Ecce Homo*, and the notes assembled as *The Will to Power*) constitutes a radical departure from Schopenhauer's.

Nonetheless, I shall argue here that on closer inspection, one finds that Nietzsche's aesthetic phenomenology does not actually leave its Schopenhauerian origins far behind. In particular, Nietzsche owes to Schopenhauer the key features of what is arguably his most central aesthetic concept, viz., that of aesthetic *transfiguration*. The idea that aesthetic transfiguration can invest human experience with positive value—that despite its suffering, strife, and pointlessness life can be 'aesthetically justified'—is a thought already implicit in Schopenhauer's account of artistic activity. Nietzsche did not, I believe, achieve a significantly different conception of aesthetic experience from that he inherited from Schopenhauer. Yet that may turn out to be a virtue, not a failing, of his project.[2]

[2] This claim will seem implausible if one assumes that Schopenhauer's aesthetics are conceptually inseparable from his ethics of resignation. That assumption is ubiquitous in Schopenhauer scholarship, and typically frames interpretations of Nietzsche's work as well. It is, for instance, a key premise of Young's argument that Nietzsche's project of life-affirmation is a failure, never managing to transcend Schopenhauer's view of art as 'an intimation of, a pointer towards, the "correct" stance to life and the world, asceticism: the denial of the will and the world' (Young, 1992, 118). A rather different picture emerges, however, if one distinguishes Schopenhauer's metaphysical speculations (and their ethical implications) from his phenomenological descriptions. That seems to me a wise move to make in any case, for Schopenhauer did not excel as a metaphysician. Indeed, his metaphysics arguably constitute and uneasy mix of Kant, Spinoza, and eastern religion that seldom rises above the level of speculative theology. In his philosophy of art, by contrast, Schopenhauer offers subtle and profound descriptions of human psychology, requiring no support from the metaphysical constructs and ethical prescriptions which frame them. Like Nietzsche, Schopenhauer excelled at articulating phenomena in which the affective and cognitive dimensions of experience interact in complex ways—as occurs aesthetic and moral experience. Of course, he himself wove these phenomenologies into metaphysical tapestries, and that fabric is not always easy to disentangle. But no blame attaches to being revisionist in respect of work which benefits from revising: to find what is of value in Schopenhauer's phenomenology of aesthetic experience one should distinguish his worthwhile psychological observations from the speculative uses to which he put them.

2 ILLUSTRATING TRANSFIGURATION: TORQUATO TASSO

> Saying Yes to life even in its strangest and hardest problems ... that is what I called Dionysian, that is what I guessed to be the bridge to the psychology of the tragic poet.
>
> (*TI*, X, 5)

2.1

Art is valued for its transformative powers, and in particular for its potential to transform human experience into something worth affirming. This is not a novel idea; theorists from Plato to the present day have recognized that, in the hands of a master, artistry can refashion what is otherwise ugly or banal into a thing of grandeur and beauty. The special genius of a Sophocles or a Dante or a Tolstoy is to take as materials the more painful and fearful aspects of our experience and to make of them something magnificent. As Nietzsche observed in *The Birth of Tragedy*, classical tragedies vividly exemplify this idealizing capacity of artistic activity, putting dreadful events and insalubrious characters into the service of some of the most noble and thrilling narratives of literary history. But while tragedy may provide a paradigm of transfiguration, the basic capacity is, for Nietzsche, a feature of *all* art that deserves the name. It is precisely because of its transfigurative power that art plays the vital role it does for Nietzsche: through art, we learn to see human experience for what it is, and yet to love and honour it—we learn to view life honestly, yet optimistically. But what exactly is transfiguration and how is it realized through the creation and experience of works of art?

Aesthetic transfiguration features in Nietzsche's work in two, related contexts: first, there is the transfiguration by the work of art of the material of which it treats—its content or subject. Secondly, there is self-transfiguration—the project by which we can exploit aesthetic strategies to transfigure ourselves, acting as artists in a broad sense of that term, recreating our own characters and destinies. These two are not, of course, unrelated; the latter kind of transfiguring relies on some of the same resources as the former, and works of art play an important causal role in Nietzsche's account of self-transfiguration. I am concerned here, in the first instance, with the first form of transfiguration: the way in which artworks effect a transfiguration of their target or content. That said, I begin, however, with a work that illustrates both: Goethe's dramatic masterpiece, *Torquato Tasso*.

2.2

Nietzsche described Goethe as 'the last German for whom [he felt] any reverence' (*TI*, X, 51), and Schopenhauer used Goethe's *Torquato Tasso* to illustrate his claim that artistic 'genius proper rests on the *absolute* strength and vigour of the intellect' (*WWR*, II, 283). On a biographical level, the composing of *Torquato Tasso* certainly required 'strength and vigour' of its author; during the years of its composition Goethe's personal circumstances paralleled in striking ways the difficult historical ones of its protagonist. Both were bound by financial pressures to the service of philistine noblemen; both occupied the ambivalent social space of the highly talented, yet low-born; both harboured amorous longings for hopelessly unattainable, aristocratic women; both struggled in their daily lives and their art to reconcile the contradictory demands of worldly ambitions and artistic ideals; and while each was valued by his benefactors for the prestige that he brought to the courts, neither could hope to be considered a true equal: Tasso was forever the indigent son of an inspired but failed chancer, and Goethe would always be a burgher's son. The ensuing conflicts, fears, and frustrations that marked Tasso's tragic life—and which very likely contributed to his eventual madness and early death—did not, however, defeat Goethe. He turned them into art, making of his own life a tale of transfiguration in which banal and luckless beginnings eventually yield a triumphant and grand biography—a tale of bringing style, shape, purpose, and beauty to the hapless accidents of nature.

Likewise, artistic transfiguration is the principal theme of *Torquato Tasso*. The Italian poet, Tasso, is portrayed as an inspired, idealistic genius, spiritually imprisoned by the wealthy and powerful Courts on whom he relies. His remarkable talents are both admired and exploited by his commercial masters; he is beholden to a world of political and social complexities in which his genius is misunderstood, and his social naiveté puts him utterly out of his depth. In Goethe's play, this hostile world is distilled in the figure of Antonio, a scheming Court advisor and politician who is the epitome of the Machiavellian Renaissance statesman, ever ready to justify the means by the end. Antonio is the ultimate usurer: he represents the 'real-world' forces of expediency and profit, in polar opposition to Tasso's ideal, poetic visions—forces that drive Tasso first to rage and then near to madness. In this detail, Goethe's art does not depart far from life: the historical Antonio in fact did much to undermine Tasso's favour with his principal benefactor (Duke Alphonso II), and Tasso was probably a victim of adult schizophrenia. He suffered psychotic and paranoid episodes from his late teens, and was subject to volatile and often bizarre outbursts which estranged him from his supporters and eventually contributed to his death.

Goethe's drama becomes historically inventive, however, in the dynamic of reconciliation it develops between Tasso and Antonio, culminating in an enlightened moment of recognition in the final scene. That scene follows one of climactic conflict, in which Tasso is provoked to draw his sword on Antonio, a transgression for which he is banished from the Court, isolated and destitute. Antonio regrets his provocations and has second thoughts, as does the beneficent Duke; at the Duke's behest Antonio goes to Tasso to reason with and calm him. He recognizes that the grandeur of his Court needs Tasso's inspiration and genius, and that the poet cannot survive and flourish without the Court. At the play's dramatic culmination, Antonio takes Tasso's hand, and Tasso responds with a metaphorical acknowledgement of their mutual dependence, affection, and respect:

> Oh, noble man! thou standest firm and calm,
> While I am like the tempest driven wave.
> But be not boastful of thy strength. Reflect!
> Nature, whose mighty power has fixed the rock,
> Gives to the wave its instability.
> She sends her storm, the passive wave is driven,
> And rolls and swells, and falls in billowy foam.
> Yet in this very wave the glorious sun
> Mirrors his splendor, and the quiet stars
> Upon its heaving bosom gently rest.
> Dimmed is the splendor, vanished is the calm!—
> In danger's hour I know myself no longer,
> Nor am I now ashamed of the confession.
> The helm is broken, and on every side
> The reeling vessel splits. The riven planks,
> Bursting asunder, yawn beneath my feet!
> Thus with my outstretched arms I cling to thee!
> So doth the shipwrecked mariner at last
> Cling to the rock whereon his vessel struck.
>
> (Act V, v. 3434–53)

With this reconciliation of contradictory forces, Goethe's *Torquato Tasso* reveals itself as a drama of transfiguration on more than one level. In the narrative, Tasso and Antonio transform a destructive conflict into a union of opposites, through their mutual recognition of the way in which each is necessary to the other; in Goethe's own life, the drama presciently charts the course of the author's psychological negotiation between the bitter facts of worldly survival and those of poetic transcendence. And on a third level, *Torquato Tasso* provides the spectator with his own opportunity for transformative thought, offering him a vision of a tragic life which ennobles and elevates it beyond its natural circumstances.

'Life is *never* beautiful', Schopenhauer observed, 'but only in the pictures of it, namely in the transfiguring mirror of art or of poetry' (*WWR*, II, 345). Within Goethe's mirror, Tasso's life is no longer an arbitrary and pointless tale of suffering and distress. Given a coherent form and meaningful trajectory by Goethe's artistry, it now illustrates for us certain essential, timeless truths—certain universals—of human psychology. In Nietzsche's terms, life is 'idealized' by Goethe's art: both creator and spectator are implicated in a move of aesthetic transformation, in which natural circumstances that are morally abhorrent, incoherent, and personally distressing are made aesthetically intelligible. And we, being creatures that delight in understanding ourselves and our place in the universe, find that transfigured tale very beautiful indeed. How exactly does Goethe's drama bring all of that about? How exactly does this work—or any work of art—lead us to reconceive nature's grim offerings in terms that elicit our admiration and endorsement? As Nietzsche asked, 'What means have we for making things beautiful, attractive and desirable', given that 'they are never so in themselves' (*GS*, 299)? His answer is aesthetic transfiguration.

2.3

Nietzsche's account of the transformative power of art differs in detail from his earliest to his last works, but from start to finish it is what makes art 'the truly *metaphysical* activity of man' (*BT*, 'Attempt', 5, 22). A 'metaphysical activity' is, at the least, an activity affecting our metaphysical assumptions and beliefs—the highly general commitments in terms of which experience is both had and interpreted. In this sense, 'doing' metaphysics is not so much a matter of endorsing this or that belief as a matter of circumscribing, articulating, and revising the framework within which our beliefs arise. If creating and appreciating art, or at least good art, is such an activity, then one sense of what it means for art to be 'transfigurative' is clear enough: it is capable of altering the framework within which emerge certain of our beliefs, and specifically our evaluative beliefs.

What is less clear is just what that might mean in *psychological* terms. By what specific psychological operations does art effect fundamental changes in our evaluative framework? Consider Goethe's drama, for instance: how exactly does one's engagement with it work to reconfigure the way in which one conceives the tragedy of Tasso's troubled nature and his conflicted relationship to Antonio? Goethe provides us with no new facts of the case; neither does he romanticize the known facts, making them more palatable or less devastating for the protagonist. Yet *Torquato Tasso* vividly illustrates the paradox of tragedy, so-called: we find pleasure in engaging with Tasso's grim trajectory as Goethe tells it.

On one level, we might think of aesthetic experience as providing an alternative framework of evaluative concepts and standards—*aesthetic* concepts and standards—in terms of which to assess human experience and its objects. This is surely part of what Nietzsche had in mind when he recommended that we 'view morality from the perspective of art' (*BT*, 'Attempt', 5). Aesthetic evaluation proceeds in largely different terms than moral evaluation; the values in which it deals move us 'beyond [the concepts and standards of] good and evil' to the values of, *inter alia*, beauty, originality, and authenticity—to the allure of created forms and the intensity and illumination of the experiences these afford. On another level, however, aesthetic experience provides a model of the phenomenology of one kind of transfiguration: the particular cognitive and affective conditions under which beautiful conceptions of human experience are constructed. So conceived, transfiguration may be characterized naturalistically, as a distinctive psychological process or complex of processes. In Sections 3 and 4 I will explore two such dimensions of transfiguration: what I call 'attunement' and 'self-transcendence'. Both, I argue, are central to Nietzsche's account of transfiguration, and both are directly inherited from Schopenhauer's aesthetic psychology.

3 THE ATTUNEMENT CONDITION

> In the mind of a man who is filled with his own aims, the world appears as a beautiful landscape appears on the plan of a battlefield.
>
> (*WWR*, I, 145)

3.1

We sometimes encounter works of art without attending to them properly, and even when we do so attend we may find that they fail to capture our interest or elicit a significant response. Contemporary audiences, for instance, are clearly less likely to be absorbed by Tasso's difficulties or to resonate emotionally with the social intrigues which ensnare him than would have a struggling and impoverished poet in nineteenth-century Weimar. Great art can leave us cold. Such occasions are often mentioned as counterexamples to 'aesthetic attitude' theories, as evidence that even unequivocally great art can fail to elicit any distinctive form of psychological engagement. They are of no interest here, however, because they play no part in the positive phenomenologies of art offered by either Schopenhauer or Nietzsche: neither thinker has *any* interest in dispassionate, detached, or casual spectatorship. Their concern is with aesthetic creation and appreciation 'proper'—namely, acts and experiences which are focused, fully attentive, and wholly involved. It may even be fair to say that these are the conditions under which an experience counts as an aesthetic one at all. Neither thinker offers an explicit argument for demarcating the territory of the aesthetic in this way, but it is clearly assumed by most of what each has to say. I, too, will assume it in my use of the term 'aesthetic': engaged aesthetic experience is what is here at stake. Aesthetic experience of other kinds, if such exists, is irrelevant.

So how does engaged aesthetic experience transfigure the psychology of the subject whose experience it is? Engaged experiences of works of art are often described as effecting a kind of *attunement* to the target of experience, in which the contents of the subject's perceptual, affective, and cognitive states are largely determined by the focal object of attention: his consciousness is 'filled' with its target on all of these levels. This is a familiar feature of focused attunement to music, for instance, and of our experiences of dancing and moving to music. It can also occur, if less obviously, in response to a captivating novel or an arresting moment of poetry, and it is familiar enough too at the theatre and cinema. On such occasions one may be aptly described as immersed in the work, as oblivious to the world beyond it, or as 'taken over' by it. (Were it not so clumsy, a better term than 'attunement' might be 'entrancement', owing to its associations with hypnotic trances and states of consciousness that compromise the subject's independent agency.)

More precisely, let us say that a subject is aesthetically attuned to a target, experiential object just when *an accurate and detailed phenomenology of his first-personal experience would make no or little mention of anything other than the object itself.* To put the same thought differently: a subject counts as attuned to a target object of attention just if there is little or nothing remaining to say about 'what it is like' for him to experience it, beyond itemizing the features of the object that occupy him. In aesthetic attunement, then, the distinction between the subject and the object is phenomenologically mitigated; the subject ceases (episodically) to be aware of himself as distinct from the object, and his ability to identify the content of his experience as distinct from its object is correspondingly diminished. So, for instance, if you are attuned to a performance of *Torquato Tasso* at the rapturous moment of recognition mentioned earlier, an accurate and detailed account of your first-personal psychological condition will not go far beyond being an accurate and detailed description of the performance itself—the sights and sounds it presents, the emotions expressed, the thoughts articulated. Of course you may be subject to some responses that are elicited by, but not embodied in, the drama: you may feel pity for Tasso when what *he* expresses is not pity, but despair. But to feel that pity you must first sympathetically identify and track his despair; your elicited emotion is a second-order response to your first-order attunement to the aesthetic object.

3.2

It is indisputable that Nietzsche took engaged aesthetic experience to be intense, impassioned, and cognitively captivating in something like this way. He often uses the term '*Rausch*' to capture this aspect of aesthetic experience. 'What', he asks, characterizes 'the psychology of the artist'? His answer is that 'If there is to be art, any aesthetic doing and seeing, one physiological condition is indispensable—*Rausch*' (*TI*, IX, 8). It may seem, however, that *Rausch* is a more specific or narrower concept than that of attunement. Certainly, Nietzsche's use of '*Rausch*' is, if not inconsistent, then at least highly variable in the connotations it carries in different textual contexts. That variability is reflected in the different translations offered for it. '*Rausch*' is sometimes translated as 'ecstasy' or 'rapture'; unfortunately, both terms carry various senses in different contexts, not all of which are appropriate. They may mean something like 'intense joy', in which case they sit uncomfortably as descriptions of profound attunement to the many 'difficult' works of art which Nietzsche identified as potential catalysts for *Rausch*—Antigone or Hamlet, or most of Wagner's operas, for instance, as well as *Torquato Tasso*. The quasi-religious or spiritual sense of 'ecstasy' is somewhat better than rapture, perhaps, suggesting as it does a moving above or beyond one's normal state of consciousness to a perspective that is affectively heightened and cognitively enlightened. But again, it implies perhaps too exclusive an association with purely positive emotions, such as elation or joy.

Another common translation of '*Rausch*' is 'intoxication', which likewise carries more and less appropriate connotations; there is something right in its suggestion of a state in which free agency is compromised (as in drunkenness), and also in the idea that one has been overpowered by something affecting all levels of thought, feeling, and perception. As Nietzsche comments, 'art appears in man like a force of nature and disposes of him *whether he will or no*' (*WP*, 798, my emphasis). But the idea that the subject of *Rausch* is thereby cognitively impaired, or that he necessarily views the world in a distorted and defective manner, is not consistent with Nietzsche's typical use of the term. That dimension of 'intoxication' sits very uneasily with the role of *Rausch* as offering profound insight and attunement to the true nature of things, and this is a role Nietzsche repeatedly mentions—from the closing sections of *The Birth of Tragedy* to *The Will to Power*. Finally, '*Rausch*' has been translated as 'frenzy', which again succeeds in some contexts (such as Nietzsche's references to sexual *Rausch*) but fails in others, particularly if one regards *Rausch* as closely connected with the joyous attitude of life-affirmation described in *Thus Spoke Zarathustra*. In the penultimate section of that work, for instance, the condition of passionate attunement is inextricably bound up with an attitude of life-affirmation: '[A]ll joy wants the eternity of all things, wants honey, wants dregs, wants drunken midnight, wants tombs, wants tomb-tears' comfort, wants gilded evening glow'.

We should thus be wary of forcing upon '*Rausch*' a single, highly determinate interpretation. While '*Rausch*' may refer, in any particular textual appearance, only to a certain species of attunement, attunement is common to them all: it is the species to which belong the many different conditions that Nietzsche names with the term. It is Nietzsche's 'indispensable physiological condition' of all aesthetic activity.[3] Art affords us infinitely many and varied occasions for entrancement, rapture, joy, ecstasy, intoxication, and the rest; in all of them, however, one's consciousness is fully attuned to the experiential target such that both the content and character of one's experience are determined by it.

The protagonist of *Torquato Tasso* illustrates this phenomenon well: Tasso—representing the artistic psychology—is largely defined and distinguished by his capacity for profound attunement to his aesthetic targets in such a way that he no longer functions as a free, deliberative agent but is, as it were, at the mercy of the experiences that are delivered to him. This loss of self-conscious agency is the source of his worldly troubles, but it is also the well-spring of his artistic creativity and insight. The ambitious Antonio, by contrast, never loses himself in this way: his intellect and imagination remain firmly harnessed to his practical, personal aims. As Schopenhauer observes,

> In the contrast between Tasso and Antonio, Goethe has given us an illustration of the opposition in which . . . two entirely different kinds of capacity . . . stand to each other. The frequently observed kinship of [artistic] genius with madness rests chiefly on that very separation of intellect from the will, essential to genius yet contrary to nature.
>
> (*WWR*, II, 387)

Schopenhauer's reference to Goethe's drama is no mere aside; he takes *Torquato Tasso* to vividly illustrate his own account of how intense attunement transfigures the subject of aesthetic experience. When aesthetically engaged with some object, Schopenhauer says, we

> relinquish the ordinary way of considering things, and cease to follow under the guidance of the forms of the principle of sufficient reason . . . we no longer consider the where, the when, the why and the whither in things, but simply and solely the *what*. . . . [We] . . . devote the whole power of our mind to perception, sink ourselves completely therein, and let our whole consciousness be filled by the calm contemplation of the natural object actually present, whether it be a landscape, a tree, a rock, a crag, a building, or anything else. We *lose* ourselves entirely in this object . . . we forget our individuality, our will . . . so that it is as though the object alone existed without anyone to perceive it and thus we are no longer able to separate the perceiver from the perception, but the two have become one.
>
> (*WWR*, I, 178)

[3] Nietzsche sometimes explicitly articulates *Rausch* in such terms; as Daniel Came has remarked, Nietzsche 'quite clearly conceives of [*Rausch*] . . . as entailing both a dissolution of self-consciousness and a (phenomenological, if not metaphysical) falling away of spatial and temporal awareness' (Came, 2009, 99). Came in fact offers the phrase 'such intoxication' in place of the bracketed '*Rausch*', having opted for that translation of the term.

Schopenhauer here calls attention to three aspects of the attuned consciousness. First, it is a state in which the subject ceases to consider how the target is causally or conceptually related to other things (regarding it 'outside' of the principle of sufficient reason). Secondly, it is a state in which the character and content of the subject's first-personal experience is wholly determined by the target. And finally, in this state the subject ceases to be aware of himself as distinct from the object—he is no longer a subject of self-conscious thought nor (accordingly) self-directed agency. These features likewise characterize Nietzschean *Rausch* insofar as the usual ways of locating oneself in terms of spatial, temporal, and causal relations give way to, as Nietzsche once put it, a 'mysterious primal Oneness' with the object of aesthetic attention (*BT*, 17).

Are there not, however, other features of Schopenhauerian attunement which have no place in Nietzsche's account—namely, tranquillity and disinterestedness?

3.3

The importance Nietzsche assigns to emotion and desire in *Rausch* is often thought to radically distinguish it from the 'contemplative' aesthetic condition allegedly envisaged by Schopenhauer. Christopher Janaway claims, for instance, that 'Schopenhauer... posits an out-of-the-ordinary state, a mind whose consciousness is temporarily cleared of the will, of all desire, emotion, and felt need' (Janaway, 2009, 56). Likewise, Julian Young takes it as given that 'in Schopenhauer's account the aesthetic state is a condition of pure passivity.... a cessation of all... activity' in which 'the mind becomes... a reflecting *tabula rasa*' (Young, 1992, 122). Taking much the same view, Aaron Ridley tells us that 'what is fundamentally wrong' with Schopenhauer's aesthetics is 'the misconstruction of the engagement with beauty as residing in a quite particular form of passivity', whereas for Nietzsche, 'that engagement is not only essentially active and wilful, but, indeed,... derives from 'an erotic whirl' (Ridley 2002: 121). And even Came—in some respects an apologist for Schopenhauer's aesthetics—remarks that 'complete will-lessness' is, for Schopenhauer, a 'necessary condition of genuine aesthetic pleasure' (Came, 2009, 94). In short, there seems to be a consensus that Schopenhauerian attunement and Nietzschean *Rausch* differ greatly in respect of the role taken in each by affective states.

The role of affect or emotion in Schopenhauer's aesthetic psychology is, however, more complicated and nuanced than this consensus would suggest. Schopenhauer, it is true, was clearly eager to forge a connection between aesthetic experience on the one hand, and his endorsement of evaluative nihilism and prescription for asceticism on the other. He clearly wants to maintain that aesthetic experience in *some* way prepares one for a wholesale resignation of the will. Books III and IV of *The World as Will and Representation* both repeatedly emphasize the former as a temporary exercise paving the way for the latter (although Schopenhauer admits that actual artists and spectators—or 'beholders', as he prefers—seldom make the transition). For instance, he famously refers to aesthetic experience as a 'Sabbath of the penal servitude of willing' (*WWR*, I, 196), and comments that it offers us a glimpse of 'how blessed must be the life of a man in whom the will is silenced not for a few moments, as in the enjoyment of the beautiful, but for ever' (*WWR*, I, 390). Are such remarks, however, part of his *psychology* of aesthetic experience? Or are they rather a *metaphysical interpretation* of it, pointing ahead to the metaethics and normative prescriptions of Book IV?

It is one thing to describe an experience type; it is another to try to justify its power and significance. Schopenhauer's association of aesthetic experience with resignation is an exercise of the latter, not the former, kind. It is a *use* to which he hopes to enlist his aesthetic psychology, not a part of that psychology itself. Moreover, there is nothing in his account of aesthetic experience that *entails* the later ethical prescriptions—although Schopenhauer himself often seems unaware of that fact. Indeed, he elides altogether the quite pronounced tension between his aesthetic psychology and the ascetic denial of the will he aims to recommend.

In sum, there is a crucial difference between the will-lessness prescribed in Book IV and the aesthetic attunement of Book III, a difference that is overlooked by both the standard, 'consensus' reading of Schopenhauer and by Schopenhauer himself: aesthetic experience displays an intensely active and emotion-imbued phenomenology, even by Schopenhauer's own account. I will explain.

Contrary to the consensus reading, to be 'liberated from the will' in Schopenhauerian aesthetic experience is decidedly not to become inactive or 'will-less' in every way. Schopenhauer writes,

> What is called the awakening of [artistic] genius, the hour of inspiration, the moment of rapture or exaltation [which] is nothing but the intellect's becoming free, when, relieved for a while from its service under the will, *it does not sink into inactivity of apathy but is active... entirely alone and of its own accord.*
>
> (*WWR*, II, 380, my emphasis)

As this passage indicates, aesthetic experience is not a state of complete 'passivity'. Rather, the subject is liberated only from a particular species of will, leaving behind or transcending a certain ordinary *species* of activity, viz., the fulfilment of individual and egocentric aims and desires. One is freed from the will only in the sense that one becomes indifferent to the ordinary, local ambitions and projects that occupy the 'merely practical man', and moved to attend to things without regard to their utility. In effecting this move, one's intellect and imagination are anything but passive; rather they are freed *for* a different, exceptionally intense, mode of creative activity.

Moreover, such activity is required of both spectator (or beholder) and artist. 'This ability', says Schopenhauer, 'must be inherent in all men in a . . . degree, as otherwise they would be just as incapable of enjoying works of art as of producing them' (*WWR*, I, 194). Although it is manifested to a 'higher degree' in the latter, they do not differ in kind. 'We must . . . assume as existing in all men that power . . . of divesting themselves for a moment of their personality', Schopenhauer writes,

> unless indeed there are some who are not capable of any aesthetic pleasure at all. The man of genius excels them only in the far higher degree and more continuous duration of this kind of knowledge . . . aesthetic pleasure is essentially one and the same whether it be called forth by a work of art, or directly by the contemplation of nature and life.
>
> (*WWR*, I, 195)

I noted earlier that Schopenhauer is often portrayed (e.g., by Ridley and Janaway) as conceiving of aesthetic experience solely from a 'passive, spectatorial' standpoint. This not only overlooks entirely the many painstaking pages Schopenhauer devotes to describing the psychology of the 'genius' (creative artist), but the fact that the beholder's experience is simply a less emphatic version of the same experience type. The psychology of the beholder as much as that of the artist is distinguished not by passivity but by a consciousness that is 'energetically active without being spurred on by the will' (*WWR*, II, 381). In ordinary, non-aesthetic experience, by contrast, one is

> immersed in the whirl and tumult of life . . . his intellect is filled with the things and events of life.
>
> (*WWR*, II, 381)

> For example, we regard houses, ships, machines and the like with the idea of their purpose and their suitability therefore; human beings with the idea of their relation to us . . . and . . . according to their position and vocation, perhaps judging their fitness for it, and so on. . . . In most cases and as a rule, everyone is abandoned to this method of consideration.
>
> (*WWR*, II, 372)

For Schopenhauer, then, it is the individual's freedom to 'follow its own laws', no longer enslaved by his practical aims, that sets apart the aesthetic consciousness—*not* passivity or the absence of emotional engagement. 'On this point hinges', Schopenhauer says, 'the difference between the capacity for *deeds* and that for *works*' (*WWR*, II, 387). He remarks:

All great theoretical achievements . . . are brought about by their author directing all the forces of his mind to one point. He causes them to be united at this point and concentrates them so vigorously, firmly, and exclusively, that all the rest of the world vanishes for him, and his object for him fills all reality. It is just this great and powerful concentration, forming one of the privileges of [artistic] genius. . . . even in the case of the objects and events of . . . everyday life. Brought under such a focus, these are then magnified to such monstrous proportions that they appear like the flea that . . . assumes the stature of the elephant. The result of this is that, by trifles, highly gifted individuals are sometimes thrown into emotions of the most varied kind. To others such emotions are incomprehensible, for they see these individuals reduced to grief, joy, care, fear, anger and so on by things that would leave the ordinary man quite unruffled. *Therefore genius lacks coolness or soberness, which consists simply in our seeing in things nothing more than actually belongs to them . . . in respect of our possible aims; hence no cool or sober man can be a genius. With [this] . . . is also associated . . . the vehemence and passionateness of willing, which is likewise a condition of genius.*

(*WWR*, II, 389; my emphasis)

Later in the same passage, Schopenhauer refers again to Goethe's Tasso as an exemplar of the aesthetic psychology, that is, of a psychology capable of intense emotion combined with an indifference to the aims of the personal, egocentric will—the liberation from the (individual) will which makes aesthetic vision possible:

From all this very readily arise that extravagance of disposition, that vehemence of the emotions, that quick change of mood under prevailing melancholy which Goethe has presented to us in *Tasso*. What reasonableness, quiet composure, comprehensive survey, complete certainty and regularity of conduct are shown by the well-equipped normal man in comparison with the now dreamy and brooding absorption and now passionate excitement of the genius, whose inner affliction is the womb of immortal works! . . . The train of thought of the intellect which is detached from its maternal soil, the will, and which only periodically returns thereto, will soon differ in every way from that of the normal intellect which still cleaves to its stem.

(*WWR*, II, 389–90)

First-personal aesthetic experience, then, is far from being dispassionate and passively receptive. Rather, the subject's psyche is freed from its usual, dreary servitude to the individual's practical aims and purposes, and redirected to a different mode of activity: 'If, by way of exception, it happens that we experience a momentary enhancement of the intensity of our intuitive intelligence, we see things with entirely different eyes', Schopenhauer observes, for we then consider things 'without any personal participation in them', leaving the intellect (and imagination) to 'freely follow its own laws, and as pure subject mirrors the objective world, *yet from its impulse is in the highest state of tension and activity*, goaded by no willing' (*WWR*, II, 373; my emphasis).

One may, of course, question the very intelligibility of the account of aesthetic experience emerging from these passages. Exactly how, for example, can one be in the 'highest state of tension and activity', while 'goaded by no willing'? If we interpret the 'silencing of the will' to which Schopenhauer alludes in this context as entailing either passivity or absence of affect, then his position is truly incoherent. It makes good sense, however, if by 'will-lessness' Schopenhauer is referring only to a liberation from the usual tyranny of those desires, aims, and purposes given to the individual *independently* of his experience of the target object. The word 'will' here can mean only the individual will—the pursuit by the individual of the satisfaction of his own independently given desires.

This circumscription of the meaning of Schopenhauer's terminology, it must be said, is not explicitly acknowledged in Volume I of *The World as Will and Representation*. Worse yet, it is not consistent with Schopenhauer's account of the term 'will' earlier, in Book II. There, the term is assigned two other senses: a metaphysical one (referring to the inchoate, noumenal essence of all that is), and a wide, psychological one, in which *every* act—however trivial—and *every* motivationally characterized mental state, including all emotions and 'calm passions', are affections of the will. The fact remains that neither of these senses is consistent with how Schopenhauer uses the terms in Book III, or in the Supplemental Essays of Volume II spelling out in detail the character of aesthetic experience. So what is to be sacrificed, one may wonder: the overall coherence of Schopenhauer's grand system or the local credibility of his aesthetic phenomenology? In general, Schopenhauer was less a master of systemic coherence than of phenomenological insight. Perhaps, given the wider confusions and inconsistencies in his overall metaphysics, we may give up on the former without too much regret.

3.4

I have argued that Schopenhauer's notion of aesthetic attunement, by his own account, involves a 'silencing of the will' only in a very specific and limited sense of that phrase: it is not all modes of willing but only, as it were, egocentric willing that is dissipated in aesthetic experience. Unfortunately, his commitment in Books I and II to a dichotomy of 'will' and 'intellect' leaves him with few resources to articulate this point. Having signed up to their 'complete independence', as he puts it, he finds it difficult to articulate the ways in which emotion, cognition, and imagination work together in Book III. When he says, for instance, that one becomes a 'pure knowing subject' in aesthetic experience, this would seem to exclude any active contribution by one's will to the existence and nature of the thing experienced. But Schopenhauer himself explicitly denies this: aesthetic engagement, as he describes it, is not a condition of 'passive receptivity', but an intensely active and creative one marked by affective arousal, imagination, and creative activity. The aesthetic subject, it is true, is freed from a certain pedestrian kind of servitude to his usual practical, pedestrian ends and aims. But that is only the beginning, not the end, of the story.

Consistent with this, the more detailed Supplementary Essays of Volume II reveal that Schopenhauer—like Nietzsche after him—is less interested in the psychology of spectatorship than in the perspective of the artist. Both, I noted earlier, require active and creative engagement. Schopenhauer insists that, 'Everyone who reads the poem or contemplates the work of art must of course contribute from his own resources', and he further reminds us that

> [This] cooperation of the beholder, required for the enjoyment of a work of art, rests partly on the fact that every work of art can act only through the medium of the imagination. It must therefore excite the imagination, which can never be left out of the question and remain inactive. This is a condition of aesthetic effect, and therefore a fundamental law of all the fine arts.
>
> (*WWR*, II, 407, my emphasis)

The beholder's and the artist's psychologies differ only in degree, not in kind: both must be capable of *active* attunement, just as in Nietzschean *Rausch*. Moreover, Schopenhauer's *paradigm* of aesthetic experience is, like Nietzsche's, the experience of the creative artist, not the spectator. The psychology of the spectator is simply a diminished version of the 'rapture' of creative 'genius', and even then spectatorship interests Schopenhauer only insofar as it is that of the engaged 'connoisseur'.[4] What distinguishes the 'ordinary man' from the artistic Genius (and his engaged, connoisseurial counterpart) is *not* an absence of affect and emotion in the former, but the fact that he, unlike the serious artist or the enlightened connoisseur, is imprisoned by the drive to pursue satisfaction of his given desires; he is a slave to his practical aims and personal ambitions, condemned to value the world around him in purely instrumental terms. The creative genius/connoisseur, by contrast, is naturally disposed to perceive and respond to the world as a thing of *intrinsic* interest, beauty, and wonder. He is transported out of himself and his merely personal sphere of concerns and ambitions by the allure and intrigue of the world he inhabits—'whether he will it or no', as Nietzsche said. But he does not thereby become a mere intellect—a vehicle for 'the mere *concept*... which can be... communicated coldly and dispassionately by words' (*WWR*, II, 408–9). Schopenhauer has nothing but

[4] This point is easily passed over in Volume I of *The World as Will and Representation*, although even there the artist/genius, rather than the spectator, provides for Schopenhauer the paradigm of aesthetic experience. In the Supplementary Essays of Volume II, however, the central role of the creative genius as the model and pinnacle of that experience-type is unambiguous.

disdain for 'merely' intellectual works of art in which 'we see the distinct, limited, cold dispassionate concept glimmer and finally appear'. Such works (as in, for example, allegories) rightly elicit our 'disgust and indignation, for we see ourselves deceived and cheated of our interest and attention' (*WWR*, II, 409). Aesthetic creativity, although the child of a special 'intuitive intellect', does not convey dispassionate thought. It is rather a matter of affectively charged inspiration:

> In the lyrical poem proper, the mere song, in which the deeply felt mood of the present and the impression of the surroundings flow forth as if involuntarily in words, whose metre and rhyme are realized automatically . . . all these . . . have the great merit of being the purer work of the rapture of the moment, of the inspiration, of the free impulse of genius, without any admixture of deliberation and reflection. They are therefore delightful and enjoyable through and through.
>
> (*WWR*, II, 409)

So it seems that Schopenhauer's 'pure knowing subject' of aesthetic experience, enjoying his 'sabbath' from all willing, is not quite as such phrases suggest nor as so often portrayed. Rather than a passive, spectatorial, intellect he is given over to 'the spontaneous inspiration, of the . . . free impulse of genius' *without* 'deliberation and reflection', and only thus does he enjoy the special delight of the aesthetic 'free moment of rapture'. The seeds of Nietzsche's *Rausch*—and the affirmative delight in existence to which it gives rise—are evidently already alive in Schopenhauer's phenomenology. Indeed, they are fully conceived, waiting only to be transplanted to an arena of values in which they are able to flourish.

4 DISINTERESTED SELF-TRANSCENDENCE AND AESTHETIC DELIGHT

4.1

The active and affectively charged character of aesthetic attunement lies at the heart of Schopenhauer's account. But attunement is not achieved without cost, and in Schopenhauer the price to be paid is the elimination of the subject's personal, extra-aesthetic concerns, aims, and desires. The aesthetic subject transcends whatever local, instrumental interests he may have taken in the object: he becomes, in a word, *disinterested*. Disinterestedness is a species of self-transcendence: on Schopenhauer's view, the attuned subject transcends his ordinary, instrumental attitudes and valuations towards some object of attention. Rather than assessing it with a view to its personal usefulness, as means to his independently given ends, his attitude is one of 'reflective disengagement from all considerations of utility, which considers only what the object is "in itself"' (Came, 2009, 95). He may, of course, take a second-order interest in the pleasure that such a state delivers, but the first-order state itself is one of impersonal enjoyment of the object for its own sake, not as a means to some extrinsic end. It is this, in fact, which connects the experience of the beautiful to that of the sublime. Both are active and impassioned conditions, but they are also disinterested: the subject leaves behind his personal wants, desires, and ambitions Disinterested self-transcendence thus goes hand-in-hand with attunement, as I have described it: the first-personal phenomenology of any artist-beholder genuinely immersed in his *object* of attention will feature only, or almost only, those cognitive and affective states that are internal to his experience of it—that represent and respond to the object itself.

This is not, of course, a novel idea. 'Self-transcendent disinterestedness' so characterized, is another label for what theorists now sometimes call the 'aesthetic attitude'. As Jerome Stolnitz defines it, the aesthetic attitude is a 'way of directing and controlling our perception' when we attend to something; it is 'disinterested and sympathetic attention to and contemplation of any object of awareness whatever, for its own sake alone' (Stolnitz, 1989, 25). As he elaborates this claim, it becomes clear that 'disinterested' means 'with no ulterior purpose'; 'sympathetic' means 'accepting the object on its own terms to appreciate it' (ibid.).[5] On one level, the idea that there exists a distinctive aesthetic

[5] Stolnitz proceeds to argue that the entire subject matter of aesthetics should be demarcated by this distinctive way of attending to an object. That is, he proposes that aesthetic experience 'is the total experience had while this attitude is being taken; and that the "aesthetic object" is the object toward which this attitude is adopted; and that "aesthetic value" is the value of this experience of its object' (1989, 25). Eliseo Vivas (1955) offers a characterization in similar terms, saying that the aesthetic attitude is 'an experience of rapt attention which involves the intransitive apprehension of an object's immanent meanings and values in their full presentational immediacy'. The key terms to note in Vivas's attempt are 'intransitive' and 'immediate'. The first indicates that the experiencing subject is not motivated by a further aim or purpose (he is not 'interested in' the object for this or that end, but just interested, full stop). The second indicates attention to the thing as presented in its own distinctive form, not as falling under this or that concept.

This agenda can appear quite extravagant in its global and reductive ambitions. Little stands to be gained by attempting to define a complex cluster of concepts related to art and aesthetics in terms of some one distinctive psychological stance or state of mind. Even if we confine ourselves to works of art, it is doubtful that there is any one such distinctive state of mind as may be induced by or adopted towards any and all particular artworks or kinds of art: we are unlikely to find a single state of mind that characterizes our proper attention to, one and all, a performance of some Schubert Lieder, a view of a field of tulips, the latest Tarantino film, and a Fra Angelica painting. Indeed, the suggestion that there is some state common to our proper attention to each is nothing short of preposterous, and George Dickie (1964) has declared that the 'myth' of the aesthetic attitude is 'no longer useful and in fact misleads aesthetic theory'. Dickie argues that there are no identifiable psychological states or conditions that are distinctive of the 'proper attention' to artworks. Rather, there is simply: (1) attending with different kinds of motive (for instance, listening to a piece of music in order to pass a

phenomenology of this kind is unremarkable in the context of Schopenhauer's account, explicitly committed as it is to a significant mitigation of the experienced distinction between subject and object. In the context of Nietzsche's aesthetic psychology, however, the situation is more complicated, not least because Nietzsche values aesthetic experience as an incentive to the will—as a way of arousing our passions and imagination in a creative, productive, life-affirming way. Can disinterested self-transcendence of this sort really have any place in Nietzsche's aesthetic solution to the 'problem of existence'?[6]

4.2

Nietzsche himself denied that aesthetic experience is disinterested, and excoriated the part he thinks it plays in Schopenhauer's aesthetics. However, at the time of *The Birth of Tragedy*, he had found a place for something very much like disinterestedness within the Apollonian realm of beautiful illusions. He refers there to cases in which the spectator is mindful of the fact that even the most captivating work of art is an illusion, 'mere appearance' (*BT*, 7); the spectator thereby remains at a remove from the spectacle it presents, engaging with the universals of the work on one level, while on another never forgetting that it is a fiction:

music theory test, or to relax, or to relieve boredom, or to enjoy the sounds); and (2) attending more and less closely (from absent-mindedly noting the music in the background to giving it one's full cognitive focus). On this view, disinterestedness does not mark any 'perceptual distinction', only motivational and attentional ones (Dickie, 1964, 58). Dickie fails to appreciate, however, that the motivational and attentional differences *cause* perceptual ones: under 'aesthetic' conditions, what one perceives and cognizes may be different in kind.

[6] Ridley dismisses this possibility out of hand on the ground that Nietzsche's conception of aesthetic experience (or at least the developed conception that emerges in, for instance, *Twilight of the Idols*) targets art from the standpoint of the artist rather than the spectator, so emphasizing the prominence of 'will' (where that is some combination of affective intensity and creative drive). It is true that Nietzsche often argues that the standpoint of the artist has been overlooked by the philosophical tradition: '[T]he experiences of *artists*' he writes, 'are "more interesting", and Pygmalion was in any event *not* necessarily an "unaesthetic man"' (*GM*, III, 6).

But this explanation misses the mark for at least two reasons. First, it is clear that Nietzsche's doubts about Schopenhauerian disinterestedness extend to the experience of the spectator; he is equally adamant that '*all* beauty incites to procreation—that precisely this is the *proprium* of its effect, from the most sensual regions up into the most spiritual' (*TI*, IX, 22). He says further that 'the effect of works of art is to excite *the state that creates art*' (*TI*, IX, 21), and that art generally manifests 'the will to live, life's form of exuberance' (*WP*, 821). As Julian Young says, '[T]here is, in short, a psychological condition that is uniquely identifiable as "*the* aesthetic state" a state that is common to the creator of art and the "genuine" spectator. The question of its nature constitutes "*the* aesthetic problem"' (Young, 1992, 26). Ridley overlooks altogether the extent to which Nietzsche repeatedly concerns himself with the aesthetic experience of the spectator rather than the artist from the beginning of his work to its end. Finally, and most significantly, this too-simple answer overlooks the fact that, despite Nietzsche's protests against Schopenhauerian disinterestedness, Schopenhauer too conceived of aesthetic experience from the perspective of the artist-genius, and regarded the experience of the 'beholder' as a diminished form of the same experience-type.

It is not only the agreeable and friendly images that he experiences as something universally intelligible.... [T]he whole divine comedy of life, including the inferno, also pass before him, not like mere shadows on a wall—for he lives and suffers with these scenes—and yet not without that fleeting sensation of illusion. And perhaps many will, like myself, recall how amid the dangers and terrors of dreams they have occasionally said to themselves in self-encouragement... 'It is a dream! I will dream on!'

(*BT*, 7)

Nietzsche here acknowledges, *inter alia*, two important features of engaged aesthetic experience. First, the spectator's suspension of disbelief permits him safely to engage emotionally with the work—to 'live and suffer' with the scenes it presents to him—and to do so with intensity and passion. At the same time—and this is the second feature—the spectator retains a protective distance from what he witnesses: he never entirely identifies his own circumstances, desires, and concerns with those of the spectacle. This does not mean that he responds to it dispassionately, without feeling, of course. If we are properly engaged with a (worthwhile) work of art, we respond to the 'universally intelligible' images of 'the serious, the troubled, the sad, the gloomy' by experiencing them first-personally—albeit not as we would in ordinary, day-to-day life. In ordinary life, such circumstances demand that we *act*; we are not left to appreciate them 'free of interest', for our own welfare directly depends on what we *do* in response to them. In aesthetic experience, by contrast, we are able to regard them—and engage with them—without our vision being clouded by Schopenhauerian 'pressures on the will', or demands for practical action. Nonetheless, the subject experiences their *motivating force*, as it were—their emotional and other affective qualities—on their own, independent of their usual relation to intention and action. (This requires a certain self-restraint, of course: small children, for instance, often fail to divorce powerful cinematic images from real life, and so pathologically transport the fear and excitement they evoke into their everyday beliefs and expectations.) Hence Nietzsche remarks later in *The Birth of Tragedy*:

[W]e must also include in our image of Apollo that delicate boundary which the dream image must not overstep lest it have a pathological effect (in which case mere appearance would deceive us as if it were crude reality). We must keep in mind that measured restraint, that freedom from the wilder emotions, that calm of the sculptor god.

(*BT*, 15, 16)

Even in *The Birth of Tragedy*, however, this image of 'freedom from the wilder emotions' sits uneasily with the picture of Dionysian *Rausch* that the essay finally endorses. And when we move on to Nietzsche's mature conception of aesthetic experience, the image of Apollo—and with it the positive role of disinterested aesthetic distance—is notably transformed. Whereas *The Birth of Tragedy* characterizes the Apollonian in terms of comforting 'dreams' and tranquilizing 'illusions', which cover reality with a 'beautiful veil', the Apollonian later becomes just one way in which aesthetic *Rausch* is manifested or realized (specifically in visual aesthetic experience, which 'excites the eye so that it gains the power of vision' (*TI*, IX, 10)). It is *Rausch* itself—formerly Dionysian *Rausch*—that becomes for Nietzsche the indispensable, necessary condition of aesthetic experience:

> If there is to be any aesthetic doing and seeing, one physiological condition is indispensable: *Rausch*. *Rausch* must first have enhanced the excitability of the whole machine; else there is no art. All kinds of *Rausch*, however diversely conditioned, have the strength to accomplish this; above all, the *Rausch* of sexual excitement... Also the *Rausch* that follows all great cravings, all strong affects; the *Rausch* of feasts, contests, feats of daring, victory, all extreme movement; the *Rausch* of cruelty; the *Rausch* in destruction; the *Rausch* under certain meteorological influences, as for example the *Rausch* of spring; or under the influence of narcotics; and finally the *Rausch* of an overcharged and swollen will.[7]
>
> (*TI*, IX, 8)

In itself, this passage (and others like it) do not tell at all against the idea that aesthetic experience is disinterested. All that they imply is that there are many causal sources of *Rausch* or attunement, taking many different targets, and that some of those sources are classic instances of 'desire-driven' immersion. Nothing follows about the specific source of the *Rausch* that is involved in 'aesthetic doing and seeing'. It may or may not be desire-driven. For instance, it may be (as Schopenhauer claims) that we value aesthetic experience in part because of the pleasure associated with our release from ordinary, practical desires: hence we develop a passionate desire for the aesthetic reprieve from desires of other kinds, as well as a positive desire for the 'delight in the mere knowledge of perception as such, in contrast to the will' (*WWR*, I, 200).

More importantly, the fact that some desire—of this or any other kind—*causally motivates* attuned aesthetic experience is neither here nor there as regards the *content* of that experience. The close association of states of *Rausch* with intense desire in other contexts, and even the fact that aesthetic *Rausch* may

[7] In *The Will to Power*, *Rausch* is more specifically associated with the manifestation of instinctual and specifically sexual energy, commenting, for instance, that 'without a certain overheating of the sexual system a Raphael is unthinkable' (*WP*, 800), and that 'the demand for art and beauty is an indirect demand for the ecstasies of sexuality' (*WP*, 805). These latter remarks seem to be speculations about a common causal source of the energy that finds expression in aesthetic rapture, rather than an attempt to characterize its phenomenological nature, however. It would, I think, be a mistake to reductively interpret *Rausch* as a direct manifestation of sexual feeling.

have its causal origins in this or that desire or instinctual drive, does not tell against the thesis that the latter involves a disinterested self-transcendence. Nietzsche himself comments on the mechanism by which such passions are transformed in aesthetic experience—namely, by sublimation. I will say a bit more about that mechanism shortly; for the moment, it is noteworthy that the causal sources of *Rausch* mentioned in this passage are just the sort of nature-given drives (sexual desire, competitiveness, cruelty) which are paradigmatic candidates for Freudian sublimation, and the satisfaction of such drives is often associated with states of 'abandon' in which the usual condition of rational, self-interested agency no longer obtains. In many cases, we do not so much possess these drives as are possessed by them, and there is a clear sense in which they overpower rather than promote our capacity for independent, self-interested agency—our ability to think and act on objects instrumentally.

4.3

Disinterested self-transcendence may yet, then, characterize Nietzschean states of *Rausch*. That is, aesthetically motivated *Rausch* could involve a 'disinterested and sympathetic attention to and contemplation of' an object 'for its own sake alone', whatever its causal source. Nonetheless, Nietzsche himself flatly denies that possibility and ridicules the very notion of aesthetic disinterestedness as it is used by both Kant and Schopenhauer. In Kant, Nietzsche says that the association of the aesthetic with the disinterested arises out of 'a lack of any refined first-hand experience [of the beautiful]' and 'reposes in the shape of a fat worm of error':

> 'That is beautiful', said Kant, 'which gives us pleasure *without interest*'. Without interest! Compare with this definition one framed by a genuine 'spectator' and artist—Stendhal, who once called the beautiful *une promesse de bonheur*. At any rate he *rejected* and repudiated the one point about the aesthetic condition which Kant had stressed: *désintéressement*. Who is right, Kant or Stendhal?
>
> (*GM*, III, 6)

In response to this question Nietzsche turns to Schopenhauer and the latter's association of aesthetic experience with asceticism—the ideal of resigning the claims of the will:

> [Schopenhauer] never wearied of glorifying *this* liberation from the 'will' as the great merit and utility of the aesthetic condition.... Schopenhauer described *one* effect of the beautiful, its ability to calm the will—but is it even a regular effect? Stendhal, a ... more happily constituted nature than Schopenhauer, emphasized ... a different effect: 'the beautiful *promises* happiness'—to him the fact seems to be precisely the *arousal of the will* ('of interest') through the beautiful. And could one not finally urge against

Schopenhauer himself that he was quite wrong in thinking himself a Kantian in this matter... that he, too, was pleased by the beautiful from an 'interested' viewpoint, even from the very strongest, most personal interest: that of a tortured man who gains release from his torture?

(*GM*, III, 6)

Two allegations are made here against Schopenhauer. The first is that Schopenhauer's aesthetic theory incorrectly characterizes 'the aesthetic condition' as a dispassionate state in which the will is tranquilized and becalmed; the second allegation is that Schopenhauer himself does *not* regard the beautiful 'disinterestedly', since he enlists it in the service of 'the very strongest, most personal interest', namely, to find relief from the restless suffering and strivings of the will.

What is one to make of these scathing remarks? The first thing to note is that they make use of and conflate two very different notions of disinterestedness. Nietzsche first identifies disinterestedness with an absence of passion or affect or will, and identifies its (putative) opposite—interestedness—with Stendhal's 'arousal of the will'. He then, however, fixes on a different distinction altogether—namely, whether or not one appreciates 'the beautiful' instrumentally, as a mere means to the end of being freed from the torturous 'penal servitude of volition'. By conflating these two senses of 'disinterested', Nietzsche also conflates two different objections to Schopenhauer's views. The first objection is that Schopenhauer wrongly characterizes aesthetic experience as passive and dispassionate; the second is that Schopenhauer *himself* valued aesthetic experience in instrumental, 'interested' terms, as a means to the satisfaction of some very personal—and extra-aesthetic—interest or aim.

Neither objection hits a legitimate mark. The first trades on an almost embarrassingly crude confusion, viz., supposing that 'disinterested' means 'dispassionate and *un*interested'. While one might excuse this confusion in a reading of Kant's account of disinterestedness (although there too it would be misplaced), we have seen that it finds no target whatever in Schopenhauer. For Schopenhauer, 'disinterested' simply does not mean 'dispassionate' in the sense of an absence feeling or motivation. Nietzsche's muddle on this score merits little comment.

What of his second objection, with its imputation of hypocrisy to Schopenhauer? This too, misses the mark, and for two reasons. First, Schopenhauer himself insisted that aesthetic experience both affords and is motivated by the pleasures we take in it, and these are not confined to the negative pleasure of release from suffering (the pleasure of 'a tortured man who gains release from his torture'). The state of aesthetic perception is also one which 'makes us feel positively happy' in itself, from the 'immediate, unreflective, yet also inexpressible pleasure that is excited in us by the impression of colours' to the 'beneficent, soothing and exalting' effect of the full moon in a night sky (*WWR*, II, 375).

There is, furthermore, the pleasure arising from the understanding that art affords, from the clarity of the ideas we achieve through it, as when

> a symphony of Beethoven presents us . . . with the most vehement conflict which is transformed in a moment into the most beautiful harmony. . . . a true and complete picture of the nature of the world, which rolls on in the boundless confusion of innumerable forms. . . . all the human passions and emotions speak from this symphony: joy, grief, love, hatred, terror, hope and so on in innumerable shades.
>
> (*WWR*, II, 450)

It may be that, as Nietzsche says, the beautiful does not *promise* happiness for Schopenhauer as it does for Stendhal. Rather, the perception of the beautiful effectively *is* happiness, for creatures like us—and a happiness in which we have the keenest interest. That this is so tells not at all against the claim that aesthetic experience itself is disinterested in Schopenhauer's technical use of that term. For his point is that *within* engaged, attuned aesthetic encounters we cease to pursue our personal, independently given desires and ambitions; that the *having* of such experience interests us is another matter altogether.

Thus Nietzsche's second objection seems also to rest on a confusion—namely, supposing that an experience which itself is 'disinterested' is also of no interest or importance. Art was of exceptional importance to Schopenhauer, and he believes it to be equally important for almost all of us. His reasons for so thinking, moreover, were reasons not far removed from those that lead Nietzsche to dignify it as the 'truly metaphysical activity' (*BT*, 'Attempt', 5) of man: it transfigures the human condition as given to us by nature and reworks it into a thing of beauty.

5 TRANSFIGURATION AND SELF-OVERCOMING

> Nature, artistically considered, is no model. It exaggerates, it distorts, it leaves gaps. Nature is chance.
>
> (*TI*, IX, 7)

> [T]he genuine artist . . . surpasses nature . . . [He] understands nature's half-spoken words. He expresses clearly what she merely stammers. He impresses on the hard marble the beauty of the form which nature failed to achieve in a thousand attempts, and he places it before her, exclaiming as it were, 'This is what you desired to say!
>
> (*WWR*, I, 45)

5.1

I have argued that Nietzsche raises no cogent objections to Schopenhauer's claim that aesthetic experience is inherently disinterested. His two main criticisms—that aesthetic experience is active and passionate in nature, and that it is an experience type which we value for extra-aesthetic reasons—both turn on conflations regarding what it *is*, in Schopenhauer's view, for us to regard an object 'free of interest'. Even if Nietzsche's confused remarks finally tell us nothing about the merits of the disinterestedness thesis, however, they are instructive in what they reveal about Nietzsche's own view of aesthetic transfiguration. In particular, they illuminate Nietzsche's contempt for the notion of '*l'art pour l'art*', and his insistence on valuing art 'from the perspective of life'—that is, valuing it above all for its capacity to transfigure not just this or that object of experience, but to transfigure the general framework of experience. (It is in this sense, recall, that art is a *metaphysical* activity.) This capacity is realized, according to Nietzsche, when the target of aesthetic experience—the aesthetic object, so to speak—is nothing other than the experiencing subject himself. Somewhat ironically, an attitude very much like disinterested self-transcendence plays a central and indispensable role in Nietzsche's psychology at this point. To see this, one must turn to the second level of transfiguration I mentioned earlier: the aesthetic transfiguration of the subject's conception of himself and of his life.

In Nietzsche's mature work, a driving force behind his high regard for art and artistic creativity is the existential goal of *amor fati*: the love of what fate has given, the endorsement of what is, just as it is.[8] The essence of the attitude of *amor fati* is that one no longer wills that one's life and one's self were other than they are: it is a refusal to condemn what blind nature has made of us and for us, combined with a recognition of one's own ability to 're-form' how we experience and how we evaluate life, and thereby to create a new identity for ourselves. The role of artistry in achieving this attitude is not to obscure or veil the less palatable aspects of experience (as it perhaps was in *The Birth Tragedy*). In Nietzsche's mature work, its role is rather to present reality in a transfigured form which reshapes our thoughts about it and the evaluative attitudes with which we respond to it:

> A psychologist... asks: what does all art do? Does it not praise? Glorify? Choose? Prefer? With all this it strengthens or weakens certain valuations. Is this merely a 'moreover'? an accident? Something in which the artist's instinct has no share? Or is it not the very presupposition of the artist's ability? Does his basic instinct aim at art, or rather at the sense of art, at life? At a desirability of life? Art is the great stimuli to life: how could one understand it as purposeless, as aimless, as *l'art pour l'art*?
>
> (*TI*, IX, 24)

[8] I have in mind especially *Twilight of the Idols,* Part IV of *Thus Spoke Zarathustra*, and *The Will to Power*. The pre-eminent objective of *amor fati* also features in *Beyond Good and Evil* and *On the Genealogy of Morality*, although these texts do not so directly address the role of art in achieving it.

Put less dramatically, to regard the world aesthetically is to regard it, like the artist, creatively and affirmatively. Doing that, we find that art enables us both to understand reality more deeply and to value it. For Nietzsche, as for Schopenhauer, art affords the former—the deeper understanding—in part by eliciting our fully attuned attention to its objects, such that the one is absorbed by or immersed in them to such an extent that the contents of one's consciousness can only be identified in relation to them. As Julian Young remarks, 'in the aesthetic state [the] normal categories of experience are suspended, thereby enabling us to become alive to usually unnoticed aspects and construals of objects: in Nietzschean language, the object undergoes 'transfiguration' (Young, 1992, 124). Art affords the latter—the positive re-evaluation—in part by suspending our standard, habitual (and largely instrumental) evaluative attitudes, and inviting us instead to enjoy its objects independently of their everyday utility. Artistically conceived objects are objects more coherent and intelligible art illuminates their necessary or essential or defining features; it lends them drama, intensity, and a sense of significance; it makes them *interesting* in themselves. Moreover, it does this in perceptual modes that excite our imaginations, emotions, and other psycho-physiological responses, thereby intensifying our visceral sense of being alive.

In all of this, Schopenhauer and Nietzsche agree. But Nietzsche further proposes that the subject *himself* can be the ultimate work of art—or can be for those possessing the strength of the true artist:

> Only artists, and especially those of the theatre, have given men eyes and ears to see and hear with some pleasure what each man *is* himself, experiences himself, desires himself; only they have taught us to esteem the hero that is concealed in everyday characters; only they have taught us the art of viewing ourselves as heroes—from a distance and, as it were, simplified and transfigured.
>
> (*GS*, 78)

This is the transfigurative project of 'self-overcoming', of becoming who one (truly) is and, in the process, becoming 'one of those who make things beautiful. *Amor fati*' (*GS*, 276). It is arguably Nietzsche's most important and original contribution to the aesthetic psychology he inherited from Schopenhauer. Yet, as this passage reveals, the project depends critically on the Schopenhauerian resource of 'distanced' self-transcendence.

5.2

Nietzsche's proposed project of self-overcoming is the highest aspiration and application of our capacity for aesthetic transfiguration. Self-overcoming is, *inter alia*, a matter of 'giving style' to one's character—an art 'practiced by those who survey all the strengths and weakness of the nature and then fit them into an artistic plan until every one of them appears as art and even weakness delight the eye' (*GS*, 290). Put most simply, it is a project of self-creation, in which one stands back from one's character—one's given desires, dispositions, ambitions, values—rather as the painter stands back from his easel. Like the artist, one uses this distance to decide how one shall organize, arrange, and manipulate them according to an artistic vision. As early on as *Human, All Too Human*, Nietzsche recognizes the importance of gaining authority over one's desires and impulses—with a view not to eliminating them, but to *mastering* them so that one may choose how they are realized and what will develop from them:

> The man who has overcome his passions has entered into possession of the most fertile ground; like the colonist who has mastered the forests and swamps. To *sow* the seeds of good spiritual works in the soil of the subdued passion is then the immediate urgent task. The overcoming itself is only a *means*, not a goal; if it is not so viewed, all kinds of weeds and devilish nonsense will quickly spring up in this rich soil now unoccupied, and soon there will be more rank confusion than there ever was before.
>
> (*HH*, 'Wanderer', 53)

While he does not mention Schopenhauer here by name, Nietzsche is surely pointing an accusing finger at him as one who mistakes the means for the goal—who supposes that transcending one's desires and aims and interests is an end in itself. The accusation does not actually hit its mark with respect to the place of self-transcendence in Schopenhauer's *aesthetic* psychology. However, what matters here is that Nietzsche recognizes a distinction between these two ways of valuing self-transcendence, and clearly recognizes its instrumental value. Earlier in the same text he has observed that when the 'philosophical blindworms speak of the *terrible character* of the passions' they fail to acknowledge the responsibility each of us has for mastering and transforming them, making of them something one can endorse:

> Through ... a lack of self-observation and observation of those who are to be brought up, it is you yourselves who first allowed the passions to develop into such monsters that you are overcome by fear at the word 'passion'! It was up to you, and is up to us, to *take from* the passions their terrible character and thus prevent their becoming devastating torrents.—One should not inflate one's oversight into eternal fatalities; let us rather work honestly together on the task of transforming the passions of mankind one and all into joys.
>
> (*HH*, 'Wanderer', 83)

In Nietzsche's next book, *Daybreak*, he again uses the metaphor of organic cultivation to describe mastery of one's will, reminding us that 'One can dispose of one's drives like a garden and, though few know it, cultivate the shoots of anger, pity, curiosity, vanity as productively and profitably as a beautiful fruit tree on a trellis' (*D*, 560). Both passages describe part of what is required for self-overcoming: the redirecting or sublimating of one's 'willings' so that they are creatively transformed 'into all joys' and 'beautiful fruit'. In Schopenhauerian aesthetic experience, likewise, the will is neither eliminated nor abandoned; rather, it is liberated from its usual bonds to the individual's interests and redirected to the 'intensely active' task of attunement or, in the genius, artistic creation.

Nietzsche later takes this move of self-transcendence an important step further, characterizing artistic activity as the vehicle of self-overcoming *par excellence*—a vehicle by which we not only transform our drives into the creation of aesthetic objects (as in Schopenhauer) but transform *ourselves* into such objects. In Book V of *The Gay Science* this further step becomes explicit:

> *What one should learn from artists.* What means have we for making things beautiful, attractive and desirable, when they are not so?—and I suppose they are never so in themselves! We have here something to learn from physicians, when, for example, they dilute what is bitter or put wine and sugar into their mixing bowl; but we have still more to learn from artists, who, in fact are continually concerned in devising such inventions and artifices. To withdraw from things until one no longer sees much of them, until one has even to see things into them *in order to see them at all*—or to view them from the side, and as in a frame—or to look at them through colored glasses, or in the light of the sunset—or to furnish them with a surface or skin which is not fully transparent: we should learn all that from artists, and moreover be wiser than they. For this fine power of theirs usually ceases with them where art ceases and life begins; *we*, however, want to be the poets of our lives, and first of all in the smallest and most commonplace matters.
>
> (*GS*, 299)

The project of being 'poets of our lives'—making our own, individual lives 'beautiful, attractive and desirable'—is the proper goal of artistic activity for Nietzsche. But it depends entirely on our ability to transcend our given, individual natures, to master our passions in their given, natural forms, just as artists must master their personal materials and subject matter (whatever 'terrible monsters' it contains). 'Nature is chance', Nietzsche remarks, but art can transfigure such monsters into objects sufficiently magnificent and far reaching to immerse the spectator's attention and command his admiration and endorsement. Classical Greek tragedies rose to this task in a particularly vivid manner: they reconceived their inherited myths of destruction and chaos so that they no longer tell mere tales of this or that individual's regrettable misfortunes, of this or that unhappy event. These particulars are aesthetically transformed into universals: the great tragedies dramatize necessary dynamics and rhythms of human experience such that even suffering and conflict become part of what is intriguing, magnificent, and beautiful in life. Thus Nietzsche's novel insight, and the move that takes his aesthetic psychology beyond Schopenhauer's, is to see that, far from provoking resignation, such art invites one to immerse oneself in its images, and that immersion in turn moves one to transcend the individual point of view even in relation to oneself. Even one's *own* sufferings and conflicts, that is, are revealed to be a part of the great drama of existence:

> The psychology of the orgiastic as an overflowing feeling of life and strength where even pain still has the effect of a stimulus, gave me the key to the concept of tragic feeling... Tragedy is so far from proving anything about the pessimism of the Hellenes, in Schopenhauer's sense, that it may, on the contrary, be considered its decisive repudiation and counter-instance. Saying Yes to life even in its strangest and hardest problems, the will to life rejoicing over its own inexhaustibility even in the very sacrifice of its highest types—*that* is what I called Dionysian, that is what I guessed to be the bridge to the psychology of the *tragic* poet. *Not* in order to be liberated from terror and pity, not in order to purge oneself to a dangerous affect by its vehement discharge—Aristotle understood it that way—but in order to be *oneself* the eternal joy of becoming, beyond all terror and pity—that joy which included even the joy in destroying. And herewith I again touch that point from which I once went forth: *The Birth of Tragedy* was my first reevaluation of all values.
>
> (*TI*, X, 5)

Nietzsche found this passage important enough to quote it at length in *Ecce Homo*, and it is not difficult to see why: it highlights two key aspects of aesthetic transfiguration. First, it emphasizes the capacity of art to transfigure its objects, even where, as in tragedy, those objects are the terror and destruction that marks human experience; aesthetically transfigured, 'even pain still has the effect of a stimulus', and the work of art manifests a joy which includes 'even the joy in destroying'. Secondly, the passage makes explicit the transfigurative effect this has on the psychology of the subject 'orgiastically' attuned to such art—namely, that one becomes '*oneself* the eternal joy of becoming, beyond all terror and pity'.

The conjunction suggested here of both *union* with and *transcendence* of 'terror and pity' is as central to Nietzsche's thought as it was to Schopenhauer's. On the one hand, the subject is transfigured by being unified with that which produces or manifests terror and destruction—the 'inexhaustibility' of life, and the perseverance of the will to life 'even in its strangest and hardest problems'. On the other hand, and at the same time, one transcends or moves '*beyond* terror and pity' in that one no longer assesses them in relation to one's individual aims and purposes. This is not, critically, a matter of being purified of or eliminating these responses. Rather, one transcends one's (ordinary, nature-given) perspective of a self-interested, individual agent concerned with the fulfilment of his local, personal, practical aims. From that perspective the tragic dimensions of life can only be feared and condemned, and never affirmed. The aesthetically transfigured agent, however, moves beyond this negative valuation of life and 'interested' evaluation of the experiences it offers. No longer identifying himself as a particular being located in a particular space at a particular time, he recognizes himself as an instantiation of universals that transcend individuality, space, and time: he is a manifestation of the eternal cycle of birth, becoming, and destruction. By facilitating such self-transcendence, art can transfigure not only its objects (what it represents or expresses) but also its subjects—those who create it and those to whom their creations are communicated:

> We must appeal to the artists themselves. What does the tragic artist communicate of himself? Is it not precisely that state *without* fear in the face of the fearful and questionable that he is showing? *This* state itself is a great *desideratum*; whoever knows it honours it with the greatest honours.... He communicates it—*must* communicate it, provided he is an artist, a genius.... Courage and freedom of feeling before a powerful enemy, before a sublime calamity, before a problem that arouses dread—this triumphant state is what the tragic artist chooses, what he glorifies.
>
> (*TI*, IX, 24)

Nietzsche's reference to the sublime in this context is telling. The experience of the sublime is a paradigmatic case of disinterested self-transcendence: it occurs precisely when one is confronted with a circumstance that would ordinarily inspire terror and profound aversion. Experienced as sublime, however, that same circumstance, as Schopenhauer observes, 'raises us above the will and its interest, and put us in such a mood that we find pleasure in the sight of what directly opposes the will' (*WWR*, II, 433). In *Twilight of the Idols* (and thereafter) our capacity for such self-transcendence is the beating heart of Nietzsche's notion of aesthetic transfiguration, and of the spirit of *amor fati* it generates. Through it, art is '*the redemption of the sufferer*—as the way to states in which suffering is willed, transfigured, deified, where suffering is a form of great delight' (*WP*, 53).

Schopenhauer likewise regarded aesthetic experience as transfigurative and redemptive, and offered a strikingly similar psychological account of why it is so. He drew very different implications from that phenomenon, of course, and in particular inferred a very different prescription for how best to address the 'problem of existence'. He notoriously avers, for instance, that:

> What gives to everything tragic, whatever the form in which it appears, the characteristic tendency to the sublime, is the dawning of the knowledge that the world and life can afford us no true satisfaction, and are therefore not worth our attachment to them.
>
> (*WWR*, II, 433–4).

Nietzsche's insight was to hold fast to what is internal to Schopenhauer's psychology of aesthetic experience itself: by respecting its intrinsic experiential character—including the 'intense activity', the 'pleasure' and 'delight' that Schopenhauer insisted it could afford—Nietzsche found in it the formula for *amor fati*, rather than resignation.

5.3

Or did he? Against this conclusion, Julian Young argues that Nietzsche's project of aesthetic redemption is ultimately a failure—an exercise in 'escapist inauthenticity' (Young, 1992, 147). Young, unlike many scholars, recognizes the affinity of Nietzsche's mature conception of aesthetic experience with Schopenhauer's own. He concludes, however, that the kind of self-transcendence to which this commits Nietzsche is incompatible with his project of life-affirmation, and represents a betrayal of the courageous vision expressed in the doctrine of eternal recurrence as it appears in Nietzsche's earlier work. Young interprets that doctrine (correctly, in my view) as a litmus test of one's preparedness to endorse all that life has to offer:

> In *The Gay Science* and in *Zarathustra* . . . that which—if I am a non-convalescent, fully healthy, Dionysian *Übermensch*—I will is the eternal recurrence of *my* life: the totality of the deeds and experiences which constitutes my exact life as an individual being
>
> (Young, 1992, 138).

However, the kind of affirmation one finds later on (for instance, in *TI*, X, 5) Young complains, is of a quite different order. There, he objects, Nietzsche endorses a 'transcendence of individuality' in which 'one identifies not with any of the individuals who are vulnerable to pain and death', and becomes

> 'oneself the eternal joy of becoming, beyond all terror'; one loses one's identity as an individual and identifies instead with 'the will to life rejoicing over *its* own exhaustibility' . . . The tragic effect, in short, is as it was in both *The Birth of Tragedy* and in Schopenhauer's account of tragedy, identified as the feeling of the *sublime*. As in *The Birth*, what tragedy does for life is to bring one the 'metaphysical comfort' of feeling oneself to be at one with the 'primal unity' or, as Nietzsche says, 'the will to life'.
>
> (Young, 1992, 137)

By my own account, Nietzsche's later work does indeed hold fast to some key ingredients of Schopenhauer's aesthetic psychology, while drawing out of them radically different implications and ethical prescriptions. For Young, however, this move (in *Twilight of the Idols* and *The Will to Power*) is a cowardly *retreat* from Nietzsche's original ambition of life-affirmation. Specifically, he accuses Nietzsche of abandoning the hard task of affirming one's own, *individual* existence, and indulging instead in an identification with a 'trans-individual' being:

> The fate I love [in *The Gay Science* and *Thus Spoke Zarathustra*] is the fate I experience as an individual *within* the world of becoming and pain. Such love and affirmation, if

I achieve it, manifests *genuine* courage, for... then I face the world 'honestly': I acknowledge its horrors and terrors, I acknowledge that pain and ultimately death are part of *my* inexorable lot. What, however, Dionysian man as conceived in *Twilight of the Idols* wills to recur is just *life*.... The only sense it makes to speak of him willing his own return is if he identifies himself with a trans-individual entity that lives on in his children and in the human species.

(Young, 1992, 138)

This characterization of Nietzsche's position in *Twilight of the Idols* effectively presents art as a vehicle for abdicating, rather than affirming, one's individual identity and the experiences that have shaped it. Worse yet, Young's account has Nietzsche resurrecting an identity in terms not far from the traditional notion of God ('a trans-individual entity that lives on in his children'). If correct, this verdict is a damning one indeed.

Young's target, I aver, misses its target rather widely. In particular, it trades on a critical elision which, we saw earlier, also misled Schopenhauer: it elides the crucial distinction between the *phenomenology* of aesthetic experience, on the one hand, and, on the other, the *evaluative implications* of that experience. Failing to distinguish these two dimensions of Nietzsche's account, Young supposes that if Schopenhauerian self-transcendence contributes to the former, it must inevitably compromise Nietzsche's 'antipodal' account of the latter. Let us briefly consider each in turn once more.

We saw earlier that Nietzsche, like Schopenhauer, recognizes the transcendence of individuality as an ineliminable condition of the kind of engaged, aesthetic experience that concerns him; only when we view a thing non-instrumentally are we free to recognize it as it is 'in itself', our vision unclouded by our usual concerns with personal, practical utilities. This much must be contributed by the *subject* of aesthetic activity, whether in the person of artist or beholder. This subjective transformation works in concert with the distinctive ways which in which such activity transforms the *objects* on which it is targeted. Nietzsche—following a long theoretical tradition before him—holds that art penetrates beyond the contingencies of ordinary perception to reveal what is truly *necessary* in its object. This is what Nietzsche (rather idiosyncratically) calls artistic 'idealizing':

Out of this feeling one lends to things, one *forces* them to accept from, one violates them—this process is called *idealizing*. Let us get rid of a prejudice here: idealizing does not consist, as is commonly held, in subtracting or discounting the petty and inconsequential. What is decisive is rather a tremendous drive to bring out the principle traits, so that the others disappear in the process.

(*TI*, IX, 8)

Recall now that Nietzsche characterizes his project of *amor fati* as precisely demanding that he 'learn more and more to see as beautiful *what is necessary in things*' (*GS*, 276, my emphasis). The connection with artistry is clear: it is the activity best placed to present 'what is necessary in things'. (As Aristotle famously expressed the point, well-formed works present timeless 'universals' through artistically conceived particulars.) This is something that does not occur naturally—without artistic reconstruction. As things are presented in nature they are chaotic and formless: 'Nature, artistically considered, is no model. It exaggerates, it distorts, it leaves gaps. Nature is *chance*' (*TI*, IX, 7). The model for the psychology of seeing 'what is necessary in things' is rather the artist's creative idealizing—a matter of bringing out 'the principle traits' or universals:

> A born psychologist instinctively guards against seeing for the sake of seeing; the same applies to the born painter. He never works 'from nature'—he leaves it to his instinct, his *camera obscura*, to sift and strain 'nature', the 'case', the 'experience'.... He is conscious only of the *universal*, the conclusion, the outcome: he knows nothing of that arbitrary abstraction from the individual case.
>
> (*TI*, IX, 7)

Goethe's *Tasso* offers a vivid illustration of this aspect of aesthetic transfiguration. In its final epiphanic recognition scene, Tasso's artistry permits him to transcend his personal fears and his hostility towards Antonio, revealing how profoundly and inescapably each man's character and actions are bound up with the other's. Tasso offers a series of poetic images of their relationship: he is, first, a wave made to sparkle when it sprays against the rocks, then a wave-tossed ship breaking against them, and finally the shipwrecked sailor clinging to one of these rocks to survive. Antonio is, by turns, the rock that both creates and destroys Tasso; he is an inescapable force of nature with which Tasso must contend and on which he ultimately depends. In these images, the identity of each man is shaped by the dynamics of their conflict. Bringing out 'what is necessary' in a thing is a matter of illuminating the features that make it the very thing that it is, and this requires in turn that one transcend the point of view of personal, instrumental interests. This is just what Goethe's 'idealization' of his protagonist's suffering achieves: an artistic reforming of nature's chance events, revealing the ways in which we exist not only as contingent particulars, but also as instantiations of necessary universals. Moreover, the insights afforded Tasso in his self-transcendent reverie scarcely allow him to *escape* his relationship with Antonio. To the contrary, they require him to see it as necessary and inescapable, and this is a fact in which he has the greatest personal interest; indeed, his future survival as an individual and as an artist turn on it entirely.

Young's interpretation of Nietzschean transcendence as cowardly escapism fails entirely to appreciate these dynamics of artistic idealization. Attunement to a work of art (including the work of one's own life, as in Tasso's case) does require disinterested, self-transcendence in order to effect the 'idealizing' of what is otherwise an arbitrary and senseless sequence of natural events. But that is not the end of the story for Nietzsche, any more than it is for Tasso. For Nietzsche, the evaluative *consequences* of this sort of aesthetic insight likewise reintroduce the interested, individual subject. Indeed, that subject re-emerges with a vengeance as the *Übermensch*, that ultimate artist who is prepared to take on the task of creating his values from the ground up. Such transformed valuations are, Nietzsche insists, art's ultimate *raison d'être*. (Hence art ultimately is to be viewed 'from the perspective of life'.) Art, not nature, is the proper paradigm for the psychologist—and for each of us—because it shows us what artistic reconstruction is capable of doing, viz., realigning our evaluative dispositions at the deepest level, proposing novel and creative ways of framing human experience. Thus realigned, we discover that it is necessarily painful, but also painfully *beautiful*. 'Only in this way', Nietzsche writes,

> can we deal with some base details in ourselves. Without this art we would be nothing but foreground and live entirely in the spell of that perspective which makes what is closest at hand and most vulgar appear as if it were vast, and reality itself.
>
> (*GS*, 78)

Tasso's epiphany aptly illustrates this transcendence of the 'foreground'. He is an artist throughout, but only at the epiphanic moment of self-transcendence does he realize his greatest work of art: himself. Always a professional master of transfiguration, Tasso becomes more than that when he creatively transfigures *himself*. This is, to be sure, a matter of moving from mere artistry to metaphysics. But is it also, as Young suggests, an abdication of his personal, individual, and highly particular circumstances? It is more natural, surely, to understand it as a revelation of who Tasso truly is in relation to Antonio, and of the ways in which the sufferings inflicted by the latter figure among the 'necessities' of his own nature. Tasso's personal failings represent, on the one hand, a familiar and common reality, yet he is also an artist in Nietzsche's sense: he transports his circumstances out of the realm of nature and reconfigures them into a coherent work of universal significance. As such, he constitutes a psychological vindication of Nietzsche's claim that an attitude of *amor fati* is *consistent* with a courageous realism about what human experience does and does not have to offer. Both attuned and transfiguring, Tasso manifests Nietzsche's real advance over Schopenhauer's aesthetic psychology: the possibility of affirming, rather than condemning, 'the future promised and hallowed in the past; the triumphant Yes to life beyond all death and change . . . ' (*TI*, X, 4).

I aver that my diagnosis of the Schopenhauerian nature of Nietzsche's aesthetic phenomenology does not, despite Young's allegations, spell disaster for the wider project of a positive re-evaluation of human experience. Indeed, if the account I have developed here is accurate, *both* Schopenhauer and Nietzsche emerge as offering powerful strategies for resisting a 'moral interpretation' of life. Schopenhauer identified attunement, transcendence, and transfiguration as the key strategies for such resistance—strategies which survive intact in Nietzsche's aesthetics from start to finish. Nietzsche, for his part, turned those strategies to a new end—namely, our aesthetic revaluation of our own natures. The inspiring theory of value and bold worldview that resulted was the culmination of a joint project that neither philosopher could have achieved on his own.

I have tried along the way to show, too, that Schopenhauer's role in this achievement has not been properly appreciated. This is no doubt due in part to Nietzsche's tendency to advertise his best appropriations as his own creations, a tendency owed in turn to his need to cultivate a view of himself as wholly self-formed, autonomous, and original. But we need not endorse that conceit; neither need we deny to Nietzsche what he genuinely achieved. His relationship with Schopenhauer's thought was more entangled, unstable, and conflicted than is often recognized, yet most readers will agree that it yielded an undeniably prescient and transformative turn in the history of the theory of value. Perhaps the best summation and assessment of their remarkable dynamic is to be found not in scholarly analyses at all, but in Goethe's poetic vision:

> *Two men they are, who therefore are opposed,*
> *I've felt it long, because by Nature cast*
> *In moulds so opposite, that she the twain*
> *Could never weld into a single man.*
>
> Goethe, *Torquato Tasso*, Act III, Scene 2 (1704–7)

REFERENCES

Came, D. 2009. 'Disinterestedness and Objectivity', *The European Journal of Philosophy*, 17/1: 91–100.

Dickie, G. 1964. 'The Myth of the Aesthetic Attitude', *American Philosophical Quarterly*, 1/1: 56–65.

Gardiner, P. 1997. *Schopenhauer* (Bristol: Thommes Press).

Janaway, C. 2009. 'Responses to Commentators', *The European Journal of Philosophy*, 17/1: 132–51.

Nietzsche, F. 1968. *The Will to Power*, Kaufmann, W. and Hollingdale, R. (trans.) (New York: Vintage Press).

Nietzsche, F. 1978. *Thus Spoke Zarathustra*, Kaufmann, W. (trans.) (Harmondsworth: Penguin).

Nietzsche, F. 1996. *Human, All Too Human*, Schacht, R. (ed.), Hollingdale, R. J. (trans.) (Cambridge: Cambridge University Press).

Nietzsche, F. 1997. *Daybreak*, Clark, M. and Leiter, B. (eds.) (Cambridge: Cambridge University Press).

Nietzsche, F. 1998. *On the Genealogy of Morality*, Clark, M. and Swensen A. (trans.) (Indianapolis: Hackett).

Nietzsche, F. 1999. *The Birth of Tragedy*, Geuss, R. and Speirs, R. (eds.), Speirs, R. (trans.) (Cambridge, Cambridge University Press).

Nietzsche, F. 2001. *The Gay Science*, Williams, B. (ed.), Nauckhoff, J. and del Caro, A. (trans.) (Cambridge: Cambridge University Press).

Nietzsche, F. 2005. *Ecce Homo*, in *The Anti-Christ, Ecce Homo, Twilight of the Idols, and Other Writings*, Ridley, A. (ed.), Norman, J. (trans.) (Cambridge: Cambridge University Press).

Nietzsche, F. 2005. *Twilight of the Idols*, in Ridley, A. (ed.), Norman, J. (trans.) *The Anti-Christ, Ecce Homo, Twilight of the Idols, and Other Writings* (Cambridge: Cambridge University Press).

Ridley, A. 2002. *Routledge Guidebook to Nietzsche on Art* (London: Routledge).

Schopenhauer, A. 1969. *The World as Will and Representation*, Vols. I and II, Payne, E. F. J. (trans.) (New York: Dover).

Stolnitz, J. 1989. 'The Aesthetic Attitude,' in Dickie, G., Sclafani, R., and Roblin, R. (eds.), *Aesthetics: A Critical Anthology* (New York: St Martin's Press; 2nd edition).

Vivas, E. 1955. *Creation and Discovery* (London: Gateway).

Young, J. 1992. *Nietzsche's Philosophy of Art* (Cambridge: Cambridge University Press).

9

Nietzsche on Distance, Beauty, and Truth

Sabina Lovibond

1

This chapter attempts to clarify some of the elements of a Nietzschean taste, and to see how these might be linked with the rest of Nietzsche's thought. It is not concerned with his 'official' philosophy of art in *The Birth of Tragedy*, but focuses mainly on three wide-ranging texts which he published in the 1880s: *The Gay Science*, *Beyond Good and Evil*, and *Twilight of the Idols*. These texts articulate a self-conscious and highly self-assured aesthetic sensibility, which is disclosed in part through pronouncements on the excellence or otherwise of individual writers and composers[1] ('Goethe is the last German before whom I feel reverence' (*TI*, IX, 51), 'Plato is boring' (*TI*, X, 2), George Eliot is a 'little blue-stocking' (*TI*, IX, 5)). But Nietzsche's attitudes emerge just as vividly through the discourse of physical condition and bodily self-expression which supplies him with so much of his evaluative vocabulary. He notices, and finds a world of meaning in, the way people move; their gestures and demeanour; how much or how little they talk, and in what tone of voice; whether or not they are working up a sweat.[2] His preferences on these points are very consistent. They owe something, no doubt, to a vitalist or biologically reductive mode of thought, as reflected in the following passage:

Reckoned physiologically, everything ugly weakens and afflicts man. It recalls decay, danger, impotence... Every token of exhaustion, of heaviness, of age, of weariness, every kind of

[1] Nietzsche has relatively little to say about the visual arts, but he refers frequently and in some detail to music; in fact, 'Without music life would be a mistake' (*TI*, I, 33).

[2] Bizet's *Carmen* seems perfect to Nietzsche because—in contrast to Wagner—it 'does not sweat' (*CW*, 1).

unfreedom, whether convulsive or paralytic, above all the smell, colour and shape of dissolution, of decomposition, though it be attenuated to the point of being no more than a symbol—all this calls forth the same reaction, the value judgement 'ugly'.

(*TI*, IX, 20)

Yet they spin free of any epistemic dependence on physiological 'theory', and issue in a spontaneous flow of comment on the expressive qualities of individuals, movements, and nations.

Contrary to the superficial process of association by which we might be tempted to link the 'will to power' or the *Übermensch* with ideas of sheer brute force, it is clear that among Nietzsche's main objects of aesthetic esteem are levity, delicacy, poise, nuance, 'halcyon' self-sufficiency, and calm—in contrast to coarseness, vehemence, noisy assertion, and emphatic gesture. Among his favourite images for the free (yet disciplined) movement of thought is that of dancing. 'Our first questions about the value of a book, of a human being, or a musical composition are: Can they walk? Even more, can they dance?' (*GS*, 366). Or again:

Who among Germans still knows from experience that subtle thrill which the possession of intellectual *light feet* communicates to all the muscles!—A stiffly awkward air in intellectual matters, a clumsy hand in grasping—this is in so great a degree German that foreigners take it for the German nature in general... *dancing* in any form cannot be divorced from a *noble education*, being able to dance with the feet, with concepts, with words.[3]

(*TI*, VIII, 7)

Too much of what we know as 'philosophy' suffers, in Nietzsche's view, from a disabling heaviness. In fact, as he asks in the famous opening words of *Beyond Good and Evil*: 'Supposing truth to be a woman—what? is the suspicion not well founded that all philosophers, when they have been dogmatists, have had little understanding of women?' (*BGE*, P). The intellectual failure of such thinkers, he goes on to suggest, is due to 'the gruesome earnestness, the clumsy importunity with which they have hitherto been in the habit of approaching truth' (ibid.);[4] by contrast, he tells us near the end of the book that 'if gods too philosophize... I do

[3] Cf. *CW*, 10 on what 'we halcyons' miss in Wagner: 'light feet, wit, fire, grace; the great logic; the dance of the stars; the exuberant spirituality; the southern shivers of light; the *smooth* sea—perfection.' (Unless otherwise stated, emphasis in quotations are always in the original.)

[4] Cf. *BGE*, 220, where he returns to the theme of the philosopher as suitor: 'truth has so much to stifle her yawns here [on the subject of "disinterestedness"] when answers are demanded of her. She is after all, a woman: one ought not to violate her'.

not doubt that while doing so they also know how to laugh in a new and superhuman way—and at the expense of all serious things!' (*BGE*, 294).

Those who can serve as our models in avoiding 'gruesome earnestness' display two distinct, yet complementary virtues: their mode of expression is both *easy* and *restrained*. 'Everything *good* is instinct—and consequently easy, necessary, free. Effort is an objection' (*TI*, VI, 2). Restraint is the mark of those who do not feel the need to insist or to force themselves on the attention of others. 'Anyone with a very loud voice is almost incapable of thinking subtleties . . . The mistrustful speak emphatically; the mistrustful also make others emphatic' (*GS*, 216, 226). In any event, 'We no longer have a sufficiently high estimate of ourselves when we communicate. Our true experiences are not garrulous' (*TI*, IX, 26). The 'ease' that appeals to Nietzsche, then, is not the kind that results from throwing decorum to the winds, even if this action is in fact typical of the 'mad and fascinating semi-barbarism' (*BGE*, 224) of nineteenth-century Europe: instead, it reflects the rigorous internalization of a system of rules, to the point where these rules become as proper to us as our own body, and no less apt for the framing of our own (effortless) gestures.

> Every artist knows how far from the feeling of letting himself go his 'natural' condition is, the free ordering, placing, disposing, forming in the moment of 'inspiration'—and how strictly and subtly he then obeys thousandfold laws which precisely on account of their severity and definiteness mock all formulation in concepts . . . The essential thing 'in heaven and upon earth' seems . . . to be a protracted *obedience* in *one* direction: from out of that there always emerges and has always emerged in the long run something for the sake of which it is worthwhile to live on earth, for example virtue, art, music, dance, reason, spirituality—something transfiguring, refined, mad and divine.
>
> (*BGE*, 188)

2

All this, however, would be arbitrary—a mere matter of subjective preference—were it not for the integration of these elements in the Nietzschean aesthetic with other concerns which are more overtly moral (in the sense of 'pertaining to character') and, ultimately, political. Such integration is of course hardly surprising, given Nietzsche's attitude to the 'moral' worldview as we are likely to understand that term pre-philosophically—that is, as an outlook informed by Judaeo-Christian notions of personal responsibility, duty, guilt, and blame.[5] As

[5] This is the 'morality' promoted by Bernard Williams to the status of a technical concept, contrasted with the more free-wheeling 'ethics': see Williams (1985), especially chapter 10.

an alternative to the familiar task of self-improvement whose purpose is to limit our propensity to wrongdoing, Nietzsche proposes the aim of 'giving style' to one's character:

> a great and rare art! It is practiced by those who survey all the strengths and weaknesses of their nature and then fit them into an artistic plan until every one of them appears as art and reason and even weaknesses delight the eye... In the end, when the work is finished, it becomes evident how the constraint of a single taste governed and formed everything large and small. Whether this taste was good or bad is less important than one might suppose, if only it was a single taste!
>
> (*GS*, 290)

That is, he proposes the aesthetically motivated project of adapting or transforming one's character (drawing boldly on the resources offered by one's particular psychological endowment, however idiosyncratic) into something that can be contemplated with pleasure. And this project too can be governed by a variety of different aesthetic values or ideals, not all equally admirable or congenial to Nietzsche, although he leaves room for a certain pluralism of appreciation:

> It will be the strong and domineering natures that enjoy their finest gaiety in such constraint [the 'constraint of a single taste'] and perfection under a law of their own... Conversely, it is the weak characters without power over themselves that *hate* the constraint of style. They feel that if this bitter and evil constraint were imposed upon them they would be demeaned; they become slaves as soon as they serve; they hate to serve. Such spirits—and they may be of the first rank—are always out to shape and interpret their environment as *free* nature: wild, arbitrary, fantastic, disorderly, and surprising. And they are well advised because it is only in this way that they can give pleasure to themselves.
>
> (ibid.)

A major point of interest in this well-known passage is the link it provides between 'morals' (in the post-Christian, aesthetics-of-character sense) and politics as areas for the exercise of a Nietzschean taste. Those who 'hate the constraint of style' because, in general, they *hate to serve* (and experience constraint as a kind of slavery) are recognizable as specimens of the same type that we will meet again in *Beyond Good and Evil* as a representative of the 'democratic form and formlessness of life... "Away with all masters!"—that is what the plebeian instinct desires here too' (*BGE*, 204).[6] Even the idea that *nature* conforms to law is redolent, for Nietzsche, of a politics he despises. 'Everywhere equality before the law—nature is in this matter no different from us and no better off

[6] 'Here' refers to the contemporary tendency of 'science' (*Wissenschaft*) to usurp the authority of philosophy.

than we': for him this implicit conviction of modern physics bespeaks a 'vulgar hostility towards everything privileged and autocratic' (ibid.).

> '*Ni dieu, ni maître*'—that is your motto too: and therefore 'long live the law of nature'—isn't that so? But . . . that is interpretation, not text; and someone could come along who, with an opposite intention and art of interpretation, knew how to read out of the same nature and with regard to the same phenomena the tyrannically ruthless and inexorable enforcement of power-demands.[7]
>
> (*BGE*, 22)

What Nietzsche admires at the level of artistic expression—including, centrally, the qualities reviewed in Section 1—is associated in his thinking with *noblesse* as opposed to commonness: he credits the favoured aesthetic attributes with a 'noble' genealogy. The choice of a French word here is calculated; for 'European *noblesse*—of feeling, of taste, of custom, in short *noblesse* in every exalted sense of the word—is the work and invention of *France*, European vulgarity, the plebeianism of modern ideas, that of—*England*' (*BGE*, 253).[8] 'Modern ideas' for Nietzsche comprise all those democratic and egalitarian tendencies (so deeply indebted, despite the pronouncement just quoted, to the French Revolution) which are the political manifestation of *ressentiment*, that is, the angry repudiation of whatever we experience as placing us in an inferior position—or as Nietzsche might prefer to put it, of whatever serves to remind us of our own inferiority.

> 'If I am *canaille*, you ought to be so too': on the basis of this logic one makes revolutions . . . Whether one attributes one's feeling vile to others or to *oneself*—the Socialist does the former, the Christian for example the latter—makes no essential difference. What is common to both, and *unworthy* in both, is that someone has to be to *blame* for the fact that one suffers.
>
> (*TI*, IX, 34)

His references to 'socialist dolts and blockheads' and to the 'anarchist dogs which now rove the streets of European culture' (*BGE*, 203; 202) are characteristic; also singled out for censure are 'international courts in place of war' and 'equal rights for women' (*GM*, III, 25), the advocacy of the latter being condemned by Nietzsche as a 'clumsy and indignant parade of all of slavery and bondage that woman's position in the order of society has hitherto entailed and still entails (as if slavery were a counter-argument and not rather a condition of every higher

[7] Later, at *BGE*, 202, '*ni dieu ni maître*' is quoted again and described as a 'socialist formula'.

[8] Cf. *TI*, IX, 38 on 'the contemptible sort of well-being dreamed of by shopkeepers, Christians, cows, women, Englishmen and other democrats'.

culture, of every enhancement of culture)' (*BGE*, 239). ('Indignant' is a term of opprobrium for Nietzsche; at any rate he thinks the lover of knowledge 'should in general lend an ear whenever anyone speaks *without* indignation' (*BGE*, 26, my emphasis).)

Another, older source of our problematic 'modernity' is the Protestant Reformation, which according to Nietzsche

> shares the responsibility for the degeneration of the modern scholar, for his lack of reverence, shame and depth . . . in short, for that *plebeianism of the spirit* which is a peculiarity of the last two centuries . . . 'Modern ideas' also belong to this peasant rebellion of the north against the colder, more ambiguous and mistrustful spirit of the south that built its greatest monument in the Christian church.[9]
>
> (*GS*, 358)

This 'peasant', or plebeian, inheritance—consolidated now by the legacy of the Enlightenment—is visible in our own cultural surroundings in an incipient 'rule of the rabble', whose 'heavy, overcast sky makes everything leaden and opaque' (*BGE*, 287). And our (modern) sensibility is further compromised by the historicism which defines the intellectual life of Nietzsche's own age, with its general attitude of sympathy for the phenomena of process and development:

> that which we men of the 'historical sense' find hardest to grasp, to feel, taste, love, that which at bottom finds us prejudiced and almost hostile, is just what is complete and wholly mature in every art and culture, that which constitutes actual nobility in works and in men, their moment of smooth sea and halcyon self-sufficiency, the goldness and coldness displayed by all things which have become perfect. Perhaps our great virtue of the historical sense necessarily stands opposed to *good* taste, or to the very best taste at any rate.
>
> (*BGE*, 224)

The mentality described in this passage, though hardly 'plebeian' in any obvious sense, is nonetheless liable to place some of the highest aesthetic achievements of the European tradition beyond our reach. For example, it will militate against the kind of pleasure Nietzsche has gained from the odes of Horace:

> this mosaic of words in which every word, as sound, as locus, as concept, pours forth its power to left and right and over the whole, this minimum in the range and number of signs which achieves a maximum of energy of these signs—all this is Roman and, if one

[9] 'North' and 'south'—the latter seen here in unexpected juxtaposition with the idea of (emotional) 'coldness'—are important aesthetic signifiers for Nietzsche in their own right: thus phase 3 of *TI*, 'How the "Real World" at last Became a Myth' (the era of the Kantian *noumenon*): 'Fundamentally the same old sun, but shining through mist and scepticism; the idea grown sublime, pale, northerly, Königsbergian' (*TI*, IV); *BGE*, 50: 'the whole of Protestantism lacks southern *delicatezza*'; *BGE*, 254: Bizet 'has discovered a region of the *south in music*'; whereas *CW*, 2: 'Wagner represents the *damp* north'.

will believe me, *noble par excellence.* All other poetry by comparison becomes somewhat too popular.[10]

(*TI*, X, 1)

Nietzsche takes seriously—that is, with the particular kind of seriousness his own 'gay science' permits or requires—the detailed effect of these long-term tendencies on our day-to-day aesthetic experience. One striking result of democratization is the growing authority of the 'Protestant ethic',[11] which venerates labour and has practically forgotten the ancient, aristocratic distaste for it. Of his American contemporaries, Nietzsche says that

the breathless haste with which they work—the distinctive vice of the new world—is already beginning to affect old Europe with its ferocity... One thinks with a watch in one's hand, even as one eats one's midday meal while reading the latest news of the stock market... If sociability and the arts still offer any delight, it is the kind of delight that slaves, weary of their work, desire for themselves.

(*GS*, 329)

This change in the social rhythm is destroying our collective 'eye and ear for the melody of movements' and generating a 'universal demand for *gross obviousness*' (ibid.) in human relationships. It also provokes in Nietzsche some more specific reflections on the evolution of German music:

[W]e might ask whether the contempt for melody that is now spreading more and more and the atrophy of the melodic sense in Germany should be understood as democratic bad manners and an after effect of the Revolution. For melody delights so openly in lawfulness and has such an antipathy for everything that is still becoming, still unformed and arbitrary, that it sounds like an echo of the *old* order in Europe and like a seduction to go back to that.[12]

(*GS*, 103)

There is another kind of slowness to which Nietzsche also attaches value, namely, slowness of emotional response—not as a symptom of sluggish or laborious physiological functioning, but rather as a sign, so to speak, of the high standard one sets for anything that is to command one's attention.

One has to learn to *see*, one has to learn to *think*, one has to learn to *speak* and *write*: the end in all three is a noble culture.—Learning to *see*—habituating the eye to repose, to patience, to letting things come to it... All unspirituality, all vulgarity, is due to the

[10] The reference is to Horace's successful transposition into Latin of Greek lyric verse metres (Sapphic, Alcaic, etc.) with their strict rules governing the occurrence of long and short vowels.

[11] This term is due not to Nietzsche but to the sociologist Max Weber (1864–1920).

[12] For a development of this theme in relation to more recent music, but with some avowed Nietzschean influence, see Scruton (1997, 500–6).

incapacity to resist a stimulus—one *has* to react, one obeys every impulse... A practical application of having learned to see: one will have become slow, mistrustful, resistant as a learner in general. In an attitude of hostile calm one will allow the strange, the novel of every kind to approach one first—one will draw back one's hand from it. To stand with all doors open, to prostrate oneself submissively before every petty fact, to be ever itching to mingle with, *plunge into* other people and other things, in short our celebrated modern 'objectivity', is bad taste...[13]

(*TI*, VIII, 6)

This is why Nietzsche is at pains to point out that even in relation to the 'classical' literature of the ancient world his own taste, 'which may be called the opposite of a tolerant taste, is... far from uttering a wholesale Yes: in general it dislikes saying Yes, it would rather say No, most of all it prefers to say nothing at all' (*TI*, X, 1).[14]

Yet this 'noble culture' has another face, to be turned towards those rare objects that succeed in penetrating its defences. Just as the longing for freedom has its home in 'slave morality', says Nietzsche, so

the art of reverence and devotion and the enthusiasm for them are the regular symptom of an aristocratic mode of thinking and valuating.—This makes it clear without further ado why love *as passion*—it is our European speciality—absolutely must be of aristocratic origin: it was, as is well known, invented by the poet-knights of Provence, those splendid, inventive men of the '*gai saber*'.[15]

(*BGE*, 260)

And in one of Nietzsche's most remarkable passages the motif of devotion, a devotion perhaps reluctantly bestowed yet destined to endure, is brought into connection with aesthetic value-judgment: in music, he says, we have to progress from *learning to hear* a melody in the first place (or to 'delimit it as a separate life'), via a phase of exertion in which we try to *tolerate* it in spite of its strangeness, to the moment when we become *used* to it and realize that its absence would be felt as a loss:

But that is what happens to us not only in music. That is how we have *learned to love* all things that we now love. In the end we are always rewarded for our good will, our patience, fairmindedness, and gentleness with what is strange; gradually, it sheds its veil and turns out to be a new and indescribable beauty. That is its *thanks* for our hospitality.

(*GS*, 334)

[13] Cf. also *BGE*, 213 on 'the slow eye which seldom admires, seldom looks upward, seldom loves'.

[14] Note that the thought in a non-metaphysical passage like this one needs to be kept separate from our more familiar image of Nietzsche as a 'Yes-sayer', which is associated with ideas such as *amor fati* and eternal recurrence.

[15] *Gai saber*: gay science.

3

The idea emerging in the last few passages cited—that of an emotional distance which restrains the noble, or aristocratic, type from any facile impulse to 'plunge into' the life around him—can be regarded as one of many variations on the theme of distance played out in Nietzsche's thought. Again, this theme connects a certain pattern of response to straightforwardly 'aesthetic' phenomena with other—more pervasive or structural—features of the Nietzschean mentality.

A batch of remarks in the early books of *The Gay Science* show distance to be important for Nietzsche, in the first place, as a necessary condition for *getting an adequate view*—for instance, of large objects such as mountains. A mountain may give charm and significance to the surrounding landscape, yet when we climb it we may be disappointed: 'We had forgotten that some greatness, like some goodness, wants to be beheld only from a distance' (*GS*, 15). But even ordinary human character tends to look better when placed at arm's length, as it is in the theatre. Our dramatists have 'taught us the art of viewing ourselves as heroes—from a distance and, as it were, simplified and transfigured' (*GS*, 78), and religion has perhaps made use of the same technique: 'By surrounding him with eternal perspectives, it taught man to see himself from a distance and as something past and whole' (ibid.). Sometimes, too, this procedure offers aesthetic benefits for the sense of hearing:

> All great noise leads us to move happiness to some quiet distance. When a man stands in the midst of his own noise, in the midst of his own surf of plans and projects, then he is apt to see quiet, magical beings gliding past him and to long for their happiness and seclusion: *women* . . . Yet! Yet! Noble enthusiast, even on the most beautiful sailboat there is a lot of noise, and unfortunately much small and petty noise. The magic and the most powerful effect of women is, in philosophical language, action at a distance, *actio in distans*; but this requires first of all and above all—*distance*.[16]
>
> (*GS*, 60)

All these examples appeal in their different ways to the thought that many things can be seen, or in general experienced, to the best advantage by standing back. Nietzsche's designs on the concept of 'standing back', however, reach far beyond this comparatively homely point. The 'hostile calm' that protects us from inferior forms of stimulation is allied, in his view, to a proper recognition of our own distance from any superior objects or persons we may encounter. Just as those who have 'learned to see' will not be found eagerly reaching out to meet new facts

[16] In a more practical vein, see also the opening lines of *GM*, III, 8 on 'what [philosophers] can least do without: freedom from compulsion, disturbance, noise, from tasks, duties, worries'.

and sensations half-way, so they will refrain in their role as observers from crowding in on things and, as it were, putting them out of countenance:

> He whose task it is to explore the soul ... will test it for its *instinct of reverence* ... Much has been gained when the feeling has at last been instilled into the masses (into the shallow-pates and greedy-guts of every sort) that there are things they must not touch ... Conversely, there is perhaps nothing about the so-called cultured, the believers in 'modern ideas', that arouses so much disgust as their lack of shame, the self-satisfied insolence of eye and hand with which they touch, lick and fumble with everything.
>
> (*BGE*, 263)

The *noblesse* Nietzsche celebrates is expressed, by contrast, in a respect for the aloofness or self-withholding quality of certain persons and ideas, and in a sympathetic acceptance of the impulse to concealment. For '[e]very profound spirit needs a mask: more, around every profound spirit a mask is continually growing' (*BGE*, 40);[17] and 'it is part of a more refined humanity to have reverence "for the mask" and not to practise psychology and inquisitiveness in the wrong place' (*BGE*, 270). Nietzsche's advocacy of the 'mask', which when taken out of context may appear to be promoting a kind of postmodernist tricksterism, is better read as an element in his complex (and of course self-referential) portrayal of the plight of the culturally 'homeless', those who 'prefer to live on mountains, apart, "untimely", in past or future centuries' (*GS*, 377).

We are concerned here with a value-judgment belonging to the domain of taste (as evidenced by Nietzsche's haughty rhetoric of touching, licking, and fumbling), but also to that of intelligence: there is much that cannot be understood by those who are unable to keep their distance, or to operate tactfully in the presence of something undisclosed.

But the motif of distance as it connects with concealment or withholding can once again be identified in a section of *The Gay Science* with a more immediate bearing on the appreciation of works of art. Resuming his discussion of the dramatic distancing of (mundane) ordinary life,[18] Nietzsche reflects that we positively require art forms such as theatre and opera to hold back, in the interest of aesthetic gratification, from the realistic portrayal of speech: taking our cue from the ancient Athenians, he says, 'we are delighted when the tragic hero still finds words, reasons, eloquent gestures, and altogether intellectual brightness, where life approaches abysses and men in reality lose their heads and certainly linguistic felicity'; opera retreats even further from lifelike representation of the

[17] Cf. *BGE*, 289: 'Every philosophy also *conceals* a philosophy; every opinion is also a hiding-place; every word also a mask'.

[18] *GS*, 78, cited above.

human scene, since words of any description are now eclipsed by music—'that is the beautiful *unnaturalness* for whose sake one goes to the opera' (*GS*, 80).

4

Nietzsche's esteem for 'distance', then, exerts a wide-ranging influence on his aesthetic reflections. But this preoccupation too turns out to be all of a piece with his moral and political worldview. In particular, the experience of *looking down from a great height*—the prerogative of the mountain dweller—is rich in political associations for him. These associations take more definite shape in the idea of a 'pathos of distance', a feeling for the natural 'order of rank' among persons (or rather among 'men'), which Nietzsche of course believes to be endangered by modern social developments:

> 'Equality', a certain actual rendering similar of which the theory of 'equal rights' is only the expression, belongs essentially to decline: the chasm between man and man, class and class, the multiplicity of types, the will to be oneself, to stand out—that which I call *pathos of distance*—characterizes every *strong* age.[19]
>
> (*TI*, IX, 37)

Nietzsche leaves us in no doubt of the importance he attaches to this mode of consciousness:

> Every elevation of the type 'man' has hitherto been the work of an aristocratic society—and so it always will be: a society which believes in a long scale of orders of rank and differences of worth between man and man and needs slavery in some sense or other. Without the *pathos of distance* such as develops from the incarnate differences of classes, from the ruling caste's looking out and looking down on subjects and instruments and from its equally constant exercise of obedience and command, its holding down and holding at a distance, that other, more mysterious pathos could not have developed either, that longing for an ever-increasing widening of distance within the soul itself, the formation of ever higher, rarer, more remote, tenser, more comprehensive states.
>
> (*BGE*, 257)

The supreme achievements of human self-formation and self-expression must therefore be credited to the 'intolerant' social disciplines imposed (according to Nietzsche) by every aristocratic morality (*BGE*, 262), and to the 'protracted obedience in one direction' (*BGE*, 188) enforced by such moralities. In the absence of these conditions they would not have been forthcoming, so the artistic

[19] Cf. *BGE*, 62 on the 'abysm of rank between man and man'. (Here at any rate Nietzsche is at one with Plato, for whom the philosophical element in society is '*naturally* the smallest', *physei oligiston genos*: *Republic* 428e9–429a1.)

and cultural heritage that receives lip service from the 'newspaper-reading *demi-monde* of the spirit' (*BGE*, 263) is the fruit of a way of life that could not be acceptable to any conscientious modernist.

However, the element of scandal in texts like these lies not in the familiar point that (for example) the 'classic' art of the ancient world was produced by a slave-owning society, but rather in the practical inference Nietzsche draws from this point—that is, in his insistence on the 'elevation of the type "man"' as a value superior to anything proposed by 'modern' (egalitarian) ideas. On this question of priorities Nietzsche is, in his own words, 'anti-liberal to the point of malice' (*TI*, IX, 39).[20] He shakes his head over working-class militancy:

> The stupidity, fundamentally the instinct degeneration which is the cause of *every* stupidity today, lies in the existence of a labour question at all. About certain things *one does not ask questions*: first imperative of instinct.—I simply cannot see what one wants to do with the European worker now one has made a question of him. He finds himself far too well placed not to go on asking for more, or to ask more and more impudently . . . But what does one *want*?—to ask it again. If one wills an end, one must will the means to it: if one wants slaves, one is a fool if one then educates them to be masters.
>
> (*TI*, IX, 40)

Our exemplars of 'actual nobility' (*BGE*, 224) in the ordering of society can be drawn from the aristocratic communities of the past ('Venice, say, or an ancient Greek *polis*' (ibid., 262)), or from Russia, 'the *only* power today which has durability in it, which can wait, which can still promise something' (*TI*, IX, 39).[21]

5

Allied to the theme of distance, and similarly indebted to Nietzsche's anti-egalitarian convictions, is that of *rarity* as a mark of aesthetic value. This idea is not confined to a narrowly political application, since an experience can also be 'rare' by virtue of occurring infrequently, or perhaps on a single, unique occasion. And there are in fact objects, or so Nietzsche suggests (again with the help of

[20] The work of Walter Kaufmann has expunged the early twentieth-century image of Nietzsche as a proto-Nazi, and there now seems to be a striking reticence about the 'anti-liberal' aspect of his thought. An important influence here will no doubt be Kaufmann's portrayal of him as 'basically "anti-political"' (1974, 412), which, however, is too respectful of Nietzsche's self-description in *Ecce Homo* as 'the last anti-political German'. In the same vein, for example, Tracy B. Strong maintains that 'Nietzsche is available to a wide range of political appropriations, indeed perhaps to all', and that 'with the exception of what he says here and there on political themes, Nietzsche does not write about political matters' (1996, 138). A refreshing contrast to this tendency is to be found in Landa (1999).

[21] This was not one of Nietzsche's more prescient moments.

mountain imagery), in regard to which a moment of perfect illumination is the most one can hope for:

> For seeing the ultimate beauties of a work, no knowledge or good will is sufficient; this requires the rarest of lucky accidents: The clouds that veil these peaks have to lift for once so that we see them glowing in the sun... But what does unveil itself for us, *unveils itself for us once only*... Yes, life is a woman.
>
> (*GS*, 339)

In a less speculative vein, however, Nietzsche can speak simply enough of 'high culture' as something with which he and his putative reader are familiar; and in this kind of context a political motive promptly reappears. Mass higher education, for Nietzsche, is an oxymoron, for any 'higher' curriculum 'belongs to the exceptions alone... Great and fine things can never be common property' (*TI*, VIII, 5). There are, no doubt, books 'for everybody', but these 'are always malodorous books: the smell of petty people clings to them' (*BGE*, 30). In general, we must remember that 'what can be common has ever but little value... great things are for the great, abysses for the profound, shudders and delicacies for the refined, and, in sum, all rare things for the rare' (*BGE*, 43).

These claims certainly relate (both for Nietzsche and for us) to a topical issue in educational politics. But they also point towards something more abstract in Nietzsche's thinking which might be described as a *politics of communication*. Here the main idea would be that since to communicate is, literally, to *render common*—that is, to present one's mental states in such a way that others can enter into them and share them—the whole business of speech, by which our thoughts are continually 'translated back into the perspective of the herd' (*GS*, 354), is rigged in favour of the ordinary or average human being; whereas 'the more select, subtle, rare and harder to understand are liable to remain alone, succumb to accidents in their isolation and seldom propagate themselves' (*BGE*, 268).

Surfacing in remarks on the way language can betray its superficial promise to connect us with others, the Nietzschean 'pathos of distance' can take on a tone of melancholy or self-pity.[22] At the same time, that contempt for the 'obvious' already registered in Nietzsche's condemnation of loud or 'emphatic' utterance

[22] 'People in general seem to understand one another—at any rate they chat away merrily enough—but no one understands *me*!' This state of mind, so normal phenomenologically yet so questionable as metaphysics, is the one over which Wittgenstein achieves a brilliant critical victory with his 'private language argument', which demonstrates that—in the relevant, metaphysical, sense—'*nothing* is concealed' (1967, §435, my emphasis). For a discussion of the motif of moral isolation in Wittgenstein, which suggests some interesting points of comparison with Nietzsche, see Tanesini (2004).

(see Section 1) is apt to spill over into a kind of narcissistic displeasure, provoked by the feeling that one has strayed too far in the direction of accessibility. 'One no longer loves one's knowledge enough when one has communicated it' (*BGE*, 160); for after all, 'Must not anyone who wants to move the crowd be an actor who impersonates himself? Must he not first translate himself into grotesque obviousness and then present his whole person in this coarsened and simplified version?' (*GS*, 236).

Nietzsche does have (and does not disavow) the normal human desire to communicate, but the persona he constructs in the works I have been discussing is defined by a refusal to lose sight of the distinction between good and bad company—and '*all* company is bad company except the company of one's equals' (*BGE*, 26, my emphasis). He therefore feels obliged to maintain a moral and intellectual exclusion zone, enforced by the device of an anti-democratic mode of expression:

> One does not only wish to be understood when one writes; one wishes just as surely *not* to be understood. It is not by any means necessarily an objection to a book when anyone finds it impossible to understand: perhaps that was part of the author's intention—he did not want to be understood by just 'anybody'. All the nobler spirits and tastes select their audience when they wish to communicate; and choosing that, one at the same time erects barriers against 'the others'. All the more subtle laws of style have their origin at this point: they at the same time keep away, create a distance, forbid entrance... while they open the ears of those whose ears are related to ours.
>
> (*GS*, 381)

To make one's thoughts available to others involves a kind of hospitality, but not necessarily the kind that promises a warm welcome to all comers. 'One knows hearts which are capable of *noble* hospitality, which have curtained windows and closed shutters: they keep their best rooms empty' (*TI*, IX, 25).[23]

Such passages seem to confirm the perceptive observation of Henry Staten that Nietzsche engages, psychologically, in the 'all-too-human' subterfuge of forestalling attack by getting one's own attack in first—that he 'preempts [his audience's] ability to reject him by having already, since long before, put himself, or found himself, beyond their reach' (Staten, 1990, 39).[24] Ironically, as Staten points out, the likely motive for this manoeuvre is nothing other than *ressentiment*, 'the

[23] Cf. *TI*, IX, 51: 'who knows, after all, whether I even *wish* to be read today [as opposed to becoming a creator of "things upon which time tries its teeth in vain"]?'

[24] Staten draws an analogy with the famous '*fort-da*' game invented by Freud's baby grandson and described in *Beyond the Pleasure Principle* (1920, §II), in which (according to Freud) a cotton-reel on a string represents the child's mother and helps him come to terms with her periodic absences by letting him imagine that he controls them.

vengefulness of the impotent against those who have power over them: for example, the vengefulness of a speaker or writer against an audience that ignores him or jeers at him' (38). At all events there is a kind of distance that one puts between oneself and others for defensive purposes, or by retreating.

6

The same exclusionary impulse makes itself felt in Nietzsche's discussions of truth, and may help to shed light on what would otherwise look like a rather crude case of self-contradiction. Some of the most celebrated of these discussions are those containing his reductive analysis of the 'will to truth' as a manifestation of the ascetic ideal, in which he points to the positivist demand for 'nothing but the facts' (the will to renounce all subjective interpretation of experience) and comments that 'all this expresses, broadly speaking, as much ascetic virtue as any denial of sensuality (it is at bottom only a particular mode of this denial)' (*GM*, III, 24). Already in *Beyond Good and Evil* he had posed the question of the value of truth, asking '*Why not rather* untruth? And uncertainty? Even ignorance?' (*BGE*, 1).[25]

Such questions pose an obvious challenge to the status of truth as a cultural value.[26] Yet Nietzsche is also to be found affirming *truthfulness* as a virtue (contrasted with evasiveness or mendacity), and insisting that a warlike temperament is needed in order to understand his ideas. *Ecce Homo*, one of Nietzsche's last works, is a rich source for this theme:

> How much truth does a spirit *endure*, how much truth does it *dare*? More and more that became for me the real measure of value. Error (faith in the ideal) is not blindness, error is *cowardice.*
>
> (*EH*, P, 3)

The problem raised by the coexistence of these two tendencies is that they make Nietzsche's philosophy appear pragmatically self-discrediting. One can construct a dialectical argument against Nietzsche on the following lines: if no claim to truth, to insight into the nature of reality, *deserves* to be accepted as true (or if none amounts to more than an 'interpretation' which we can take or leave

[25] Cf. *BGE*, 4: 'To recognize untruth as a condition of life: that, to be sure, means to resist customary value-sentiments in a dangerous fashion, and a philosophy which ventures to do so places itself, by that act alone, beyond good and evil.'

[26] On the historically privileged position of this value cf. Collingwood (1940, 140): 'If European civilization is a civilization based on the belief that truth is the most precious thing in the world and that pursuing it is the whole duty of man, an irrationalist epidemic if it ran through Europe unchecked would in a relatively short time destroy everything that goes by the name of European civilization'.

according to temperament),[27] then this must also apply to the very proposition just stated (the Nietzschean proposition)—so it will follow that Nietzsche's condemnation of truth does not deserve to be accepted either.[28]

There is of course a risk here of judging Nietzsche by standards which he himself rejects, since for him—as befits a philosopher of 'difference'—'the will to a system is a lack of integrity' (*TI*, I, 26). Still, we do normally assume that to *speak* (philosophically, or in any other intentionally controlled way) is implicitly to present oneself as a 'centred' subject, one whose belief-and-attitude-set is sensitive to the norm of non-contradiction. And it is against this background that the question arises: what is the relation between Nietzsche's *critique of truth* and his *appeal to truth*, or truthfulness, as a test of spiritual quality? Can we see these two gestures as proceeding, lucidly, from a single author?

The question of the intended truth-status of Nietzsche's own utterances has been amply discussed by recent commentators, and could take us far beyond the bounds of a study of his aesthetics.[29] However, it may be helpful to bring this question into connection with the theme of distance which has been my main concern in the present paper. Much of twentieth-century philosophy takes for granted the essentially social nature of language, and hence of the thought-contents it enables us to express; so too does Nietzsche,[30] but for him the idea is mediated by a sense of his own intellectual and emotional distance from others. Thus '*One* is always wrong, but with two, truth begins. *One* cannot prove his case, but two are irrefutable' (*GS*, 260).[31]

For every so-called 'truth', he is suggesting here, there has to be a community to originate the sign-system within which that 'truth' is expressed, and to validate it *as* a truth (since '*One* is always wrong'). But what community can play such a

[27] See again *BGE*, 22.

[28] This 'table-turning' argument against views that deny the existence of objective truth goes back a long way: cf. Plato, *Theaetetus* 169d–171c.

[29] It is broached, for example, in the opening pages of Nehamas (1985) and of Clark (1990), and is addressed at several points in Williams (2002). Clark's resolution of the problem relies on a distinction, which for present purposes I have ignored, between 'truth' *simpliciter* (or 'empirical truth') and something called 'metaphysical truth', or 'correspondence to things as they are in themselves' (22); and on the claim that after 1886, as Nietzsche himself becomes aware of this distinction, he abandons the kind of all-out attack on truth that characterizes the pre-1886 period. Personally, I am not persuaded that a reading under which Nietzsche 'does not require us to abandon logic, argument, or the commitment to truth' (23) can do full justice to his animus against democratic values (see Section 4).

[30] See Section 5 on his 'politics of communication'.

[31] Cf. *GS*, 265: 'What are man's truths ultimately? Merely his *irrefutable* errors'—which looks like a hostile reworking of Aristotle's statement that 'what everyone agrees upon, we call true' (*Nicomachean Ethics* 1172b36–1173a1), although the echo may well be accidental, since Nietzsche pays much less attention to Aristotle than to Plato.

role in relation to those insights which Nietzsche is inclined (at least in a certain mood) to regard as *simply* true, and for which he thinks courage is needed? A possible answer is: one that exists in Nietzsche's imagination, the community of 'friends' and equals whom he pictures awaiting him in the future[32]—in fact, an anti-egalitarian counterpart of Kant's (equally notional) 'kingdom of ends'.

Perhaps this character that Nietzsche creates for himself—the character of a speaker with, for all he knows, no one to speak to—provides as good an explanation as any for the coexistence in his writings of destructive criticism of truth as a value or ideal, and the defiant brandishing of '*my* truth' that we find in *Ecce Homo*.[33] 'His truth' is so called proleptically, in the hope of its reception one day by an intelligent audience. But in imagining this moment, Nietzsche does not enter into the kind of relationship with 'generalized others' demanded by a regime of epistemic democracy: that is, he does not acknowledge that *each* of his fellow cognitive subjects is in principle just as likely as himself to hold views that deserve to prevail.

We might ask at this point: how does Nietzsche think he came into possession of the system of meanings within which he is advancing 'his truth'? Nietzsche's thoughts, like those of other people, depend constitutively on language—a language that someone had to teach him. So he will be making use of the socialization he has received from the 'herd' in order to do the thinking that will overcome their 'truth' and install his own in its place. In another context, this behaviour might invite the label 'exploitative' (helping oneself to the teaching, then spitting out the teacher); but such criticism can hardly gain any leverage on one who holds that 'Life operates *essentially*... through injury, assault, exploitation', and that 'whatever exists, having somehow come into being, is again and again reinterpreted to new ends, taken over, transformed and redirected by some power superior to it' (*GM*, II, 11, 12).

The whole business of socialization is one about which Nietzsche shows a striking ambivalence. It is something about which he can on occasion be very positive—more so than the liberal-individualist tradition generally teaches us to be.[34] However, at the same time, something in him feels that *all* communication—and so by implication every use of language—vulgarizes;

[32] See, again, *GS*, 381 and *BGE*, 26; and cf. *EH*, III, 1: 'Some are born posthumously'.

[33] *EH*, IV, 1: 'my truth is *terrible*; for so far one has called *lies* truth'; *EH*, IV, 3: 'Zarathustra is more truthful than any other thinker'.

[34] Thus *BGE*, 260, 'Deep reverence for age and the traditional... is typical of the morality of the powerful; and when, conversely, men of "modern ideas" believe almost instinctively in "progress" and "the future" and show an increasing lack of respect for age, this reveals clearly enough the ignoble origin of these "ideas"'; and cf. *BGE*, 188, cited in Section 1.

consciousness itself is an imperfection; 'everything good is instinct'. So one at least of the products of 'age' and 'tradition', namely language, turns out also to lead in the direction of vulgarity and shallowness.

But if we reflect further, we may find a certain consistency here. Reverence for age and tradition may *reinforce* the view that language vulgarizes the inner life. Nietzsche's thinking may be that if we have such reverence, then—unlike the men and women of 'modern ideas' whom he so despises—we will no longer feel the need to insist on having everything explained, justified, provided for in advance, and so forth, but will consent to take things on trust and to wait until such time as we have become attuned to the mental habit of our elders, so that we no longer require explanations. There are connections here both with conservative anti-theoreticism in political theory (such as Burke's *Reflections on the Revolution in France*),[35] and with the sort of anti-theoreticism in recent moral philosophy that derives from the later Wittgenstein, and ultimately from the Aristotelian tradition.

Possibly what we have in the case of Nietzsche is an instance of the 'tacit knowledge' tradition as mediated by a philosopher for whom coexistence with other human beings is a constant source of distress or 'nausea', even though it is recognized as unavoidable (not just for our natural survival but also for our moral and intellectual life).[36] Perhaps he is one of those thinkers whom feminist critics have diagnosed as 'transcendental narcissists',[37] elevating into metaphysics their own discomfort with the facts of dependency and connectedness. Or perhaps he dreams from time to time of a condition in which one would just *be* what is of value—that is, express it in one's own person and life, not chatter about it—and in which, however violent one's personal impact on the world, one would not need to *say* 'no' to anything.[38] But despite the presence of this anti-social, anti-verbalizing theme in Nietzsche, we should also remember that he is unsurpassed at recording the emotional significance of attachment—even if what is in question here is not specifically attachment to people.[39] Connection is desirable—but with the right objects (or persons, if such exist). There can be no compromise.

References

Braidotti, R. 1991. *Patterns of Dissonance* (Cambridge: Polity Press).

35 Burke (1968). 36 Cf. *GS*, 364: 'The hermit speaks'. 37 Cf. Braidotti (1991, 51).

38 Cf. *GS*, 276: '*Looking away* shall be my only negation'. This seems to be the condition of the happily unreflective nobility pictured in *GM*, I.

39 See again *GS*, 334, discussed in Section 2.

Burke, E. 1968. *Reflections on the Revolution in France*, O'Brien, C. C. (ed.) (Harmondsworth: Penguin).
Clark, M. 1990. *Nietzsche on Truth and Philosophy* (Cambridge: Cambridge University Press).
Collingwood, R. G. 1940. *An Essay on Metaphysics* (Oxford: Clarendon Press).
Freud, S. 1920. *Beyond the Pleasure Principle and Other Writings* (Harmondsworth: Penguin).
Kaufmann, W. 1974. *Nietzsche: Philosopher, Psychologist, Antichrist* (Princeton: Princeton University Press; 4th edition).
Landa, I. 1999. 'Nietzsche, the Chinese Worker's Friend', *New Left Review*, 236: 3–23.
Nehamas, A. 1985. *Nietzsche: Life as Literature* (Cambridge, MA: Harvard University Press).
Nietzsche, F. 1967. *The Case of Wagner*, Kaufmann, W. (trans.) (New York: Random House).
Nietzsche, F. 1968. *Twilight of the Idols*, Hollingdale, R. J. (trans.) (Harmondsworth: Penguin).
Nietzsche, F. 1969. *Ecce Homo*, Kaufmann, W. (trans.) (New York: Random House).
Nietzsche, F. 1969. *On the Genealogy of Morals*, Kaufmann, W. and Hollingdale, R. J. (trans.) (New York: Random House).
Nietzsche, F. 1973. *Beyond Good and Evil*, Hollingdale, R. J. (trans.) (Harmondsworth: Penguin).
Nietzsche, F. 1974. *The Gay Science*, Kaufmann, W. (trans.) (New York: Random House).
Scruton, R. 1997. *The Aesthetics of Music* (Oxford: Oxford University Press).
Staten, H. 1990. *Nietzsche's Voice* (Ithaca, NY: Cornell University Press).
Strong, T. B. 1996. 'Nietzsche's Political Misappropriation', in Magnus, B. and Higgins, K. M. (eds.), *The Cambridge Companion to Nietzsche* (Cambridge: Cambridge University Press): 119–47.
Tanesini, A. 2004. *Wittgenstein: A Feminist Interpretation* (Cambridge: Polity Press).
Williams, B. 1985. *Ethics and the Limits of Philosophy* (London: Fontana).
Williams, B. 2002. *Truth and Truthfulness: An Essay in Genealogy* (Princeton: Princeton University Press).
Wittgenstein, L. 1967. *Philosophical Investigations*, Anscombe, G. E. M. (trans.) (Oxford: Basil Blackwell; 3rd edition).

10

Nietzsche and Music

Aaron Ridley

There are comparatively few philosophers in whose musical tastes it would be proper to take a strictly philosophical interest. Adorno is obviously one; as too, perhaps, is Schopenhauer: certainly it is difficult not to feel a measure of theoretical disquiet at his enthusiasm for Rossini, given the place assigned to music in his, Schopenhauer's, metaphysics. More marginally, although still justly, one might be puzzled at Kant's deafness to music in general or at Collingwood's to the later Beethoven's in particular. But move much further out than this, and—however wonderful it would be to learn, say, that Spinoza had been a devotee of Monteverdi—the interest becomes predominantly biographical.

But it is surely Nietzsche who must take the laurels in the present context. This, after all, is the philosopher who claimed, of what he seemed to think his finest work, that 'the whole of *Zarathustra* may be reckoned as music' (*EH,* III, *Z,* 1), intending thereby to talk it up; who thought that, 'without music, life would be an error' (*TI,* I, 33); who embarked upon his philosophical career as the champion of a composer whom, at the conclusion of that career, he devoted many of his remaining energies to denouncing. Music and conceptions of music run through and up and down Nietzsche's philosophy in a way that is true of no one else's.[1]

In such a case it must be important to know what music he liked—and why. This essay starts from there. In Section 1, I try to say something about what Nietzsche's musical tastes actually were; in Section 2, I ask what it was about

[1] In many contexts, it is important to bear in mind that Nietzsche's thought developed quite sharply during the brief period of his philosophical activity, and so necessary to be cautious in attributing to the Nietzsche of *Beyond Good and Evil,* say, views that he had expressed in, for example, *Human, All Too Human.* The present context, however, is not a case in point: with the exception of his (very significant) *volte face* about the value of Wagner, Nietzsche's thinking about music remained pretty constant throughout.

music that led him to accord it such a prominent place in his thinking; in Section 3, I try to understand the sense in which he thought that philosophy, especially his own, could *be* music; in Section 4, I explore the significance of his late preference for Bizet over Wagner; and finally—if only very briefly—I attempt, in Section 5, to assess the importance of music for an appreciation of Nietzsche.

1 NIETZSCHE'S TASTES

Nietzsche himself was adamant that a person's tastes are uniquely revealing of his or her most fundamental nature. 'In the end', as he puts it, 'it must be as it is and always has been: great things remain for the great, abysses for the profound, nuances and shudders for the refined, and, in brief, all that is rare for the rare'; which is why, as he also puts it at the same place, '"My judgement is *my* judgement": no one else is easily entitled to it' (*BGE*, 43). So Nietzsche would have agreed that it makes sense to enquire into his tastes, at any rate if we wish to understand *him*; and all the more so, surely, if we wish to understand him as the peculiarly 'musical' philosopher that he took himself to be.

One perhaps tempting way into the question of Nietzsche's musical tastes would be to turn to the evidence of his own compositions (for he was, from quite an early age, a keen amateur composer, and also, apparently, a gifted improviser at the piano). That evidence, however, makes for uncomfortable listening. It would seem to indicate a taste for two main styles of music: an earlier, self-consciously 'academic' style, much given to counterpoint and to less than fully convincing efforts at Lutheran chorale; and a subsequent, much less disciplined style that is vaguely reminiscent, at best, of late Schumann on a more than usually bad day.[2] On the strength of these indications, I suspect, one would doubt that Nietzsche really *had* any musical tastes,[3] and so would doubt that music could possibly have had the significance for his philosophy that he appears to suggest.

But Nietzsche himself warns us against the attempt to extrapolate to a person's taste from his artistic activities:

[2] Perhaps the least unknown of his works is the *Hymn to Life*, which sets a text by Lou Salomé to music recycled from Nietzsche's early compositional style. Michael Tanner's cruelly apt description of it, as sounding 'like a Congregational Church' hymn 'with a few wrong notes' (1994, 21), acquires an added piquancy when set beside the final sentence of Nietzsche's own, rather more admiring discussion, of the work: '(Last note of the A-clarinet, c flat, not c: misprint)' (*EH*, III, *Z*, 1).

[3] I.e. one would think him possessed not so much of *bad* taste, as of no taste properly to be considered musical.

> Don't we have to admit to ourselves, we artists, that there is an uncanny difference within us between our taste and our creative powers? They stand oddly side by side, separately, and each grows in its own way . . . A musician, for example, might create his life long what is utterly at odds with what his refined listener's ear and listener's heart esteem, enjoy, and prefer—and he need not even be aware of this contradiction.
>
> (*GS*, 369)

One should be inclined, I think, to construe this passage as testament, among other things, to Nietzsche's self-awareness: he wasn't a good composer; far more accomplished musicians than he had told him so, and he knew it. But one should also take seriously what it says. For Nietzsche is surely right, and not only in his own case, to insist that 'one's taste can easily grow far beyond the reach of the taste of one's powers' (ibid.). If he were not right, after all, it would be hard to explain why so few of the very best critics have been practicing musicians of any calibre. So his compositions are not the place to turn to for a guide to his preferences.

If one consults instead the more usual kinds of biographical source (i.e., what he said, what others said he said, what concerts he went to, what scores he owned, etc.) the picture that emerges is broadly this. At the beginning of his musical life—which is to say, until the earlier 1860s (he was born in 1844)—Nietzsche was something of a conservative. His idols were Bach, Handel, Haydn, and Beethoven; and he showed considerable resistance, despite the efforts of friends to convert him, to what was then called 'the music of the future', as exemplified, for instance, in the works of Berlioz and Liszt. His early tastes thus already stretched further than 'the reach of the taste of [his] powers': there is nothing in his compositions of that or any other period to suggest the least assimilation of Haydn or Beethoven.

He did, in due course, succumb to the blandishments of 'the future', however, most urgently in the form of Richard Wagner's music dramas (*Tristan und Isolde* especially), to which he remained unreservedly devoted until some point in the mid-1870s. His first book, *The Birth of Tragedy* (1872), is, among much else, a blatant piece of Wagnerian propaganda, hailing Wagner as the second coming of Aeschylus. But by the time that he published 'Richard Wagner in Bayreuth' (the fourth of the *Untimely Meditations*) in 1876, outwardly another exercise in propaganda, the inner fires had cooled; and shortly afterwards he attempted to break with Wagner and his music altogether.

He never did shake off his enthusiasm for *Tristan*. Nor, during the Wagner years or afterwards, did he repudiate his early taste for the German 'classics'. But what appears to have replaced Wagner, and to have taken up residence in his tastes alongside those classics, is the music of southern Europe, in which—

especially Italy—he increasingly spent as much time as he could. Bizet, perhaps as a kind of honorary Spaniard,[4] and Rossini, as an indubitable Italian, are the subjects of warm encomia from Nietzsche in his final sane years.

What is most striking, I think, about this brief sketch of Nietzsche's preferences is just how conventional they are. It would have been quite an achievement, for a German born when he was into his class and background, *not* to have revered Handel and Beethoven, say. Nor, when he converted to it, was Wagnerianism exactly a minority interest: half of musical Europe was in its throes. And when of course he repudiated that enthusiasm, the other half of musical Europe was there waiting for him, even if he here perhaps did show a more original streak.

The standard refuge from 'the music of the future' at that time lay in the works of Brahms, held by the anti-Wagnerians to be the continuation of the great tradition of the classics; and, on past form, one might have expected Nietzsche to have nailed his colours to that mast. But no: he didn't care for Brahms. Brahms's melancholy, Nietzsche wrote, 'is the melancholy of incapacity; he does *not* create out of an abundance, he *languishes* for abundance... He is too little a person, too little a centre... In particular, he is the musician for a certain type of dissatisfied woman' (*CW*, Second Postscript). And so instead his tastes migrated to the South—although not, it has to be said, to any particularly out-of-the-way portions of it.

Is this conservatism of taste surprising? In one way it is. After all, one thinks of Nietzsche as a radical, as a philosopher busy and keen to expose the totems of contemporary culture as merely hollow idols. Viewed in this light, one might have anticipated that his preferences would be far more iconoclastic. But viewed in another light, his conservatism is not just not surprising, it is integral and essential to the character of his achievement. For it *is* as a critic of contemporary culture that Nietzsche stands out; and his strictures and complaints about it simply *could* not have been half so telling, half so accurate or devastating—so dangerous, even—had they not proceeded from somewhere very close to that culture's heart. Taken in this way, it is his conservatism that, as a form of deep intimacy, permitted him such a clear sighted and often merciless perspective upon his chosen targets. More radical tastes might have clouded his view.

2 WHY MUSIC?

Of all the arts, it is clear that Nietzsche revered music the most. He also regarded it as the most fundamental, as the following (unpublished) remark of 1871

[4] Or, indeed, an honorary African: see *CW*, 2.

indicates: music, he says, 'represents for us art *as a whole* and the artistic world' (*KSA*, 7, 307). Music also represents life. In a section of *The Gay Science* headed '*Why we are no idealists*', Nietzsche remarks that 'Formerly philosophers were afraid of the senses': 'Having "wax in one's ears" was then almost a condition of philosophizing; a real philosopher no longer listened to life insofar as life is music; he *denied* the music of life—it is an ancient philosopher's superstition that all music is sirens' music' (*GS*, 372); whereas 'we' non-idealists, clearly, are willing to listen.

This combination of convictions—that music is in some sense the fundamental art, and that it is immediately related to the essence of life—is, again, just what one would expect to find in a German of Nietzsche's period and condition. When Schopenhauer, by whom Nietzsche was much influenced, said that music went metaphysically deeper than the other arts (by being a 'copy' of the will itself, rather than being a mere distillation of its representations), and that 'in the melody, in the high, singing, principal voice, leading the whole and progressing with unrestrained freedom... I recognize the highest grade of the will's objectification, the intellectual life and endeavour of man' (*WWR*, I, 256–63), he himself was only translating the *zeitgeist* into his own idiom.

For the idea had taken hold—once music had ceased to be regarded as just an ancillary to words or dancing, and had become a 'fine art' in its own right—that its apparent lack of representational content, together with its manifest air of meaningfulness and logic, made it special. Music, if it seemed to be about anything, seemed to be about itself, about its own processes and developments. And yet—an ancient thought—it also seemed to echo, and to cause to resonate, the inner life of the spirit; and so, to the extent that spirit and world are one, as the German Romantics had held them to be, to echo the innermost nature of the world.

Lydia Goehr puts it nicely when she notes that thinkers of the period came to 'accept a double-sided view of musical meaning, that it be transcendent, embodied spirituality and purely musical at the same time. In sum, the new romantic aesthetic allowed music to mean its purely musical self at the same time that it meant everything else' (1992, 156–7)—which of course made music the most *philosophical* of the arts. As Schopenhauer has it:

> supposing we succeeded in giving a perfectly accurate and complete explanation of music which goes into detail, and thus a detailed repetition in concepts of what it expresses, this would also be at once a sufficient repetition and explanation of the world in concepts, or one wholly corresponding thereto, and hence true philosophy.
>
> (*WWR*, I, 264)

Nietzsche's version of this thought is phrased more exuberantly, but it is plainly coming from the same place: 'I am convinced that art'—he means music—'represents the highest task and the truly metaphysical activity of this life' (*BT*, 'Attempt', 5). And 'In this', as Georges Liébert rather splendidly observes, 'he who was so contemptuous of all things German shows himself to be wholly in conformity with his origins. One could not be more German, and the explosive product of a long gestation' (2004, 10).

So Nietzsche was hardly unusual in thinking of music in the general terms that he did. What makes his thought distinctive is his connection of these, as it were, freely available elements with questions concerning the *valuation* of life, questions that he regarded as central to understanding what he took to be the decadent malaise of modernity.

Nietzsche's chief objection to contemporary culture, refracted through a kaleidoscopic range of issues, is based on the charge that it is in (largely self-deceived) thrall to a set of values that denigrate and deny life and the world in favour some non-existent 'beyond'—the values of modern morality, with its roots in the no longer believable teachings of Christianity, being only the most obvious cases in point.

These values arose in order to rescue us from the terrors of an existence of meaningless suffering: they '*offered man meaning!* It was the only meaning offered so far; any meaning is better than none at all' (*GM*, III, 28). But now that the 'whole mysterious machinery of salvation' which the Christian 'interpreted . . . into suffering' (*GM*, II, 7) has become incredible, that meaning—even if we haven't noticed the fact—is withdrawn, and we are left only with a set of values which, decoupled from the Christian's 'machinery', do nothing but deny life.

In Nietzsche's view, therefore, those values are ripe for a 're-evaluation'—'*the value of these values themselves must . . . be called into question*' (*GM*, P, 6)—as part of an attempt to achieve a new table of values through which, without appeal to the 'beyond', without appeal to anything that is not worldly from top to bottom, life might be celebrated and affirmed, its inevitable sufferings notwithstanding. And to that task, Nietzsche regards art, and especially music, as having an important contribution to make.

Nietzsche's most basic conception of art construes it as a matter of giving form. In speaking of the creators—the 'artists'—of states, for example, he says 'Their work is an instinctive creation and imposition of forms; . . . wherever they appear something new soon arises, a ruling structure that *lives* . . . in which nothing whatever finds a place that has not first been assigned a "meaning" in relation to the whole' (*GM*, II, 17).

Form-giving is thus also a matter of giving meaning; and the meanings that are given are, because sustained by their place in a 'ruling structure', parts of a living whole. Nietzsche's understanding of form, that is, is a thoroughly Romantic, organicist one.[5] It is also, not unexpectedly, a model of form in whose terms it was widely felt that music was most naturally to be conceived—music, in which there are, as it were, no pre-assigned meanings at all, in which one and the same note or chord can mean many different things depending exclusively upon the place that it is given in relation to a particular whole.[6] Indeed, music might well, from this point of view, be regarded as the form-giving art *par excellence*, since, considered in 'its purely musical self', as Goehr has it, it is nothing *but* form.

But that is not the whole of Nietzsche's story. 'What does all art do?', he asks: 'does it not praise? does it not glorify? does it not select? does it not highlight? By doing all this it *strengthens* or *weakens* certain valuations' (*TI*, IX, 24). In the case of the non-musical arts, this strengthening or weakening of valuations is an effect of the patterns of (ordinary, referential) meaning that result from the form that has been imposed. In the case of music, on the other hand, that strengthening or weakening is accomplished much more powerfully and directly. Enjoying, as it does, an intimate and more than 'purely musical' connection to the inner life—in its aspect, that is, as 'transcendent, embodied spirituality'—music echoes, and so causes to resonate in the listener, particular evaluative dispositions of the soul (Nietzsche refers to these as 'living crystallizations' of 'subtle feelings of value and differences of value' (*BGE*, 186)).[7]

In Nietzsche's view, then, music is a uniquely potent medium for the transmission of values. Indeed, assuming that a soul could, through music, become so imbued with life-affirmation that this became second nature to it, music might even be the agent by which the worn-out, life-denying values of traditional morality are finally laid to rest. It is for this reason that Nietzsche's central critical preoccupation when thinking about music—as can be seen, for example, throughout *The Case of Wagner*—is whether this or that work speaks for or against life.[8] For a healthy culture, in his settled view, is one which both produces and is sustained by life-affirming art—life-affirming music above all—a condition of which our own falls painfully short.

[5] He insists on this conception repeatedly—see, e.g., *CW*, 7, in which a failure of form means that 'The whole no longer lives at all', and in which one of Wagner's alleged flaws is said to be 'his incapacity for giving organic form'.

[6] So, for example, the chord that would be a tonic triad in a piece composed in C major would be a dominant in a piece composed in F, a subdominant in a piece composed in G, and so on.

[7] Cf. *BGE*, 268: 'The values of a human being betray something of the *structure* of his soul'.

[8] Cf. *GS*, 370.

From this perspective, one might say that Nietzsche's version of 'the music of the future' is a music that would cure us of our still-Christianized pathology, and leave us, as he puts it in a not unrelated context, 'well disposed' towards ourselves and towards life (*GS*, 341). And this is a vision that, for the reasons I have given, draws its sense from the peculiarly Romantic tradition of theorizing about music of which Nietzsche was so fully a part.

3 PHILOSOPHY AS MUSIC

In ways that have already been touched on, Nietzsche thought of philosophy and music as being very closely related to one another. Indeed, he longed for a synthesis of the two. In *The Birth of Tragedy*, he calls for a '*Socrates who practices music*' (*BT*, 15); in the 'Attempt at a Self-Criticism' appended to that book 14 years later, he remarks of his earlier self that 'It should have *sung*, this "new soul"—and not spoken!' (BT, 'Attempt', 3.); and, as we have already seen, he appears to think, or at least says, that 'the whole of *Zarathustra* may be reckoned as music' (*EH*, III, *Z*, 1).

If this is Nietzsche being to some extent whimsical, it is not only that. He reliably thinks of writing, philosophical writing included, in musical terms—as, for example, in the following well-known passage:

> there is *art* in every good sentence! Art that wants to be discerned to the extent that the sentence wants to be understood! A misunderstanding about its tempo, for instance, and the sentence itself is misunderstood! To have no doubts as to the rhythmically decisive syllables, to feel breaks in the most stringent of symmetries as deliberate and attractive, to extend a patient and subtle ear to every *staccato* and every *rubato*, guessing the meaning of the order of vowels and diphthongs and how tenderly and richly they can change colour and change it again when put next to each other—who among book-reading Germans... [has] 'the ear for it[?]'
>
> (*BGE*, 246)

This, as well as being brilliant, is clearly intended entirely seriously; and it tells us a good deal about how Nietzsche, not without reason, thinks about his own written style: he writes *musically*. And this matters to him not, as one might put it, on merely aesthetic grounds, but because of the powers that he holds music to have, and because of what he wants his writing to achieve.

Something of the character of Nietzsche's musico-philosophical ambitions is made explicit in a short dialogue that he wrote a few years earlier (I quote most of it):

> *Music as an advocate.*—'I am thirsting for a composer,' said an innovator to his disciple, 'who would learn my ideas from me and transpose them into his language; that way I should reach men's ears and hearts far better. With music one can seduce men to every

error and every truth: who could refute a tone?'—'Then you would like to be considered irrefutable?' said his disciple. The innovator replied: 'I wish for the seedling to become a tree. For a doctrine to become a tree, it has to be believed for a good while; for it to be believed it has to be considered irrefutable. The tree needs storms, doubts, worms, and nastiness to reveal the nature and strength of the seedling; let it break if it is not strong enough. But a seedling can only be destroyed—not refuted'.

(*GS*, 106)

So music, on this conception, reaches 'men's ears and hearts far better' than mere talk can. And, once established in their hearts, the seedlings of the ideas implanted there can take root and grow into trees, at which point—but not before—they can be tested by the 'storms, doubts, worms, and nastiness' of attempted refutation. In the form of mere talk, on the other hand, the same ideas are vulnerable to pre-emptive destruction: they may, because not bedded-in well enough to be refuted, be regarded as merely odd, eccentric, or pointless. Certainly that was Nietzsche's own experience in attempting to impart ideas.

The thought here is clear enough, and is made still clearer once we recall the larger character of Nietzsche's philosophical project. He wants to detach us—by whatever means: by argument, by rhetoric, by seduction, by bullying—from a set of values that he regards as life-denying, so that we might attach ourselves instead to values from the perspective of which life is to be embraced as good, indeed as worthy of *gratitude*.[9] The 'ideas' or 'doctrine' that *he* wishes to convey, that is, concern those 'living crystallizations' of 'subtle feelings of value' that he regards music (as 'embodied spirituality') as so perfectly equipped to impart, and to impart, moreover, directly into the soul. Small wonder, in light of this, that Nietzsche should have wanted his philosophical prose to be genuinely 'musical'—and small wonder, either, that he should have wanted to think of what he took to be his best work as musical without the inverted commas, however hyperbolic that thought might be.

The way in which Nietzsche envisaged a properly musical philosophy as working—that is, as working directly upon its audience's soul—owes a good deal to Wagner's ideas about music, which the younger Nietzsche had imbibed enthusiastically. In the face of a true music drama, said Wagner, 'Nothing should remain for the synthesizing intellect to do ... [W]e must become *knowers* through *feeling*'.[10] And this, of course, for the reasons that we have seen, is exactly how

[9] See, for example, the inscription placed between the preface and the first chapter of *Ecce Homo*: 'On this perfect day, when everything is ripening and not only the grape turns brown, the eye of the sun just fell upon my life: I looked back, I looked forward, and never saw so many and such good things at once ... *How could I fail to be grateful to my whole life?*'

[10] From Richard Wagner, *Opera and Drama*, cited in Tanner (1996, 9).

Nietzsche hoped that a philosophy transposed into the 'language' of music would affect its readers (or listeners). The priority of 'feeling' in this mechanism is noteworthy: both he and Wagner are committed to the view that cognition, ordinarily so-called, is (or can be) *consequent* upon feeling. And this is a commitment that Nietzsche emphasizes elsewhere: 'We still draw the conclusions of judgements we consider false', he says, 'of teachings in which we no longer believe—our feelings make us do it' (*D*, 99). And, when it comes to our moral judgments, 'We have to *learn to think differently*—in order at last, perhaps very late on, to attain even more: *to feel differently*' (*D*, 103).[11]

The most that a non-musical philosophy might achieve, on this picture, is, indeed, to get us to '*think differently*' (in the hope that a transformation of feeling will follow); whereas a philosophy transposed into music should be able to cut to the chase, and get us to '*feel differently*' first (with the side-effect that we would then think differently too).[12] And in light of this conception of the issues, Nietzsche's call for—perhaps, indeed, his wish to *be*—a '*music-practicing Socrates*' (*BT*, 17) scarcely looks whimsical at all. It seems, in fact, to be just what a crusading philosopher of value, with a strongly Romantic musical aesthetic, *ought* to be after.[13]

4 CARMEN *CONTRA* PARSIFAL

I noted in Section 2 that Nietzsche's primary critical question, given his larger re-evaluative project, is whether this or that work speaks for life or against it. Here, I propose to look briefly—even, in a sense, parenthetically—at that style of critical assessment in action.

It is safe to say that Wagner's final music drama, *Parsifal*, did not find favour with Nietzsche; perhaps not wholly accurately, he would come to attribute his break with Wagner to what he, Nietzsche, regarded as that work's outright capitulation to Christianity. Wagner, he wrote, 'suddenly sank down helpless and shattered before the Christian cross' (*HH*, II, P, 3):

[11] Thus, as he puts it later, 'moralities'—i.e. explicit systems of evaluation—are 'merely a *sign-language of the affects*' (*BGE*, 187).

[12] This is clearly all central to the affective dimension of Nietzsche's 'perspectivism' (as stated in, e.g., *GM*, III, 12); for an extended (and excellent) reading of the *Genealogy* as an attempt to work on our thoughts *via* our feelings, see Janaway (2007). Janaway doesn't put it in these terms, but his is, in effect, a reading of the *Genealogy* as an exercise in musical philosophy.

[13] For a somewhat tendentious attempt to read *Twilight of the Idols* as an exercise in musical philosophy, see Gillespie (1988). For a much more convincing series of reflections on the place of music in that book, see Strong (1997).

Did *hatred of life* gain control over him...? Because *Parsifal* is a work of malice, of vindictiveness, a secret poisoning of the presuppositions of life, a *bad* work.—The preaching of chastity remains an incitement to perversion: I despise anyone who does not regard *Parsifal* as an attempt to assassinate ethics.

(*NCW*, 'Wagner as Apostle of Chastity', 3)

Indeed, the effect of it is to cast 'a shadow over Wagner's earlier art—which now seems too bright, too healthy. Do you understand this? Health, brightness having the effect of a shadow? almost of an *objection?*' And all of this because

There is nothing weary, nothing decrepit, nothing fatal and hostile to life in matters of the spirit that his art does not secretly safeguard... He flatters every nihilistic (Buddhistic) instinct and disguises it in music; he flatters everything Christian, every religious expression of decadence. Open your ears: everything that ever grew on the soil of *impoverished* life, the whole counterfeit of transcendence and the beyond, has found its most sublime advocate in Wagner's art... His last work is in this respect his greatest masterpiece.

(*CW*, Postscript)

And there is more in the same vein, perhaps collectively comprising the most exhilarating critical assault in the history of music.

In Nietzsche's view, then, *Parsifal* speaks (rather warmly) *against* life, and is hence 'a *bad* work'; and his overarching reason for claiming this is, through the dizzying sparkle of his rhetoric, that *Parsifal* is complicit, even joins forces, with the nihilistic and decadent instincts that give birth to 'transcendence and the beyond'—that give birth, that is, to a non-existent 'other' in whose favour life and the world are to be denied.

At one level, it seems almost point-missing to ask whether Nietzsche was actually right about this: perhaps one should simply enjoy the display (much as, for example, one might enjoy the July fireworks in Paris without wondering unduly whether the 'storming' of the Bastille was an event to merit them). But, at another level, if one takes Nietzsche's concerns seriously, it would surely be point-missing *not* to ask whether he was right. If music has the powers that he claims for it, and if our existing values are in as sorry a state as he says, it might matter very much whether *Parsifal* is 'a *bad* work' or not.

Several commentators have taken issue with Nietzsche's assessment of *Parsifal*, and in my view they are right to have done so. Georges Liébert, for example, argues that Wagner's final music drama is merely a development of his earlier works, noting that 'the fact that Wagner considered it to be "the most sacred of his works" indicates that to his eyes there was just a difference of degree, not one of nature between it and those that preceded—the very pagan *Ring*, *Tristan*, where the word God is never pronounced'; and what that development culminates in, according to Liébert, is a conception in which art *replaces* religion (i.e., the term 'sacred' becomes proper to art), so that 'the agent of [the] "redemption" that Parsifal represents on-stage, is no other, in reality, than the artist himself' (2004, 121).

I think that there is something to be said for this interpretation; certainly it accords well enough with what we know *Wagner* to have believed. But it doesn't address what, in my view, is the heart of Nietzsche's critique—namely, that *Parsifal* colludes with various 'religious' and 'nihilistic' instincts in the 'counterfeit of transcendence and the beyond'; for it might still do that, even if the 'beyond' that is counterfeited is, as it were, a purely artistic one.

Much more powerful, I think, is Michael Tanner's response to Nietzsche, which one might in fact regard as a refutation. I can't begin to do justice here to the power and subtlety of Tanner's argument; at most I can attempt to indicate its outlines. But the headline news is that while *Parsifal* is '*about* religion', is *about* the longing for transcendence, is, indeed, 'the most penetrating study we have of the psychopathology of religious belief in artistic terms', the work itself is not a religious one, but is an exercise in 'the refusal to transcend' (1979, 205–9).[14]

At the heart of the drama, as Tanner reads it, is the thought, of which the various protagonists only gradually, and unevenly, become aware—that 'neither the way of desire nor the way of asceticism will bring salvation' (1979, 212); which is to say that neither erotic love nor its renunciation (chastity) will bring salvation.[15] And it is this false alternative—figured as Nature, animality, sensuality, on the one hand, and as anti-Nature, life-denial, lust for the 'beyond', on the other—whose dialectic is played out until, in the 'Good Friday Music' of Act III, Nature itself is transfigured, and Parsifal finds *there* 'what he had been looking for *beyond* Nature'. In Wagner's 'anti-transcendental vision', that is, Nature, 'although it has never been painted in more exquisite colours,... is none the less no longer, in its unconscious loveliness, a temptation: it looks up to man who, in transcending Nature, has no need to transcend himself' (1979, 216)—the transcending of Nature being, as it were, an immanent transcendence (i.e., one that neither requires nor offers a move to the 'beyond').[16]

[14] Tanner doesn't note, although he might have done, that in the Eucharist-like scenes of the drama, instead of wine being transmuted into other-worldly blood, as it would be in Catholic ritual, blood is transmuted into all-too-worldly wine. This reversal, as Wagner's wife, Cosima, remarked, 'permits us to return our gaze refreshed back to earth, whereas the conversion of wine into blood draws us away from the earth' (C. Wagner, 1978, 1:984); which is one reason why, as she puts it elsewhere, '*Parsifal* has nothing in common with any Church, nor indeed with any dogma' (cited in Borchmeyer, 1991, 401–2, n. 59).

[15] Tanner does a brilliant job, by the way, if only in passing, of skewering those who, like Nietzsche, fail to attend to the astonishing complexities of Wagner's psychological explorations, and hear only a 'preaching of chastity'. See Tanner (1979, 211).

[16] It is in keeping, I think, with the fully immanent character of *Parsifal*'s dramatic resolutions that the work should end as it does. For such is the harmonic fluidity of the long, wonderful

What Tanner's reading convinces one of so completely, in my view, is that far from *flattering* 'every nihilistic' instinct, 'every religious expression of decadence', as Nietzsche claims, Wagner sets out in *Parsifal* to understand and inhabit those instincts and expressions, so as to diagnose and *overcome* the impulses lying behind 'the whole counterfeit of transcendence and the beyond'. Wagner's art, that is, is engaged in an enterprise that is Nietzschean to its core. It is, in fact, an exercise in just the kind of musical philosophy for which Nietzsche longed most ardently.

So Nietzsche got it wrong about *Parsifal.* He also got it wrong, according to many, in his late championing of *Carmen* instead—in his apparent suggestion that what would-be life-affirmers could really do with is a solid diet of Bizet. Nietzsche assures us that he is not joking: 'it is not merely pure malice', he says, 'when I praise Bizet in this essay at the expense of Wagner' (*CW*, P). And his enthusiasm seems genuine:

Yesterday I heard—would you believe it?—Bizet's masterpiece for the twentieth time... How such a work makes one perfect!... Really, every time I heard *Carmen* I seemed to myself more of a philosopher, a better philosopher, than I generally consider myself... This music seems perfect to me. It approaches lightly, supplely, politely. It is pleasant, it does not *sweat*... This music is evil, subtly fatalistic: at the same time it remains popular—its subtlety belongs to a race, not to an individual. It is rich. It is precise. It builds, organizes, finishes... Have more painful tragic accents ever been heard on the stage? How are they achieved? Without grimaces. Without counterfeit. Without the *lie* of the great style.

(*CW*, 1)

The valuations that *Carmen* 'strengthens or weakens'—what it praises and glorifies—are also to Nietzsche's liking:

This work, too, redeems... From Mérimée it... has the logic in passion, the shortest line, the *harsh* necessity... Another sensuality, another sensibility speaks here, another cheerfulness. This music is cheerful, but not in a French or German way; its cheerfulness is African; fate hangs over it; its happiness is brief, sudden, without pardon. I envy Bizet for having had the courage for this sensibility... Finally, love—love translated back into nature. Not the love of a 'higher virgin'!... But love as *fatum*, as fatality, cynical, innocent, cruel—and precisely in this a piece of nature... Such a conception of love (the only one worthy of a philosopher) is rare: it raises a work of art above thousands.

(*CW*, 2)

These are remarkable passages—especially when one bears in mind the fact that, despite certain features of his self-image to the contrary, Nietzsche was generally

concluding bars that the final A flat major chord, for all its radiance and serenity, has a provisional air about it—even an air of arbitrariness—as if the music needn't have ended there, as if the events of the drama had not been, perhaps could not be, brought to a close once and for all.

much more at home, much more energized, when attacking and demolishing than when celebrating.

Tanner thinks that these passages are remarkable, too—remarkable for expressing a preference (for Bizet over Wagner) that he finds 'bathetic' (1994, 67), a view supported, he suggests, by Adorno's great essay 'Fantasia sopra *Carmen*'. I'm not so sure, however. It is true that that essay argues, as Tanner says, that in *Carmen* everything is ultimately denied meaning: as Adorno puts it, 'the inhumanity and hardness, even the violence of the form, has been used to obliterate the last token of meaning, so as to forestall any illusion that anything in life could have any meaning over and above its obvious one'. Yet the effect of this, as Adorno also argues, is that 'In *Carmen*, which appropriates nature for itself without any sacral aura, one can breathe freely. The unsentimental, undiluted depiction of natural passion achieves what the inclusion of any consoling meaning would deny to the work'—it 'destroys the illusion that nature is anything more than mortal. This is the precise function of music in *Carmen*' (1992, 62–3).

If Adorno is right about Bizet's music—and to me it seems that he is—it is unclear why there should be anything 'bathetic' in Nietzsche's late enthusiasm for it. It is true that *Carmen* hasn't the depth or the complexity of a *Parsifal*—very little has. But there is, as one might put it, more than one way of refusing to transcend. One way is to feel the allure of the 'beyond', to explore it—and to overcome it. That is Wagner's way. Another way is to remain oblivious to the allure, to be so constituted that the 'beyond' is simply *not* alluring. That is Bizet's way. And one can see why, in Nietzsche's view, the latter of these alternatives might appear to be the healthier. Perhaps Bizet is, as Nietzsche once said of the Greeks, one of those who is 'superficial—*out of profundity*' (*GS*, P, 4).

5 THE MUSICAL PHILOSOPHER

'Of *what* do I suffer when I suffer of the fate of music?', Nietzsche asks. 'That music has been done out of its world-transfiguring, Yes-saying character'—an answer that continues his quarrel with the composer of *Parsifal*. It also, however, underlines the depth of his commitment to the importance of music: he experiences its vicissitudes as immediately as any sufferings of his own (*EH*, III, *CW*, 1). Indeed, it is not too much to say that, for Nietzsche, the 'fate of music' is intimately tied up with the fate of the world itself, at any rate insofar as that world is (or ought to be) of interest to human beings. For music has the potential, on his view, to *redeem* the world—whether all by itself, or in its guise as transfigured philosophy—so that existence becomes a source of gratitude and joy, rather than constituting an insistent, and perhaps in the end overwhelming, seduction to one or another sort of nihilism.

Even by Nietzsche's standards, these are large thoughts, apocalyptic in their implications; and it seems to me that we would do well to bear it in mind that he had them whenever we approach his work, for they are, quite plausibly, its ground bass even when they are not its leading theme. And if I am right about this, it follows that we should also bear in mind the conservatism and romanticism that made such thoughts possible for him.[17]

Only someone so deeply invested in his culture could have seen through so much of it so decisively; and only someone whose culture conceived of music in *that* way could have offered music—in all deep seriousness—as the cure for our ills. That a prescription of this sort would nowadays strike most of us as laughable does not, I think, speak unambiguously of our progress in the meantime. For us, by and large, life 'without music' would be an 'error' only in the sense that it would be a bit more boring, or emptier. For Nietzsche, by contrast, it would be an error because it would be robbed of its chance to be most truly itself—to be, like happiness, 'brief, sudden, without pardon'. It would be frustrating if we had 'grown out of' the resources to think this.

A final thought. Suppose, for a moment, that 'the whole of *Zarathustra*' actually *can* 'be reckoned as music', at any rate in the sense in which Nietzsche held that writing can be 'musical'. And suppose that the ideas expressed there, like those of the 'innovator' of section 106 of *The Gay Science*, were to be transposed into music in the ordinary sense, so yielding music to the power of music. In Nietzsche's view, presumably, the result ought to implant his preferred evaluative stance into his listeners' souls with unparalleled force and directness.

It would be interesting, in light of this, to turn a critical eye on the actually existing attempts to, indeed, transpose *Thus Spoke Zarathustra* into music. I have in mind the garrulous bombast of Richard Strauss's eponymous effort, perhaps most faithful, in its way, to the 'music' of Nietzsche's own *Zarathustra*; the oddly uninvolving solemnity of Mahler's setting of the so-called 'Midnight Song',[18] made still remoter, if anything, by the outward *schmaltz* of its solo string figures; and, above all, the anxiously nostalgic *pastorale* that is Delius's *A Mass of Life*, the work of a composer

[17] I should probably say here that, at odds with what seems to be the contemporary orthodoxy, 'conservative' and 'romantic' have never struck me as being obviously terms of abuse, let alone of condescending abuse; and that is not how I use them in this essay. As far as I can see, both conservatism and romanticism have their richnesses and depths. And if both also have their shortcomings, then so, at least as evidently, do any of the readily available alternatives.

[18] The words are in fact those of *Z*, III, 15 and the setting constitutes the fourth movement of Mahler's third symphony.

who could no more write music to dance to than Nietzsche, it is hard not to feel, wrote a text to merit it—at any rate in *Zarathustra*. It would be fascinating—on another occasion—to see what came out.[19]

REFERENCES

Adorno, T. 1992. *Quasi una Fantasia* (London: Verso).

Borchmeyer, D. 1991. *Richard Wagner: Theory and Theatre* (Oxford: Clarendon Press).

Gillespie, M. 1988. 'Nietzsche's Musical Politics', in Gillespie, M. A. and Strong, T. (eds.), *Nietzsche's New Seas* (Chicago: Chicago University Press): 117–53.

Goehr, L. 1992. *The Imaginary Museum of Musical Works* (Oxford: Oxford University Press).

Janaway, C. 2007. *Beyond Selflessness: Reading Nietzsche's* Genealogy (New York and Oxford: Oxford University Press).

Liébert, G. 2004. *Nietzsche and Music* (Chicago: Chicago University Press).

Nietzsche, F. 1966. *Beyond Good and Evil*, Kaufmann, W. (trans.) (New York: Vintage Books).

Nietzsche, F. 1967. *The Birth of Tragedy*, Kaufmann, W. (trans.) (New York: Vintage Books).

Nietzsche, F. 1969. *On the Genealogy of Morals*, Hollingdale, R. J. and Kaufmann, W. (trans.) (New York: Vintage Books).

Nietzsche, F. 1969. *Thus Spoke Zarathustra*, Hollingdale, R. J. (trans.) (London: Penguin).

Nietzsche, F. 1974. *The Gay Science*, Kaufmann, W. (trans.) (New York: Vintage Books).

Nietzsche, F. 1986. *Human, All Too Human*, Hollingdale, R. J. (trans.) (Cambridge: Cambridge University Press).

Nietzsche, F. 1997. *Daybreak*, Hollingdale, R. J. (trans.) (Cambridge: Cambridge University Press).

Nietzsche, F. 1997. *Untimely Meditations*, Hollingdale, R. J., (trans.) (Cambridge: Cambridge University Press).

Nietzsche, F. 2005. *The Case of Wagner*, Norman, J. (trans.) (Cambridge: Cambridge University Press).

Nietzsche, F. 2005. *Ecce Homo*, Norman, J. (trans.) (Cambridge: Cambridge University Press).

Nietzsche, F. 2005. *Nietzsche Contra Wagner*, Norman, J. (trans.) (Cambridge: Cambridge University Press).

Nietzsche, F. 2005. *Twilight of the Idols*, Norman, J. (trans.) (Cambridge: Cambridge University Press).

Schopenhauer, A. 1969. *The World as Will and Representation*, Payne, E. F. J. (trans.), 2 vols. (New York: Dover).

Strong, T. 1997. 'Introduction', in Nietzsche, F., *Twilight of the Idols* (Indianapolis: Hackett).

Tanner, M. 1979. 'The Total Work of Art', in Burbidge, P. and Stutton, R. (eds.), *The Wagner Companion* (London: Faber): 140–224.

Tanner, M. 1994. *Nietzsche: A Very Short Introduction* (New York and Oxford: Oxford University Press).

Tanner, M. 1996. *Wagner* (London: Harper Collins).

Wagner, C. 1978. *Cosima Wagner's Diaries*, Gregor-Dellin, M. and Mack, D. (eds.), Skelton, G. (trans.), 2 vols. (New York: Harcourt Brace Jovanovich).

[19] My thanks to Alex Neill and David Owen for their comments on earlier versions of this essay.

11

Nietzsche on Wagner

Roger Scruton

Wagner was the most philosophical of musicians and Nietzsche the most musical of philosophers, so a philosophy of music ought to be implied somewhere in their conflict. However, Nietzsche's early adoration of Wagner distorted his later rejection, so that the serious thinking has to be discerned within a cloud of self-loathing. Maybe Nietzsche's reaction would have been more moderate had he not at first offered the unquestioning discipleship that Wagner demanded, presenting Wagner, both in *The Birth of Tragedy* (1872) and in *Richard Wagner in Bayreuth* (1876) as the greatest modern artist and the saviour of German culture. At any rate, the dispute between Wagner and Nietzsche was a divorce, rather than a disagreement.[1] In reacting against Wagner, Nietzsche was also reacting against himself, vomiting forth a poison that he thought he had swallowed, but to which his metabolism had made its own peculiar contribution.

Matters are made worse by the subsequent demonization of Wagner and canonization of Nietzsche. It is hard to go back to this controversy now, without regretting the tone taken by Nietzsche, and the tone taken subsequently by just about everyone else. Nietzsche's attack on Wagner is an attack on the art, the institution, and the man, and it was echoed by Theodor Adorno, so as to foreground those aspects of Wagner which are most objectionable to the modern reader—anti-Semitism, the focus on national myths and racial heroes, the use of orchestral magic to fill every moment with an emotion that might seem to be, in Nietzsche's word, 'counterfeit'.[2] And it is partly thanks to Nietzsche that Wagner-criticism has become stuck in this groove.

Meanwhile Nietzsche himself has become a kind of idol. Despite his antagonism towards democracy and mass culture, despite his unashamedly racist attack

[1] For the intricacies of the story, see Köhler (1998). [2] Adorno (2004).

on the Germans and all things German, despite his advocacy of 'health' and strength against the 'sickness' of compassion, despite his contempt for socialists, vegetarians, feminists, and women generally—despite committing every sin condemned by the morality of 'political correctness', Nietzsche is now a cult figure.

His perspectival approach to truth and knowledge, his debunking of morality in general and Christian morality in particular, his genealogical approach to art and culture, and his emphasis on power and domination as the real 'truth' of the human condition—all these give him a head-start in the postmodern search for anti-authoritarian authorities. His texts are therefore read for what they permit—which is just about everything—rather than for what they condemn—which is also just about everything.

The result is that, in the Nietzsche-Wagner stand off, Nietzsche is dealt all the winning cards. And this is a pity since it obscures the very real strength of Nietzsche's position, and the seriousness of the grounds on which he questions Wagner's art. Although Wagner the artist can be defended against the charges levelled by Nietzsche, those charges force us nevertheless to explore the music dramas at the deepest level. And they contain interesting hints of a philosophy of music.

Nietzsche expressed his adoration towards Wagner in his first published work, *The Birth of Tragedy*, which appeared in 1872. Fourteen years later Nietzsche reissued *The Birth of Tragedy* with 'an attempt at self-criticism', in which he dismisses the book as 'badly written, ponderous, embarrassing, image-mad and image-confused, sentimental, in places saccharine to the point of effeminacy, uneven in tempo, without the will to logical cleanliness' (*BT*, 'Attempt', 3) and much more to similar effect. And certainly *The Birth of Tragedy* has none of the lapidary quality that we associate with the later works.

For all that, it is an important work, and one that is vital to understanding Nietzsche's conception of the artistic enterprise.[3] It registers a decisive break with a reading of Greek art and literature that had been orthodox in German-speaking countries since Winckelmann and Goethe. According to this reading, Greek civilisation epitomized the human spirit in its sunlit, self-knowing form. The art of the Greeks was an art of reason, and their literature an exploration of the virtues through which the rational being confronts and overcomes adversity.

[3] This view is endorsed by Young (1992), although for reasons slightly different from those I give. In my view *The Birth of Tragedy* is the only one of Nietzsche's works that contains an argument detachable from the author of it.

The Greek ideal was one of clarity and harmony, and this ideal was conveyed by their poetry, their architecture, and their art.

Nietzsche was not the first to cast doubt on that wishful picture. In *The Art Work of the Future* (1859) Wagner had pointed to the religious nature of Greek tragedy, to the connection between tragedy and religious ritual, and to the paradigmatic nature of tragedy as an art.[4] *The Ring of the Nibelung* was conceived with the *Oresteia* in mind, and Wagner understood the Greek gods in Aeschylus in the same spirit as he depicted the German gods in *The Ring*, namely as personifications of the unconscious forces by which the human will is governed.

Nietzsche went further, identifying Dionysus, the god of tragedy, as one of two dominant psychic principles, the other being Apollo, the god of philosophy. While Apollo represents the reason and enlightenment that had been singled out by Winckelmann and Goethe, Dionysus was the god of dark passions, unconscious yearnings, and ritual destruction. Tragedy invites this god into the public arena where his demands can be acknowledged and purged. And the true vehicle of tragedy is not words, in which the rational and critical intellect is sovereign, but music and dance, in which bodily rhythms and animal passions find their expression.

Nietzsche argued that Greek civilisation had been misjudged by Winckelmann, Goethe, and Schiller, and that a new understanding had since supervened, one that acknowledged the function of Greek religion in presenting and appeasing the irrational aspects of the human psyche. This thesis is one to which Nietzsche returns in later works, writing, for example, in *Twilight of the Idols* (1888), that 'it is only in the Dionysian mysteries ... that the *basic fact* of the Hellenic instinct finds expression' (*TI*, X, 4). And he connects that 'basic fact' with life, health, and sexuality. The thesis was later defended by E. R. Dodds in *The Greeks and the Irrational* (1951), and has been effectively normalized by modern scholarship.[5] But it was associated in *The Birth of Tragedy* with the new German spirit, manifest in the art of Wagner. Like the Greeks, the Germans had their myths and legends, in which the unconscious forces of life claim recognition and acknowledgement. If the Germans were really to do what Winckelmann and Goethe wished for them, and to replicate the achievements of Greek civilisation, it would not be through philosophy but through music—not through reason and enlightenment, but through myth and legend.

Here Nietzsche introduced a theme that was to dominate his later thinking: the theme of health. Myth, he argued, is the healthy part of a culture: 'myth alone saves all the powers of the imagination and of the Apollonian dream from their

[4] Wagner (1887–1888). [5] Dodds (1951).

aimless wanderings' (*BT*, 23). Without myth the Apollonian principle of reason has no life on which to reflect. Hence the 'Socratism which is bent on the destruction of myth' is the sign of an unhealthy and degenerate culture. And Nietzsche discerned this unhealthy 'Socratism' in the Germany of his day, arguing that 'now the mythless man stands eternally hungry, surrounded by all past ages, and digs and grubs for roots, even if he has to dig for them among the remotest antiquities' (*BT*, 23).

In the face of this disinherited condition, Nietzsche implies, the Wagnerian rebirth of tragedy through music and myth brings with it the possibility of a return to health. Nothing less is at stake in the destiny of German music than the defence of German culture from decadence. The terms are those that Nietzsche would later use to condemn the art of Wagner; but they are here used to praise it. So, right from the start, Nietzsche's discussion of Wagner presents us with two major questions in aesthetics: on what grounds can we distinguish healthy from decadent art, and what is the aesthetic significance of the distinction?

In the last work published in his lifetime, *Twilight of the Idols*, Nietzsche ventures an explicit account of his aesthetic: 'The "beautiful in itself" is scarcely a term', he writes,

> not even a concept. In the beautiful man sets himself up as a measure of perfection; in certain cases he prays to himself therein. Nothing is beautiful; the human alone is beautiful: in this naivety all aesthetics is contained—it is the first truth of aesthetics. Let us add a second truth at once: nothing is ugly save *decadent* humanity (*der entartende Mensch*).
>
> (*TI*, IX, 19)

Nietzsche is here giving the *central* place in aesthetic judgment to the distinction between healthy and decadent forms of human life. He adhered to this position throughout his literary career. As he puts the point in *The Case of Wagner*, 'what has most profoundly occupied me is in effect the problem of decadence', and in taking up arms against decadence, he was 'joining forces against everything sick in me, including Wagner, including Schopenhauer, including the whole of modern "humaneness" (*Menschlichkeit*)' (*CW*, P). And he raises the same point in *The Gay Science*, arguing that 'my objections to the music of Wagner are physiological objections: why should I trouble to dress them up in aesthetic formulas? After all, aesthetics is nothing but a kind of applied physiology' (*GS*, 368). Wagner's music, he suggests, is the cause and effect of a bodily sickness.

Nietzsche was not the first philosopher to place the idea of health at the centre of his worldview—Feuerbach had defended a 'healthy sensuality' in his *Principles of the Philosophy of the Future* (1843), a work that profoundly influenced

Wagner.[6] And the concepts of decadence and degeneration were moving to the centre of intellectual life at the time of Nietzsche's mature works. Krafft-Ebing's *Psychopathia Sexualis* appeared in 1886, and in a compendious and influential work published in 1892 Max Nordau summarized the *fin-de-siècle* as the period of decadence, taking Nietzsche himself, along with Baudelaire, Zola, Wagner, Poe, and many more, as symptoms of the disease.[7] Nevertheless, Nietzsche was probably the first thinker to take the distinction between health and disease as definitive of what is at stake in the artistic enterprise. And this distinction had an added importance for him on account of his genealogical method.

This method conditions all Nietzsche's fundamental positions in philosophy, so that for him to describe a work of art as decadent, and to say that it arises from and is rooted in a decadent form of life, are ultimately equivalent claims. Tragedy, according to *The Birth of Tragedy*, is healthy precisely in what is most obscure, and what flows unconsciously beneath the reasoned clarity of the conscious motives. For health means life, life belongs to the body, the body belongs to the community, and the community is true to its inner nature only when responding to the unconscious forces by which it endures. In the collective dance the social organism lives and renews itself.

The tragic hero is precipitated out of the dance through the fault of consciousness, and for this fault he must pay. Hence the original dichotomy—Dionysus versus Apollo—shows itself in another: that between the formless flow of unconscious life and the *principium individuationis* that asserts itself in defiance of life. Those Schopenhauerian terms are used to alert the reader to the danger of the enlightened, Apollonian spirit that stands outside the collective life of a culture, in a posture of critical isolation. That, for Nietzsche, is the primary source of decadence. The tragedy reaffirms the original flux, in which human life constantly renews itself through negating the claims of individuality. Nietzsche quotes Isolde's dying words by way of explaining what he means:

In des Wonnemeeres
wogendem Schwall,
in der Duft-Wellen
tönendem Schall,
in des Weltathems
wehenden All –
ertrinken—versinken
unbewusst—höchste Lust.

(*BT*, 22)

[6] Feuerbach (1986). [7] Nordau (1895).

Isolde's 'highest joy' lies in the renunciation of the individuated self, sinking at last into the unending flux of becoming—the world breath's wafting whole, which is the equivalent in Wagner of Schopenhauer's directionless and ever restless Will.

Nietzsche was later to turn his back on Schopenhauer as he turned his back on Wagner. But some of the most important ideas adumbrated in *The Birth of Tragedy* survive into his mature writings on music. For Nietzsche the primary musical phenomenon is dance, and dance is organized by rhythm. Dance is a social phenomenon: we dance *with* others, and usually in groups. So music is one part of a complex social whole, which is the group or tribe *moving together*, in response to a pulse whose significance lies deeper than reason. The primary form of this collective movement is religious ritual, and it is from religious ritual that tragedy is born. The art of tragedy, Nietzsche claims, delayed the destruction of the Greek myths, by perpetuating the Dionysian ritual in which music and dance occupied a central place.

Those ideas are more suggested than dwelt upon in *The Birth of Tragedy*. But they are of considerable importance in understanding the dispute with Wagner. Equally important is the conception of art that both men shared, and which they had inherited from Hegelian philosophy. Art, for both Nietzsche and Wagner, was the highest of human activities—higher than science, and higher too than religion. Indeed the destiny of art, according to both Wagner and Nietzsche, is to rescue through symbols the human truth that religion conceals, the truth about *us*. This truth is not what religion tells us, but it is what religion *means*. (This is the theme of Wagner's powerful essay on Art and Religion: *Gesammelte Schriften*, vol. 10, 211. It is also the original inspiration for *The Ring*.) And both thinkers turned to music as epitomizing the spiritual transformation that is the true goal of every artist. 'Only music', wrote Nietzsche, 'placed beside the world, can give us an idea of what is meant by the justification of the world as an aesthetic phenomenon' (*BT*, 25).

Here, then, is a suggestion as to the source of the dispute with Wagner. Both men believed that the human world is in need of justification. They believed that the *religious* justification was either empty (Wagner) or pernicious (Nietzsche). But both believed that the religious need is a non-accidental feature of the human psyche, and one that demands satisfaction. This satisfaction is to be found in art, which supersedes religion and provides an *aesthetic* justification of the world ('the justification of the world as an aesthetic phenomenon'). And for Nietzsche, at least, no other justification is possible: hence the need for tragedy, which involves the overcoming of horror by aesthetic means.

The difference between Nietzsche and Wagner begins at this point. For Nietzsche, an aesthetic justification of the world is one that affirms life and health against decline and sickness. It is in direct conflict with the Christian justification, which elevates meekness, compassion, and other such life-denying virtues over the life-affirming virtues on which the future of mankind depends, and of which Nietzsche went on to give an alarming description. As he puts it in *On the Genealogy of Morals*: 'The *sickly* are the greatest danger to man: *not* the wicked, *not* the "beasts of prey"' (*GM*, III, 14).

For Wagner, by contrast, the aesthetic justification of the world involves foregrounding our capacity for renunciation. Art is not a vindication of life but a redemption from it, and the theme of redemption is the recurring motive of the Wagnerian music-drama, from *The Flying Dutchman* to *Parsifal.* The music drama retains, for Wagner, the fundamental significance of the Greek tragedy. That is to say, it is not merely a *picture* of a moral process. It is an *enactment* of that process, into which the spectator is drawn as a quasi-participant, as in a religious ritual, so that the redemption portrayed on the stage takes place also in the psyche of the observer.

This 'Eucharistic' conception of art became ever more prominent as Wagner's art developed, so that *Parsifal* is described as a 'festival play for the consecration of the stage', in other words as a religious ceremony. And Wagner attempted to confine the performance of *Parsifal* to the sacred precinct of Bayreuth (mercifully without success). In some way the work of art *redeems* the one who stands within its emotional ambience. The spectator *undergoes* the music drama, and his emotions are rearranged by it, as they are rearranged by the religious ritual. The hunger of the knights of the Grail for the Eucharistic meal is a symbol of the hunger that calls out in all of us, for a spiritual transformation that art alone can now provide. This transformation frees us from our enslavement to the world, and gives us the strength and the serenity to renounce it. And—if we are to follow the path taken by Tristan, Isolde, Parsifal, and Hans Sachs—we will recognize that the erotic, which seems to invite us *into* life, is in fact the original call to renunciation, the deep burning in the soul that tells us that we are 'not of this world'.

The Wagnerian idea of redemption closely corresponds to the Christian one; and it was part of Wagner's brilliance to recognize that in all its forms redemption requires sacrifice—the very sacrifice that is portrayed in the Greek tragedy and enacted in the Christian Eucharist: the sacrifice of the whole human being. The human must be 'offered up' if we are truly to transcend it: only then do we free ourselves from the resentments and conflicts with which human communities are poisoned. That which is 'offered up' is life itself—either in the promissory form of erotic yearning (Sachs, Parsifal) or in the realized form of a living victim

(Siegfried, Tristan, Brünnhilde). This idea has both a religious and a secular meaning, as is clear from *Parsifal* and *The Mastersingers*, and has since been developed in surprising and ingenious ways by René Girard.[8]

Wagner's vision of redemption through sacrifice is both a theory of human communities, and a moral exhortation. And the moral exhortation is tried and tested, not in life, but in art—in the realm of imagination, that enables the spectator of the drama to 'live through' a sacrifice that he cannot actually live. (If he did so, life itself would cease.) That vision of redemption was once available through religion. In *Parsifal*, however, art replaces religion, taking the instruments of redemption and infusing them with an *aesthetic* life.

For Nietzsche the whole idea of redemption, conceived in that way, is a denial of life and an invocation to decadence. In the third essay of the *Genealogy*, devoted to the demolition of asceticism, he ridicules *Parsifal*, wondering whether the composer had not intended the work as a kind of satyr play, a grotesque sequel to *The Ring*. And in *The Case of Wagner* he sets out to demonstrate the decadent quality of the Wagnerian hero, who is not a hero at all but an *entartete Mensch*. He also sets out to show the *aesthetic* disaster that ensues, when such a character is made central to a large-scale music drama.

The goal of the book is to reject Wagner's moral vision, and also to suggest that the attempt to build that vision into a sustained work of art leads to music that is fundamentally sick. The moral faults of the vision translate directly into aesthetic faults in the music, and at the same time an immersion in the music involves a corruption in the soul of the listener, whose psyche is jeopardized by this surrender to a polluted ideal.

Claims of that kind place an enormous critical onus on the one who makes them, and it is fair to say that Nietzsche does not discharge that onus. He does not succeed in showing that the Wagnerian philosophy of redemption is either decadent in itself or aesthetically destructive. Nor does he succeed in showing just *how* a moral vision displays itself in musical form, and just *how* music invites the sympathy (and possibly corrupt sympathy) of the listener. The belief that music has a moral and character-forming potential is at least as old as Plato; and the belief that works of art are to be judged in terms of the life contained in them has survived into our times as a critical commonplace, although one that stands in need of a philosophical underpinning. But it seems to me that Nietzsche does not really provide that underpinning.

Nietzsche's attack has three parts. First there is the accusation of decadence, which is directed not only at Wagner but at the world of which Wagner was a

[8] Girard (1972; 1978).

part, and specifically at the *German* conception of that world. Then there is the attack on the claims that Wagner makes for his art. For Wagner, his *Gesamtkunstwerk* involved an adventure of music into new expressive domains, so as to explore the depths of the human condition through the 'endless melody' that speaks to what is unconscious and hidden. Against these claims Nietzsche argues that Wagner is really a 'miniaturist', that his musical techniques are incapable of generating real development, and that the whole thing is a kind of confidence trick, a simulation of musical life, which ignores the real source of music in rhythm and dance.

Finally, Nietzsche argues that the heroic in Wagner is a sham. His characters need to be unmasked, to be deprived of their mythic costumes and returned to the bourgeois context from which they have been lifted into legend. Wagner's portentous music does not offer them redemption, since it merely disguises the fact that they are the ordinary sick refuse of nineteenth-century society—as far from tragic grandeur as Flaubert's Emma Bovary. The Wagnerian drama is a species of 'counterfeiting', in which the heroic passions and vast deeds reveal themselves, when held up to the critical light, as thin wisps of sickly passion, puffed up by musical bombast. The promises of 'redemption' and 'transcendence' both depend on the forgery conducted by the music, and the fact that these promises are taken so seriously by so many is indicative of the equally decadent and counterfeit nature of the surrounding culture.

Those powerful criticisms issue in off-putting passages like this:

> Wagner's art is sick. The problems he presents on the stage—all of them problems of hysterics—the convulsive nature of his affects, his overexcited sensibility, his taste that required ever stronger spices, his instability which he dressed up as principles, not least of all the choice of his heroes and heroines—consider them as physiological types (a pathological gallery!)—all of this taken together represents a profile of sickness that permits no further doubt . . . Precisely because nothing is more modern than this total sickness, this lateness and overexcitement of the nervous mechanism, Wagner is *the modern artist par excellence.*
>
> (*CW*, 5)

Nietzsche is aware that to justify his claims he must say something about the music—about what it *does* and *how* it does it. His attack is directed against all three musical dimensions—melodic, rhythmic, harmonic—as Wagner makes use of them. Nietzsche claims that Wagner's supposedly 'infinite' or 'endless' melody conceals an absence of genuine melodic inspiration.[9] He implies that

[9] That Wagner was the enemy of melody was a critical commonplace in the early reception of his works. An article in *The Times* of 21 July 1853 claims that Wagner's music 'threatens to exclude melody altogether'. Wagner's champion Francis Hueffer responded with *Richard Wagner and the*

there is even a kind of *fear* of melody in Wagner—certainly fear of those gripping tunes that Nietzsche identifies in *Carmen*, and which he associates with 'French' finesse, as against 'German' bombast. (This reverses a thesis of *The Birth of Tragedy*, which had contrasted the healthy world of German myth, with the unhealthy clarity of French civilisation, applying in a local way the contrast between *Kultur* and *Zivilisation* made fashionable by Herder.)

The real melody, for Nietzsche, is the melody that gives direct and immediate pleasure to the listener, the melody that engages with the spontaneous will to dance. He is short on examples, other than *Carmen*, but we can all agree that the *Habañera* from that great work is quite another kind of thing from the Prize Song from *The Mastersingers*, which constantly develops, and reaches closure only as a temporary pause in its seemingly unending growth towards the final chorus.

Nietzsche is dismissive towards the Wagnerian 'leitmotif', which he compares (obscurely) to a '*toothpick*, used to get rid of the remainders of food' (*CW*, 8). And he associates the Wagnerian musical process with a 'degeneration of the sense of rhythm' (*CW*, 'Postscript'), while praising Wagner for having inspired the study of rhythmics, then being initiated by Riemann.[10] In *Contra Wagner*—the fragments collected in Turin in 1888—Nietzsche takes this criticism further, interestingly connecting the '*endlöse Melodei*' with the rhythmic disintegration, as he perceived it, of Wagner's music—its inability to *dance*. He illustrates through an image that occurs also in *The Case of Wagner*:

> One walks into the sea, gradually loses one's secure footing, and finally surrenders oneself to the elements without reservation: one must *swim*. In older music, what one had to do in the dainty, or solemn, or fiery back and forth, quicker and slower, was something quite different, namely, to *dance*. The measure required for this, the maintenance of certain equally balanced units of time and force, demanded continual *wariness* of the listener's soul—and on the counterplay of this cooler breeze that came from the wariness and the warm breath of enthusiasm rested the magic of all *good* music. Richard Wagner wanted a different kind of movement; he overthrew the physiological presuppositions of previous music. Swimming, floating—no longer walking and dancing.
>
> (*NCW*, III, 1)

Music of the Future (1874), defending the Wagnerian conception of melody as inseparable from the musical and dramatic texture. (Thanks to Gulliver Ralston for these references.)

[10] See the now unjustly neglected Riemann (1903). In unpublished work Kathy Fry has drawn attention to Nietzsche's phrase-structure analysis in the 1870–1871 notebooks of *Tristan*, Act III, Scene II (the passage of rhythmical disorder, as Tristan tears the bandage from his wound). Nietzsche here attempts to show that a strophe/antistrophe form emerges at the higher level, so that what looks like disorder is in fact another kind of order. I am grateful to Kathy Fry for drawing my attention to this passage, which again shows Nietzsche praising Wagner for an aspect of his work that would later draw forth severe condemnation. See Colli and Montinari (1993, 192).

The faults Nietzsche discerns concern Wagner's attitude to the listener. The composer's floating rhythms are denying the impulse to move with the music in a healthy and reciprocal way: Wagner is not responding to, nor *wary* of, the listener's soul. Finally Nietzsche is dismissive of Wagnerian harmony, which he describes (in connection with *Parsifal*) as 'a rope of enharmonics', on which ugly things perform their gymnastics (*CW*, 5). He means, I take it, that the harmonic progressions are not genuine, but the result of taking chords whole from one tonal centre to another, as in the enharmonic changes used in classical music for special effect, and normalized by Schubert in his *Lieder*.

This use of enharmonics, Nietzsche implies, negates true harmonic movement, so that the music slops around like a sea, instead of moving forward like a river. Thus Wagner's music is a failure in all three dimensions of musical order: melody, rhythm, and harmony. And the failure stems from the adverse *use* of music, to inflate the sentiments attached to scenes and characters that do not really contain them. To put the point directly: the defects of form stem from defects of content. Because the content is faked, so is the form.

Nietzsche was of course aware of the originality and brilliance of Wagner's music. In an illuminating study Georges Liébert has shown the extent to which Nietzsche's love–hate relation with Wagner was really a love–hate relation with himself, and in particular with his own self-image as a musician. Liébert shows how deeply self-deceived the philosopher was, both in his initial admiration for the composer, and in his subsequent petulant break with him.[11] At the very moment when he was publicly denouncing *Parsifal* as a work of sickness, decadence, and deception, Nietzsche sent to Peter Gast a wonderful description of the Prelude to that work, and confessed, in his notes written prior to *Beyond Good and Evil*, that he knows 'of nothing that grasps Christianity at such a depth and that so sharply leads to compassion'.[12] *Parsifal* captures the dramatic and emotional logic of the Christian vision, and Nietzsche's own musicality compelled him to recognize this, and to see it as an artistic triumph.

Furthermore, the faults that Nietzsche discerns in Wagner's music are very obviously the faults shown by his own compositions. These have now been published, and many issued on CD. There are some charming songs in the manner of Löwe, some grandiose attempts at choral and orchestral fantasias, and massive splurges for piano with fraught romantic titles like 'Hymn to Friendship'. Nietzsche was at best what he so unjustly and outrageously accused Wagner of being (*CW*, 6)—a miniaturist, whose short-breathed successes are inspired by solitary and lachrymose emotions that could not be pursued at

[11] Liébert (2004). [12] Letter to Peter Gast (Heinrich Köselitz), January 1887.

greater length without morbidity. The works for which he would have wished to be remembered are formless improvizations, with lunatic bass-lines and grotesque progressions, entirely devoid of melodic or harmonic logic.

Nietzsche knew this, of course, and had turned to literature with a sense of opting for second best. He even described *Thus Spoke Zarathustra* as a work of music, hoping to gain by metaphor what he could not achieve in fact. And throughout his troubled and lonely literary career he took what consolation he could from the fact that he, unlike his critics, had the soul of a musician, and could hear his way into the secret heart of things. His prose was an attempt to convey the wordless truths, the primeval needs and hopes, that find their true voice in music. But the spirit of Dionysus eluded him, who claimed it as his own, and in his attack on Wagner's music he was taking revenge for this.

According to Nietzsche, Wagner's music only *pretends* to the emotions that it claims. Hence the dramas themselves fall apart. The characters are real only by moments, and only in those histrionic gestures that show Wagner's art to be the art of the showman. True drama, Nietzsche holds, is not theatrical, and it is precisely Wagner's mastery of the theatrical idiom that disqualifies his dramas from bearing the meaning that he wishes for. Wagner is an actor, a showman, and everything he does is devoted to *effect*, even though there is no dramatic content in terms of which the effect could be justified. Hence the seemingly paradoxical description of Wagner as a 'miniaturist'. It is only by moments that the magic works. But, in a famous passage, Nietzsche turns that criticism around, acknowledging that some of those moments, at least, are not mere theatre, but sparks of lyrical insight without compare in the history of music:

> There is a musician who, more than any other musician, is a master at finding the tones in the realm of suffering, depressed, tortured souls, at giving language even to mute misery. None can equal him in the colours of late autumn, in the indescribably moving happiness of the last, truly last, truly shortest joy; he knows a sound for those quiet, disquieting midnights of the soul, where cause and effect seem to be out of joint and where at any moment something might originate 'out of nothing'. He draws most happily of all out of the profoundest depths of human happiness, and, as it were, out of its drained goblet, where the bitterest and most repulsive drops have finally and evilly run together with the sweetest. He knows that weariness of the soul which drags itself, unable to leap or fly any more, even to walk; he masters the shy glance of concealed pain, of understanding without comfort, of the farewell without confession—indeed, as the Orpheus of all secret misery he is greater than any; and some things have been added to the realm of art by him alone, things that had hitherto seemed inexpressible and even unworthy of art—the cynical rebellion, for example, of which only those are capable who suffer most bitterly; also some

very minute and microscopic aspects of the soul, as it were the scales of its amphibian nature: indeed he is the master of the very minute. But he does not *want* to be that!

(*NCW*, I)

Take away those moments, however, and what remains? A great work of counterfeit: fake transcendence, fake characters, fake emotions, and—in the end—a fake redemption offered without cost by Parsifal, the 'holy fool'. None of this is believable, since none of it comes from the heart—it is all icy abstraction, rooted in the Hegelian conception of music as a vehicle for the 'Idea'. Thus 'everything that ever grew on the soil of *impoverished* life, all of the counterfeiting of transcendence and beyond, has found its most sublime advocate in Wagner's art'.

Nietzsche does not spell out this criticism in detail, but it is clear that he believes, not merely that the raw material provided by Wagner's characters is insufficient to meet their allegorical and metaphysical purpose, but also that it is impossible that any characters *should* meet that purpose, and moreover that it is decadent to *want* to meet it. For the longing for redemption, as Wagner presents it, is a sickness, a renunciation of life and health for the sake of a bogus spiritual purity.

Although Nietzsche does not explicitly say so, I suspect that he regarded the Wagnerian 'redemption' as a kind of cliché, an idea worn thin by too much use, brought in to the later dramas only because the characters, lacking the will and integrity that makes true tragedy possible, have to be content with 'redemption' as second best. Hence Nietzsche's ironical comment, regarding the placing of a wreath on the composer's grave by the German Wagner Society, on which was inscribed the last words of *Parsifal*: 'Redemption for the Redeemer': 'Many (strangely enough) made the small correction: "Redemption from the Redeemer". One breathed a sigh of relief' (*CW*, 4).

In response to those charges I will say only this: Nietzsche's advocacy of 'life' is at best an excusable compensation for the invalid existence that the philosopher was obliged to lead, at worst a surrender to all that is most destructive in human nature. If compassion for the weak is decadence, if sacrifice is decadence, if the transcendence of sexual desire is decadence, if the renunciation of power for love, and divine arrogance for human pity are decadence—then roll on decadence. And if health comes only with a life 'beyond good and evil', in which pity and renunciation play no part, then away with health.

But enough of that. There is truth in Nietzsche's claim that the Wagnerian characters do not always live up to the metaphysical and moral burdens that he places on them. Only every now and then—alone in the forest, confronting the Rhine-daughters, dying in a long-delayed access of consciousness—does

Siegfried represent the tragic truth of human freedom. And whatever we think of his personal qualities and allegorical meaning, Siegfried is certainly very far from the 'marvellously accurate archetypal youth' whose portrait Nietzsche praises in 'Richard Wagner in Bayreuth' (the fourth of Nietzsche's *Untimely Meditations* (1876)). Only in the encounter with Kundry as seductress does Parsifal become fully alive as a human being. On the other hand, there are few creations that are as hair-raising and persuasive as Wagner's Kundry. There is nothing since the Greeks to compare with the portrait of Wotan, and nothing outside Dickens and Victor Hugo to match Alberich or Mime.

Much more interesting philosophically is Nietzsche's sketchy attempt to read the charge of decadence into the *music*, to associate the moral failure (as he saw it) of the dramas with a failure of musical form. The insight that inspired *The Birth of Tragedy* is of lasting importance. Music is not a conceptual idiom. All attempts to assimilate the organization of music to the organization that we know from language are, it seems to me, doomed.[13] We understand music by moving with it, and what we understand is not a thought but a 'field of sympathy' into which we are inducted by the music as we are inducted into a ritual by the gestures of a priest. Dance is the primary form of this collective movement, and dance has a place in religious ritual for that very reason.

If there is corruption in the music of Wagner it must be found, therefore, in the musical movement. In this Nietzsche is right; and he is right to question the melodic, rhythmic, and harmonic organization of the Wagnerian idiom in those terms. What kind of human being is it, that the listener is invited to 'move with' in this music? In surrendering to this movement am I surrendering something of myself that I should be withholding? Or am I, as Wagner wants me to believe, entering a sacred place, in which the sympathetic response to the music will effect a new order in my feelings? Can I through this music achieve the order of sacrifice and renunciation that will bring the peace and quiescence that the Greeks sought through tragedy, and which we moderns must seek through a new form of art—the 'artwork of the future' that will replace religion not by refuting it, but by doing its work, and doing it better?

Wagner believed that he had to refashion all the ways in which music moves. His endless melodies are not, however, the redundant contraptions that Nietzsche claimed them to be. Nor does his music display a rhythmic disintegration. The use of the broken triplet of the 'look' motive in the prelude to *Tristan and Isolde* is one of the finest examples in music of a syncopated rhythmic order generated from the smallest possible cell, which spreads its accent through the

[13] I have argued this at length in Scruton (1997).

whole entity of which it is a part. The result is not rhythmic disintegration but integrated rhythm *without closure*. Likewise the harmonic movement of the prelude is not a tightrope of enharmonic changes, but a supreme instance of voice-led modulation *without closure*. And the melody is moving according to the same principle and in a way that enters the memory of every musical person. This is musical art of the highest order. This three-dimensional movement without closure is used to convey a state of mind 'from within' and without words—without even the possibility of words.

That having been said, however, Nietzsche's questions need to be answered. What would show this supreme musical competence to be also moral competence, so to speak—the expression of uncorrupted human life, of a kind that invites and deserves our sympathy? The sting might be drawn from Nietzsche's charge of decadence, without conferring on the Wagnerian drama the supreme significance that it claims for itself. Not counterfeit, but not necessary either—a byway of modern life that teaches us nothing.

Such might be the moderated judgment of a Nietzschean today. But we have reached the point at which Nietzsche's onus needs to be discharged. His own advocacy of life is far more obviously a sham, in my view, than Wagner's post-Christian philosophy of redemption. And his defence of closed rhythms and catchy tunes is too short-breathed to carry any intellectual weight. One wonders what Nietzsche would say in response to Lady Gaga, Meshuggah, or EDM, or in response to a popular movie culture dominated by 'special effects', ludicrous metamorphoses, and relentless violence without any moral or emotional rationale. Would he be thereafter a little less inclined to apply the label 'decadent' to Wagner, or would he recognize that there are forms of 'life' to which a dose of old-fashioned decadence might reasonably be preferred?

References

Adorno, T. 2004. *In Search of Wagner*, Livingstone, Rodney (trans.) (London: Verso).

Colli, G. and Montinari, M. 1993. *Nietzsche, Werke II: 3 Vorlesungsaufzeichnungen 1870–1871* (Berlin: de Gruyter).

Dodds, E. 1951. *The Greeks and the Irrational* (Los Angeles: University of California Press).

Feuerbach, L. 1986. *Principles of the Philosophy of the Future*, Vogel, Manfred (trans.) (Indianapolis: Hackett).

Girard, R. 1972. *La violence et le sacré* (Paris: Grasset)

Girard, R. 1978. *Des choses cachées depuis la fondation du monde* (Paris: Grasset).

Hueffer, F. 1874. *Richard Wagner and the Music of the Future* (London: Chapman and Hall).

Kaufmann, W. (ed.) 1954. *The Portable Nietzsche* (New York: Viking Portable Library).
Köhler, J. 1998. *Nietzsche and Wagner: A Lesson in Subjugation* (New Haven, CT: Yale University Press).
Liébert, G. 2004. *Nietzsche and Music*, Pellauer, D. and Parkes, G. (trans.) (Chicago: University of Chicago Press).
Nietzsche, F. 1967. *The Birth of Tragedy* and *The Case of Wagner*, Kaufmann, W. (trans.) (New York, Vintage Books).
Nietzsche, F. 1969. *On the Genealogy of Morals*, Hollingdale, R. J. and Kaufmann, W. (trans.) (New York: Vintage Books).
Nietzsche, F. 1997. *Untimely Meditations*, Hollingdale, R. J. (trans.), Breazeale, D. (ed.) (Cambridge: Cambridge University Press).
Nietzsche, F. 2005. *Twilight of the Idols*, Norman, J. (trans.) (Cambridge: Cambridge University Press).
Nietzsche, F. 2008. *Richard Wagner in Bayreuth* (Dodo Press).
Nordau, M. 1895. *Degeneration*, Anon (trans.) (New York: Appleton and Co.).
Riemann, H. 1903. *System der musikalischen Rhythmik und Metrik* (Leipzig: Breitkopf u. Härtel).
Scruton, R. 1997. *The Aesthetics of Music* (Oxford: Oxford University Press).
Wagner, R. 1887–88. *Gesammelte Schriften* (Leipzig: E. W. Fritzsch; 2nd edition).
Young, J. 1992. *Nietzsche's Philosophy of Art* (Cambridge: Cambridge University Press).

Index

Printed and bound by CPI Group (UK) Ltd, Croydon, CR0 4YY